50
Strategies for Teaching English Language Learners

SIXTH EDITION

Adrienne L. Herrell

Florida State University, Retired
California State University, Fresno, Emeritus

Michael Jordan

California State University, Fresno, Retired

Director and Publisher: Kevin M. Davis
Portfolio Manager: Drew Bennett
Managing Content Producer: Megan Moffo
Content Producer: Yagnesh Jani
Portfolio Management Assistant: Maria Feliberty
Managing Digital Producer: Autumn Benson
Digital Studio Producer: Lauren Carlson
Development Editor: Jeffrey Johnston
Executive Product Marketing Manager: Krista Clark
Procurement Specialist: Deidra Headlee
Cover Design: Pearson CSC, Jerilyn Bockorick
Cover Art: ©FatCamera/Getty
Full Service Vendor: Pearson CSC
Full-Service Project Management: Pearson CSC, Gowri Duraiswamy
Editorial Project Manager: Pearson CSC, Martin 'Tinah' Aurea
Printer/Binder: LSC Communications, Inc
Cover Printer: LSC Communications, Inc
Text Font: PalatinoLTPro-Roman

Chapter opening photos (left to right): © Petro Feketa/Fotolia; © Monkey Business/Fotolia; © Rob/Fotolia;
© Monkey Business/Fotolia.

Credits and acknowledgments for material borrowed from other sources and reproduced with permission,
appear on the appropriate page within this textbook.

Every effort has been made to provide accurate and current Internet information in this book. However, the
Internet and information posted on it are constantly changing, so it is inevitable that some of the Internet
addresses listed in this textbook will change.

Copyright © 2020, 2016, 2012 by Pearson Education, Inc. 221 River Street, Hoboken, NJ 07030. All
Rights Reserved. Manufactured in the United States of America. This publication is protected by Copyright, and
permission should be obtained from the publisher prior to any prohibited reproduction, storage in a retrieval
system, or transmission in any form or by any means, electronic, mechanical, photocopying, recording, or
likewise. For information regarding permissions, request forms, and the appropriate contacts within the Pearson
Education Global Rights & Permissions department, please visit www.pearsoned.com/permissions.
PEARSON and ALWAYS LEARNING are exclusive trademarks in the United States and/or other countries owned
by Pearson Education, Inc. or its affiliates.

Library of Congress Cataloging-in-Publication Data

Names: Herrell, Adrienne L., author. | Jordan, Michael, 1944- author.
Title: 50 strategies for teaching English language learners / Adrienne L.
    Herrell, Michael Jordan.
Other titles: Fifty strategies for teaching English language learners
Description: Sixth edition. | Hoboken : Pearson, [2018] | Includes
    bibliographical references.
Identifiers: LCCN 2018041648| ISBN 9780134986616 | ISBN 013498661X
Subjects: LCSH: English language—Study and teaching—Foreign speakers.
Classification: LCC PE1128.A2 H467 2018 | DDC 428.2/4071—dc23 LC record available
    at https://lccn.loc.gov/2018041648

ISBN 10:   0-13-498661-X
ISBN 13: 978-0-13-498661-6

To Susan McCloskey for her years of dedicated teaching of English learners and for all the things we have learned by observing in her classroom.

AH & MJ

Contents

About the Authors

Adrienne Herrell is retired as a visiting professor and ESOL Coordinator at Florida State University. She taught classes in early literacy, assessment, and strategies for teaching English language learners at California State University, Fresno, until her retirement in 2004. *50 Strategies for Teaching English Language Learners*, Sixth Edition, is her eighteenth book for Pearson.

Michael Jordan is retired from California State University, Fresno, where he coordinated the multiple subjects (elementary) credential program and taught classes in Curriculum and Instruction, Social Foundations of Education, and Psychological Foundations of Education. *50 Strategies for Teaching English Language Learners*, Sixth Edition, is his eleventh book for Pearson.

Preface

New to This Edition

This sixth edition of *50 Strategies for Teaching English Language Learners* presents a major focus in identifying and teaching students at their language development level. With adoption of the Common Core State Standards (CCSS), educators across the United States are reflecting on exemplary practices and research in strategies for supporting intellectual and educational growth in students of all ages. Common Core does, however, present additional challenges for students who are in the process of acquiring English. In this edition, you will notice the following:

- **A new chapter** is included that addresses the choice and use of technology strategies based on the needs of your students.
- **Additional adaptation charts** have been provided for matching the teaching strategies to the language levels of your students
- **Additional teacher self-evaluation rubrics** are included throughout this new edition to support teachers in ensuring that they are fully implementing exemplary strategies. These rubrics also provide ideas for improving teacher implementations.
- **Video links** have been added to demonstrate the use of strategies, support the reader's understanding of the strategies, or discuss implementation issues.

Acknowledgments

We are extremely appreciative of the professors who took the time to review the fourth edition and give us suggestions for improving the fifth edition. This is a time-consuming task, but improving educational strategies is obviously a priority to these professors: Daniel Gilhooly, University of Central Missouri; Tom Salsbury, Washington State University; Lena Shaqareq, University of North Florida; and Ana Torres, Texas Tech University.

An Introduction to the Strategies

The 50 strategies included in this edition have been sequenced to represent their importance and complexity of implementation. The first 15 strategies are presented to support some very basic requirements in any classroom that contains English language learners (ELLs) or limited English experience students (LEEs). Limited English experience students are those whose first language is English but who have limited vocabularies and experiences engaging in social or academic English. In today's busy society the students we teach sometimes have not had the experiences or verbal interaction opportunities they might have had in times past (Trelease, 2013).

It is crucial that classrooms provide multiple opportunities for students to practice verbal interaction in both social and academic English (Goldenberg, 2008). It is also important for teachers to establish an accepting and supportive classroom environment. The strategies included in this edition provide multiple ways to accomplish these goals on a daily basis. This video links address the importance of providing opportunities for interaction in the classroom. As you watch it, think about the following question:

Enhanced eText
Video Example i

- What can you as a teacher do to provide an environment in which all students are accepted and all languages valued?

The cultures that students bring to the classroom have an effect on their learning as well. Some cultures stress sharing, and students find it difficult not to share answers, even in a testing situation. They don't necessarily think of sharing as "cheating." They just have been deeply acculturated to share everything. Some other cultural considerations are explored in the video links, which address additional areas that teachers must consider in order to teach the whole child. Think about the following questions as you watch:

Enhanced eText
Video Example ii

- Why are a student's former educational experiences important for a teacher to understand?
- How does a teacher discover information about a student's beliefs and cultural background?

A teacher's job in a culturally rich society presents many challenges. We offer the strategies in this edition to support teachers in providing an environment and learning community in which they and their students will thrive. All of the strategies have been field-tested in classrooms in several states and have received powerful feedback:

"These strategies WORK with both our ELLs and our English-only students."—Susan McCloskey, Fresno Unified School District

"Many of my English-only students have very limited vocabularies and all the students have greatly benefited from the strategies in this book."—Jennifer Bateman, Dahlonega, Georgia

References

Goldenberg, G. (2008). Teaching English language learners: What the research does—and does not—say. *American Educator, 32*(2), 8–44.

Trelease, J. (2013). *The read-aloud handbook* (7th ed.). New York, New York: Penguin Books.

Theoretical Overview

In this section of *50 Strategies for Teaching English Language Learners*, you are introduced to the **basic theory**, **principles**, and **assessment strategies** underlying the effective teaching of students who are in the process of acquiring English as a second language.

This section provides the research and **exemplary practices** on which the 50 teaching strategies are built. It is vital that teachers make good choices in their everyday **interactions** with students, particularly students for whom English is not their first language. To make good choices in the way they plan instruction, interact verbally, correct mistakes, and assess English language learners, teachers must understand how language is acquired.

Educators are encountering a growing number of **English language learners (ELLs)** in their classrooms. They have become the fastest growing segment of the population in public schools today, with more than 9 percent of students in schools in the United States attending public schools coming from a home where a language other than English is spoken as their first language. This is a growth of 32% compared to numbers a decade ago, while overall student enrollment only gained 4.9% (United States Department of Education, 2017). To add to the challenge, accountability requirements of the **No Child Left Behind Act of 2001 (NCLB)**, **Race to the Top (RTT)**, and the **Common Core State Standards (CCSS)** include English learners in the legal requirements for assessment. Their scores are often required to be factored into the determination of whether a school is making **adequate yearly progress (AYP)**. All of these elements add to the critical need for teachers to find effective strategies for teaching all learners. To learn more about each of these federal initiatives, you might want to explore the following websites:

NCLB—en.wikipedia.org/wiki/No_Child_Left_Behind_Act
RTT—en.wikipedia.org/wiki/Race_to_the_Top
CCSS—en.wikipedia.org/wiki/Common_Core_State_Standards_Initiative

This sixth edition of *50 Strategies for Teaching English Language Learners* incorporates and blends both the Common Core and the National Standards for Teaching English Language Learners published by Teachers of English to Speakers of Other Languages (TESOL). While the Common Core focuses on a nationally consistent "shared set of standards" for English and language arts and mathematics, it initially made limited provisions for supporting academic language acquisition while simultaneously learning academic content. TESOL standards provide teachers with clear guidelines in supporting ELLs as they become more proficient in speaking, writing, and comprehending social and academic English. "TESOL's *PREK–12 English Language Proficiency Standards* (ELPS, 2006) provide a resource to blend both the CCSS and the individual state standards so that ELLs are prepared to meet the goals of college and career readiness" (TESOL, 2013). This ongoing quest for ways to build and maintain proficient bilingual students in schools can only be achieved with teachers who understand the value of good teaching. These are teachers who can teach the language of the content, differentiate instruction, and scaffold learning to produce academically successful students who stay in school and are given every opportunity to participate fully and equitably.

Theoretical Overview

The research in language acquisition has been rich and productive during the past 25 years. Working together, linguists and educators have discovered effective ways to support students in their acquisition of new languages and content knowledge (Crawford & Krashen, 2007). It is vital that classroom teachers understand the implications of language acquisition research so they can provide the scaffolding and verbal interactions necessary for their students to be successful in the classroom.

Language Acquisition Theory and the Classroom Teacher

For classroom teachers to make good decisions about instructional practices for English language learners, they must understand how students acquire English and how this acquisition differs from the way foreign languages have traditionally been taught in the United States (Collier, 1995). Many teachers have experienced classes in Spanish, French, or other languages in which they have practiced repetitive drills and translated long passages using English–French (or Spanish) dictionaries. While these approaches have been used to study languages for many years in the United States, it should be noted that linguists such as Jim Cummins and Stephen Krashen have been researching and offering new approaches to language acquisition.

Seminal research in language acquisition was conducted in the 1980s and has been built upon continuously since that time. In his 1982 study of language acquisition, Krashen makes a distinction between language acquisition and language learning that is vital to the support of students' gradual acquisition of fluency in a new language. He states that **language acquisition** is a natural thing. Young children acquire their home language easily without formal teaching. However, teachers must also keep in mind other factors such as gender, ethnicity, and the learner's immigrant or "non-native" status, and how these affect language learning (Canagarajah, 2006). Language acquisition is gradual, based on receiving and understanding messages, building a listening (receptive) vocabulary, and slowly attempting verbal production of the language in a highly supportive, nonstressful setting. It is exactly these same conditions that foster the acquisition of a second language. The teacher is responsible for providing the understandable language—**comprehensible input**—along with whatever supports are necessary for the students to internalize the messages. To explore the importance of comprehensible input and the role the teacher plays in making language understandable, view this video and think about ways you, as a teacher, can provide instruction that is comprehensible. Ask yourself:

- How is planning important in providing comprehensible input?
- What habits do teachers need to develop in order to be more understandable?

Using approaches and materials that add context to the language—props, gestures, pictures—contributes to the child's language acquisition and eventually to the production of the new language. Recent trends in language acquisition support in the classroom rely heavily on

Enhanced eText
Video Example TO.1

- using assessment of the learner's needs,
- present level of functioning, and
- individual motivation to acquire the target language in structuring the teaching methods to be employed (Canagarajah, 2006).

Krashen and Terrell (1983), even in their earliest research, stressed the need for English language learners to be allowed to move into verbal production of the new language at a comfortable rate. Students must hear and understand messages in the target language and build a listening vocabulary before being expected to produce spoken language. This does not mean that the English language learners should be uninvolved in classroom activities but that the activities should be structured so that they can participate at a comfortable level. Questions asked of them should be answerable at first with gestures, nods, or other physical responses. This language acquisition stage is called the silent or **preproduction period**, and it is a vital start to language acquisition. The subsequent stages and implications for teaching and learning are explained in Chapter 15, Leveled Questions. For a description of the language development stages, see Figure TO.1.

It is important to recognize that levels of language proficiency are dynamic; that is, they change as students grow and learn. TESOL has adopted a slightly different description of the levels of language proficiency that accounts for the changes that take place as students make progress in acquiring English proficiency and emphasizes the ongoing changes that take place. TESOL's descriptors are organized into five levels: starting, emerging, developing, expanding, and bridging. Figure TO.2 shows the levels and their characteristics.

Researchers around the world have explored approaches to teaching language. German researcher Leo van Lier insists that the most important aspect of effective teaching is understanding the learner. He ascribes to Vygotsky's theory (1962) that teaching and assessing in the child's **zone of proximal development (ZPD)** is vital, as is the role of verbal interaction. The "AAA curriculum" (van Lier, 1996) is based on three foundational principles: awareness, autonomy, and authenticity. In the area of awareness, van Lier sees focusing attention and the role of perception as vital for teachers and learners. Both students and teachers must (1) know what they are doing and why, (2) be consciously engaged, and (3) reflect on the learning process. Autonomy involves **self-regulation**, **motivation**, and **deep processing**, all of which include taking responsibility, being accountable, and having free choice in learning activities. Van Lier believes that all these

FIGURE TO.1 Stages of Language Development

Preproduction (also known as the silent period) Characteristics:
- Communicates with gestures, actions, and formulaic speech
- Often still in silent period
- Is building receptive vocabulary

Early Production Characteristics:
- Can say, "I don't understand."
- Can label and categorize information

Speech Emergence Characteristics:
- Uses language purposefully
- Can produce complete sentence

Intermediate Fluency Characteristics:
- Can produce connected narrative
- Can use reading and writing within the context of a lesson
- Can write answers to higher-level questions
- Can resolve conflicts verbally

FIGURE TO.2 Performance Definitions of the Five Levels of English Language Proficiency

English language learners can understand and use . . .

Level 1 Starting	Level 2 Emerging	Level 3 Developing	Level 4 Expanding	Level 5 Bridging
. . . language to communicate with others around basic concrete needs.	. . . language to draw on simple and routine experiences to communicate with others.	. . . language to communicate with others on familiar matters regularly encountered.	. . . language in both concrete and abstract situations and apply language to new experiences.	. . . a wide range of longer oral and written texts and recognize implicit meaning.
. . . high-frequency words and memorized chunks of language.	. . . high-frequency and some general academic vocabulary and expressions.	. . . general and some specialized academic vocabulary and expressions.	. . . specialized and some technical academic vocabulary and expressions.	. . . technical academic vocabulary and expressions.
. . . words, phrases, or chunks of language.	. . . phrases or short sentences in oral or written communication.	. . . expanded sentences in oral or written communication.	. . . a variety of sentence lengths of varying linguistic complexity in oral and written communication.	. . . a variety of sentence lengths of varying linguistic complexity in extended oral or written discourse.
. . . pictorial, graphic, or nonverbal representation of language.	. . . oral or written language, making errors that may impede the communication.	. . . oral or written language, making errors that may impede the communication, but retain much of its meaning.	. . . oral or written language, making minimal errors that do not impede the overall meaning of the communication.	. . . oral or written language approaching comparability to that of English-proficient peers.

Source: From PreK–12 English Language Proficiency Standards, 2006, TESOL. Copyright 2006 by the Teachers of English to Students of Other Languages. Used with permission.

principles apply to both learners and teachers, and he encourages teachers to provide opportunities for autonomy for the students as teachers make curriculum choices that address the needs of individuals. This is in direct opposition to packaged curricula that require all students to move through the activities in the same manner and pace.

The third principle of van Lier's approach is authenticity. He defines **authenticity** as teaching and learning language as it is used in life, being relevant, and basing all learning activities on true communication. All the aspects of authenticity involve a commitment to learning, integrity, and respect on the part of both learner and teacher. Hart and Risley (2003) concur with van Lier. They found that a child's experience with language mattered more than **socioeconomic status**, race, or anything else they measured.

The role of practice in language learning is addressed by van Lier in his principles. He identifies two aspects of practice that must be considered: focus and control. Although he agrees that learning a language requires lessons that focus on various aspects of the language, he believes that activities such as guided dialogues, role takings, and simulations are not so narrowly focused. They require language learners to problem-solve and choose their own words instead of simply parroting standard responses.

A summary of van Lier's thoughts on language activities and specifically language practice includes the following five points:

1. Quality of exposure and interactions is more important than quantity. Thoughtfully designed activities that engage students and encourage authentic language participation are more valuable than numerous, repetitive parroting exercises.
2. The quality of the interaction is determined by a student's access. The comprehensibility of the activity, the context in which it takes place, the student's familiarity with the topic and the others engaged, and the student's self-confidence are all factors that make an activity work to advance language understanding.
3. Students must be receptive to participation in activities. In order for this to take place, students must feel that they can be successful and will receive support if needed.
4. In order for the language activities to become a part of a student's language **repertoire**, the student must process the material both cognitively and socially.
5. In order for new learning to be remembered and accessible, various forms of practice, including rehearsal, may be necessary (van Lier, 1996).

The principles noted by van Lier have an important impact on the types of activities we plan for our language learners. Keep in mind his emphasis on considering students' interests, personalities, and motivation; actively engaging students; and assuring students that they will be supported as they participate.

The role of the classroom environment in supporting children's language acquisition cannot be ignored. Meaningful exposure to language is not enough. Students need many opportunities for language interaction. Swain and Lapkin (1997) propose that a classroom where children work together to solve problems and produce projects supports their language development in several ways. It gives them authentic reasons to communicate and support in refining their language production. It also helps students understand that their verbal communication is not always understood by others. This realization helps to move children from **receptive, semantic processing** (listening to understand) to **expressive, syntactic processing** (formation of words and sentences to communicate). If children are simply left to listen and observe without the opportunity or necessity to communicate they remain in the **preproductive stage** for an extended period of time. The structure of **communicative classroom activities**, those that necessitate communication and verbal interaction, prevents this from happening. As far back as 1991, a shift in classroom structures for English learners was under way (Brown, 1991). The shift includes a number of areas as illustrated by the following:

We are moving from:	**and shifting to:**
A focus on product	a focus on process
Teacher-controlled classrooms	student-involved classrooms
Preplanned, rigid curricula	flexible, open-ended curricula
Measuring only performance	gauging competence and potential
Praising correct answers	building on approximations

Source: Adapted from Brown (1991).

The values underlying these shifts are clear. "Teaching practices that are **process-oriented, autonomous**, and **experiential** are considered empowering. The shift from the previous product-oriented and teacher-fronted **pedagogies** certainly reduced passivity of students and encouraged greater involvement" (Canagarajah, 2006; Zhang, Munawar, Nui, Anderson, 2016).

In addition to the shift in teaching focus in the 1990s, the focus of the Common Core standards added another challenge to teachers and students alike. Teachers implementing Common Core are expected to raise **student interactions** to include requiring that students explain the processes they use to obtain answers in mathematics as well as strategies they use in solving problems or reading for understanding. This change in requirements provides an additional challenge to both teachers and ELLs. Standards provide a tool for identifying the language as well as the content that ELLs are expected to achieve. **English Language Proficiency Standards (ELPS)** act as a starting point for identifying the language that ELLs must develop to access and negotiate **content** successfully. They provide the bridge to the **content-area standards** expected of all students (Fenner & Segota, 2012).

Current Research Related to Teaching Reading to English Language Learners

It is widely recognized that limited language proficiency hampers reading development in English (August & Shanahan, 2006). Reading proficiency is central to student learning in all content areas and, because of this, has generated a large number of research studies in recent years (Brown, 2007). In 2012, the Educational Testing Service published an extensive review of literature concerned with teaching reading to English language learners (Turkan, Bicknell, & Croft, 2012). This report identifies successful strategies for teachers who want to become effective teachers of English language learners and groups the approaches into three areas of importance for ELLs:

1. Teachers should recognize that literacy skills in the ELLs' native languages might influence their processing of linguistic information in English.
2. Teachers should facilitate active learning of academic vocabulary and the linking of new vocabulary to everyday experiences.
3. Teachers should be able to guide ELLs with metacognitive reading strategies that help them monitor and repair comprehension problems.

Literacy Skills in the First Language

Although it is widely recognized that students who already know how to read in their first language have an advantage in learning to read English, there are some ways that reading knowledge in one language may interfere with comprehension in English, or any second language. Several studies found that phonological awareness in Spanish supported the growth of phonological awareness in English (Leafstedt, Richards, & Gerber, 2004; Lindsey, Manis, & Bailey, 2003). There has been some attention to the possible interference caused by false cognates in English. Cognates are words in English that sound similar to Spanish words. False cognates are words that are similar in spelling in both languages but have different meanings in English (Durgunoglu, 2002). This becomes problematic when teachers have limited or no knowledge of the students' first languages. There are resources available to teachers, however. In *Learner English*, Swan and Smith (2001) examine the types of interference students of various languages encounter when they are in the process of acquiring English. By identifying the differences between various languages and English, the book helps teachers pinpoint difficulties in reading, writing, and speaking that may be due to the interference of rules and formats from a student's first language (see Chapter 24, Cognate Strategies). There are also lists of cognates and false cognates available online that provide teachers with knowledge of when to draw on students' cognate knowledge and when to warn them of false cognates. Several good lists of cognates and non-cognates are available online.

Vocabulary Instruction

Calderon (2007) highlighted the importance of teachers understanding the levels of lexical challenge presented by different English words. Based on the work of Beck, McKeown, and Kucan (2002), Calderon suggests that teachers distinguish words as belonging to one of three tiers:

Tier one words are common, everyday words in English that are probably understood in the students' first language. These words can often be taught by providing a visual or referring to a word in the students' first language.

Tier two words are more academic words that are used across disciplines. Many of these words are prepositions and conjunctions that are used across all content areas, for example: *so, at, into, within, by, if,* and *then*. Understanding the relationship implied by these words supports the students' comprehension of academic language. Without this understanding, comprehension of tier three vocabulary becomes more challenging.

Tier three words are infrequently used words that may be content-specific. These words often have cognate words in the students' first language.

Townsend and Collins (2009) drew on the findings of an intervention study to suggest that teachers provide multiple exposures to target words in multiple texts so students have many opportunities to use words in meaningful contexts (see Chapter 7, Collecting and Processing Words and Chapter 6, Vocabulary Role-Play).

Calderon (2007) and Herrera, Perez, and Escamilla (2010) suggest several additional instructional approaches. Teachers should:

- preteach vocabulary including contextualization to support the text to be read;
- differentiate their vocabulary instruction based on students' language development level;
- choose words from the correct tier to enable students to comprehend;
- use graphic organizers to support vocabulary understanding (see Chapter 30, Graphic Organizers);
- make vocabulary collections (see Chapter 7, Collecting and Processing Words);
- incorporate oral activities to give students practice in using the new vocabulary (see Chapter 19, Verb Action); and
- provide multiple opportunities to use the new vocabulary in several contexts during the school day.

Several researchers have focused on the importance of contextualizing vocabulary. McIntyre, Kyle, and Chen (2008) found that the connections made between new vocabulary and students' past experiences are vital in supporting the students' retention and use of the vocabulary, both orally and in writing. The research done by McIntyre et al. (2008) and Marzano and Pickering (2006) also found that repeated practice with new vocabulary serves a vital role in the retention and use of words. Other recommendations include:

- using Total Physical Response with beginning-level ELLs (see Chapter 2, Total Physical Response), and
- acting out word meanings (see Chapter 6, Vocabulary Role-Play) .

Rieg and Parquette (2009) present the idea that ELLs' comprehension of vocabulary and text is enhanced through music, drama, and reader's theater activities (see Chapter 12, Repeated Readings). Porter (2009) suggests several strategies:

- using adapted texts or abridged versions of texts;
- reading summaries of text before reading the actual text; and
- using visual aids such as maps of character relationships, student-produced storyboards, and student illustrations depicting characters or scenes in the text.

Zhang et al (2016) present an approach to conducting discussion groups focused on interactions among students after reading a common text. The teacher's questioning provided support for both students' involvement in the group and their deeper understanding of the text.

Focusing on text "structure" is identified by Dreher and Grey (2010) as a vital part of supporting ELLs in comprehending text. Very often ELLs are not familiar with sentence structures such as *compare* and *contrast*. Providing direct instruction in comprehending sentence structure as well as specific vocabulary connected with varying sentence structure supports both vocabulary and comprehension development. Terms such as *unlike, similar to, compared to*, and *resembles* require identification, definition, and practice in use. Combining reading and writing instruction by discussing, identifying, and then writing sentence structures like compare-and-contrast statements supports student understanding and presents an opportunity to assess student achievement in an authentic way.

Several researchers (Cummins, 2003; Shanahan & Beck, 2006) have noted that teachers should emphasize vocabulary but also emphasize comprehension. Research supports the use of a reading instruction approach that balances an emphasis on word recognition with the teaching of high-level reading strategies. This is also emphasized in the Common Core, where much attention is paid to high-level comprehension skills such as recognizing motivation in characters and the way in which word choice changes the nuances of meaning. These types of reading strategies require that students use self-monitoring or metacognition skills.

Improving Metacognition Skills

Herrera et al. (2010), p. 142) define metacognition skills as the "ability to think about [one's] own thinking." Proficient readers are able to monitor their own understanding of text, identify problems when they are not comprehending, and find resources to build their understanding (e.g., bilingual dictionaries, reading strategies, and asking clarifying questions). Other exemplary practices for ELLs identified in the research include:

- teaching students to verbalize their thought processes while reading (Herrera et al., 2010; Vacca & Vacca, 2008);
- teaching students to use think-aloud strategies combined with (1) making predictions, (2) developing images from the text as its being read, (3) linking to information to past knowledge or experience, and (4) demonstrating strategies they employ to explain how they got their information (Vacca & Vacca, 2008);
- providing explicit instruction in strategies such as questioning, making inferences, monitoring, summarizing, visualizing, and identifying main ideas (Mokhtari & Sheorey, 2002; Taboada, 2010); and
- explicitly modeling strategies and ensuring that students have repeated **guided practice** in using them.

Supporting English Language Learners in Constructing Meaning

Making meaning is defined by Ajayi (2008) as "a process by which learners gain critical consciousness of the interpretation of events in their lives in relation to the world around them" (p. 211). This concept stresses that meaning is created by individual learners, and that they construct meaning after reading a story or watching a video while being influenced by their own social, cultural, and historical experiences.

The role of the teacher is important in supporting students in building on their background knowledge and cultural experiences (Herrera et al., 2010). Successful strategies found for facilitating students' abilities to integrate past knowledge and experience with understanding of texts being read include:

- using literature logs to encourage students to think about the meanings of words, ideas, and themes in text (see Chapter 7, Collecting and Processing Words);
- promoting students' extended verbal and written interactions by *working the text*—reading it, rereading it, discussing it, and writing about it (see Chapter 11, Close Reading);
- using literature circles to support students' in making text-to-self, text-to-text, and text-to-world connections (Farris et al., 2007); and
- using multiple modalities to communicate meaning by providing pictures, songs, textbooks, narratives, spoken and written words, gestures, films, or videos that support understanding (Ajayi, 2008; see Chapter 4, Visual Scaffolding).

Many researchers (Krashen, 1982; Krashen & Terrell, 1983; McLaughlin, 1990) have studied the role of emotions in the acquisition of language. Krashen calls the effect of emotions on learning the **affective filter**. When a learner is placed in a stressful situation in which language production or performance is demanded, the student's ability to learn or produce spoken language may be impaired. This underscores the responsibility of the teachers to provide a supportive classroom environment in which students can participate at a comfortable level without having to worry about being embarrassed or placed in a situation where they will be made to feel incompetent. Krashen's affective filter hypothesis stresses that for a student to learn effectively, the student's motivation and self-esteem must be supported while anxiety is diminished. This provides an opportunity for the English language learner to take in information, process vocabulary, and eventually produce language because stress levels are lowered and the affective filter is not interfering with thinking and learning.

Motivation and Competition as they relate to English Language Learners

Motivation is generally recognized as a key factor in language learning. In first language learning, the basic need to communicate wants and desires is highly motivational. Ushioda (2013) asserts that motivation is a key factor in second language learning, as well. Because of this factor, teachers must recognize that their ability to motivate is extremely important to their teaching effectiveness. A major factor in students' development of autonomy is the teacher's ability to support them in acquiring techniques that support their learning success through individual effort and the use of strategies and self-regulation methods (Kormos & Csizer, 2013).

Competition is a motivational approach used in many classrooms. Its success has been shown to be dependent upon students' confidence and perception of themselves as learners.

Two types of competition are typically used in the classroom: self and social. In self-competition, students try to achieve personal bests by improving their performance and tracking their progress. The teacher helps by setting up a record-keeping system and consistently celebrating student achievements. Self-competition is seen as a more positive approach with English Language Learners until their abilities to communicate in English become more closely aligned to their peers (Zhi-Hong, 2014).

An alternate approach used by some teachers allows the use of both systems at the same time. The idea is to have some students track their own personal achievements while others compete and compare with one another. For example, if teams are doing math problems on the board, self-competitors do the same problems at their seats and keep track of their own successes. That way everyone gets the practice, some individual and some social. This allows students who are motivated by team competition the enjoyment of "comparing" while others can choose to compete solely with themselves. Self-competitors should be encouraged to keep track of their growth in a small notebook in much the same way that athletes keep track of their "personal bests".

Language Demands on the Student

Jim Cummins's research (2000) contributes to the understanding of language acquisition and effective classroom practice in several ways. First, Cummins differentiates between social language, called **basic interpersonal communication skills (BICS)**, and **academic language**, called **cognitive academic language proficiency (CALP)**. Though students may acquire BICS and be able to communicate in English while on the playground or when asking and answering simple questions, this is not the same thing as having the level of language proficiency necessary to benefit fully from academic English instruction without additional support. As you watch this video in which Dr. Cummins explains his theories, think about the following questions:

Enhanced eText
Video Example TO.2

- What indicators of a student's acquisition of BICS would a teacher be able to observe?
- How would indicators of CALP differ from those of BICS?

Cummins's theory of the differences between social and academic language has been criticized, especially by proponents of the whole language approach. Although Cummins responds to these criticisms in his book *Language, Power, and Pedagogy* (2000), he still maintains that, although social and academic language are not mutually exclusive, differences between the two are real. He also maintains that instruction in academic language does not have to be reduced to "drill and kill." One of the criticisms of his theory is based on the definition of academic language as "decontextualized." One of the important approaches to teaching academics to English learners is the use of **visuals**, manipulatives, and **multiple examples** to provide **context** and promote understanding. Cummins also emphasizes the power of academic language in promoting success for English learners, both in school and in life (Cummins, 2000).

Cummins helps us understand what must be added to instruction to make it comprehensible to students. He identifies two **dimensions of language**: its **cognitive demand** and its **context embeddedness.** Using a **quadrant matrix**, Cummins (1996) demonstrates how the addition of context supports students' understanding of all verbal communication and is vital with more

FIGURE TO.3 Cummins's Quadrant Demonstrating the Dimensions of Language

Source: Adapted from "Primary Language Instruction and the Education of Language Minority Students" (p. 10), by J. Cummins, 1996, *Schooling and Language Minority Students: A Theoretical Framework,* 2nd ed. Los Angeles, CA: Evaluation, Dissemination, and Assessment Center, School of Education, California State University, Los Angeles. Copyright 1996 by Charles F. Leyba, Reprinted with permission.

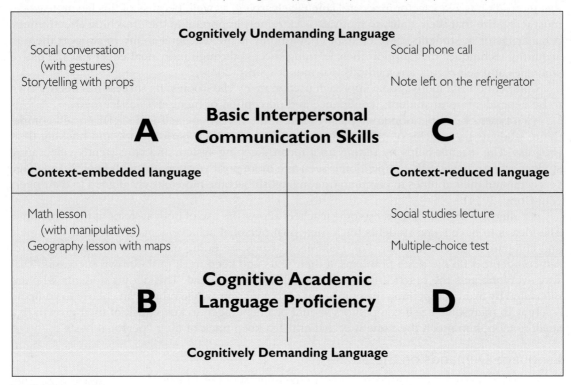

cognitively demanding language such as the language of content instruction in the classroom. Figure TO.3 points out the interaction of these linguistic elements.

By examining Cummins's quadrant, teachers can see that even social language is made more understandable by the addition of context. Directions given orally with gestures are more easily understood than the same words spoken over the telephone without the aid of gestures. This becomes even more important in the classroom, where teachers use academic terms that may be unfamiliar to the English language learner or use them in a way that might be different from the customary social meaning. Figure TO.4 demonstrates this possible confusion with one English language learner's illustration of a riverbed in response to a geography lesson. The student's understanding of the word *bed* was linked to his prior knowledge of the word and did not support his understanding of the term when used to describe a geographic feature.

FIGURE TO.4 An English Language Learner's Concept of a Riverbed

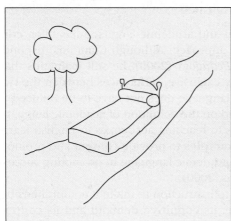

The Underlying Theory Base of Instruction for English Language Learners

In recent years, the research base addressing effective teaching strategies for English learners has grown as more teachers experience the need to prepare themselves to better serve this population. Basic techniques to support English learners in the classroom have been employed widely. These techniques include such things as slower speech, clear enunciation, use of visuals and demonstrations, vocabulary development, making connections to student experiences, and the use of supplementary materials (Genesee, 1999).

With the initial publication of *50 Strategies for Teaching English Language Learners* (Herrell, 1999) and *Making Content Comprehensible for English Learners: The SIOP Model* (Echevarria, Vogt, & Short, 2000), teachers have concrete strategies for effectively supporting the learning of English learners in their classrooms. These resources provide strategies that support the progress of English learners in the classroom and include such vital components as:

- planning language objectives for lessons in all curricular areas;
- building academic vocabulary development into all lessons;
- building and activating background knowledge;
- providing opportunities for extended academic English interaction;
- integrating vocabulary and concept review throughout lessons; and
- providing both modeling and feedback related to language usage in both speech and writing (Short & Echevarria, 2004/2005).

Strategies are defined in this book as approaches that can be used across curricular areas to support the learning of students. The strategies described in this book are based on the theories of the linguists described in this introductory section. The goals of the strategies are to enhance learning. To provide this enhancement, one or more of the underlying premises of effective instruction of English language learners are emphasized in each of the strategies. These five premises are as follows:

1. Teachers should provide instruction in a way that ensures students are given *comprehensible input* (material presented in a manner that leads to a student's understanding of the content, i.e., visual, manipulative, scaffolded in the child's first language [L1], etc.).
2. Teachers should provide opportunities to increase verbal interaction in classroom activities.
3. Teachers should provide instruction that contextualizes language as much as possible.
4. Teachers should use teaching strategies and grouping techniques that reduce the anxiety of students as much as possible.
5. Teachers should provide activities in the classroom that offer opportunities for active involvement of the students.

According to Díaz-Rico and Weed (2002) and Ovando, Collier, and Combs (2003), teachers who consistently use scaffolding strategies (contextual supports, simplified language, teacher modeling, visuals and graphics, and cooperative and hands-on learning) to help English learners organize their thoughts in English, develop study skills, and follow classroom procedures, support their students in making significant gains in knowledge of both academic English and curriculum content.

As teaching strategies like the scaffolding strategies previously listed are explained in the following chapters, the reader will be reminded of the national TESOL standards by means of a feature at the end of each chapter entitled "Examples of Approximation Behaviors Related to the TESOL Standards." They connect the strategy to the reasons for its appropriateness to English language learners. Strategies are related to the goals deemed by TESOL to be important in supporting students who are acquiring English. Making the connection between the TESOL goals and the students' levels of English development enables teachers to select activities that best suit the needs of their learners. The strategies in this book are not meant to be used in isolation. By combining strategies, teachers can plan innovative lessons that will motivate students to learn. The examples that are included in each chapter demonstrate ways the strategies can be combined and used effectively.

The Role of Assessment in Teaching English Language Learners

Students who are in the process of acquiring English often have difficulty expressing themselves in conveying their understanding of the content they are learning. Beginning English learners often understand much more than they are able to express. Their receptive English grows at a much faster rate than their expressive English. For this reason, teachers must create a variety of ways for English learners to demonstrate their understanding. It is important that teachers provide ways of documenting the learning of ELLs so that appropriate lessons can be planned. It is also vital that English learners be able to show that they are learning and be included in classroom interactions. Assessment strategies are included as part of this theoretical overview because teachers will need to adjust their teaching strategies on the basis of their knowledge of students' growing competencies. Because assessment can be extremely language-based, requiring exact vocabulary to read and answer questions, assessment strategies must be adjusted to find out how well students understand the concepts being taught. Less formal assessment also provides an opportunity for teachers to learn more about their learners' understanding of English vocabulary and use of sentence structure.

Assessment strategies appropriate for English learners include the use of observation and anecdotal records by the classroom teacher and paraprofessionals (watching and documenting the students' reactions and responses, as well as documenting their growth). In addition, performance sampling, in which students complete certain tasks while teachers observe and document their responses, are very effective in monitoring and documenting growth. The third assessment strategy, portfolio assessment, is a way to maintain records of observations, performance sampling, and ongoing growth. These three assessment strategies, when combined, provide a rich store of information about English learners that give a more complete picture of their individual growth and learning development.

Anecdotal Records

Anecdotal records (Rhodes & Nathenson-Mejia, 1993) are a form of assessment that allows teachers to document the growth and accomplishments of students. Anecdotal records are based on a teacher's observations of students as they engage in classroom activities. This form of assessment and documentation is especially appropriate for English language learners because the teacher can ask questions of students, record language samples, and note ways in which students demonstrate understanding (Genishi & Dyson, 1984).

Teachers are free to discuss observations with students and celebrate the growth that is documented. This encourages and motivates students and may even serve to lower classroom anxiety, thereby increasing participation and learning (Garcia, 1994). An anecdotal record always includes the student's name, the date of the observation, and a narrative of what was seen and heard by the teacher. It is not intended to be a summary of behavior but instead a record of one incident or anecdote observed by the teacher. Such things as quotes, descriptions of interactions with other students or teachers, and demonstrations of knowledge through the use of manipulatives or learning centers are easily documented through these narratives. If anecdotal records are taken regularly and placed in sequential order, they provide a good indication of a student's progress and a basis for instructional planning. A sample of an anecdotal record of a first-grade child working at the writing center is shown in Figure TO.5.

FIGURE TO.5 Anecdotal Record for an English Language Learner

Maria	**4/15**	**Writing Center with Dolores**

Maria and Dolores are sitting at the writing center looking at labeled pictures of birds. On the table is a collection of books about birds. The students are to write one page for a book about birds they are compiling this week.

"What this word?" Maria asks Dolores, pointing to the word *eagle*. Dolores answers "eagle." Maria: "That a pretty bird. I write about eagle." She writes, "Eagle is a prty brd." and draws a very detailed picture of the eagle. The teacher asks her why she thinks the eagle is pretty. Maria says, "Eagle have shiny feathers." The teacher asks if she can write that. Maria smiles, and says, "I try." She writes, "Eagle hv shne fethrs."

Step-by-Step

The steps in implementing anecdotal records are the following:

- *Decide on a system*—Decide what system you will use for keeping anecdotal records. They can be kept on index cards, in a notebook, on peel-off mailing labels (later transferred in sequence to an anecdotal record form), or in any format that helps keep track of student progress.
- *Choose what to document and schedule*—Decide what you want to document and make a schedule for observing the students. A sample schedule allowing a teacher to observe a class of 20 students—4 per day—in four areas a month is shown in Figure TO.6.
- *Conference and set goals*—Set up a conference schedule and discuss your observations with the students and/or parents. This is also a good time to discuss language development and the setting of language and content-area goals.
- *Use records for planning*—Use the records to plan appropriate lessons for your students or to focus on language acquisition goals and progress. See the "Language Framework Planning" section in Chapter 34 for an example of how this could be done.

FIGURE TO.6 Schedule for Conducting Observations for Anecdotal Records

Focus Area	Monday	Tuesday	Wednesday	Thursday	Friday
Writing Center	Ana Blia Carol Helen	Dan Irana Maria Susana	Jose Earl Patrick Wally	Luis Rosa Tomas Franco	Gina Karen Ned Pablo
Literature Circles					
Writing Conference					
Guided Reading					

Performance Sampling

Performance sampling is a form of authentic assessment in which students are observed in the process of accomplishing academic tasks and evaluated on how the tasks are done. The word *authentic* indicates that the tasks students are asked to do are similar or identical to actual tasks that students routinely accomplish in the classroom setting, unlike more traditional forms of assessment, which tend to be unlike everyday classroom activities.

Performance samples are well named because the teacher observes a sample of the student's performance in a given academic task. Examples of the types of tasks used in performance sampling are the following:

- working a mathematics problem that involves reading the problem, setting up an approach to finding a solution, and finding a reasonable solution;
- responding to a writing prompt by webbing a short piece of writing, writing a draft of a written piece, working with a peer to elicit feedback on the draft, revising the piece, and working with a peer to edit the piece for mechanics and spelling; and
- researching a topic in social studies and documenting the information gained by completing a data chart.

Performance samples are documented in several ways. The teacher might write an anecdotal record of the observation. The teacher might design a scoring **rubric** and evaluate the student's performance on the rubric as seen in Figure TO.7. Figure TO.8 shows a teacher's checklist for evaluating student performance.

FIGURE TO.7 Example of a Scoring Rubric for Performance Sampling

5	**Exemplary Performance**
	The student:
	planned the task in an outstanding way
	followed the plan to achieve a high-level product
	proofread and corrected all errors
	produced a unique product
4	**Strong Performance**
	The student:
	planned the task
	followed the plan to complete the product
	proofread and corrected the majority of errors
	produced a good product
3	**Acceptable Performance**
	The student:
	performed the task to an acceptable end
	corrected some errors
	showed some understanding of what was required
2	**Weak Performance**
	The student:
	showed some confusion about what was expected
	left out some important steps in the process or didn't finish the task completely
	failed to correct errors
1	**Very Weak Performance**
	The student:
	showed only minimal understanding of the task
	completed a very small portion of the task
0	**No Performance**
	The student failed to complete the task

FIGURE TO.8 Example of a Checklist for the Assessment of Performance Sampling

_____ The student read the problem.
_____ The student made an attempt to find a solution to the problem.
_____ The student demonstrated planning to devise a solution.
_____ The student followed the plan created.
_____ The student found a solution to the problem.
_____ The student found multiple solutions to the problem.
_____ The student evaluated the solutions found and recognized the most unique or viable one.
_____ The student was able to communicate viable reasons for his/her choice of solutions.
_____ The student was able to explain the methods used in finding the solution to the problem.

Note: Dates should be included.

Performance sampling is a particularly appropriate form of assessment for English language learners because their approach to academic tasks is observed and documented and their assessment is based on their ability to perform the task rather than their fluency in English, which is sometimes the case in more traditional forms of assessment (Hernandez, 1997).

Step-by-Step

The steps in performance sampling are the following:

- *Choose an assessment task*—Decide on the academic area to be assessed and choose a task for the students to perform that will demonstrate their understanding of the content that has been studied. Design an observation instrument such as a rubric or **checklist** (Figures TO.7 and TO.8) or structure an anecdotal record that will itemize the abilities documented by the student.
- *Set up a schedule*—Set up a schedule so that you can observe all the students within a reasonable amount of time.
- *Design the task*—Gather materials and set up the task so that you can observe the students and document their performance. Plan an assignment for the rest of the class to do so that you will be able to observe without interruption.
- *Observe and give feedback*—Observe the students, complete the observation instrument, and give them feedback on their performances.

Making Classroom Assessments Comprehensible to English Language Learners

Writing equitable classroom assessments for maximum success without watering down the content requires following some guidelines (Siegal, Wissehr, & Halverson, 2008). In order for test questions to be comprehensible to English learners, several considerations must be employed.

- The learning, instructional goals, and assessment questions must match.
- The conceptual and scientific goals should be assessed.
- The language demands of the lesson and the assessment must match.
- Make assessments linguistically and culturally comprehensible by using shorter sentences, bulleting ideas, and adding visuals.

Language Development Profiles

Language development profiles are a form of rubric based on language acquisition stages. Typical language usage and structures are listed along with the language development stage. The teacher uses these profiles to document the progress of an English learner by noting examples of the student's language usage along with the date the sample was noted. Language development profiles are most effective when combined with short anecdotal records and included in a portfolio that provides samples of the student's class work.

Step-by-Step

The steps in using language development profiles are the following:

- *Identify the state or national language development standards to be used*—Since teachers are responsible for addressing the language development standards of their own state, it makes sense to use those standards as a basis for observing and documenting the progress of the English learners for whom they are responsible. Figure TO.9 provides an example

FIGURE TO.9 Language Development Profile

Student's Name: Jose Garcia
Grades K–2 Listening and Speaking

Early Production	Speech Emergence	Intermediate Fluency	Full Fluency
Speaks single words or short phrases	Beginning to be understood when speaking (may still have inconsistent use of plurals, past tense, pronouns)	Asks and answers instructional questions using simple sentences	Listens attentively to stories and information on new topics and identifies key concepts and details both orally and in writing
8/29/05 Jose asked, "I come?" when I asked his table group to move to the carpet.	10/12/05 Jose said, "They same size." when asked why he put two figures together in a sorting activity.		

Grades K–2 Reading Fluency and Vocabulary Development

Early Production	Speech Emergence	Intermediate Fluency	Full Fluency
Reads aloud simple words (nouns, adjectives)	Reads aloud an increasing number of English words	Uses decoding skills to read more complex words independently	Recognizes words that have multiple meanings in texts
9/15/05 Jose read his name and Angelica's on the duty chart.	10/14/05 Jose read all the color words aloud when playing a game.		

Please note that this is a small section of the K–2 English Development Profile, used for an example, only. For the complete profile, please see the Teacher Resource section of this text.

of a language development profile based on the California English Language Development Standards. A complete profile is also included in the Teacher Resources section.

- ***Prepare a functional profile for classroom use***—Using the English language development standards for your state, compare them to the example given in this text. Make any adaptations needed to address the standards for which you are responsible. The profile should clearly describe an example of the type of language the student will be able to produce at each level. Structure the profile so that you have space for dating and documenting the language samples that you observe (see Figure TO.9 for an example).
- ***Familiarize yourself with the profile***—It is easier to recognize growth when you are very familiar with the stages and examples given on the profile. Keep an example of the profile handy to guide you in the beginning. As you interact with students, practice identifying the stages at which they are communicating. The stages will soon become very familiar to you.
- ***Plan regular observations***—Until this process becomes a part of your regular teaching routine, plan times for observing. Whenever you have an opportunity to interact verbally with English learners in your classroom, document their levels of language development.
- ***Document the students' language development progress***—Make a habit of jotting down the date and a few words to help you remember the content and context of verbal interactions that can be documented on the profiles. You may start by using sticky pads and attaching your notes on a blank profile. However, you should always take a few minutes at the end of each day to update your profiles. Once your notes become cold, it's hard to remember exactly what you wanted to document. (Again, refer to Figure TO.9 for an example of documentation.)
- ***Share the language development progress with students and parents***—Plan time to share the progress you are seeing. You will find that the developmental profiles support you in celebrating student growth by giving you very specific language samples to share with your students and their parents.
- ***Store the profiles***—The profiles are valuable to you in documenting student growth, writing comments on report cards, and passing on information to other teachers and support personnel. If you are maintaining portfolios, they provide a perfect place for storing the profiles. Some teachers have found that they prefer to keep the profiles in a separate folder within easy reach so that they can be constantly updated.
- ***Use technology in the process***—Many teachers use a computer to add the documentation to their developmental profiles. They take informal notes, as previously described, but then update the profiles on the computer. This provides an ongoing file of information that can (and should be) updated and printed out periodically for safekeeping.

Portfolio Assessment

Portfolio assessment refers to a system for gathering observations, performance samples, and work samples in a folder or portfolio; regularly analyzing the contents of the portfolio; and summarizing the students' progress as documented by the contents of the portfolio (Herrell, 1996). Often, students are involved in selecting the work to be kept in the portfolio. Students are also involved in the review and summarization of the work, setting goals for future work, and sharing the contents of the portfolio with parents (Farr & Tone, 1998). English language learners can demonstrate their growth over time by being actively involved in selecting items to be included in their portfolios. This video demonstrates how students reflect on their own work while teachers help them identify ways in which they have grown and areas that still need focus. After you view the video, think about:

Enhanced eText
Video Example TO.3

- How does the teacher use the work samples to celebrate growth with the students?
- How does the teacher use the work samples to suggest areas that still need improvement?

This approach to assessment is particularly appropriate for English language learners because it enables assessment based on actual sampling of students' work and the growth they are experiencing, with less dependence on scores on standardized tests, which are often difficult for English language learners to understand (Hernandez, 2000). Portfolio assessment allows students to demonstrate their content knowledge without being so dependent on English fluency. The focus in this approach to assessment is celebration of progress rather than dwelling on weaknesses. Figure TO.10 looks at examples of the contents of a student portfolio.

FIGURE TO.10 Examples of the Contents of a Portfolio

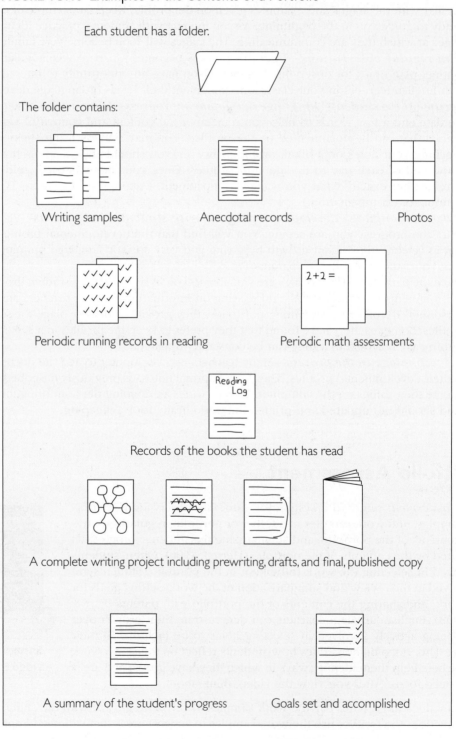

Each student has a folder.

The folder contains:

Writing samples

Anecdotal records

Photos

Periodic running records in reading

Periodic math assessments

Reading Log

Records of the books the student has read

A complete writing project including prewriting, drafts, and final, published copy

A summary of the student's progress

Goals set and accomplished

Step-by-Step

The steps in implementing portfolio assessment are the following:

- *Choose portfolio contents*—Decide what curricular areas you want to include in the portfolio and obtain baseline work samples, performance samples, or observations for each student, in each area to be included.
- *Introduce the portfolio to the students*—Explain the portfolio system to the students, stressing their active involvement in the selection of materials to be included in the portfolio. Also explain the use of baseline samples and the fact that future work samples will be selected to demonstrate the students' progress. Involve them in setting up the portfolio and labeling the samples of work that will be used as baseline samples.
- *Schedule performance and work samples*—Establish a schedule of observations and performance and work sampling that will serve to document periodic checks on the students' progress and provide updated samples of their work.
- *Schedule conferences*—Schedule periodic conferences with the students and their parents to review the contents of their portfolios, celebrate their growth, and involve them in setting goals for themselves.

Using Assessment to Differentiate Instruction

The purpose of formative assessment is to determine exactly what students understand in order to provide effective instruction that meets individual needs. Identifying students' language development level is always an approximate determination that can fluctuate according to the activity and context. Language development levels are used in Figure TO.11 to demonstrate adaptations that can be made to individualize instruction that meets students' needs.

FIGURE TO.11 Differentiating Instruction Based on Language Development Level

Activity: Read-Aloud	
Language Development Stage	**Teacher's Action**
Preproduction	Point to pictures to show words.
Early Production	Have students repeat word.
Speech Emergence	Ask simple questions.
Intermediate Fluency	Ask students to predict verbally.
Fluent	Ask students to summarize.
Activity: Writing a Story on a Chart	
Language Development Stage	**Teacher's Action**
Preproduction	Ask students to add periods.
Early Production	Ask students to write initial consonants they can identify.
Speech Emergence	Ask students to add high-frequency word (with support).
Intermediate Fluency	Ask students to write entire word.
Fluent	Ask students to reread entire sentence after group works together to write it.
Note: Students can all be listening to the same story. The teacher simply involves them according to their language development level.	

Conclusion

It is important for teachers of English language learners to recognize the essential ways in which they must adapt lessons and assessment to meet the unique needs of these students. Teachers need to understand the basic support that must be provided for English language acquisition in the classroom context. English learners can comprehensively acquire language and content if they receive the appropriate scaffolding and are assessed in ways that allow them to demonstrate their understanding and knowledge.

This new edition of *50 Strategies for Teaching English Language Learners* is specifically formatted to help teachers recognize how these students must be supported so that they can be successful in classes taught in English. The strategies are arranged in order of their recommended use according to the English language development levels of the students. Strategies typically used for preproduction students are explained first, and strategies for more advanced English learners are presented in order of their effectiveness with students as they increase in English proficiency. For each strategy, adaptation techniques show how to add support for English learners at different levels. Because it is vital that teachers continually assess and keep track of the English language development levels of students, approaches for assessing the understanding and needs of students are included and recommended for each strategy.

The strategies to support English learners are many. It is recommended that teachers implement them slowly so neither the teacher noe the students become overwhelmed. To quote Canagarajah (2006), "There are no easy answers for teachers here. They are themselves compelled to learn from students and develop engaged positions of agency as they provide learning environments that better enable critical negotiating language. The most important attribute of a successful teacher of English learners is the confidence they place on the learners and their abilities as teachers to work together in building comprehension (Gibbons, 2015).

References

Ajayi, L. (2008). Meaning-making, multimodal representation, and transformative pedagogy: An exploration of meaning construction instructional practices in an ESL high school. *Journal of Language, Identity, and Education, 7*, 206–229.

August, D., & Shanahan, T. (Eds.). (2006). *Developing literacy in second-language learners: A report of the National Literacy Panel on Language-Minority Children and Youth.* Mahwah, NJ: Erlbaum.

Beck, I., McKeown, M., & Kucan, L. (2002). *Bringing words to life.* New York, NY: Guilford Press.

Brown, C. L. (2007). Supporting English language learners in content-reading. *Reading Improvement, 44*(1), 32–39.

Brown, H. D. (1991). TESOL at twenty-five: What are the issues? *TESOL Quarterly, 25*, 245–260.

Calderon, M. (2007). *Teaching reading to English language learners, grades 6–12. A framework for improving achievement in the content areas.* Thousand Oaks, CA: Corwin Press.

Canagarajah, A. S. (2006). TESOL at forty: What are the issues? *TESOL Quarterly, 40*(1), 9–34.

Collier, V. P. (1995). Acquiring a second language for school. *Directions in Language & Education, 1*(4). National Clearinghouse for Bilingual Education.

Crawford, J., & Krashen, S. (2007). *English language learners in American classrooms: 101 questions, 101 answers.* New York, NY: Scholastic Teaching Resources.

Cummins, J. (2000). *Language, power, and pedagogy: Bilingual children in the crossfire.* Bristol, England: Multilingual Matters.

Cummins, J. (2003). Reading and the bilingual student: Fact and friction. In G. G. Garcia (Ed.), *English learners: Reaching the highest level of English literacy* (pp. 2–33). Newark, DE: International Reading Association.

Díaz-Rico, L., & Weed, Z. (2002). *The crosscultural, language, and academic development handbook* (2nd ed.). Boston, MA: Allyn & Bacon.

Dreher, M. J., & Gray, J. L. (2010). Compare, contrast, comprehend: Using compare-contrast text structures with ELLs in K–3 classrooms. *Reading Teacher, 63*(2), 132–141.

Durgunoğlu, A. Y. (2002). Cross-linguistic transfer in literacy development and implications for language learners. *Annals of Dyslexia, 52*, 189–205.

Echevarria, J., Vogt, M., & Short, D. (2000). *Making content comprehensible for English learners: The SIOP model.* Boston, MA: Allyn & Bacon.

Farr, R., & Tone, B. (1998). *Portfolio and performance assessments: Helping students evaluate their progress as readers and writers* (2nd ed.). New York, NY: Wadsworth.

Farris, P. J., L'Aller, S., & Nelson, P. A. (2007). Using literature circles with middle school ELLs. *Middle School Journal, 38*(4), 38–42.

Garcia, G. E. (1994). Assessing the literacy development of second-language students: A focus on authentic assessment. In K. Spangenberg-Urbaschat & R. Pritchard (Eds.), *Kids come in all languages: Reading instruction for ESL students* (pp. 180–205). Newark, DE: International Reading Association.

Genesee, F. (Ed.). (1999). *Program alternatives for linguistically diverse students.* (Educational Practice Report 1). Santa Cruz, CA, & Washington, DC: Center for Research on Education, Diversity, & Excellence.

Genishi, C., & Dyson, A. H. (1984). *Language assessment in the early years.* Norwood, NJ: Ablex.

Gibbons, P. (2015). *Scaffolding language, scaffolding learning: Teaching English language learners in the mainstream classroom* (2nd ed.). Portsmouth, NH: Heinemann.

Hart, B., & Risley, T. (2003). *Meaningful differences in the everyday experiences of American children.* New York, NY: Brookes.

Hernandez, H. (1997). *Teaching in multicultural classrooms.* Upper Saddle River, NJ: Merrill/Prentice Hall.

Hernandez, H. (2000). *Multicultural education: A teacher's guide to linking context, process, and content* (2nd ed.). Upper Saddle River, NJ: Pearson.

Herrell, A. (1996). Portfolios and young children, a natural match. *Kindergarten Education: Research, Theory, and Practice, 1*, 1–10.

Herrell, A. (1999). *50 strategies for teaching English language learners.* Upper Saddle River, NJ: Merrill/Prentice Hall.

Herrell, A., & Jordan, M. (2011). *50 strategies for teaching English Language Learners* (4th ed.). Upper Saddle River, NJ: Pearson.

Herrera, S. G., Perez, D. R., & Escamilla, K. (2010). *Teaching reading to English language learners: Differentiated literacies.* Boston, MA: Allyn & Bacon.

Kormos, J., & Csizer, K. (2013). The interaction of motivation, self-regulatory strategies, and autonomous learning behavior in different learner groups. *TESOL Quarterly, 47*(3) 1–25

Krashen, S. (1982). *Principles and practices of second language acquisition.* Oxford, England: Pergamon Press.

Krashen, S., & Terrell, T. (1983). *The natural approach: Language acquisition in the classroom.* Oxford, England: Pergamon Press.

Leafstedt, J. M., Richards, C. R., & Gerber, M. M. (2004). Effectiveness of explicit phonological-awareness instruction for at-risk English learners. *Learning Disabilities Research & Practice, 19*(4), 252–261.

Lindsey, K. A., Manis, F. R., & Bailey, C. E. (2003). Prediction of first-grade reading in Spanish-speaking English-language learners. *Journal of Educational Psychology, 95*(3), 482–494.

Marzano, R. J., & Pickering, D. J. (2006). *Building academic vocabulary: Teacher's manual.* Alexandria, VA: Association for Supervision and Curriculum Development.

McIntyre, E., Kyle, D. W., Chen, C.-T., Kraemer, J., & Parr, J. (2008). *Six principles for teaching English language learners in all classrooms.* Thousand Oaks, CA: Corwin Press.

McLaughlin, B. (1990). *Myths and misconceptions about second language learning: What every teacher needs to unlearn.* Santa Cruz, CA: National Center for Research on Cultural Diversity and Second Language Learning.

Mokhtari, K., & Sheorey, R. (2002). Measuring ESL students' awareness of reading strategies. *Journal of Educational Psychology, 94*(2). 249–259.

Ovando, C., Collier, V., & Combs, M. (2003). *Bilingual and ESL classrooms: Teaching multicultural contexts* (3rd ed.). Boston, MA: McGraw-Hill.

Porter, C. (2009). Words, word, words: Reading Shakespeare with English language learners. *English Journal, 99*(1), 44–49.

Rhodes, L., & Nathenson-Mejia, S. (1993). Anecdotal records: A powerful tool for ongoing literacy assessment. *The Reading Teacher, 15*, 503–509.

Rieg, S. A., & Paquette, K. R. (2009). Using drama and movement to enhance English language learners' literacy development. *Journal of Instructional Psychology, 36*(2), 148–154.

Shanahan, T., & Beck, I. (2006). Effective literacy teaching. In D. August & T. Shanahan (Eds.) *Developing literacy in second-language learners: Report of the national literacy panel on language minority children and youth*. Mahwah, NJ: Erlbaum.

Short, D., & Echevarria, J. (2004/2005). Promoting academic literacy for English language learners. *Educational Leadership. 62*(4) 8–13.

Siegel, M., Wissehr, C., Halverson, K. (2008). Sounds like success: A framework for equitable assessment: How to revise written assessments for English language learners. *The Science Teacher, 75*(3), 43–50.

Swain, M., & Lapkin, S. (1997). Problems in output and the cognitive processes they generate: Steps toward second language learning. *Applied Linguistics, 16*, 371–391.

Swan, M., & Smith, B. (Eds.). (2001). *Learner's English* (2nd ed.). Cambridge, MA: Cambridge University Press.

Taboada, A. (2010). English-language learners, vocabulary, and reading comprehension: What we know and what we need to know. *College Reading Association Yearbook, 30*, 307–322.

TESOL. (2010). *ESL standards for pre-K–12 students*. Alexandria, *VA*: Author

TESOL International Association. (2013). *Overview of the Common Core State Standards for ELLs*. Alexandria, VA: Author.

Townsend, D., & Collins, P. (2009). Academic vocabulary and middle school English learners: An intervention study. *Reading and Writing, 22*(9) 993–1019.

Turkan, S., Bicknell, J., & Croft, A. (2012). *Effective practices for developing literacy skills of English language learners in the English language classroom*. Princeton, NJ: Educational Testing Service.

United States Department of Education, National Center for Student Statistics, Common Core of Data (2017). Retrieved from http://nces.gov/ccd/elsi

Ushioda, E. (2013). Motivation and ELT. Global issues and local concerns. In E. Ushioda (Ed.), *International perspectives on motivation: Language learning and professional challenges* (pp. 1–17). Palgrave, N.H. Macmillan.

Vacca, R. T., & Vacca, J. L. (2008). *Content area reading: Literacy and learning across the curriculum* (9th ed.). Boston, MA: Pearson.

van Lier, L. (1996). *Interaction in the language curriculum: Awareness, autonomy, & authenticity*. New York, NY: Longman.

Vygotsky, L. S. (1962). *Thought and language*. Cambridge, MA: MIT Press.

Zhang, J., Niu, C., Manuwar, S., Anderson. R. (2016).What makes more proficient discussion group in English learners' classrooms? Influence of teacher talk. Research in the Teaching of English. 51 (2). Downloaded from Questa.com April 30, 2018.

Zhi-Hong, C. (2014). Learning preferences and motivation of different ability students for social-competition or self-competition. *Journal of Educational Technology & Society 17* (1), 283–293.

Predictable Routines and Signals

Reducing Anxiety

Predictable routines and signals in the classroom are highly important in structuring a positive and nurturing environment and reducing anxiety of English language learners (Ferlazzo & Sypnieski, 2011; Krashen & Terrell, 1983). Because English learners do not always understand everything that is said in the classroom, having set patterns, routines, and signals helps them relax and not worry as much about being able to follow the sequence of events and activities during the school day. If they know what to expect, they can focus more of their energy on the instruction and less on what they will be expected to do next. Predictable routines can include the sequence of the subjects to be taught, places within the classroom where certain things are stored and accessible to students, a certain spot on the chalkboard or bulletin board where reading or homework assignments are posted, a daily list that gives the routine in sequence, and hand or flashing light signals that indicate the close of one activity and the beginning of another (Goldenberg, 2008). Watch this video to see how teachers keep their students focused and alert, enabling students to connect to instruction rather than worry about what they are supposed to do next.

Enhanced eText
Video Example 1.1

- How does the use of routines and procedures enhance the learning environment?
- How do English language learners benefit from the use of routines and procedures in the classroom?

Figure 1.1 provides a list of predictable routines and signals that support English language learners in the classroom.

Although implementing predictable routines and signals is usually associated with elementary classrooms, this practice is also vital in secondary classrooms. In addition to classroom routines, secondary teachers must also make their academic expectations clear. As the Common Core State Standards (CCSS) are implemented and assessed, academic expectations are changing. Fisher and Frey (2013) suggest introducing students to the Common Core expectations in a gradual way during the first month of school. Planning activities that support students in understanding how the expectations have changed helps prepare them to address those standards. Fisher and Frey list several changes that students must understand and begin to practice in order to address the Common Core:

- Students will be expected to explore below the surface of academic tasks.
- Students will be expected to construct knowledge within and across curricular areas.
- Students will be required to be able to explain their solutions and how they arrived at them verbally and in writing.

FIGURE 1.1 Predictable Routines and Signals in the Classroom

Routine	Use	Benefit to English Language Learners
Morning sign-in	A way of taking roll and indicating lunch count.	Students feel a part of the class and that their presence is valued.
Set activity at the beginning of the school day	A way to engage students immediately. Such things as journal writing, reading library book; tasks such as watering plants, sharpening pencils are appropriate.	Students know what to do immediately. Have a chance to share their evening in writing, sign up to share journal entries, or chat briefly with peers and teacher.
Set place in the room where certain activities occur	Students move to certain areas for group lessons, review, sharing orally.	Students know what to expect when moved to a certain area.
A list of the day's activities and approximate times are posted in the same place each day	Helps students get their assignments in order and know which books to get out, when homework will be collected.	Students have a visual reminder of the day's activities; less reliance on oral directions.
Consistent use of modeling and contextualizing of oral directions	Helps students to follow directions.	Students waste less energy wondering what to do next.
Use of hand signals, light signals	Helps student to redirect their energies, know when activity changes are coming.	Students alerted to upcoming events, drawing to a close of activities and events.
Posting of assignments, page numbers, long-term assignments, homework	Helps students stay on task.	Students are aware of expectations.
Set place to submit assignments and get materials	Fosters reliability and self-reliance.	Students are aware of expectations.

All of these changes put additional stress on students learning to speak and write in English. For this reason, teachers are advised to provide training exercises from the beginning of the year so that all students are aware of the expectations.

Step-by-Step

The steps in implementing predictable routines and signals are as follows:

- *Set up your room*—Set up your room with certain areas designated for group activities, free reading, and partner work. Establish these areas with the students by **modeling** their use and asking questions like, "Will you work with other people in this area?" or "Where will you sit if you want to read a book by yourself?" Use your computer to create clear, legible, large-print signs and graphics to help guide students.
- *Establish routines*—Establish set places for students to turn in assignments, pick up needed materials, and keep their book bags, lunch boxes, and other personal belongings. Model putting these things in the established places.
- *Model routines*—Model each new routine as it is established, and be careful to maintain the routines once they've been established. Anytime a student shows confusion about a classroom routine or expectation, determine if a set routine would lessen the student's confusion.
- *Contextualize directions*—Be **consistent** about modeling as you give directions. For example, "Take out your math book" should be accompanied by your holding up the math book. "Open to page 21" should be modeled and *page 21* should be written on the board. Modeling, gestures, and demonstrations are all vital ways to **contextualize instructions**. Be consistent!
- *Evaluate your use of routines and procedures periodically to identify areas that can be improved*—Periodically use the **self-evaluation rubric** shown in Figure 1.2 to identify areas in which you can improve the use of routines and procedures in your classroom.

FIGURE 1.2 Routines and Procedures Teacher Self-Evaluation Rubric

Beginning	Developing	Accomplished	Exemplary
Establish routines and procedures for some activities.	Routines and procedures are established and rarely changed.	Routines and procedures are established and changed when students are observed needing different or additional support.	Routines and procedures are established and changed when needed. Students are given periodic reviews. Areas of the classroom are labeled to support students' use of them.
Routines and procedures are explained orally.	Routines and procedures are explained orally and modeled.	Routines and procedures are explained orally and modeled, and visual supports are added. Teacher observation is used to determine when changes are needed.	Routines and procedures are explained, orally and modeled, and visual supports are used. Their use is observed and changes are made to improve student understanding and success. Student input is a part of the planning for change.

FIGURE 1.3 Checklist for Observing Student Use of Classroom Routines and Signals

Names	Date	No Response	Watches Others Before Responding	Responds to Signal or Verbal Direction

Suggested Interventions
No response: Assign a partner.
Watches others: Offer verbal encouragement.
Responds appropriately: Offer positive nonverbal acknowledgment.
Establish a signal that indicates "I need help."

• *Assess to determine appropriate follow-up instruction*—When giving directions in the classroom, be aware of how your English learners respond. Note whether they need visual cues, for instance watching others before responding. You may want to use a simple checklist to focus your observations and keep track of students' progress in classroom participation. See Figure 1.3 for a sample checklist.

Applications and Examples

Mr. Castle's kindergarten students know exactly what to expect when he starts singing, "Time to clean up." They immediately begin to put their materials away. They seem to shift into high gear when they see their teacher pick up a book and go to sit in the rocking chair. They all know it's story time. They quickly clean up and go sit on the carpet. They love to hear Mr. Castle read stories.

Mr. Castle uses a set of predictable routines and signals with his 5-year-olds. Using consistent and predictable routines is especially effective for his English learners. His students know that when the light on the overhead projector comes on, Mr. Castle wants them to quiet down. He has several songs he sings to give them signals about changing activities and he always puts notices to go home on top of the bookshelf by the door. If Mr. Castle forgets to give out the notices, he hears from 20 youngsters, "You forgot to give us our notes!"

* * * * *

Ms. Newsome teaches high school economics. A number of her students are English language learners, so she has assigned study partners for them. Ms. Newsome uses a simple routine to signal to her students when an assignment can be done with the study partners. She writes the names of both partners on the top of the assignment page when she determines that the assignment can be done in collaboration. When she thinks the assignment is one that her English language learners can handle on their own, she doesn't write the names on the assignment paper.

Ms. Newsome has established a set routine that also serves as a signal to her students for when collaborative work is acceptable. She also has some lessons she records, and the English language learners are instructed to use the listening station to listen to the tape and follow the directions step-by-step. Her English language learners know when she wants them to move to the listening station because Ms. Newsome simply hands a tape to Joaquin, which signals that it is his job to go by and tap the others on the shoulder. Ms. Newsome doesn't have to say a word.

Conclusion

Predictable routines and signals save a lot of time in the classroom because a short signal or standard routine lets students know what is expected of them. Signals and routines also serve to lower students' anxiety and help them feel they are fully participating in the classroom community, which is especially important for English learners.

Examples of Approximation Behaviors Related to the TESOL Standards

PreK–3 students will:

- restate information given.
- give or ask for permission.

4–8 students will:

- follow directions from modeling.
- associate labeled realia with vocabulary.

9–12 students will:

- ask for information and clarification.
- negotiate solutions to problems.

References

Ferlazzo, L., & Sypnieski, K. (2011). *The ESL/ELL teacher's survival guide.* San Francisco, CA: Jossey-Bass.

Fisher, D., & Frey, N. (2013). *The First 20 Days: Common Core Edition.* Newark, DE: International Reading Association.

Goldenberg, G. (2008.) Teaching English language learners: What the research does—and does not—say. *American Educator, 32*(2), 8–44.

Krashen, S., & Terrell, T. (1983). *The natural approach: Language acquisition in the classroom.* Oxford, England: Pergamon Press.

Total Physical Response and Total Physical Response Storytelling (TPR and TPRS)

Integrating Movement into Language Acquisition

Total physical response (TPR) (Asher, 1982, 2009) is an approach to second-language acquisition based on first-language acquisition research. In first-language acquisition, children follow a sequence: a) they listen and acquire receptive language before attempting to speak, b) they then develop understanding through moving their bodies, and c) they are not forced to speak until they are ready. Repetition and active involvement are vital to the retention of new vocabulary (Nation, 2005).

In total physical response (TPR), teachers build on the natural sequence of language acquisition. Teachers gradually introduce commands, acting them out as they say them. Initially, students respond by performing the actions as the teacher demonstrates. Gradually, the teacher's demonstrations are removed, and the students respond only to the verbal commands. Teaching classroom routines through total physical response helps students gain confidence in classroom participation (Díaz-Rico, 2013).

Further research in the practice of TPR (Seely & Romijn, 2006) has identified uses for this strategy beyond learning basic vocabulary, directions, and procedures. Research suggests that total physical response storytelling greatly enhances language fluency. According to language acquisition expert Stephen Krashen, "TPR storytelling is much better than anything else out there" (quoted in Seely & Romijn, 2006, p. 39).

Step-by-Step

The steps in teaching a total physical response lesson are the following:

- *Choose vocabulary to physicalize*—Choose vocabulary that will be used in the classroom, such as verbal directions, colors, and parts of the body, and list the words that students will need to know. For older students, select directions and vocabulary that are relevant to the current lesson. Choose simple commands that incorporate the target vocabulary and that require a movement response such as "Stand up," "Sit down," "Touch your head," or "Show me the red block."

• *Introduce vocabulary gradually*—Introduce two or three commands at first. Give a **command** while demonstrating it physically. For example, "Stand up" is accompanied by standing up. Motion for the students to do it with you. Introduce the next command and demonstrate. After you have introduced three commands, randomly alternate the commands and continue modeling and encouraging the students' responses.

• *Drop the physical modeling*—After students have practiced the commands as you model them, and once they appear to know what to do without waiting for your demonstration, drop the demonstration and encourage students to respond to the verbal commands.

• *Add additional commands*—Add new commands, but no more than three at a time. Always start with a demonstration when introducing a new command, practice until the students appear to understand, and then stop modeling the behavior.

• *Add additional responses*—Find new ways for students to demonstrate their understanding of the vocabulary being practiced—such as pointing to pictures, drawing pictures, and taking turns demonstrating commands. Increasing the variety of activities will promote practice and improve student confidence. Total physical response can be included in many lessons, especially when reviewing concepts. View this video to see TPR being used to review math concepts while practicing following English directions. As you watch, consider the following questions:

• What other types of activities would lend themselves to the use of TPR?
• How does this activity format support English language learners?

• *Play games for additional practice*—Once the students gain confidence, play a game that involves a student volunteer giving the commands. Gradually encourage new student volunteers to give the commands as they become comfortable speaking the words. Never force students to speak the commands. Wait until they are confident enough to volunteer.

Enhanced eText
Video Example 2.1

• *Assess student progress and understanding*—Because students are responding to commands with physical movements, it is easy to document their progress. Make a checklist of the commands you have taught and keep track of the commands that students know automatically and those that still require modeling. Be sure to document when students volunteer to be leaders in the games being played for practice. Share with students the progress you have documented and celebrate together.

• *Periodically review your use of total physical response and plan to improve and expand your use of the strategy*—Use the teacher self-evaluation rubric in Figure 2.1 to determine your present level of implementation. Plan to improve your use of the strategy by adding the descriptors given at the next highest level.

Step-by-Step for TPR Storytelling

• *Start with basic TPR*—Give a command and perform the corresponding action to demonstrate its meaning. Restate the command and have students move in response to it. Don't expose students to more than three new words at a time.

• *Incorporate hand TPR*—Add the use of hand gestures or hand signs to represent words or concepts. Examples of **hand TPR** include a stroking motion to represent *cat* and raising hands and wiggling fingers as the hands are brought down to represent *rain*. These hand gestures can be combined with whole-body TPR.

• *Ask some questions that can be answered with one word*—**Pantomime** putting a hat on your head, then ask, "What is on my head, a hat or a dog?" The students should respond, "*Hat.*" This step helps to build the students' vocabulary and confidence in responding to questions in English. Repeat this step several times to build vocabulary for future activities like telling mini-stories.

FIGURE 2.1 Total Physical Response Teacher Self-Evaluation Rubric

Beginning	Developing	Accomplished	Exemplary
TPR is used for demonstrating directions and/or simple vocabulary.	TPR is used for teaching basic directions, simple vocabulary, and other words that students don't seem to understand (based on observation).	TPR is used for a variety of lessons whenever new vocabulary is introduced.	TPR is used for a variety of lessons with students of various English language development levels. New vocabulary, procedures, and the sequence of actions are all frequently introduced using TPR.
TPR is used only for introductory lessons.	TPR is used for a variety of lessons. It may be used very briefly at times to introduce new procedures.	TPR is used almost daily for brief lessons, and whenever new vocabulary or procedures are introduced.	Students are encouraged to use TPR to demonstrate vocabulary and/or procedures to other students.

- *Start telling mini-stories and have students repeat them*—After you have introduced the vocabulary for the mini-story, tell the story and have the students pantomime the words. For example, you may tell this mini-story after introducing and having the students use a combination of hand and whole-body TPR for the words *I, ran, school, morning, raining, wet,* and *cold.*

- I ran to school this morning because it was raining. I got very wet and cold.

The students should act out the words as you tell the story several times. If you have students who can retell the story, ask them to retell it while other students continue acting it out.

- *Do not require students to repeat the words after the storyteller*—The students should demonstrate their comprehension of the story by acting out key words. Give them an opportunity to retell the story when they gain the confidence to do so.
- *Teach the students to tell their own stories*—Encourage students to make up a simple story (two or three sentences) and teach the vocabulary using hand and whole-body TPR. Work with students to help them identify vocabulary to teach and ways to make the vocabulary understood. Support their initial efforts by writing the vocabulary words on the board. After a student tells a mini-story, encourage other students to ask questions about the story that can be answered with gestures as well as words.
- *Continue to observe your students to determine when lessons should be repeated*—Observe your students during TPR and TPR storytelling to identify areas of confusion and document vocabulary growth. Also document any increased willingness to participate in activities, which is a strong indicator of language development and confidence.

Applications and Examples

Mr. Tong's kindergartners are learning the names of body parts. Because he has many English language learners in the class, Mr. Tong decides to use total physical response to support their understanding of the English names for body parts. He begins the lesson by saying, "Point to your head," as he demonstrates. He motions for the students to join him in touching their heads, and nods and smiles as they follow his lead. He then introduces, "Touch your chin," as he demonstrates. He alternates the two commands for a few minutes and then adds and models, "Touch your nose."

Mr. Tong repeats these three commands several times before he drops the demonstrations and gives just the verbal commands. He watches the students carefully after he stops modeling to make sure they are following along. Mr. Tong continues this game for a few days until the students respond to commands to touch or point to their heads, chins, noses, ears, eyes, shoulders, feet, toes, knees, hands, arms, and elbows.

Mr. Tong changes games once he observes the students responding to verbal commands to identify each part of the body. The new game will help them understand the uses of each body part. He adds this game to address the Common Core standard for students to "identify real-life connections between words and their use." Mr. Tong asks the students to point to the body parts according to their uses. For example:

What helps you see? What helps you hear? What helps you walk?

Mr. Tong notices that several of the students are using body part names when communicating verbally in the classroom, so he plans a game that will requires students to give directions in English. First, Mr. Tong pairs the students and tells them to touch their heads while he demonstrates with a partner. Then, he tells them to touch their hands as he demonstrates. Next, Mr. Tong asks a volunteer to give the directions, and one child eagerly raises his hand. Mr. Tong helps the volunteer to demonstrate the commands as the student gives the directions and the others follow along. This game is played for a few minutes a day for about a week to give additional volunteers a chance to be the leader. Even the native English speakers enjoy playing.

* * * * *

Ms. Lopez teaches seventh-grade science, and she is concerned about student safety. She wants to begin addressing the Common Core science standard related to scientific procedures that requires students to "follow precisely a multistep procedure when carrying out experiments, taking measurements, or performing technical tasks." To make sure that everyone understands the safety procedures, she uses a total physical response lesson. She introduces the terms *pitcher*, *beaker*, and *Bunsen burner*, and the directions "Tip the beaker" and "Pour carefully" at the beginning of the lesson with the burners turned off. She demonstrates exactly how to tip the beakers to make sure the liquid doesn't splash as she says, "Tip the beaker slowly toward the pitcher and pour carefully."

After Ms. Lopez is sure that the students understand the terms and directions with the accompanying demonstration, she repeats the directions without a demonstration as she walks around the room.

Ms. Lopez observes the students as they practice transferring liquids from the pitchers to the beakers and placing the beakers into the holders, and she feels much more confident about their understanding of the safety procedures. The next day, Ms. Lopez will introduce how to light the burners and what procedures to follow during emergencies. However, Ms. Lopez will review today's lesson before introducing the new one.

Conclusion

Although the total physical response strategy is generally used with young children or English language learners who have very little English knowledge, the method can be used to introduce new procedures and vocabulary at almost any level. Figure 2.2 shows many ways in which this strategy is effective.

Total physical response is an active learning approach for supporting comprehension in a low-anxiety atmosphere (Krashen & Terrell, 1983). For this reason, it is very popular with English language learners and teachers alike. Total physical response is also highly effective in teaching vocabulary associated with **content-area knowledge**. Teachers can introduce vocabulary and

FIGURE 2.2 Applications for Total Physical Response

- Movement directions (stand up, sit down, line up, walk, run, kneel, hop, etc.)
- Students' names
- Color words
- Number words
- Shapes
- Body parts
- Prepositional phrases
- Directions (up, down, left, right, high, low, etc.)
- Classroom procedures
- Content vocabulary/picture sorts

have students respond by drawing, pointing, putting pictures in order, or engaging in any other physical response that encourages active involvement and verifies understanding.

TPR storytelling has been shown to facilitate the development of verbal fluency in English language learners (Seely & Romijn, 2006). Having students use hand gestures and whole-body responses encourages their participation as they acquire new skills.

Examples of Approximation Behaviors Related to the TESOL Standards

PreK–3 students will:

- observe and imitate motions of others.
- use practiced motion appropriately in class.

4–8 students will:

- use knowledge of the classroom setting to determine acceptable behavior.

- use observations to determine appropriate physical responses.

9–12 students will:

- observe and imitate the speech and actions appropriate in a particular situation.
- vary oral responses according to social settings.

References

Asher, J. (1982). *Learning another language through actions: The complete teachers' guidebook.* Los Gatos, CA: Sky Oaks.

Asher, J. (2009). *The total physical response (TPR): Review of the evidence.* Retrieved from http://www.tpr-world.com/review_evidence.pdf

Díaz-Rico, L. (2013). *The crosscultural, language, and academic development handbook: A complete K–12 reference guide* (5th ed.). Boston, MA: Pearson Education.

Krashen, S., & Terrell, T. (1983). *The natural approach: Language acquisition in the classroom.* Oxford, England: Pergamon Press.

Nation, I. S. P. (2005). *Teaching and learning vocabulary.* In E. Hinkel (Ed.), *Handbook of research on second language teaching and learning* (pp. 581–596). Mahwah, NJ: Erlbaum.

Seely, C., & Romijn, E. K. (2006). *TPR is more than commands—at all levels* (3rd ed.). Berkeley, CA: Command Performance Language Institute.

3

Modeled Talk

Demonstrating as You Talk

Modeled talk (Herrell, 1999) or **scaffolded instruction** (Gibbons, 2015), the **concurrent** verbal explanation and physical demonstration of directions or concepts, is one of the simplest and most powerful strategies to use with English language learners. It takes some planning and practice but can quickly become a habit for effective teachers. Modeled talk involves the use of gestures, visuals, and demonstrations as explanations are made (Echevarria, Vogt, & Short, 2012). Gestures and modeling provide examples for learners to follow and lower learners' anxiety since they know exactly what to do because they have seen the directions or content modeled (Peregoy & Boyle, 2011).

Step-by-Step

The steps in implementing modeled talk are the following:

- *Identify the lesson and gather materials*—Identify the lesson to be taught and the materials to be used. Think about what you plan to say to explain the lesson and the directions to the students. Prepare the materials students will use so that you have an example to show and, if necessary, examples in various stages of completion. Create physical gestures that will help students understand exactly what will be expected of them without having to rely solely on English vocabulary for understanding.
- *Practice your modeled talk*—Practice your talk in front of a mirror to determine if your instructions, modeling, and gestures convey the message you want the students to understand.
- *Design a visual of directions*—Design a standard visual that will be used regularly if the lesson or directions require that students follow a sequence of instructions. This will help students become accustomed to looking for this visual for support in remembering the sequence. Simple numbered drawings work well for this. A set of standard drawings created and saved on the computer, printed, laminated, and placed in sequence on the chalkboard can be used again and again for different activities. A picture of a pair of scissors, for example, always reminds the students that the next step is to cut, while a picture of a crayon reminds them to color.
- *Review the steps to be taken*—Review the steps students are to take after you have delivered your modeled talk. Use the visuals you have created to reinforce the students' reference to them for support in remembering what to do. When the students are performing the activities you have explained, refer to the visuals whenever there is a question about what to do next so that the students practice using them. Figure 3.1 provides suggestions for props and visuals that support modeled talks.

FIGURE 3.1 Props and Visuals to Support Modeled Talk

Props	Visuals
Any textbooks to be used	Numbered charts showing sequence to be followed
Scissors, tape, rulers, pencils, notebooks that will be needed	Diagrams showing a recap of directions given
Realia whenever vocabulary will be new	Standard illustrations for scissors (for directions to cut), crayon (for directions to color), pencil (for directions to write), computer (when it is to be used), ruler (for directions to measure), paintbrush (for directions to paint)
Word cards for any new vocabulary to be written	
Maps, globes, manipulatives, examples of products to be made	

- ***Observe students as you model talk***—As you observe students following the directions, determine the sections that need to be re-modeled. Ask follow-up questions that students can answer by demonstrating a part of the directions you have given and modeled.

Applications and Examples

Ms. Milsovic is using modeled talk to explain the day's learning centers to her kindergarten class of English language learners. She begins by sitting in a small chair with the students sitting on the floor in front of her.

"When I play the music," Ms. Milsovic says as she points to herself and then touches the play button on the CD player so the children hear a short section of the music they use as a signal to change activities, "you (indicating the children) will go to the centers (she motions toward the centers)."

"First (she holds up one finger), you will go to the planning board," Ms. Milsovic says while signaling for them to follow her to the planning board. The **planning board** is made of a large automotive drip pan. It has photographs of each of the centers attached by magnetic tape across the top of it and room for children's names on magnets under each of the center pictures.

"You will look for your name," Ms. Milsovic continues as she shows the children the name cards, which are not yet attached to the board. She reads a few of the names so the children understand what is written on the name cards.

"If Cher's name is under this center," she points to the picture of the Art Center, "she will go to the Art Center first." She motions for the children to follow Cher to the Art Center.

At the Art Center, Ms. Milsovic shows the children exactly what they will do there. She demonstrates each step as she talks about it. On this particular day, the children are studying frogs and toads, and they are using green paper plates to make frogs with long curled tongues. Ms. Milsovic shows them how to make the frog and posts a visual with drawings that demonstrate what to do first, second, and third. After she demonstrates, she refers to the visual and asks one of the children to tell her what to do at each step. Figure 3.2 shows the directions Ms. Milsovic used.

Each center is carefully modeled, and key English vocabulary is taught and practiced. When all the centers have been explained, the children and Ms. Milsovic return to the planning board, and the names of the children are placed on the board so they know where to go first. She then asks a few of the children to show her where they will go. "Alberto, where will you go?" she asks as she points to his name on the chart. Alberto answers by pointing to his assigned center or naming the center. Once this is done, Ms. Milsovic plays the music on the CD player, signaling that it's time to move to the centers. Since the children know what to do at each center and there

FIGURE 3.2 Ms. Milsovic's Directions for the Art Center

are visuals available at each center to remind them in case they forget, Ms. Milsovic is able to work with small groups of students at the Writing Center using interactive writing to teach them how to write words describing frogs. The children are secure in their understanding of what is expected of them.

* * * * *

Ms. Delgado is demonstrating how to make four-corner books for her fifth graders, who are always looking for new ways to celebrate the books they have read. Since the students will be making their books while Ms. Delgado is holding literature discussions, she wants to make sure that they know exactly what to do. She displays a poster that shows each of the steps in their assignment, and then she gives a modeled talk demonstrating the steps in the process. Figure 3.3 shows the poster Ms. Delgado displays. She's always careful to use clear instructional illustrations so that her English learners can easily access the information.

As Ms. Delgado demonstrates how to make a four-corner book, she refers to the steps listed on the poster. "First," she says as she points to the number 1 on the poster, "you fold a piece of paper like this." She demonstrates and then points to the drawing on the poster. Ms. Delgado writes "1" on the chalkboard and puts the sample she has started under the number.

FIGURE 3.3 How to Make a Four-Corner Book

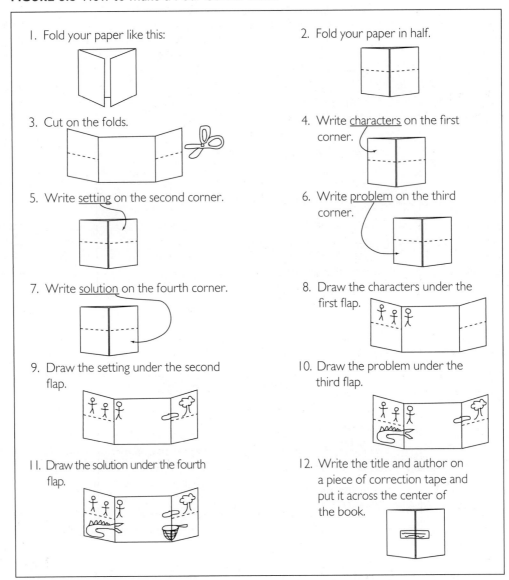

1. Fold your paper like this:

2. Fold your paper in half.

3. Cut on the folds.

4. Write <u>characters</u> on the first corner.

5. Write <u>setting</u> on the second corner.

6. Write <u>problem</u> on the third corner.

7. Write <u>solution</u> on the fourth corner.

8. Draw the characters under the first flap.

9. Draw the setting under the second flap.

10. Draw the problem under the third flap.

11. Draw the solution under the fourth flap.

12. Write the title and author on a piece of correction tape and put it across the center of the book.

"Second," she continues, as she points to the number 2 on the poster, "you fold the paper in half, this way." She takes a premade sample that was completed in step 1, demonstrates step 2, points to the drawing on the poster, writes the numeral 2 on the chalkboard, and puts the second sample under it.

"Third," she says as she points to the number 3 on the poster, "you cut on the folds you just made." She demonstrates the cutting on an additional sample, writes the numeral 3 on the chalkboard, and puts the third sample under it. At this point, samples of each stage of the process line the chalk tray for the students to examine later if necessary.

Next, she takes a premade sample of a four-corner book and writes "characters" on one corner. "You write the word *characters* on the first corner," she says as she demonstrates.

Ms. Delgado models each step, adding the word *setting* on the second corner, the word *problem* on the third corner, and the word *solution* on the fourth corner. She then lifts the flap labeled *characters* and demonstrates how to draw the main characters of her book. She repeats the process with the rest of the four corners.

Last of all, Ms. Delgado takes a piece of wide correction tape and puts it across the middle of her four-corner book and writes the title and author of the book on it. As she does each of these steps, she refers the students to the poster and leaves a sample on the chalkboard for them to examine as they are making their own books. Once she has completed the modeled talk, she puts the supplies on a table for the students to use and calls a literature discussion group together. The rest of the class is busily engaged in making four-corner books, and her group is not disturbed. They know how to make their books and know they will have an opportunity to share the books after Ms. Delgado finishes working with her groups. This was explained to them as a part of the modeled talk, and it's on the poster.

Conclusion

Modeled talk is helpful in lowering students' anxiety because they know and can respond to what is expected of them. It serves another important function when a teacher uses it consistently. English-speaking students often learn how to model talk and use it when explaining procedures and concepts to English language learners in the classroom. Students' use of modeled talk to other students increases the opportunities for English language learners to interact successfully with their peers, and it builds feelings of community within the classroom.

Examples of Approximation Behaviors Related to the TESOL Standards

PreK–3 students will:
- follow instructions from verbal and nonverbal cues.
- gather and organize materials needed to complete a task.

4–8 students will:
- follow a sequence of instruction based on verbal directions and physical actions.

- generate and ask questions to clarify expectations.

9–12 students will:
- compare and classify information based on verbal instructions and physical modeling.
- construct a chart or visual representation of information gained through oral directions and physical modeling.

References

Echevarria, J., Vogt, M., & Short, D. (2012). *Making content comprehensible for elementary English learners: The SIOP model* (4th ed.). Boston, MA: Allyn & Bacon.

Gibbons, P. (2015). *Scaffolding Language Scaffolding Learning. Teaching English Language learners in the Mainstream Classroom.* Portsmouth, NH, Heinemann.

Herrell, A. (1999). Modeling talk to support comprehension in young children. *Kindergarten Education: Research, Theory, and Practice, 3,* 29–42.

Peregoy, S., & Boyle, O. (2011). *Reading, writing, and learning in ESL* (6th ed.). Boston, MA: Longman.

Visual Scaffolding

Providing Language Support through Visual Images

Visual scaffolding is an approach in which the language used in instruction is made more understandable by displaying drawings or photographs that allow students to connect spoken English words to visual images being displayed (Echevarria, Vogt, & Short, 2010a; Greenberg, 2008). To use this strategy, the teacher builds **hard-copy** and **digital** files of visuals, such as photographs or drawings, that can be easily accessed for teaching. Photographs, illustrations, and even hand drawings can provide visual support for a wide variety of content and vocabulary concepts and can build background knowledge (Echevarria, Vogt, & Short, 2010b). In addition to visual representations, gestures used by teachers can be extremely supportive of student understanding. The meanings of gestures should be pretaught and used consistently (Díaz-Rico, 2018). 4.1 lists resources for securing visuals.

Step-by-Step

The steps in planning and implementing visual scaffolding are the following:

- *Identify the vocabulary*—Identify specific vocabulary to be taught in the lesson that can be scaffolded with visual images, such as drawings or photographs.
- *Collect visuals*—Find (or make) photos or line drawings that can be used to support visually the vocabulary needed for the students to understand the lesson. Use the Internet to search for images that can be collected in a "visuals file" on the computer for future use.
- *Reproduce and organize visuals*—Reproduce the visuals on transparency film for use on an overhead projector or capture them as digital files by searching the Internet that can then be easily shared with a digital projector or computer interface with an **interactive whiteboard** during teaching. Using a **document camera** allows the teacher to project either transparencies or hard copies of visuals. Arranging visuals and files in sequential order works well for a specific lesson, but you may want to organize your growing picture file alphabetically so that you can easily access the pictures for future lessons. Since pictures to be projected using an overhead projector need not be large, they can be stored in a shoe box or binder for easy access or on a file in the computer.
- *Engage the students*—Encourage students to use the picture files in their presentations as a way to encourage asking and answering questions. They can even be taught to help build or use a classroom picture dictionary on the computer.

FIGURE 4.1 Visual Scaffolding Resources

- Internet image resources—for example, *www.google.com* (select *images*) or *www.Altavista.com* (select *image*)
- Teacher-, student-, parent-taken photos
- Illustrations in old textbooks
- Line drawings from old black-line masters or workbooks
- Line drawings from children's coloring books
- Illustrations from big books
- Children's artwork

  (all of the above can be converted to color transparencies or digitized)
- Vacation videos
- Commercial videos
- Class-made videos

To make color transparencies and/or projectable illustrations:
- Scan the picture into your computer using an inexpensive flatbed scanner and print it out. Most printers require special transparency film.
- Take photos using a digital camera, download them to your computer, and print them out as hard copy or transparencies. The use of photo-quality printing paper will greatly enhance the quality of the hard copy.
- Download illustrations and photos from the Internet and print out as needed.
- Take standard photos and have them converted to picture CDs at your local photo shop or take them to a local copy and print center to have them converted to color transparencies, posters, calendars, and so on.
- Use a document camera to make projectable images.

Storing Resources
- A three-ring notebook with clear plastic sleeves can be used to store and organize transparencies. They can be projected without removing them from the sleeve.
- Small transparencies of individual pictures can be stored alphabetically in a shoe box (plastic or otherwise) and be kept near the overhead projector for quick access.
- Digital material may be stored on the hard drive of your classroom computer, on flash drives, or on picture CDs for quick, organized access.

- ***Build the file***—Continue to build your file on an ongoing basis. Involve the students in finding pictures to add to your files and picture dictionary.

Applications and Examples

Visual scaffolding can be used effectively at all grade levels and across curricular areas. Mr. Chavez is teaching a social studies unit on community to his second-grade class. Because his students all walk to school and their parents often use the city buses for transportation, many of the students have never been more than a few blocks away from the school. Mr. Chavez tries to plan the community unit to build the students' sense of pride in their community. Since Mr. Chavez recognizes the importance of visuals for his English learners, he takes digital photographs of local community helpers such as postal workers, crossing guards, firefighters, and police officers, and of local institutions like the post office and the neighborhood grocery store. These are all places and people with whom his students are familiar. Mr. Chavez then downloads the photographs to his computer and organizes them in files by category so that they can be easily accessed, projected, and manipulated using the classroom interactive whiteboard.

As he leads a discussion about community helpers, including where they work and what they do, Mr. Chavez uses his collection of photographs to connect the discussion to local people and places so that the new vocabulary is identified with those people and places that the students are familiar with. Hard copies of the original photographs are printed and displayed in the room with labels so that the students can begin to learn and practice the written forms of the words on the labels.

Mr. Chavez and his students then take a field trip into the central part of town where the students are introduced to a supermarket. Mr. Chavez provides some digital cameras from the school, and the students work in small groups finding, photographing, and cataloging vocabulary words. He explains that they are doing this in preparation for a discussion back in their classroom where they will compare the pictures of the supermarket with the ones of their neighborhood grocery.

"So many food!" exclaims Mercedes as she looks at the photo of the supermarket produce aisle piled high with fruit and vegetables. "Mr. Santos have only some," she says as she points to the picture of Mr. Santos's small store.

Mercedes' observations are just the beginning of the conversations Mr. Chavez hears among his students during the next few days. He has placed the photos in the writing center, and the students are writing about the sights they have seen on their bus trip to the supermarket. The photographs have expanded the students' understanding of their community. Using the photos in the writing center also provides a source of verbal stimulation and comparison that helps clarify correct usage, both spoken and written, for many days.

* * * * *

In Ms. Hammond's high school history class, the students are studying ancient Egypt. Ms. Hammond has transferred her vacation pictures of Egypt onto a picture CD, which she downloads to her classroom computer and shares on the interactive whiteboard. The students are enthralled as she describes her feeling of being extremely small when she posed for a photograph in front of the pyramids. The students are particularly interested in how the pyramids were built, and they listen intently as Ms. Hammond displays and discusses photographs she has scanned from David McCaulay's book *Pyramid* (1975). The students begin a **glossary** of words they are learning as they study ancient Egypt. They illustrate their glossary using sketches they make of the pictures she displays to support their discussion. As a follow-up to their discussion of the pyramids, the students form groups to research various segments of daily life in ancient Egypt. They add to their glossaries, work together to give oral presentations, and prepare displays of their own to demonstrate the facts they are learning about their area of research.

As the students present their reports, Ms. Hammond finds they have followed her example. All of the groups have searched the Internet for pictures and illustrations of costumes, artifacts, and reproductions of Egyptian art to support their presentations. These have been downloaded and reproduced as hard copy and digital photographs to share with others in the class. These visuals support English learners as they present their sections of the group report.

Conclusion

Although visual scaffolding requires some planning, there are abundant resources for visuals and it's an extremely powerful tool for English learners. Photos can be copied or scanned from books, magazines, and the Internet, and transferred to transparency film for use with overhead projectors or used as digitized visuals on the computer or with interactive whiteboards. If technology is limited in your classroom, then simply printing pictures or other visuals and passing them out to the students can be equally effective. Sharing these "visual clues" will lead to clearer understanding of concepts and ideas while the students are gaining content and language knowledge.

All of these enable you to build a picture file for use in scaffolding vocabulary and concept understanding. Photos taken on vacations can often be used in classroom teaching and may even make part of your trip tax-deductible. Parents can contribute photographs that you can copy or scan for your growing file. Send out a request for photos of hard-to-find items to give the parents an opportunity to lend support.

Line drawings, photographs, maps, and realia are not the only visuals that can be used in scaffolding. Video is another useful visual support. It is often possible to find brief video clips online so that students get a real-life, moving scaffold while a topic is discussed. Again, vacation video is a rich source of support and adds a powerful personal connection to the learning.

Examples of Approximation Behaviors Related to the TESOL Standards

PreK–3 students will:

- retell interesting events.
- ask questions to satisfy personal needs.

4–8 students will:

- work in cooperative groups and follow task roles.
- paraphrase directions given orally or in writing.

9–12 students will:

- use verbal communication to identify expectations for class assignments.
- assist in oral presentations as appropriate.

References

Díaz-Rico, L. (2018). *The crosscultural, language, and academic development handbook: A complete K–12 reference guide* (6th ed.). Boston, MA: Pearson Education.

Echevarria, J., Vogt, M., & Short, D. (2010a). *Making content comprehensible for elementary English learners: The SIOP model.* Boston, MA: Allyn & Bacon.

Echevarria, E., Vogt, M. E., & Short, D. (2010b) *Making content comprehensible for secondary English learners.* Boston, MA: Allyn & Bacon.

Goldenberg, G. (2008). Teaching English language learners: What the research does and—and does not—say. *American Educator, 32*(2), 8–44.

McCaulay, D. (1975). *Pyramid.* Boston, MA: Houghton Mifflin.

5

Realia Strategies
Connecting Language Acquisition to the Real World

Realia is a term for real things—concrete objects—that are used in the classroom to build background knowledge and vocabulary. Realia provide students with opportunities to build on their learning using all their senses (Echevarria, Vogt, & Short, 2010). Though using realia in the classroom is not always possible, it is usually the best choice for students to learn all they can about a topic. Realia allow students to see, feel, hear, and even smell the object being explored. In this video a teacher discusses the use of realia and shows examples of the importance of blending realia into all lessons that contain new or challenging vocabulary.

Enhanced eText
Video Example 5.1
https://www.youtube.com/
watch?v=uQk3aCJayuY

If the real thing is not available, a teacher must move down the continuum from the concrete (real thing) to a **replica** (such as a model) to a **semi-concrete** object (such as a photograph or illustration). However, each move down the continuum causes the loss of some sensory information that could be helpful in comprehension. Multiple opportunities to explore new vocabulary in different contexts deepens vocabulary knowledge (Nation, 2005). See Figure 5.1 for suggestions of classroom realia that are helpful in the presentation of powerful learning experiences.

Step-by-Step

The steps in implementing the use of realia are the following:

• *Identify opportunities to use realia*—Be aware of opportunities to include realia in lessons as you plan. Pre-read any stories that will be read aloud or used for reading instruction in order to identify vocabulary that may be unfamiliar to the students. Once the vocabulary is identified, locate realia that will be helpful in enhancing their understanding.

• *Collect realia*—Begin to collect items that can be stored in the classroom and organize them so that they can be easily accessed for instruction. Plastic tubs or large, clear plastic bags are often used for this purpose. Some items will be appropriate for only one theme or book and should be stored with that theme's materials or book. Yard sales and end-of-season sales at craft stores are good sources of realia for classroom use. Parents are often helpful in locating and supplying useful items.

• *Build a library of realia*—Collaborate with other teachers at your school or in your grade level to build a library of realia that can be shared for major theme studies. Locate local merchants, farmers, and other resources that may loan your large items, such as farm equipment or animals.

FIGURE 5.1 Realia for Powerful Learning

Category	Realia	Uses
Household items	Eating utensils, kitchen appliances (from different cultures), miniatures such as household furniture, old-fashioned items no longer commonly seen	Active experiences, vocabulary development, role-playing, story reenactment, prereading activities, oral language practice, story problems in math
Food	Fruit, vegetables, unusual items unfamiliar to children; many plastic food items are available for classroom use	Sensory experiences, vocabulary development, acting out stories, grammar activities (singular, plural)
Clothing	Different kinds of hats, gloves, sweaters, jackets, boots, any examples of ethnic clothing to support understanding	Vocabulary development, story reenactment, writing support, oral language practice
Literacy materials	Books, magazines, newspapers, encyclopedia, reference books, checkbooks, bank books	Role-playing, vocabulary development, easy access for research, exposure
Farm or occupational items	Rakes, plows, harnesses, tools, baskets, hay, nails, models of barns, silos, scarecrows, wagons, farm carts	Prereading activities, role-playing, vocabulary development, knowledge of size and weight
Flowers and plants	Examples of flowers and plants being studied or read about; unusual plants such as large sunflowers, pumpkins	Vocabulary development, sensory experiences, size comparisons
Animals	Classroom pets, house pets, farm and zoo animals, birds	Sensory experiences, vocabulary development
Crafts	Knitting, crocheting, tatting, sculpting clay, potter's wheel, spinning wheel, loom	Vocabulary development, role-playing, sensory experiences, prereading activities
Ethnic items	Piñatas, chopsticks, wok, tortilla press, tea sets, clothing	Vocabulary development, cross-cultural experiences

- *Use field trips as realia*—If it's too large to move and your students' learning would benefit by experiencing it, take a field trip. Give your students the opportunity to really understand what they are studying.
- *Assess by using realia*—Realia can be used to assess students' vocabulary and understanding of verbal directions. An example of using realia to assess vocabulary is shown in Figure 5.2. For suggestions on ways to adapt realia use for students at different levels of language development, see Figure 5.3.

FIGURE 5.2 Using Realia to Assess Vocabulary

Preproduction Level	Show two objects and ask the student to show you the _____ .
Early Production	Show two objects and ask the student to show you the one that is used for _____ .
Speech Emergence	Ask the student to name objects.
Intermediate Fluency	Ask the student to tell uses for objects.
Fluent	Ask the student to compare objects.
Note: Start a level below your estimate of the student's English development level and move to higher levels until the student is unable to respond. Return to the level at which the student is successful before stopping. End with success!	

FIGURE 5.3 Realia Uses for Students of All Ages and Language Development Levels

Preproduction	Early Production	Speech Emergence	Intermediate Fluency	Fluent
Use realia to introduce new vocabulary and pass the objects around for students to hold. Encourage them to try to say the name of the object as they hold it.	Use objects to encourage students to pronounce new vocabulary. Write the names of the objects on a chart with drawings or photographs to help them remember the names.	Encourage students to tell you the name of the object and its use (e.g., "This is a broom and I use it to sweep.").	Introduce objects related to a story. Ask students to tell you how the object was used in a story, and why it was important.	Have students role-play a situation and use the objects to enhance the role-play by showing how the objects relate to the situation being played.
Introduce two or three object names and encourage students to identify the correct object as you name it.	Introduce two or three objects and ask students to identify the correct object by its use (e.g., "Which one is used to sweep the floor?").	Encourage students to compare and contrast objects. Help them to include colors, sizes, and possible uses as they make their comparisons.	Ask students to identify additional uses for each object or tell a short story about how the object could be used. Encourage creativity.	Have students choose several objects and then tell or write a story that includes the chosen objects in traditional or innovative ways.

Applications and Examples

Ms. Castaño found a beautiful little bilingual book that she wants to use with her third graders. Many of her Hispanic students speak English very well now, but their parents are concerned that they are losing their fluency in Spanish. Ms. Castaño is always looking for ways to encourage the use of their primary language. The book she found, *My Mexico—México Mío* (Johnson, 1996), is a collection of poetry in English and Spanish. Many of her third graders will be able to read both the English and Spanish versions of the poems, and there are many opportunities for active lessons and vocabulary development in both languages.

As Ms. Castaño prepares her lessons for the next week, she also gathers realia to support the students' understanding. Her school is near a little park where she will be able to take the students on a walk to see an adobe wall like the one described in the poem "Adobe Brick." She may even be able talk her father into coming to school and demonstrating how to make adobe bricks.

Ms. Castaño has a broom in the classroom and a huge plastic cockroach given to her as a joke years ago that she will use together with the students to reenact the poem "I Am Cucaracha." She's smiling to herself now as her preparations for the use of this lovely little poetry book begin to get exciting. Ms. Castaño knows of a market where she can buy some gourds to use in making maracas as described in the poem "Gourds." She knows that her friend Marcella will be glad to bring her loom to school so the children can practice weaving as they read "I Saw a Woman Weaving."

After that experience, she can teach the children to weave paper place mats and maybe one of the mothers will come to school to make tortillas as a concluding activity on Friday. She picks up two ears of corn to take to school so the children will understand how the tortilla flour is made.

Ms. Castaño makes a list of new vocabulary words that will be learned this week and is pleased to see many new Spanish and English words on the list. Her native English speakers will be learning a lot from this week's poetry unit too.

* * * * *

Mr. Millar's sixth graders are exploring survival skills through a combined literature and science study based on several survival stories: *My Side of the Mountain* (George, 1959), *Island of the Blue Dolphins* (O'Dell, 1960), *River Rats, Inc.* (George, 1979), and *Hatchet* (Paulsen, 1987). The students are working in groups to explore the realia they have found or had relatives send to them from the areas in which the stories took place. In some cases, they have been able to actually taste the berries and boiled twigs that the characters in the books ate to survive.

Mr. Millar has contributed some of the realia used in the study, like some of the more primitive tools that are no longer readily available. In other cases, the students have used some of the raw materials described in the books to construct the tools and cooking utensils made by the characters in the stories. Now that all of the students have read one of the survival stories, they are comparing the survival strategies used in each of the books.

"Most of the tools they made in the stories depended a lot on the wood and stone and other materials that were available in the area," Johan observes.

"That is very true," Mr. Millar agrees. "What else was affected by the location of the story?"

"The problems they had," Susana replies. "Survival in the Canadian wilderness is very different from survival on a Pacific island."

"I thought it was interesting that they had different plants that they used for medicine," Teresa adds.

"The botany books we looked at listed a lot of plants that were edible or used for medicinal purposes," Jacob says. "I never knew that you could eat boiled twigs, either."

"They sure don't taste too great," Teresa says with a grin.

"What could you eat if you were stranded around this area?" Mr. Millar asks.

"Twinkies from the Minute Market," Susana jokes.

"No, seriously," Mr. Millar says. "Are there any local plants you could eat?"

"My grandmother says they used to eat dandelion salad," Johan says. "We could try that. We have a lot of dandelions growing in our yard."

"See whether you can get her recipe," Mr. Millar says with a smile. "We're going to take a survival hike in a few weeks so we need to research the plants that we may have to eat. Mr. Smithson, the botanist at the college, is coming along just to make sure we don't poison ourselves. We will also have to gather **indigenous** materials from the woods to use as tools and cooking utensils. We have some research to do before we go. All we are going to bring along is a supply of water and some very basic tools like the stone and wood hatchets and a first-aid kit. But first, let's check the Internet and see if we can find out what kinds of plants are indigenous to our local area and decide if they can be safely eaten or not. Then we will be off to gather our survival feast!"

The students looked at Mr. Millar with a wide assortment of expressions, from excitement to apprehension.

Conclusion

The use of realia in the classroom supports English learners in a wide variety of ways. Introducing real objects that can be seen, felt, and manipulated is a powerful way to connect vocabulary to real life. The use of realia motivates students because they can actually use the real objects in the way in which they are intended to be used. Realia introduces an authentic hands-on nature to many lessons. The use of real objects conveys meaning in a way that no photograph or illustration can. There is no confusion over the size, weight, texture, or smell of an object, fruit, vegetable, or tool when the real thing is actually present. In some cases it is important to provide several objects in order to see a range of possibilities, such as several different kinds of apples or tiny sunflowers to be compared with other huge examples seen in certain parts of the world. Teachers can be extremely innovative in the use of realia as demonstrated in the applications and examples found in Chapters 6 and 26 in this text.

Examples of Approximation Behaviors Related to the TESOL Standards

PreK–3 students will:

- associate written symbols and realia.
- represent story sequence with realia.

4–8 students will:

- compare and contrast real objects.

- represent information through the use of realia.

9–12 students will:

- describe change and growth in real things.

References

Echevarria, J., Vogt, M., & Short, D. (2010). *Making content comprehensible for elementary English learners.* Boston, MA: Allyn & Bacon.

George, J. (1959). *My side of the mountain.* New York, NY: Dutton.

George, J. (1979). *River rats, inc.* New York, NY: Dutton.

Johnson, T. (1996). *My Mexico—México mio.* New York, NY: G. P. Putnam's Sons.

Nation, I. S. P. (2005). In E. Hinkel (Ed.), *Handbook of research on second language teaching and learning* (pp. 581–596). Mahwah, NJ: Erlbaum.

O'Dell, S. (1960). *Island of the blue dolphins.* Boston, MA: Houghton Mifflin.

Paulsen, G. (1987). *Hatchet.* New York: Aladdin Paperbacks/Simon & Schuster.

6

Vocabulary Role-Play
Building Vocabulary through Dramatization

Vocabulary role-play (Herrell, 1998; Zwiers, 2014) is a strategy that encourages learners to make connections among their past experiences, the content currently being studied, and vocabulary that is new or being used in an unfamiliar way. Students are introduced to new vocabulary and given an opportunity to discuss and use the vocabulary in context through role-playing. Several researchers have validated the importance of multiple exposures to new vocabulary with English learners (Jordan & Herrell, 2002; Lyster, 2007; Snow & Katz, 2010; Spada & Lightbrown, 2008). Often, several groups of students are given the same vocabulary and asked to write and perform skits in which the words are used and demonstrated. Since the groups are likely to write and perform skits in which the vocabulary words are used in different contexts, the skits serve to show multiple uses of the same words. In this way, English language learners are given an opportunity to see the vocabulary words used in context, as well as demonstrations of several contexts in which the words may be used appropriately (Echevarria, Vogt, & Short, 2010).

Step-by-Step

The steps in implementing vocabulary role-play are the following:

- *Identify key vocabulary*—Determine the vocabulary words that will be used in a lesson or reading. Make cards with the words written on them.
- *Teach the lesson or read the book*—As you teach the lesson or read the book—either reading aloud or having the students read—stop when you encounter key vocabulary and discuss and act out the words. Pronounce the words carefully and have the students practice pronouncing them, especially if the words contain sounds that might be difficult for them. Be sure to reread the page fluently after the vocabulary is explored. As each word is explored, place it in a pocket chart so students can see it clearly. To see a vocabulary role-play presentation in a first-grade classroom, watch this video and note the ways in which the teacher makes the vocabulary understandable. Is this video still available? It was on our CD.
- *Connect the vocabulary to past experiences*—After the lesson is complete or the story is read, show the cards to the class, one by one, and ask the students to talk about ways in which they have seen the words used. Use this opportunity to explore multiple meanings of words.
- *Sort the words*—Further explore the words by engaging the students in word sorting. Ask them if any of the words have similar meanings or if any of them are names for things—nouns. Identify the movement words—verbs—and place them together. Students might be encouraged to do a word search using any of several of the online search engines. This gives them an opportunity

FIGURE 6.1 A Word Sort Using Words from a Vocabulary Role-Play Lesson

Movement Words	Names for Things	Descriptive Words
VERBS	NOUNS	ADJECTIVES/ADVERBS
paraded	ledge	scary
prowled	geranium	slowly
stroked	statue	quickly
winked	puddle	sparkling
stretched	park bench	leisurely

Source: Words taken from *The Third-Story Cat* (Baker, 1987).

to explore a variety of word meanings and usage. Review the word meanings in several different ways to help the students remember them. See Figure 6.1 for a typical word sort.

• *Plan ways to use the words*—Leave the words on display in the pocket chart. Use the words in directions during the day. Encourage the students to use the new vocabulary in their writing and celebrate verbally when they do. Involve the students in creating scenes using the new vocabulary by dividing the class into small groups of three to five students and giving each group a set of four or five words. Make sure that each group has at least one member who is a strong reader. Instruct each group to create a scenario in which all their words are used.

• *Give the students time to practice*—Give the groups time to work on their scripts and practice performing their scenes. Encourage the groups to make and use simple props.

• *Perform the scenes*—Give each group a chance to perform the scene that they have written. Discuss how the words were used after each scene is performed, celebrating innovative uses of the new vocabulary.

• *Focus on multiple word meanings*—Compare and contrast the uses of the words by the groups, emphasizing the differing contexts used in the skits, and the similarities and differences in the ways in which the words were used.

FIGURE 6.2 Using Vocabulary Word Play with Different Levels of English Learners

Preproduction	Early Production	Speech Emergence	Intermediate Fluency	Fluent
Demonstrate the meanings of new vocabulary with actions. Have the students repeat the pronunciations and actions. Use the students' home language to clarify when appropriate.	Use visuals or realia, "This is a ____" (pointing to the visual or realia. For verbs, have the students act out the motion and repeat a simple sentence such as "I am hopping."	Ask simple questions such as "What is the girl doing?" (pointing to a picture.) The student can respond, "The girl is hopping." Or for nouns, "What is the girl holding?" The girl is holding a jump rope."	Have the student read and illustrate the words with pictures or motions. Transfer to a visual or demonstrate a motion as they respond to questions. At this level they can write sentences or short paragraphs using the new vocabulary.	Fluent English speakers can write and act out multiple meanings of words

Applications and Examples

Ms. Lee has brought her calico cat, Muffin, to school to visit the children in her first-grade class. Many of the children express fear at the possibility of handling Muffin, but Ms. Lee wants them to become more comfortable with her. She chooses a special book about a calico cat to share with her class. As she sits in the big rocking chair in the corner of the classroom with Muffin sleeping in her lap, Ms. Lee shows the cover of the book she holds, which has no picture on it.

"The title of this book is *The Third-Story Cat*," Ms. Lee says. "There is no picture on the cover to help us guess what it is about. What do you think it might be? What is a third-story cat?"

"Maybe there were two other stories about the cat," Jacob suggests.

"That's an idea," Ms. Lee agrees.

"Have you ever heard the expression *third story* before?" she asks.

"I think my uncle lives on the third story," Tony answers tentatively. "You have to go up a lot of stairs to his apartment."

"That's right, Tony. *Third story* means the same thing as *third floor*." Ms. Lee opens the book to the title page where the students can see a lovely watercolor painting of an apartment building with three floors. In the apartment on the third floor you can see a calico cat sleeping on the window sill.

"Look up here in the window," Ms. Lee says. "Do you see a cat that looks just like Muffin?"

"O-o-o-h," the students sigh. "It does look like Muffin."

Ms. Lee then uses the illustration of the apartment building to show the meaning of the words *third story*. She sweeps her hand across the first floor of the apartment building in the picture and says, "The people who live on this floor can walk out their doors and be on the sidewalk. This is the first floor or first story." She points to the doors that open onto the sidewalk and to the sidewalk itself as she says the words.

"The people who live on the second floor, or second story, have to go up some stairs to their apartments." Ms. Lee points to the doorway and moves her hand up to the second floor as she explains.

"The people who live on the third story have to go up even more stairs," Ms. Lee explains as she points to the third floor.

"There are a lot of big words in this story," Ms. Lee says. "The author of this book, Leslie Baker, uses a lot of wonderful words to tell us about all the exciting things this cat does one day. Let's read the story and find out what adventures the cat has."

Ms. Lee reads the story aloud to the students, using the beautiful illustrations to help them understand the new vocabulary that is introduced in the story. She stops to demonstrate the meaning of the word *startled* as the cat is surprised by a butterfly flying up out of the geranium box. She has one of the children demonstrate the word *crept* as the cat is balancing along the ledge on the three-story building. As the story is read the children are exposed to a number of new words describing the ways in which cats move: *paraded*, *prowled*, *twitched*, and *leaped*. Some other words require some physical practice, like *winked* and *stroked*.

After the story is read, Ms. Lee goes through the new words again and has the children make a large circle. They walk around the room and act out the movements the cats made in the story. They wink, creep, twitch, and parade until they are all very silly. They show the difference between being startled and being frightened, between winking and blinking, between parading and prowling, and between patting and stroking. When they sit back down in the circle, Ms. Lee shows them cards with the new words printed on them and as she holds each card up, a child volunteers to act it out.

Ms. Lee leaves the new vocabulary word cards in a part of the room near the pocket chart and shows the children how they can use the cards to fill in the blanks in the pocket chart story.

They are invited to make new sentences with the cards during center time and they even have a new pointer with a calico cat on the end of it to use as they read the sentences they are making. Ms. Lee smiles as she watches the children busily building sentences with the new vocabulary words. One of the children is carrying Muffin around the room with her as she acts out the new words she has learned from *The Third-Story Cat*.

* * * * *

Mr. Valdez's fourth graders are studying Florida history. They are reading about the barefoot mail carriers who brought the mail down the beaches to the first settlements and the ways in which a variety of people came to Florida to establish permanent residences. Some of the vocabulary is unfamiliar to the students and Mr. Valdez wants to make sure that the words are understood by all his students. Going through the Florida history book, Mr. Valdez selects the words *barefoot*, *cypress*, *brackish*, *humid*, *Everglades*, and *tide pools*, and writes the words on sentence strips.

After he reads the section from the Florida history book aloud to his class, Mr. Valdez asks the students to talk about the ways in which they have heard the words used before.

Jonah starts the discussion by saying, "I like to go barefoot in the summertime. My mother is always telling me to put my shoes on."

"I know what it means to go barefoot," Katie adds. "I just don't understand why the mail carriers were barefoot."

Mr. Valdez takes the time to explain that since there were very few roads in the early days, the easiest route down the state was walking along the beach and so the mail carriers often got their feet wet. To protect their shoes, they walked barefoot until they came to places where they needed to wear shoes. Then they would stop and put their shoes back on.

Carla talked about brackish water and how her dad is often worried about the saltwater at their beach house invading the drinking water. "That's what he calls brackish water," she explains. "It's when the saltwater invades the fresh water."

"Yes," Mr. Valdez agrees. "But in some places in the state it's a natural thing for water to be brackish. Some of the rivers empty into the ocean and there is an area in which the saltwater and fresh water mix. That's also brackish water."

The discussion continues until each of the words has been discussed. Mr. Valdez then divides the students into groups of three and asks them to write a short skit in which they use as many of the new vocabulary words as they can. One member of the group is assigned as the note-taker and the skits are written. The students are given 15 to 20 minutes to make simple props and each group is given a chance to act out its skit. Some of the groups have one of the members read the script while the other two do the acting. One group chooses to do a **charade** and asks the class to guess which word they are portraying. Another group has a complete dialogue with each of the speakers emphasizing a few of the new vocabulary words. One of the groups even performs a rap routine using the new words. By the time all six groups perform, all the new words have been demonstrated multiple times in many different contexts. Mr. Valdez is confident that the new vocabulary is thoroughly understood by everyone.

Conclusion

Vocabulary role-play provides the link between learning a new word and using the word in context, or multiple contexts. Role-play enables the student to create experiences with which to link the new vocabulary. The study of words and their multiple meanings and origins can also be effective with the use of vocabulary role-play. Students can add brief videos to illustrate word meaning, create animated computer dictionaries, publish vocabulary books, and import graphics from the Internet to illustrate word posters—all of which increase their interactions with and understanding of English vocabulary and multiple meanings.

Examples of Approximation Behaviors Related to the TESOL Standards

PreK–3 students will:

- act out common verbs.
- re-create a scene from a story-book with dialogue and action.

4–8 students will:

- create a scene demonstrating multiple meanings of common words.
- communicate the meanings of words through verbalization and action.

9–12 students will:

- interact with a group to write a script demonstrating word meanings.
- use appropriate language structures to depict a variety of social contexts in dramatic action scenes.

References

Baker, L. (1987). *The third-story cat.* Boston, MA: Little, Brown.

Echevarria, J., Vogt, M., & Short, D. (2010). *Making content comprehensible for elementary English learners: The SIOP model.* Boston, MA: Allyn & Bacon.

Herrell, A. (1998). *Exemplary practices in teaching English language learners.* Fresno: California State University.

Lyster, R. (2007). *Learning and teaching languages through content: A counterbalanced approach.* Philadelphia, PA: John Benjamins.

Snow, M. A., & Katz, A. (2010). English language development: Foundation in kindergarten through grade five. In *Improving education for English learners: Research-based approaches.* Sacramento: California State Department of Education.

Spada, N., & Lightbrown, P. (2008). Form-focused instruction: Isolated or integrated? *TESOL Quarterly, 42*(2), 181–207.

Zwiers, J. (2014). *Building Academic Language, 2nd ed.* Hoboken, N.J., Jossey-Bass.

Collecting and Processing Words

Making Vocabulary Your Own

Collecting words (Herrell & Jordan, 2001; Gibbons, 2015) is a strategy for helping children develop better speaking and writing vocabularies. It also supports their understanding of the **nuances** of words that have the same or similar meanings. Research clearly indicates that the development of an extensive vocabulary and an understanding of word meanings is essential to successful and fluid comprehension in reading and verbal interactions (Allen, 2000). By "collecting" words, students are constantly building a **repertoire** of words and word meanings that will increase their understanding of oral language and stories and improve and strengthen their spoken vocabulary and eventually their writing skills.

Research in effective vocabulary instruction has identified several approaches that support effective word understanding in English learners:

1. Frequent exposure to targeted vocabulary words, such as through the repeated reading of storybooks and the discussion of the meanings of words in the context of stories, is needed to support effective understanding. (Biemiller & Boote, 2006)
2. Explicit instruction of targeted words, such as by acting out word meaning, is needed. (Biemiller & Boote, 2006)
3. Learning words taught within the context of a story is more effective than the study of definitions. (Nash & Snowling, 2006)
4. Moving from low-demand to high-demand questions promotes greater gains in word knowledge. (Blewitt, Rump, Shealy, & Cook, 2009)
5. Vocabulary instruction should include teacher-student activities and interactive activities that target new words. (Coyne, McCoach, & Kapp, 2007)

Collecting words involves making charts or digital files of words discovered by the children as they listen to or read stories or as they listen to and participate in conversations. The charting of the words supports student understanding of their meanings as the words are categorized, acted out, or connected to objects and context. The word charts provide a record of the words students acquire as they add to the collections and act as an ongoing vocabulary reference for students. As students locate and add words to the charts, they are responsible for helping other students understand the meanings and nuances of the new words. This may be accomplished through simple explanations, or it may require more elaborate picturization such as drawing, miming, or acting out to demonstrate the word meanings. Exploring the meanings of the words is a vital step because vocabulary development is directly connected to progress in reading comprehension (Beck & McKeown, 2001).

52

FIGURE 7.1 Double-Entry Word Journal

Word	The Ways We Use It.
Tiptoe	Miss McCloskey said, "Please tiptoe to your seats."
Parade	"We look like a parade when we walk with our heads and knees held high," said Miss Vang.

While the words are being collected on charts within the classroom, students engage in finding ways to process, or use, these new words. A variety of collections and methods of categorizing them for use with English language learners (See Video Example 7.1).

Enhanced eText
Video Example 7.1
https://www.youtube.com/watch?v=SICHeJAf15w

As students discover new words, they are encouraged to find ways to use the words in speech or in writing and report back to the teacher and other students about their discoveries. The teacher must set aside some time each day for word study, devoting part of this time to discussing the ways in which the new words have been used by students. In kindergarten and first grade, this revisiting of the words is done orally or by having the teacher take the children's dictation to document the word usage in a double-entry journal created by the class. This involves having the students talk about how they used the words while the teacher writes their words into a classroom journal. When students are able to write for themselves, they take over the journal entries. See Figure 7.1 for an example of a double-entry word journal.

Step-by-Step

The steps in collecting and processing words are the following:

- *Identify unfamiliar words in reading selections*—As you are reading aloud or having students read, note words that students seem to misunderstand or cannot act out or explain.
- *Write the unfamiliar words on chart paper and explore their meanings orally*—Ask students to explain the words or use them in sentences. Expand their knowledge of the words by giving multiple examples of ways the words are used.
- *Have the students act out the words whenever possible*—If some words are difficult to act out, look for a similar situation to act out that would help students understand the words.
- *Introduce synonyms and add them to the word collection with the original word*—Have the students suggest words that mean the same thing or are similar in meaning. If the meanings of the words suggested are nuances of the original word, act out the two words to try to show the differences.
- *Provide the students with vocabulary journals and challenge them to find ways to use the new words*—Using the **T-chart** format, ask students to list new words on the left side of the T and document how they used the word on the right side of the T. Kindergarten students can draw pictures to show how they used the words.
- *Assess to determine the need for further instruction*—Assessing the understanding of the new vocabulary explored through word collections and vocabulary journals involves several approaches. Observation of verbal interactions noting the use of words from the word collections allows teachers to determine which of the words are understood and being used verbally. Examining student writing for the use of new vocabulary is another effective way to determine which of the words are being integrated and which will need further exploration. The checklist shown in Figure 7.2 is one way to document findings and help teachers identify words that will require more instruction and use in guided practice.

FIGURE 7.2 Sample Checklist for Documenting Vocabulary Usage

Names	Anicea	José	Marcos	Theo
Vocabulary Used				
Walk *and forms*	*Stomped* *Tiptoed*	*Ambled* Hopped	*Trudged* *Skipped*	
Said *and forms*	*Replied*			*Yelled*
Nice *and forms*	*Friendly*	*Polite*	*Kind*	
Good *and forms*	*Super*	*Great*		Tasty
Cursive = Oral Usage		Manuscript = Written usage		

Applications and Examples

Miss Benninghoven's first graders are listening to her read *Fritz and the Beautiful Horses* (Brett, 1987). Because her class has a number of English language learners and children with limited English vocabularies, Miss B. wants to make sure that they all understand the words in the book. After she reads the book once, Miss B. reads it a second time, stopping to involve the children in acting out movement words from the story. When the horses in the story prance, she gets the children up on their feet and they practice prancing. When the horses in the story parade, she and the children parade around the room. Because Jan Brett's story contains so many descriptive movement words, the children have several opportunities to get up and move.

Once Miss B. has read through the book a second time and the children have all acted out the movement words, she has them form a circle around the outside edges of the classroom and Miss B. holds up cards with the movement words written on them. As she holds up *buck,* the children show how horses buck. They move around the classroom in a clockwise direction responding to each new movement word as it is displayed.

After the children have several more chances to act out the words from the story, Miss B. asks them to return to their desks, and she explains the next thing they will do.

"I am going to give each table five words from our story. I want you to work together and each group to write a short play using the words I give you. Each group will have a recorder and a leader. You are all to help write the play. You may use the art materials to make props and then you will have a chance to practice your skits and perform them for the class. Your play has to include the words you are given, but it doesn't have to be about horses. You can use the words in any way that makes sense."

"Before you work in groups, let's try writing a play together so you can see how it is done. Let's use the words, *prance, parade, shy, stride, and cracked.* Can you think of a setting for our play?" asks Miss B.

"We could be at a parade," suggests Thomas.

"Good idea, Thomas," nods Miss B. "That uses one of our words in a new way."

"The narrator can say that we are at a parade," says Jimmy.

"Good," says Miss B. as she writes <u>NARRATOR: The children are at a parade</u> on the overhead projector transparency.

"The trick dogs can be prancing and the trainers can be cracking their whips," suggests Lydia.

"Good idea. You've used the words in a new way, not just like they were used in the book. You're really getting the idea," replies Miss B. The class negotiates the sentence together and Miss B. writes the sentence they agree on as >_<u>"NARRATOR: As the children watch, the trick dogs prance by. The trainer cracked the whip over their heads."</u>

"How can we use the word *stride*"? Miss B. asks.

"That's hard," replies José. "The dogs can't stride. Maybe the trainer can do it."

"Oh! I know!" says Ramon excitedly. "We can add it to the sentence we just wrote. The trainer can stride as he cracks his whip."

"OK," agrees Miss B. With the children's help she changes the sentence to say, <u>"As the children watch, the trick dogs prance by. The trainer strides alongside them, cracking his whip over their heads."</u>

"Is that all right?" asks Ramon. "Our word was *cracked,* and you changed it to *cracking*."

"I'm glad you noticed that," says Miss B. with a smile. "I think that's OK. You can change the endings as long as the root word, the main part of the word, stays the same. That makes it a little easier."

"Now, how are we going to act this out as a play?" asks Miss B.

"That's easy," replies Thomas. "We have some people be dogs, one person be the trainer, and the rest of the people are the children. One person gets to be the narrator."

Miss B. divides the class, and they walk through the play several times, taking turns playing different parts.

"Now I think you are ready to do this on your own," says Miss B. She divides the class into small groups, making sure each small group has a strong reader and writer in it. She distributes word cards to each group, and they get started on writing their plays.

After the children have a chance to perform their plays, Miss B. will review the meanings of the words they have used and the many different ways they found to use them. She will punch holes in the corner of the word cards and they will be kept together as a collection from *Fritz and the Beautiful Horses*. Over the year, the word collections based on stories they read will grow almost daily. Miss B. stores the word collections on hooks placed under the chalkboard. Each collection has a picture of the storybook on the first card so that the children can remember the book they read to create the word collection. Interestingly, this system also helps the children find the words they want to access for writing projects because they actually seem to remember which words are in which story.

* * * * *

Mr. Quinn's tenth graders are reading the required play *Julius Caesar* by William Shakespeare. Because Mr. Quinn knows his students will have difficulty understanding the vocabulary and language structures in the play, he plans to use word collections and processing to support their understanding.

Each day the class reads a scene aloud, and they list the unfamiliar words on a word collection chart. After they finish reading the day's scene, Mr. Quinn leads a discussion in which they explore the meanings of the words on the word collection chart. Each student has an individual booklet entitled "Word Collections." They write each of the words from the word collection chart on a page in their individual booklet. The students add synonyms to the word collection list and take time to act out the words whenever possible.

At the end of each day's lesson, each student writes a paragraph or two to summarize the day's scene from the Shakespeare play using the words and synonyms from the word collections chart. In their individual word collections booklet, they document the ways they find to use the new words either in verbal communication or in their writing.

Conclusion

Vocabulary development has been widely researched. In the past twenty years, a number of research studies have examined the impact of vocabulary knowledge on student achievement. As a result of the vocabulary acquisition research, three main implications for instruction have been recognized: (1) the wide range of vocabulary understood by students, (2) the differences in vocabulary knowledge between low- and high-achieving students, and (3) the importance of a sustained focus on oral and written vocabulary acquisition within the reading/language arts program. Several researchers have proposed evidence that strongly links vocabulary deficiencies to academic failure in disadvantaged students in grades 3–12. Although there is no evidence that any single method of teaching vocabulary is superior, many comprehensive programs for supporting vocabulary acquisition have produced positive results (Stanovich, 1986; White, Graves, & Slater, 1990). For this reason, teachers of reading and language arts are well advised to incorporate daily vocabulary acquisition strategies into their programs.

To start students off on the right track toward the building of a rich store of vocabulary knowledge, word study must begin as early as possible. Even preschool and kindergarten students can be actively engaged in the exploration of vocabulary words. It's simply a matter of adjusting word study to their developmental level and making sure that the words are taught in context and supported with movement and multiple encounters with the words over time. Collecting and processing words through word collections, active involvement, and vocabulary journals all support this vital development.

Examples of Approximation Behaviors Related to the TESOL Standards

PreK–3 students will:

- identify words in specified categories.
- use new vocabulary in oral production.

4–8 students will:

- edit writing to include varied vocabulary.
- increase the complexity of written and oral sentences.

9–12 students will:

- include academic language in written reports.
- recognize the nuances of meaning.

References

Allen, R. (2000). *Report of the national reading panel.* Alexandria, VA: ASCD.

Beck, I., & McKeown, M. (2001). Text talk: Capturing the benefits of read-aloud experiences for young children. *The Reading Teacher, 55,* 10–20.

Biemiller, A., & Boote, C. (2006). An effective method for building meaning vocabulary in primary grades. *Journal of Educational Psychology, 98*(1),44–62. [ERIC Document Reproduction Service No. EJ734337]. Retrieved April 5, 2014, from ERIC database.

Blewitt, P., Rump, K., Shealy, S., & Cook, S. (2009). Shared book reading: When and how questions affect young children's word learning. *Journal of Educational Psychology, 101*(2), 294–304. [ERIC Document Reproduction Service No. EJ835037]. Retrieved April 5, 2014, from ERIC database.

Brett, J. (1987). *Fritz and the beautiful horses.* Boston, MA: Sandpiper.

Coyne, M., McCoach, D., & Kapp, L. (2007). Vocabulary intervention for kindergarten students: Comparing extended instruction to embedded instruction and incidental exposure. *Learning Disability Quarterly, 30*(2), 74–88. [ERIC Document Reproduction Service No. EJ786232]. Retrieved April 5, 2014, from ERIC database.

Gibbons, P. (2015). *Scaffolding Language, Scaffolding Learning: Teaching English Language Learners in the Mainstream Classroom.* Portsmouth, NH. Heinemann.

Herrell, A., and Jordan, M. (2001). Collecting and processing words: Strategies for building vocabulary in young children. *Kindergarten Education: Research and Practice, 3*, 17–25.

Nash, H., & Snowling, M. (2006). Teaching new words to children with poor existing vocabulary knowledge: A controlled evaluation of the definition and context methods. *International Journal of Language and Communication Disorders, 41*(3), 335–354. [ERIC Document Reproduction Service No. EJ747456]. Retrieved April 5, 2014, from ERIC database.

Stanovich, K. E. (1986). Matthew effects in reading: Some consequences of individual differences in the acquisition of literacy. *Reading Research Quarterly, 21*, 360–406.

White, T. G., Graves, M. F., & Slater, W. H. (1990). Growth of reading vocabulary in diverse elementary schools: Decoding and word meaning. *Journal of Educational Psychology, 82*(2), 281–290.

Manipulatives Strategies
Using Objects to Connect Concepts

8

Manipulatives are concrete devices that students can move and handle to support their thinking and learning. Manipulatives differ from **realia** in that they are usually nondescript objects such as beans or blocks that don't necessarily resemble real objects. Although they are most often used in math and science, they can effectively support language understanding in other subject areas as well. As you watch this mathematics video, note the ways in which the manipulatives are used both for teaching and practice and think about the following questions:

- How does the use of manipulatives in the teaching of a lesson enable the English learners to better understand the math concept?
- How does the teacher organize the manipulatives that the students use to ensure they are easily distributed?

Enhanced eText
Video Example 8.1

For manipulatives to be used effectively the teacher must demonstrate their use while simultaneously modeling the connection to academic language. Especially for English learners, the appropriate formal mathematics vocabulary must be layered on top of experiences, not presented abstractly (Coggins, Kravin, Coates, & Carroll, 2007).

Manipulatives can be concrete representations of the concepts being taught, as in models of the human body, which can be disassembled for study, or **representative manipulatives** such as small wooden cubes used for counting and math calculations. Concrete representation manipulatives are often used to support the development of academic vocabulary, while semi-concrete representational manipulatives are used to explain and illustrate an abstract concept such as a number. Manipulating learning materials is important for English learners because it helps them connect abstract concepts with concrete experiences (Echevarria, Vogt, & Short, 2010). Figure 8.1 provides suggestions for using manipulatives.

Step-by-Step

The steps in the use of manipulatives are the following:

- *Identify concepts to be taught and ways to represent them*—Identify the concept to be taught and the parts of the concept that could be represented by some kind of concrete object. Design a teaching plan that employs a demonstration of the concept using the manipulatives as examples.
- *Demonstrate and explain*—Demonstrate the use of the manipulatives as you explain the concept to the students. Use the demonstration to connect the manipulative, the concept, and any new vocabulary. Model the way you expect the students to use the manipulatives.

FIGURE 8.1 Manipulatives That Might Be Used in Various Subject Areas

Subject Area	Suggested Manipulative Use
Vocabulary	• Miniatures or wooden cutouts of objects • Colored blocks to teach colors, singular and plural forms • Attribute blocks to teach shapes, sizes, texture, color • Dolls to teach body parts
Mathematics	• Beans for counters • Small props for acting out word problems • Geometric shapes cut into fractional parts • Colored linking cubes for building patterns • Measuring cups and containers for studying measurement
Science	• Human body models • Realia for experiments • Styrofoam balls and toothpicks for construction • Magnets, batteries, iron filings

• *Provide guided practice*—Provide guided practice in the use of the manipulatives. Walk the students through the procedure to be used, demonstrating how to use the manipulatives and connecting the manipulatives to the vocabulary to be learned.

• *Give students time for additional practice*—Give the students time to use the manipulatives independently while you circulate around the classroom observing, giving feedback, and scaffolding language usage.

• *Celebrate and review*—Celebrate the students' demonstration of learning, again taking the opportunity to connect the manipulatives to the vocabulary and concepts learned.

• For examples of manipulative usage in mathematics that support English learners see: scholastic.com/teachers/article/10-ways-help-ells-succeed-math
• For suggestions of manipulatives useful in language arts, see: american-classroom-supply.com/language-arts-manipulatives-article.html

• *Continue to assess and improve on your use of manipulatives throughout the curriculum*—Use the self-evaluation rubric in Figure 8.2 to examine your planning and use of manipulatives in the classroom on a regular basis. Look for ways to support your students' learning in new and motivating ways.

Applications and Examples

To address the Common Core State Standards (CCSS.ELA-LITERACY.RL.2.9), Mr. Sanchez is using story props and a **Venn diagram** to teach his second graders to "compare and contrast two versions of the same story." Two hula hoops are laid on the floor, and the students sit around them. In front of each student are three or four props from one of the two versions of *Stone Soup* that the class has read together in the past few days.

"In the green hoop, we will put the props from the newer version of *Stone Soup* (McGovern, 1968) that we read first," Mr. Sanchez says as he places the McGovern version of the book in the center of the

FIGURE 8.2 Manipulatives Teacher Self-Evaluation

Beginning	Developing	Accomplished	Exemplary
Use a few manipulatives in math.	Use a few manipulatives in math and science.	Examine plans for possible manipulative use in all subjects.	Use manipulatives in all subjects to support understanding of abstract concepts and new vocabulary.
No plan is implemented to expand manipulative use.	Planning is beginning to be implemented to increase the use of more manipulatives.	Student learning is evaluated to determine the effectiveness of manipulative use.	Manipulatives are organized and their effectiveness evaluated on a regular basis.
Parents are not involved in collecting manipulatives or understanding their purpose.	Parents are involved in collecting manipulatives and understand their purposes.	Parents are given opportunities to experience manipulative use at back-to-school nights and/or parent conferences.	Workshops for parents are scheduled to encourage their understanding of manipulative use and help in collecting manipulatives.

green hoop. "In the red hoop, we will put the props from the other version of the story," Mr. Sanchez says as he places the Brown (1947) version of the book in the center of the red hoop.

"Now watch what I am going to do," he says as moves one hoop so it overlaps part of the other one. "Now we have a section of the hoops that overlap. When you see two circles that overlap like this, it is called a Venn diagram. The part that overlaps is where we will put the props that show something that was the same in both versions of the story. Who has something that was in both versions of the story?"

Petra holds up a stone. Mr. Sanchez nods and smiles as he says, "Yes, Petra. There was a stone in each version. That's why it was called *Stone Soup*. Where should we put the stone?"

Petra smiles at Mr. Sanchez but makes no move to place the stone. Mr. Sanchez continues, "Put the stone in here, Petra," he says as he motions to the overlap in the hoops. "The stone was in the first story." He makes a circular motion to indicate the green hoop and points to the first book. "The stone was in the second story." He repeats the motion with the red hoop and the second book. "So, we put the stone in here." He points to the overlap, and Petra puts the stone in the correct place.

"Very good! The stone was in both stories." Mr. Sanchez smiles at Petra and points to both books.

The process is repeated with the students making decisions about the proper placement of each of the props in the Venn diagram. As they place the props, the students talk about whether the props were in both stories. When there is disagreement Mr. Sanchez urges them to look in the book. When all the props have been placed, Mr. Sanchez pairs the students to work together on another Venn diagram. He gives each pair of students a large laminated piece of construction paper with a Venn diagram drawn on it. He gives each pair a set of pictures of the same set of props they have just used. The partners are to reenact the sorting of the props and recreate the Venn diagram they have just done as a class. The only addition to the task is a set of word cards that identify each prop. The partners must read the words and put them into the Venn diagram along with the props. There is a lot of conversation among the pairs, in home languages and English, as the students make decisions about the placement of the props and words. Occasionally, a student will come to get one of the versions of the story to prove a point. As the pairs complete their work, they raise their hands and Mr. Sanchez comes to them so they can read the words they have placed on the diagram and explain their diagram. Mr. Sanchez uses this time to reinforce word identification skills, vocabulary pronunciation, and correct use of the Venn diagram.

In this case, Mr. Sanchez used concrete manipulatives, the props. He then moved to semi-concrete manipulatives, the pictures. Finally, he provided abstract manipulatives, the words. He also used partner work to facilitate the use of home languages to communicate and solve problems and supported the students as they reported their results in English.

* * * * *

Older students also benefit from the use of manipulatives in the classroom. As Ms. Yang's sixth graders study the human body, she provides a model of each of the systems of the body that contains removable parts so the students can take the model apart, closely examine the parts, and reassemble the model. They are completing a diagram of each system as a part of a human body notebook they are compiling. In presenting the lesson in this way, Ms. Yang wants her students to "integrate qualitative or technical information expressed visually (e.g., in a flowchart, diagram, model, graph, or table)" (CCSS.ELA-LITERACY.6–8.9).

Ms. Yang has put together groups of four students to work cooperatively to disassemble the model, use the parts of the model to help them label their diagrams, and then reassemble the model. Group members work together to test one another on the names of the body parts and exactly where the parts fit into the system. Each group includes English learners, and every member is expected to help the others to learn each of the body parts, where it fits in the model, how it is spelled, and where the label goes on the diagram in their notebooks.

Everyone knows that the diagrams must be completed again on Friday as a test. Each group that has every member pass the test with at least an 80 percent will get extra recess time on Friday afternoon, so everyone is anxious to help the others learn. No one wants to be sitting inside studying for a human body retest while everyone else is outside playing on Friday afternoon.

Conclusion

Manipulatives—whether they are real objects that help students to relate language to concepts or representational objects such as blocks, counters, or beans—are often supportive of students' understanding and language development. Although traditionally manipulatives have been used in primary classrooms, there is evidence to support their use with older students and especially with English learners of all ages (West, 2011). Presenting new concepts in a concrete way, before moving to semi-concrete representations, such as pictures, and finally to abstract symbols, helps students make the gradual switch from concrete to abstract thinking. Manipulatives can be used in many ways, but consideration should be given to connecting the vocabulary, concepts, and thought processes through demonstration, in much the same way vocabulary is introduced to infants. For example, "This is a cup. We drink from a cup," as the cup is being shown and demonstrated.

Examples of Approximation Behaviors Related to the TESOL Standards

PreK–3 students will:
- use manipulatives to represent real objects.
- manipulate objects to demonstrate concepts.

4–8 students will:
- use manipulatives to solve problems.

- use manipulatives and verbal explanations to demonstrate problem solutions.

9–12 students will:
- use manipulatives to represent complex interactions.
- use manipulatives to explain concepts to others.

References

Brown, M. (1947). *Stone soup.* New York, NY: Aladdin/Macmillan.

Coggins, D., Kravin, D., Coates, G., & Carroll, M. (2007). *English language learners in the mathematics classroom.* Thousand Oaks, CA: Corwin Press.

Echevarria, J., Vogt, M., & Short, D. (2010). *Making content comprehensible for elementary English students: The SIOP model.* Boston, MA: Allyn & Bacon.

McGovern, A. (1968). *Stone soup.* New York, NY: Scholastic.

West, L. (2011). *Using physical and virtual manipulatives with eighth-grade geometry students* (Unpublished master's thesis). University of Nebraska–Lincoln, NB.

9

Choosing Technology Based on Student Needs

Advancing Progress in English Language and Content Learning

Any look into today's classroom will show the observer many changes in the ways in which we teach and learn. Technology is evident in the ways in which teachers present concepts and information as well as the opportunities students have to utilize technology to support their learning, research, and writing.

The use of technology in the classroom is not the goal in and of itself (Parris, Estrada & Hongsfeld, 2017). The Partnership for 21st Century Learning (P21), a group of educators tasked with looking at the infusion of technology information vital to education, identifies skills and themes that students will be expected to acquire in order to participate successfully in the fast-paced digital age. They include the following:

1. Content and 21st century themes.
2. Learning and innovational skills
3. Information, media, and technology skills
4. Life and career skills

The purpose of this chapter is to provide guidance to teachers of English language learners as they make technology choices to facilitate the learning of their individual students who are in the process of acquiring English. Because these students will be at a disadvantage in acquiring basic skills in English like reading, writing, listening, speaking, and learning mathematics, technology can be a great benefit in providing specific practice in these skills. Technology can also provide visual support for vocabulary development. To support these students in acquiring the English language skills needed to be successful, teachers must choose the applications, software and programs that provide them with support in the skills they are acquiring and the practice they need.

Step-by-Step

The steps in choosing effective technology for English language learners are the following:

• ***Learn the language development levels of your students.*** Before choosing appropriate technology or curricular materials, it is important to know your students.

FIGURE 9.1 Technology Appropriate for Levels of English Language Learners

Preproduction	Early Production	Speech Emergence	Intermediate Fluency	Fluent
Direct correlation between visuals, spoken words and text. Use with a fluent English partner.	Technology to improve pronunciation and basic reading and keyboarding skills. Use with a fluent English partner to increase verbal interactions.	Expand use of different apps and programs. Look for programs that require verbal or written responses.	Expand choices for students at this level. Choices should include partners as well as software.	The sky's the limit as long as the students have received instruction in the use of the chosen technology.

- *Look for technology to match both the language levels and academic needs of your students.* Many of the technology programs and tools available can be used at several levels, which allows for ongoing use as students improve in their English production and academic understandings.

- *Choose technology that increases student interaction* (Lacina, 2004). Sitting at a computer alone doesn't support the acquisition of English as effectively as sharing the experience with another student or student mentor which adds the extra opportunity for verbal interaction and clarification.

- *Provide time for English language learners to use the technology.* When students in the class are involved in group activities or other center activities, provide English language learners with time to use the specifically chosen technology to increase their skills. If before- or after-school programs are available, give the English language learners extra practice in using technology. See Figure 9.1 to determine the most appropriate technology for your students.

- *Carefully monitor students as they use technology to determine if and when they are confused or needing to advance in their use.* When students are motivated by using technology, different or more advanced use will be helpful to their further growth. If they are frustrated by the technology, and it gets in the way of their learning, make some changes. Pair them with a more technology savvy student or find an approach that can be used more easily.

- *Remember that technology should enhance learning.* NEVER use it just because it is available. If students are not benefitting from a digital tool, find one that works for them or return to teacher-based instruction.

Applications and Examples

Mrs. Affeld teaches second grade in a diverse neighborhood. She has seven students at various levels of English development. All of the students live in households where Spanish is spoken. Mrs. Affeld wants to provide her students, both English language learners and native English speakers, with opportunities to improve their English vocabulary, pronunciation, fluency and writing skills. Since her school district has provided funds for purchasing technology Mrs. Affeld prepares a proposal to submit to her principal outlining the technology she would like to implement in her classroom, the needs it will meet, and a brief explanation of how it will be used. Her proposal looks like this:

Language Master and cards for vocabulary and pronunciation development. The Language Master is a tape recording and playing device where the teacher prepares tape recorded cards that the student sends through the machine to hear the correct pronunciation of the English word. Pictures can be posted on the cards to support understanding. Whole sentences can also be posted. The student reads the card in the limited time allowed on the tape to support pronunciation and fluency. There are two tapes on each card, so the student can play the teacher's pronunciation with their own. See Video Example 9.1, showing how the Language Master machine is used.

Enhanced eText
Video Example 9.1
https://www.youtube.com/
watch?v=k1MrKXAij7M

How this technology will be used: The Language Master will be used in a center during center time. All students, both ELLs and native English speakers, who are struggling with new vocabulary and/or pronunciation will use the Language Master to review new vocabulary words and content-area terminology. Individuals can review words and practice reading fluently as needed during individual practice time after reading groups.

LeapFrog tablets.   LeapFrog learning tablets allow students to read and write with support. With just a touch, students are supplied with unknown words. Individual abilities are supported as students read. Reading levels and fluency speed adjust to the students' ability. The tablets also support writing. See Video Example 9.2, to view a LeapFrog tablet.

Enhanced eText
Video Example 9.2
https://www.youtube.com/
watch?v=jgOPIuYErL4

How this technology will be used: LeapFrog tablets will be used during sustained silent reading time so that ELLs and native English speakers needing support will be successful in their independent reading. They will also be available during center time for students to practice reading and/or writing.

* * * * * * * * * *

Because many of his students have moved from Puerto Rico or have relatives still living there, Mr. Repich uses an online discussion board, Moodle (docs.moodle.org), to pose current event questions to his tenth-grade social studies class. Moodle allows an ongoing discussion as well as the posting of visuals and/or videos which help enrich and give credence to the students' comments. He has established a set of rules to govern students' comments:

1. Limit your response to 200 words. If possible, post a visual or video to support your text.
2. The discussion will have a cut-off date and time.
3. You may NOT delete your post after it is submitted, so consider it carefully before posting.
4. Remember to make your comments polite. If you are commenting on another student's post, be courteous.
5. Try to use the social studies vocabulary that you are learning in class whenever possible. If you feel the need to define a term, do so.

Mr. Repich posts a short video from the evening news showing the destruction in Puerto Rico after Hurricane Maria and asks this question, "What do you feel the U.S. government should do to support the people of Puerto Rico in this disaster? Why?" The first few responses were posted quickly.

Andrea: I think the U.S. should send food and water but allow the Puerto Ricans to make the repairs on their own. The U.S. takes on too much around the world, and I think we should take care of our own.

Jose: Since Puerto Ricans are U.S. citizens, I think the U.S. should provide exactly what they have provided in Texas and Florida. (He posts another short news video to support his stand.) (NOTE: Fair use allows televised video to be used for educational purposes for one month.)

Alberto: I agree with Jose, and I think anyone who wants to come to the U.S. should be given free plane tickets. There should be places set up for them to live.

A few days later Mr. Repich conducts a class discussion of the posts. He and the students use a vocabulary word wall and build an online bulletin board using _Noteapp_. The bulletin board includes new vocabulary words, letters, translations of letters, and photographs that students have received from relatives in Puerto Rico.

Every week, Mr. Repich and his students discuss the progress being made on the island, and students add to their online bulletin board.

Conclusion

Many applications, software, and teacher-support materials are available for classroom use today. The numbers are increasing daily. Although many seem to be unique and beneficial to learning, there are several things to keep in mind: the language and learning levels of your students and whether or not the technology increases learning and/or motivation. Try not to overwhelm your students and infuse technology gradually, ALWAYS using it to increase motivation and learning in your students and NOT just for the purpose of integrating technology.

When choosing a technological application or software, it is important to think about HOW the technology will be used. For guidance in choosing appropriate technologies for your classroom, see Figure 9.2.

FIGURE 9.2 Choosing Appropriate Technology for English Language Learners

1. Does this application or software address a specific need?
2. Have you documented this need in one or more of your students?
3. Does this technology allow students to advance as they become more proficient?
4. Does this technology allow students to work independently or with a partner or small group?
5. Does this technology encourage the use of spoken or written English?
6. How does the technology encourage users to become more fluent English speakers or writers?

Student Need to be Met	Adaptability of Technology	Example
Basic vocabulary development	1. Can be used by individual or pairs. 2. Cards for new vocabulary can be added. 3. Sentences can be added to build fluency.	Language Master vocabulary cards and sentences
Language development within academic content areas	1. Uses a placement test to identify areas of need. 2. Individualized for student growth. 3. Uses flash cards, reading activities, games, audio/voice pronunciation, graphic organizers, writing activities, and quizzes to track progress.	Brainpop ESL
Vocabulary development and grammatical structure	1. Audio and visual aids. 2. Uses a placement test to identify level of proficiency. 3. Individualized for student growth. 4. Assessment driven. 5. Feedback and reports available.	Renaissance Learning: English in a Flash
Vocabulary, memory, and grammar development	1. Individual games 2. Video presentation 3. Worksheet follow-up availability 4. Flash cards 5. ESL e-books	ESL Games World–www.esl-gamesworld.com

Examples of Approximation Behaviors Related to the ISTE Standards

PreK–3 students will:

- *Acquire basic skills and knowledge using technology.*
- *Recognize uses for technology.*

4–8 students will:

- *Build knowledge by actively exploring online sources.*
- *Create original works or responsibly repurpose content from online information.*

9–12 students will:

- *Publish or present content that customizes the message for intended audiences.*
- *Evaluate the accuracy, perspective, credibility and relevance of online information.*

References

International Society for Technology in Education Standards downloaded October 21, 2017.

Lacina, J. (2004). Promoting language acquisitions: Technology and English language learners. *Childhood Education, 81*(2), 113. Retrieved from Questia.com.

Parris, H., Estrada, L., & Honigsted, A. (2017). *ELL frontiers: Using technology to enhance instruction for English learners.* Thousand Oaks, CA: Corwin Publishing.

10

Moving into Reading
Using Multiple Strategies to Foster Comprehension

Interactive read-aloud (Barrentine, 1996) is reading books out loud using facial expressions, different voices for different characters, and gestures while encouraging the active participation of listeners through prediction, discussion, and checking for understanding. It also involves the exploration of the structure of text and think-aloud strategies that demonstrate how readers gain meaning from text (Canagarajah, 2006). This form of read-aloud is a powerful teaching tool to use with English language learners; it provides a strong language model and reduces anxiety among students because the use of voices, illustrations, and gestures aids in improving comprehension (Reid, 2002). Students see their teachers as role models, and in interactive read-aloud, the teachers actually do, in fact, model what good readers do (Tompkins, 2009).

Read-aloud plus (Jordan & Herrell, 2001) is an extension of interactive read-aloud. It is a strategy that can be used whenever students must read "tough text." It is an especially valuable strategy to use with English language learners because it incorporates the modeling of fluent, expressive reading of English text. The additional use of techniques for stopping to clarify vocabulary and periodic checking for understanding helps to provide or activate knowledge and helps students make connections between the text and their personal experience (Short & Echevarria, 2004).

Although read-aloud has traditionally been used extensively with young children, its effectiveness with older students has been documented many times (Krashen, 1993; Trelease, 1995, 2013). This research has led many administrators of high schools with low test scores in reading and comprehension to mandate the daily use of read-aloud on a schoolwide basis. Such innovative programs have shown promising results (Trelease, 2013).

Interactive read-aloud is motivational. When students observe a teacher reading fluently and with enthusiasm, they often choose to read the same book, or another book by the same author, for leisure reading (Wood, 1994). The discussion of characters, settings, and descriptions that are involved in interactive read-aloud provides shared understanding and vocabulary that helps English language learners stretch their linguistic abilities (Swain, 1993). It's been documented that students who frequently hear books read aloud have a more extensive vocabulary than those who do not (Trelease, 2013). See Video Example 10.1 to see how the teacher engages the students and demonstrates how she uses strategies to determine the meanings of unfamiliar words.

> **Enhanced eText**
> Video Example 10.1
> https://youtu.be/00-i6m8ELiw

Shared reading (Holdaway, 1979) is a strategy that teachers use to read books, charts, and other texts with students when the text is too difficult for students to read independently. Students and teacher read the text aloud together. Even when the students cannot read along with the

FIGURE 10.1 Read-Aloud Plus Extension Activities

- Visuals—transparencies, photos, graphs, charts
- Realia—real objects related to the material being studied
- Paraphrasing—restating the material in simple language
- Rewriting—rewriting the material in simple language
- Rewriting and illustrating—adding illustrations to the rewritten material
- Comparing and contrasting—using graphics such as webs or Venn diagrams to compare and contrast material with previously read material
- Physicalization—acting out the material, sometimes adding simple props

teacher, they hear the words pronounced as their eyes follow the text. In the primary grades, large books with big print— **"big books"**—are often used with small groups of students so that everyone can see the illustrations and text (Depree & Iversen, 1996). Shared reading can also be done with multiple copies of small books, poetry charts, song lyrics, or any text for that matter, as long as the teacher and all the students can see the words (Tompkins, 2009). The introduction of interactive whiteboards and **large platform projectors** also allows teachers to work effectively in whole class settings as well as with small groups. Books can easily be digitized for presentation in a format suitable for viewing across the entire classroom. Specific words might be highlighted or colorized to provide stronger visualization for the students.

Using shared reading with English language learners is appropriate because the teacher has opportunities to use illustrations to support vocabulary development, to use think-aloud strategies to teach problem-solving approaches, and to integrate verbal interactions to support comprehension (Gibbons, 1993). When using shared reading with English language learners, it is especially important to build background knowledge and experiences that help students understand the meaning of the text. The skills and strategies that can be taught through shared reading are shown in Figure 10.2.

Interactive read-alouds and shared reading can be used together to support students as they move into English reading. The teacher begins with interactive read-aloud and gradually moves students into shared reading of texts.

Step-by-Step

The steps in implementing interactive read-aloud are the following:

- *Choose an appropriate book*—Choose a book that is above the **instructional reading level** of the students and that will give you an opportunity to provide a rich read-aloud experience through the use of different voices, excitement, and drama. Set aside a time each day when you will read aloud interactively with your students.
- *Preread and plan interactions*—Before beginning the read-aloud sessions, thoroughly read the book you have chosen. Use **sticky notes** to mark places for discussion, predictions, and connections to other books the students have read or for sharing personal experiences that relate to the story. Also think about any visuals or realia that may increase comprehension and get these items ready for use.
- *Stop for interactions*—Select a 10- to 15-minute section of the text to read each time, stopping at logical places during reading. Read with enthusiasm, using gestures and voices, and review the events of each day's reading at the end of the session. Discuss predictions for the next day's reading and involve the students in relating the events of the day to their own experiences or similar literary experiences. Use graphic devices like story mapping or daily illustrations of the events to keep students interested. See Figure 10.3 for an example of a **story map**.

FIGURE 10.2 Skills and Strategies Taught through Shared Reading

Guided Reading Applications	Example
Word boundaries	"Frame the word *caps* in this sentence."
Left-to-right progression	"Point to the words with the pointer."
Punctuation uses	"How would you say this sentence?"
Word meaning	"Show me the dahlias in the picture."
Illustrations/story meaning	"How did you know he was scared?"

Cuing systems—visual
          meaning
          syntax
	"How did you know the word was *monkeys*?"
	"Show me the picture that shows you what that word means."
	"Would we say, 'The boy went jeans'?"

Reading with expression	"How would he say that?"
Fix-it strategies	"How would it start if the word were *lantern*? Read it again."
Use of context for meaning	"Read the part that helps you understand what the word *flourish* means."
Reading for cohesion links	"Read the part that tells you that he heard the noise after he went to bed."
Reading to confirm	"Read the part that tells you why he was angry."

• ***Assess student progress and understanding***—Students' abilities to paraphrase or retell the events in a story are indicative of their understanding of the story. When English learners understand the story but don't have the vocabulary or confidence to retell or paraphrase, they can often draw illustrations or act out scenes to indicate their comprehension. To determine whether the strategy of interactive read-aloud is effective, pause occasionally to allow students to demonstrate their understanding by paraphrasing, illustrating, or acting out scenes. Anecdotal records of these types of informal assessments can be kept in individual student portfolios.

Step-by-Step

The steps in using shared reading are the following:

• ***Introduce the text***—Introduce the book or text. When using a book, examine the cover and make story predictions from the illustrations on the cover. Encourage the students to talk about personal experiences that relate to the topic of the book, chart, or poem.

FIGURE 10.3 Example of a Story Map

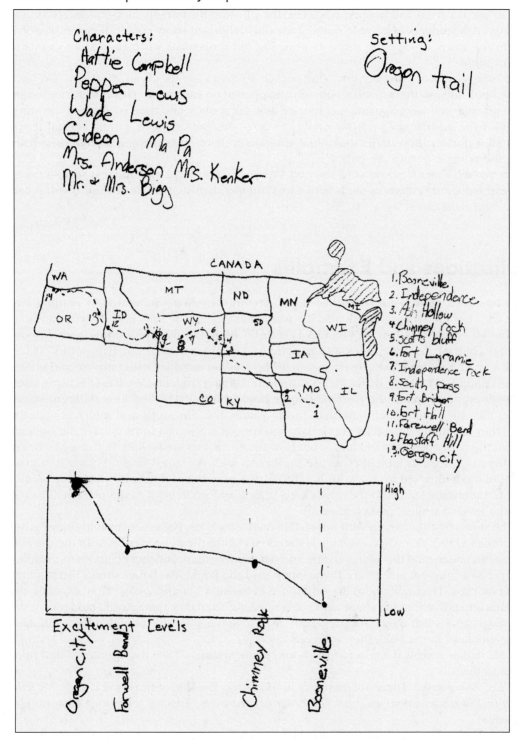

• ***Read the book and track the print***—Read the book or other text aloud, tracking the words as you read so the students can read along. Use a pointer to make sure the students are looking at and saying the words with you. They may not know all the words, but they will hear you pronounce them as you point to them.

- *Stop for discussion and prediction*—Stop at appropriate times to discuss what is happening or to predict what will happen next. Use the illustrations to help support understanding of vocabulary. Ask students to point to parts of the illustrations to show comprehension of words or events in the story. Involve the students in acting out movement words and story events to reinforce meaning.
- *Encourage verbal interactions*—Encourage students to talk about the story. Go back through the book and ask them to talk about what happened on each page. This is a chance for the students to practice oral language and incorporate new vocabulary into their retelling of the story.
- *Reread for additional practice and exposure*—Reread the book or text several times, tracking with a pointer. Encourage individual students to take turns reading a page or **refrain** aloud, use the pointer, or turn the pages.
- *Practice with small versions of the text*—After students have read the text several times, they can read individual copies of the book or text independently or illustrate their favorite part of the story and write about it.

Applications and Examples

Ms. Baker has been addressing several of the Common Core State Standards in reading language arts with her kindergarten students. She wants her students to "ask and answer questions about unknown words in a text" (CCSS.ELA-LITERACY.RL.K.4); "with prompting and support, compare and contrast the adventures and experiences of characters in familiar stories" (CCSS.ELA-LITERACY.RL.K.9); and "actively engage in group reading activities with purpose and understanding" (CCSS.ELA-LITERACY.RL.K.10). To support her young students, Ms. Baker is using interactive read-aloud as she reads the *Curious George* books (Rey, 1941). She uses different voices for George, the other animals, and the man in the yellow hat. She stops and interacts with the students as they encounter unfamiliar vocabulary and concepts. She also stops to have the students predict what might happen next and talk about how the characters are feeling. Because Ms. Baker works with young students, she likes to use big books with oversized illustrations. She's even had several of them digitized for use with her interactive whiteboard. Using an electronic pointer to highlight, underscore, and colorize words adds variety and excitement to the presentation and enhances the level of student participation.

After the students' experiences with interactive read-aloud, Ms. Baker moves into shared reading. She chooses a book that will encourage her students to use their experiences with the *Curious George* books to understand the next text. She and her kindergarten students begin shared reading with *Caps for Sale* (Slobodkina, 1968). Before they read the book, Ms. Baker shows the students some hats and caps. They talk about the difference between a hat and a cap. They examine the different caps and talk about the shape and color of each. Ms. Baker reminds the students of the *Curious George* stories that they have previously read together and tells them that they will meet some more monkeys in the book they will read today.

When Ms. Baker reveals the cover of the book, Jana exclaims, "I see the monkeys!" and hops up to point to them.

"Yes," Ms. Baker says. "There are monkeys in this story. The title of the book is *Caps for Sale: A Tale of a Peddler, Some Monkeys, and Their Monkey Business.* That's a long title. What do you think it means?"

"The man in the tree is selling caps," Kevin suggests.

"You are right, Kevin!" Ms. Baker says. "He sells caps." She points to the peddler on the cover. "He is called a peddler. A peddler sells things."

"What do you think it means when it says a tale of a peddler, some monkeys, and their monkey business?" Ms. Baker asks.

"My dad says, 'No monkey business!'" Curt says. "He says that when he wants us to be good."

"Yes, monkey business is being silly, like monkeys," Ms. Baker says. "We will see what monkey business is when we read the book." Ms. Baker opens the book and begins to read, pointing to the words as she reads them. When she gets to the refrain, "Caps! Caps for sale!" she encourages the students to read with her. When she gets to the part where the monkeys imitate everything the peddler does, she has the students act out what the peddler and the monkeys do. She stops to have the students predict several times during the story, and she points to pictures as she says words that might be unfamiliar to the students. They are all very involved in the reading of the story.

After Ms. Baker and the students read the story several times, she gets the caps out again and shows the students how to stack them like the peddler in the story did. The caps and several copies of the book are placed in the dramatic play area, where the students are told that they can act out the story later. Ms. Baker suggests that one person can pretend to be the peddler and others can take the parts of the monkeys.

"If you forget what comes next in the story, the book will be there to help you," Ms. Baker says. "Just look at the pictures and the words in the book and you will remember what happens next."

Ms. Baker often uses big books in her kindergarten classroom. The large illustrations help her to teach new vocabulary. She finds that her English language learners follow along with the rest of the students as they read the books and enjoy using the language from the books to retell the stories.

* * * * *

To support her ninth graders in achieving the Common Core State Standard to "read and comprehend literature in the 9–10 grade complexity band proficiently with scaffolding as needed at the high end of the range" (CCSS.ELA-LITERACY.RL. 9–10.10), Ms. Bosic is preparing them to attend a performance of highly acclaimed actor Hal Holbrook's reenactment of America's great storyteller, Mark Twain. The students have read several short selections written by Mark Twain and want to hear *The Adventures of Huckleberry Finn* (de Voto, 1984). Ms. Bosic knows that the students will benefit more from the theater excursion if they understand the stories they will actually be hearing and decides to expose the students to *Huckleberry Finn* through an interactive read-aloud.

After rereading the first few chapters of the book, Ms. Bosic decides to use interactive read-aloud to read the story in **dialect** and to use a few props. She finds an old flannel shirt and decrepit straw hat and uses sticky notes to mark stopping points in the story. Because Ms. Bosic is teaching the use of comprehension processes to her students, she plans to model the processes as a part of her read-aloud. Figure 10.4 explains the comprehension processes.

Ms. Bosic introduces the reading of *Huckleberry Finn* by showing the film *The Adventures of Tom Sawyer*. She asks the students what they think might happen next with Huckleberry.

"I think he's going to run away," Ramon says. "He's never going to be able to live with the Widow Douglas."

"You may be right, Ramon," Ms. Bosic says with a smile. "We get to see in the next book, *The Adventures of Huckleberry Finn*."

Ms. Bosic opens the book and says, "Mark Twain begins this book with a warning and an explanation. Do you know what a warning is?"

"Do you mean a warning like, 'Be careful'?" Kelly asks.

"Yes, Kelly. It's something you say or read that tells you to be careful or that something is dangerous. Mark Twain starts this book with these words:

"Notice: Persons attempting to find a motive in this narrative will be prosecuted; persons attempting to find a moral in it will be banished; persons attempting to find a plot in it will be shot.

By order of the author, per G. G., Chief of Ordinance."

"What do you think Mark Twain is warning us about?" Ms. Bosic asks.

The students seemed very puzzled by the quote, so Ms. Bosic decides to explore the word meanings. "Let's take the warnings one at a time. He says 'persons attempting to find a motive will be prosecuted.' What is a motive?"

Ms. Bosic leads the students through a discussion by asking them to relate the unfamiliar vocabulary to experiences they've had in the past. They relate the word *motive* to murder mysteries on TV, the word *prosecuted* to shoplifting warnings they see in stores, and the word *moral* to Aesop's Fables they've read in the past. At the end of the discussion, Ms. Bosic commends the

FIGURE 10.4 Teaching Comprehension Processes

Process	Definition	Teaching Strategies
Microprocesses	Sentence-level connections Making sense of elements within a sentence	Read-aloud, rereading for fluency, phrasing practice
Integrative processes	Connections between adjacent sentences within a selection	Finding cohesion links, referents, visualizing the connections between ideas
Elaborative processes	Making connections between personal experiences or other texts related to the text being read	Think-aloud referring to personal experiences or other texts that were similar to the one being read
Macroprocesses	Getting the main idea, overarching meaning of a whole selection	Summarizing the text, stating the main idea, finding the topic sentences
Metacognitive	Monitoring your own understanding of what is being read	Stopping and taking stock and having strategies to use to support understanding Rereading, paraphrasing, looking up words, self-correcting, and monitoring

Sources: Irwin (1991); Tompkins (1997); and Fisher, Flood, Lapp, & Frey, (2004)

students for making connections. She reminds them that other stories and television shows and movies that they have seen may help them understand stories that they read. She explains that it is these kinds of connections that good readers use to help them understand tough text.

Because Ms. Bosic reads the story with the dialect of the characters, she manages to set a tone that helps the students to relax and enjoy the story. She stops periodically to model comprehension processes like thinking aloud when something may be confusing or talking about something in the book that reminds her of the Tom Sawyer video. She stops every now and then and pretends to be confused by a pronoun, asking the students, "Who is meant by the word *he* in that sentence?" She might even reread a sentence to help the students make connections. She doesn't demonstrate these strategies constantly because she doesn't want to interrupt the flow of the story, but she gives the students a lot of ideas about how she is making meaning of the text by using her short explanations and demonstrations.

At the end of each day's reading, Ms. Bosic reviews some of the more difficult vocabulary and encourages the students to discuss the main events in the part of the story read that day. She asks questions that require the students to infer, and she encourages them to predict what might happen next. She is modeling fluent reading, obviously enjoying the story, and using the storytelling mode with the addition of the simple costume and dialect.

FIGURE 10.5 Using Reading Strategies for Different Language Development Levels

Preproduction	Early Production	Speech Emergence	Intermediate Fluency	Fluent
Read-aloud with visual support. Shared Reading	Continue read-aloud with visual support Adjustment of text level using *Newsela*	Pair with fluent reader to practice pronunciation and adjust text level using *Newsela*	Allow students to record their oral reading, work on fluency and pronunciation, and then re-record.	Encourage and affirm.

When Ms. Bosic and her students return to school after attending the Hal Holbrook performance, she distributes individual copies of *The Adventures of Huckleberry Finn*. She continues to use interactive read-aloud, and she uses dialects as she reads, but asks the students to follow along in their books. She stops periodically and asks a student to read, discussing the meaning of a word or the motivation of a character. As they continue through the book, she notices more of her students reading with expression and even attempting to use dialect. This shared reading of the text allows even her more limited English speaking students to comprehend the text and have fun in the process.

Conclusion

Interactive read-aloud and shared reading, though traditionally associated with primary classrooms, are also highly effective in supporting comprehension and vocabulary development in older students, especially those who are English learners. Even high school students benefit from hearing fluent, expressive reading of English text. By hearing literature read with the use of different voices, inflection, gestures, and body language, English language learners are supported in refining their reading and speaking skills. For a presentation of the use of interactive reading to model effective reading strategies for secondary students, see Video Example 10.2.

Enhanced eText
Video Example 10.2
https://www.youtube.com/
watch?v=JdiScrcP2Nk

As you view this video, think about how the teacher could stop in the reading of a text to demonstrate effective reading strategies and involve the students in identifying other strategies they could use to build understanding. For suggestions of strategies to use with students at different English language development levels, see Figure 10.5.

Observation is vital when teachers use shared reading and interactive read-aloud. Post-it notes can be used to note the names of students who are not participating, who need to point to illustrations in order to make themselves understood, or who seem to have trouble with comprehension. When students need more individual instruction, older students or volunteers can be trained to use these strategies effectively. It is important to keep a record of the vocabulary that is introduced so that it can be used repeatedly during the day.

Examples of Approximation Behaviors Related to the TESOL Standards

PreK–3 students will:

- listen to and join in shared reading.
- imitate actions related to storybooks.
- orally describe favorite storybook characters.

- orally describe personal experiences related to a text.

4–8 students will:

- explore alternative ways of saying things.
- make connections between stories and personal experiences.
- describe a personal hero, orally or in writing.
- use words from books read in oral and/or written communications.

9–12 students will:

- use comprehension strategies to make sense of text.
- connect new vocabulary to past experiences.
- respond to literature orally or in writing.
- participate in the performance of a scene from literature.

References

Barrentine, S. (1996). Engaging with reading through interactive read-alouds. *The Reading Teacher, 50,* 36–43.

Canagarajah, A. S. (2006). TESOL at forty: What are the issues? *TESOL Quarterly, 40*(1), 9–34.

Depree, H., & Iversen, S. (1996). *Early literacy in the classroom: A new standard for young readers.* Bothell, WA: Wright Group.

de Voto, B. (Ed.). (1984). *The portable Mark Twain.* New York, NY: Penguin Books.

Fisher, D., Flood, J., Lapp, D., & Frey, N. (2004) Interactive read-alouds: Is there a common set of implementation practices? *The Reading Teacher, 58*(1), 8–17.

Gibbons, P. (1993). *Learning to learn in a second language.* Portsmouth, NH: Heinemann.

Holdaway, D. (1979). *Foundations of literacy.* Auckland, New Zealand: Ashton Scholastic.

Irwin, J. (1991). *Teaching reading comprehension processes* (2nd ed.). Needham Heights, MA: Allyn & Bacon.

Jordan, M., & Herrell, A. (2001, November). *Read-aloud plus: Adding understanding to tough text.* Presentation at the California Reading Association State Conference. San Jose, CA.

Krashen, S. (1993). *The power of reading.* Englewood, CO: Libraries Unlimited.

Reid, S. (2002). *Book bridges for ESL students.* Lanham, MD: Scarecrow Press.

Rey, H. A. (1941). *Curious George.* Boston, MA: Houghton Mifflin.

Slobodkina, E. (1968). *Caps for sale: A tale of a peddler, some monkeys, and their monkey business.* New York, NY: HarperCollins.

Swain, M. (1993). The output hypothesis: Just speaking and writing aren't enough. *The Canadian Modern Language Review, 50,* 158–164.

Tompkins, G. E. (1997). *Language arts: Content and teaching strategies.* Upper Saddle River, NJ: Merrill/Prentice Hall.

Tompkins, G. (2009). *Literacy for the 21st century.* (5th ed.). Upper Saddle River, NJ: Merrill/Prentice Hall.

Trelease, J. (1995). Sustained silent reading. *California English, 1,* 8–9.

Trelease, J. (2013). *The read aloud handbook* (7th ed.). New York, NY: Penguin Books.

Wood, K. (1994). Hearing voices, telling tales: Finding the power of reading aloud. *Language Arts, 71,* 346–349.

11

Close Reading

Engaging with Text to Improve Reading Comprehension

Close reading is a strategy recommended to help students uncover the layers of meaning that lead to deep comprehension (Boyles, 2012; Fang, 2016). Most teachers understand the importance of teaching students to read closely, but this more structured approach to close reading, enables all students—struggling, exemplary, and English language learners—to acquire and use strategies that support the achievement of strenuous Common Core State Standards. This strategy directly addresses Common Core Reading Anchor Standard 1: "Read closely to determine what the text says explicitly and to make logical inferences from it; cite specific textual evidence when writing or speaking to support conclusions from the text." In this video, Dr. Doug Fisher, a well-known California State University at San Diego educational researcher and author, clarifies the relationship between close reading and the Common Core.

Enhanced eText
Video Example 11.1
www.youtube.com/watch?
feature=player_embedded&
v=5w9v6-zUg3Y

As you view the video, think about the following questions:

- How does close reading support the Common Core State Standards?
- What is the main purpose of close reading?

The Partnership for Assessment of Readiness for College and Careers (2011) identifies several aspects of close reading necessary to prepare students to achieve the proficiency sought in CCSS:

- engaging in complex text;
- examining meaning thoroughly and methodically;
- encouraging students to read and reread deliberately;
- focusing on the meanings of individual words and sentences, and the order in which sentences unfold; and
- developing an understanding of how the ideas develop over the course of the text.

In order to implement close reading in the classroom, teachers must thoroughly understand how close reading differs from instruction used in the past. Figure 11.1 highlights some of the differences between traditional comprehension questions and those associated with close reading.

It is recommended that teachers use short texts as they are teaching students to read closely. Using short texts allows students to reread text to both ask and answer questions leading to deeper understanding (Boyles, 2013; Coleman & Pimentel, 2012). We don't want to abandon longer texts, but using shorter ones in the beginning encourages students to ask and answer questions of themselves during the reading, an important facet of close reading. Students learn to

FIGURE 11.1 Differences Between Traditional Comprehension Questions and Questions Associated with Close Reading

What did Ethan and Alexis do to make Maya feel bad?	How did the author use dialogue to help you, the reader, understand how Maya felt when Ethan and Alexis teased her?
	(Standard 4: The use of language)
How did Maya change after Ethan and Alexis teased her?	How did the author use description to help the reader understand how Maya felt?
	(Standard 6: Point of view)
How did Maya solve her problem?	How did the author use the Tikis to demonstrate how Maya could solve her problem? (Standard 5: Text structure)

Source: Questions based on *Bullies: Playground Push-Around* by April Sopczak, 2013, published by Neon Tiki Tribe.

ask questions related to their own understanding and related to the writer's craft. The following questions are examples:

- What is being compared here?
- How did the author choose words to help us understand how the character is feeling?
- Why did the author use non-standard English in this part?

Step-by-Step

The steps in implementing close reading are the following:

- *Demonstrate close reading when you read aloud*—To demonstrate the type of thinking needed when reading closely, stop and discuss vocabulary, word choices, and plot escalation when you read aloud. If you are reading a story that uses similes, for example, discuss the simile, its meaning, and how it helps you understand the story. Follow up the oral reading with a short lesson on the structure of similes and have students write some of their own.
- *Observe and document students' individual reading levels*—In order to make close reading most effective, students should be reading material at their optimum instructional reading level. Careful monitoring of student reading levels and matching texts to those levels will enable students to acquire effectively the comprehension strategies taught.
- *Choose short texts with enough complexity to allow students to practice comprehension strategies*—Even if students are capable of reading longer texts, using short texts to teach close reading is recommended. Do not abandon longer texts. Instead, use shorter texts to support students in achieving the level of interaction with a text that is needed to thoroughly understand its meaning. The Common Core State Standards recommend a wide range of texts for teaching close reading. Appendix B of the Common Core lists numerous picture books for younger readers and English language learners. When students are learning a process, such as how to search for a recurring theme, reading short texts allows them to make more passes through the entire sequence of a text. Most literature and informational texts at the middle and high school levels can be used, as long as they are relatively short. Figure 11.2 includes suggestions for the types of texts appropriate for close reading instruction at the elementary level.

FIGURE 11.2 Appropriate Texts for Elementary-Level Close Reading Instruction

Traditional literature:
- Folktales
- Legends
- Myths
- Fables
- Short stories
- Poetry
- Scenes from plays

Informational texts:
- Short articles
- Biographies
- Personal narratives

Primary source materials:
- Martin Luther King Jr.'s *I Have a Dream* speech
- Preamble to the U.S. Constitution
- Sayings from *Poor Richard's Almanac*

FIGURE 11.3 Sample Questions That Support the Common Core State Standards

Standard	Sample Questions
Conventions of language	How would omitting the comma in this sentence change its meaning?
Word meaning	What does the word *counted* mean in this sentence? How does it convey the character's feeling?
Word relationships and nuances	How would changing *wanted* to *desired* change the meaning of this sentence? Why do you think the author chose to use *wanted*?
Domain-specific word meaning	What does the word *bed* mean in this science text? How does the word relate to the bed you sleep in at night?
Identifying central ideas or themes	What phrase is repeated throughout this essay? Why did the author use it repeatedly?
Compare and contrast texts	What do this poem and short story have in common besides the title?

   • ***Prepare questions that engage students in reexamining texts and that support their ability to meet the Common Core standards***—Familiarity with the Common Core standards for the grade level and content area you are teaching will help you prepare questions that enable students to use strategies that strengthen their abilities to meet those standards. Use direct teaching methods to help students understand the importance of the skills being taught for thorough understanding of the texts they read and for exemplary writing. Prepare questions that provide them with experience in reading and rereading texts to identify salient points and examine word choice, sentence structure, and plot building. See Figure 11.3 for examples of Common Core standards and sample questions.

FIGURE 11.4 Suggestions for Observing and Documenting Student Growth in Close Reading

Observe	Document
As you read aloud and demonstrate close reading strategies, ask students to give additional examples.	Use Post-it notes or 3-by-5 cards to write short anecdotal records of student participation and performance.
During the study of short passages, ask students to respond to questions that require them to analyze, reread, or paraphrase.	Prepare a checklist for the questions you create. List student names under the questions and use symbols next to the names to indicate students' levels of response.
As students begin to practice close reading independently, ask them to practice the use of self-questioning and document their success.	Ask students to keep a journal of the questions they ask themselves and their responses. Collect their journals periodically and evaluate student responses to plan reteaching.

- *Document students' strengths and needs for reteaching*—Throughout the process of modeling, reading, and questioning, it is vital that teachers observe and document students' levels of understanding and their abilities to use the strategies being taught. Devise a system that works well for you, and document students' performance over time. Figure 11.4 offers suggestions for observing and documenting student growth.
- *Teach students how to ask important questions about the texts they read*—As you demonstrate questioning for comprehension, involve the students by posting the types of questions you use and the Common Core standards they support. Ask students to keep a journal as they read independently, and practice close reading. Recognize students who embrace the concept, and devise questions to reach deep meaning by creating a classroom chart or class blog to highlight strong questions and what the students learned about the text from their questions. Take time to discuss student questions and how they support vital understandings. Ask students also to use self-questioning when they write to help them become more thoughtful in terms of word choice and sentence construction.

Enhanced eText
Video Example 11.2

- *Incorporate rereading for gradually uncovering deeper meaning*—Support students in learning to use close reading to deepen gradually their understanding of texts. You might change the focus of the questioning gradually, beginning with noticing and recounting details and later advancing to examining the author's craft. See Figure 11.5 for the sequence of text analysis and sample questions. This gradual process requires rereading the same passage.
- *Relate texts to the students' past experiences*—Discuss how the action in a text mirrors or differs from students' experiences. Draw attention to things they have done or other books they have read that help them to understand concepts in the text. As you follow examples of **ETR (experience text relationships)** in this video, ask yourself:

How does this strategy support understanding the text?
- Why would ETR be especially valuable to an English learner?
- *Focus on observing and analyzing*—Continue to observe, document, and analyze student responses throughout the teaching, practicing, and reteaching of close reading strategies.
- *Provide experience using close reading in a wide variety of texts*—For students to benefit from close reading instruction and make it a habit, they need opportunities to use it on a daily basis. Demonstrate the level of understanding students can achieve of their textbooks by using

FIGURE 11.5 Questioning Sequence for Deepening Comprehension

Noting and recounting details	Who is speaking in this passage? What seems to be important here? Why?
Noting the author's choice of words	What other word could be substituted here without changing the meaning?
	If I substitute _____ for this word, how does the meaning change?
Imagery including comparisons, similes, metaphors, personification, figurative language, and symbols	What symbols did the author choose to use? What other metaphor could be substituted here?
Tone and voice	Is the voice formal or informal? How does this passage help you to understand the character?
Sentence structure	Based on the order of words in this sentence, which word do you think is most important?
	Why did the author use a sentence fragment here?

close reading. Engage the students in close reading for the first few paragraphs in a text assignment before asking them to read independently. Encourage students to post good close reading questions as they use them. Recognize insightful questions by posting the "Questioner of the Day" or reviewing the questions posted and asking the author of the question to stand for a bow.

• ***Constantly reflect on your instruction and strive to improve your delivery, examples, and questioning***—Use the teacher self-evaluation rubric in Figure 11.6 to reflect on your close reading lessons to improve your implementation and to meet students' individual needs in your classroom.

Examples and Applications

Mrs. Kling's third graders include several struggling readers and about 10 second-language learners whose home language is Spanish. She is teaching lessons on figurative language so that her students can begin to engage with and comprehend texts that include these forms. Mrs. Kling decides to start with a read-aloud of *Bookstore Mouse* (Christian, 1995), which includes many examples of figurative language. As she prepares to read the first chapter of the book aloud, she discusses three words they will hear in this narrative. The words they explore are *sharp*, *tasty*, and *harsh*. She begins the lesson showing items that could be termed sharp. She shows the class a knife, a sharpened pencil, and a picture of a sword. She then asks the question, "How are these things alike?" As the students arrive at the word *sharp*, they work **collaboratively** to write a definition of the word and write it on the board. They decide that *sharp* means "having a point that could hurt you."

She then talks about another way that you can use the word by saying, "What would it mean if someone said you were sharp?" The students are confused at first, but then she explains that sharp can mean having a point that can hurt you or it can mean that you are smart. She also explains

FIGURE 11.6 Close-Reading Teacher Self-Evaluation Rubric

Beginning	Developing	Accomplished	Exemplary
Text chosen is appropriate for students but offers few opportunities for analysis.	Text chosen is appropriate for students and offers opportunities for analysis.	Text chosen is appropriate for students and offers several chances for analysis.	Text chosen is appropriate for students and offers multiple chances for analysis.
Close reading is demonstrated at least once a day.	Close reading is demonstrated several times a day in reading instruction.	Close reading is demonstrated several times a day in reading and writing instruction.	Close reading is demonstrated several times a day across content areas.
Close reading questions are sometimes prepared.	Close reading questions are prepared for every reading lesson.	Close reading questions are prepared for daily reading and writing lessons.	Close reading questions are prepared for daily lessons across content areas.
Student responses are analyzed frequently.	Student responses are analyzed and lessons adjusted in reading.	Student responses are analyzed and lessons in reading and writing are adjusted daily.	Students and self are analyzed and lessons across content areas are adjusted daily.

that it is sometimes used to say that you dress well. "If someone says you are a sharp dresser, it means that you look nice," she tells them. The group then works together to make a list of other words that can be used in place of *sharp*. Under the first definition they write *pointed, pointy*, and *like a dagger* (because they've recently learned similes). Under the definition "to have a smart mind" they write *smart, clever*, and *like a wise man*. This process is repeated for the other two words and then the first chapter of the book is read aloud.

As Mrs. Kling reads the chapter, she stops to explore the text by thinking aloud, asking herself questions such as "I wonder why the author chose these words?" She asks the students to contribute to the discussion about the words. Because the words are used figuratively in the story and the mouse actually looks for words that he can eat in each category, this requires some explanation and discussion. The term *pointed remark* requires more discussion and explanation. Some students are asked to demonstrate the making of a pointed remark. Mrs. Kling reads the chapter with expression and rereads parts after she has stopped for discussion so that students don't lose the flow of the story. As a follow-up to the reading, the class begins a word collection for each of the three words explored. The students are encouraged to add to the collections as they read and find additional words that could substitute for the original words.

* * * * *

Mr. Beale teaches 10th-grade language arts in a high school where many students speak languages other than English at home. He is introducing Shakespeare's *Romeo and Juliet* by reading a summary of the play and then reading the acts of the play that match the sections of the summary they read. Mr. Beale uses the summary of the play from *Shakespeare Stories* (Garfield, 1985). He reads aloud, stopping to explore vocabulary and situations the students may not understand. He is also demonstrating **think-aloud strategies** by asking himself questions about certain sentences, like "In old Verona where the men were bright as wasps and carried quick swords for their stings." He says, "That's an unusual sentence. I wonder why the author chose to use those words to tell us that the men carried swords. Why do you think he didn't just say, 'The men carried swords.'?" He encourages his students to talk about the different feeling you get when reading the more figurative sentence and how it sets the stage for a play in which the language is unlike everyday speech. After Mr. Beale reads and discusses the summary of the first scene, he reads the actual scene from the play, and the process of engaging with the text is repeated. He has the students create a comparison chart showing what they learned in the summary and the difference in the language used in the play. They go beyond discussing the words and phrases to exploring the feelings conveyed by the choice of words, the way the characters are created through having them speak, and the way the plot is constructed. They explore the concept of **foreshadowing** and how to recognize it. In this process the actual scene in the play is read several times as the students look for words that need explanation, words that could be changed without changing the meaning of the scene, and examples of character development and plot points.

> **Enhanced eText**
> Video Example 11.3
> www.youtube.com/watch?v=WgQYvj2U4Kw

> **Enhanced eText**
> Video Example 11.4
> www.youtube.com/watch?v=XFRClI2q18Y

Observe a first-grade teacher conducting a close reading lesson of fictional material in this video (see Video Example 11.3) and note the engaging strategies he uses with his students. Close reading offers strong support for understanding both fiction and nonfiction text.

Watch as the 10th-grade teacher in this video (see Video Example 11.4) guides her students through a reading of a more difficult nonfiction text that requires a deeper investigation of text-related issues. What do you think she means by the purpose of close reading and annotating the text?

Conclusion

With the advent of the Common Core State Standards and the assessments arising from them, teachers need support in helping students meet the higher expectations of these new standards. This support is especially important for students just learning English. Teachers must teach vocabulary all day and in every content area.

Most teachers know that teaching students to read closely is important. A series of gradual instructional approaches that helps students engage with complex text, close reading begins with teacher modeling and questioning, regardless of the content area. If students are not yet reading, teachers should read aloud, stopping to ask questions that demonstrate their thought processes. When beginning close reading instruction at any level, the teacher models through oral reading and questioning. Close reading is especially appropriate in content instruction because content textbooks present a major challenge for many students. This strategy cannot be taught or learned quickly. It requires ongoing instruction that gradually becomes more challenging, but close reading can be implemented at all grade levels, and individual practice can be accomplished with various forms of technology.

Examples of Approximation Behaviors Related to the TESOL Standards

PreK–3 students will:

- orally describe personal experiences related to a text.

- use words from books read in oral and/or written communications.

- use a balance of strategies to explore the meanings of unknown words.

4–8 students will:

- explore alternative ways of saying things by analyzing authors' word choices.
- make connections between stories and personal experiences.
- use self-questioning to make sense of text.

- monitor self-reading to evaluate personal comprehension.

9–12 students will:

- periodically stop to self-evaluate for metacognition while reading.
- explore the author's use of **figurative language**, vocabulary, and logic.
- ask questions about the author's background and knowledge base.

References

Boyles, N. (2012/13). Closing in on Close Reading. *Common Core: Now What?* 70(4), 36–41.

Christian, P. (1995). *The Bookstore Mouse.* New York, NY: Harcourt Brace.

Coleman, D. & Pimentel, S. (2012) *Revised publishers' criteria for the Common Core Standards in English Language Arts and Literacy. Grades 3-12.* Retrieved from Student Achievement Partners at www.achievethecore.org/stealthesetools

Fang, Z. (2016). *Teaching Close Reading in Complex Texts Across Content Areas.* Research in the Teaching of Reading, *51*(1).

Partnership for Assessment of Readiness for College and Careers. (2011). *PARC model content frameworks: English language arts/literacy grades 3–11.* Retrieved from www.parcconline.org on 10/12/2014.

12

Repeated Reading
Using Script Writing and Reader's Theater

Repeated reading of familiar text (Tompkins, 2006) is one of the most effective ways to support students as they develop fluency and comprehension and correct pronunciation (Cunningham & Allington, 2003). In the traditional approach to repeated reading, students are asked to read for a given amount of time, usually about a minute, and their fluency is measured by how far they can read in that given time. They are asked to reread the same passage periodically to document their growing fluency.

Enhanced eText
Video Example 12.1
https://youtu.be/NKEnroeclEw

Writing a script from a book that the students have read provides an opportunity for repeated reading and writing based on the story read. The students write a readers theatre script based on a book they have read. In the process of writing the script they read and reread portions of the book which provides opportunities for increased understanding as well as interpretive reading.

To view an example of a reader's theater script written from a children's book, reread for fluency, and performed for the class, see Video Example 12.2.

Can you see how repeated readings, writing scripts, and performing them supports understanding and fluency?

Enhanced eText
Video Example 12.2
https://www.youtube.com/watch?v=Bq0Ohvo_b1U

In Jordan and Herrell (2000) and Herrell and Jordan (2006), we found that writing and rereading reader's theater scripts was especially powerful in supporting reading fluency in English language learners. The power of rereading familiar text has been confirmed by other researchers in the field as well (Carrick, 2006, 2009; Young & Rasinski, 2009).

Step-by-Step

The steps in using repeated reading, script writing, and reader's theater are the following:

• *Select a book*—Choose a book that will be interesting to both you and the students. Make sure you match the book to the students' English development levels and their ages. Books containing lots of dialogue are best for the beginning script writing activity but later, as students further develop writing and language skills, they will enjoy creating the dialogue for characters who do not speak in the original book.

• *Read the book aloud*—Use read-aloud plus (Chapter 10) to engage the students in discussion and interaction as you read the book. Explore the vocabulary as part of the discussion of the book.

FIGURE 12.1 Script Formats

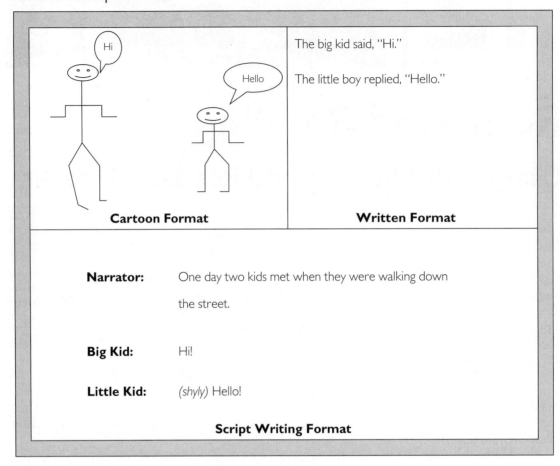

• *Demonstrate the format for writing a script*—Start by showing how dialogue is written in different literary formats. Draw a simple cartoon with speech balloons to show who is talking. Write a simple sentence including dialogue to show how to indicate who is talking and then put their words in quotes to show exactly what they are saying. Then model the writing of a script with the character's name at the left margin and the words to be spoken indented to the right. See Figure 12.1 for an example of this step.

• *Write the script using shared writing*—Demonstrate how to begin the story by using a narrator or storyteller to set the scene and describe action that does not involve dialogue. Use the author's words when they are appropriate but give students the freedom to create their own dialogue as long as it supports the story line. Use an overhead transparency, large chart, or interactive whiteboard to take the students' dictation. Stop and reread the script every time new dialogue is added. (Refer to Chapter 13 to review shared writing.)

• *Use a computer to create the script*—After each day of working on the script, type the script as far as you've gotten. Begin the next day's writing session by assigning roles to each of the students and reading aloud that part of the script that they have completed. Encourage students to add direction about how the character's lines should be read. Figure 12.2 shows how these stage directions should be added. Also encourage students to edit dialogue if they think of a better way to say things.

• *Highlight the script when it is completed*—After the script is completed, prepare enough copies so that each reader has a copy. Put the scripts into individual folders and label each folder with the character's name, **highlighting** that character's dialogue in the script.

• *Practice reading the script aloud*—Encourage students to practice reading the script with expression and fluency before they "perform" it for the class or for other classes.

FIGURE 12.2 Script with Stage Directions

Narrator:	(*excitedly*) Two kids met each other walking down the street.
Big Kid:	(*calmly*) Hi!
Little Kid:	(*shyly*) Hello.

- ***Perform the script***—Give the students an opportunity to perform the reader's theater script for their class or other classes. This involves reading the script with expression and fluency but not memorizing lines. English learners are often reluctant to perform for their class but are eager to perform for younger students.
- ***Assess the students' comprehension, reading fluency, and expression as they read, and plan additional practice for students who need it***—Observe students carefully during the process of script writing and reader's theater practice and performance to document their involvement and plan future instruction. Figure 12.3 shows a sample observation checklist for this strategy.

Applications and Examples

Finding ways for English learners to participate successfully in her fifth-grade classroom is important to Mrs. Duncan. She has a group of students at the **speech emergence level** of English development, and they are reluctant to participate in class. Mrs. Duncan also wants to introduce her students to skills they'll need to meet the Common Core standards for grade 5. She wants her students to be able to "quote accurately from a text when explaining what the text says explicitly and

FIGURE 12.3 Checklist for Documenting Behaviors in Script Writing and Reader's Theater

Student Names												
Contributes dialogue using words from the book												
Contributes original dialogue												
Contributes stage directions that show comprehension of character												
Reads with expression												
Reads confidently												
Projects voice to be heard												

when drawing inferences from the text" (CCSS.ELA-LITERACY.RL. 5.1); "determine the meaning of words and phrases as they are used in a text, including figurative language such as metaphors and similes" (CCSS.ELA-LITERACY. RL.5.4); and "explain how a narrator's or speaker's point of view influences how events are described" (CCSS.ELA-LITERACY.RL.5.6).

Mrs. Duncan chooses to read *Stellaluna* (Cannon, 1997) to her class as a literary follow-up to their study of bats. She has noticed several English learners looking at the book during their free time. She feels confident that using this book will support their fluency development, build their confidence, and address some of the Common Core standards at the same time.

Mrs. Duncan gathers the group of five English learners to work together to write a script of the story while their classmates work on individual projects about bats. They begin by rereading the book, page by page. Mrs. Duncan takes their dictation as they recreate the story, adding dialogue for the owl and other characters who don't speak in the book.

It takes about a week of short sessions for the students to complete the script. During this time, Mrs. Duncan types the script each evening, and the group practices reading it each day. They start at the beginning of the script each day and gradually add directions to tell the reader how to read the characters' words based on their analysis of the attitude of the character. They add more of the story each day.

During the second week, they practice reading the script and decide that they want to perform it for the kindergarten class where several of them have younger siblings. On the day of the kindergarten performance, the principal comes to watch and is delighted to hear several of the students in the group speak aloud for the first time. The group is so excited about their performance that they want to perform it again, this time for a first-grade class.

Four performances later, the group decides they want to perform the reader's theater script for their own class. Their confidence and fluency are markedly improved. After the performance, the other students in their class are very impressed. They make comments like, "Wow, you guys are great readers!"

* * * * *

Mrs. Arena's eighth-grade class is studying the U.S. Constitution. They participate in an in-depth study in which they complete a KWL chart (see Chapter 41) and read a number of books about the Constitution written at a wide variety of reading levels. In engaging the students in this series of activities, Mrs. Arena addresses several of the Common Core Standards in history/social sciences and literacy:

- "Identify key steps in a text's description of a process related to history/social sciences." (CCSS.ELA-LITERACY.RH.6–8.3)
- "Determine the meaning of words and phrases as they are used in a text, including vocabulary specific to domains related to history/social sciences." (CCSS.ELA-LITERACY. RH.6–8.4)
- "Cite the textual evidence that most strongly supports an analysis of what the text says explicitly as well as inferences drawn from the text." (CCSS.ELA-LITERACY.RI.8.1)

While reading *A History of US: From Colonies to Country* (Hakim, 1993) and *Shh! We're Writing the Constitution* (Fritz, 1987), students are especially impressed with the personal information they learn about the members of the Constitutional Convention. The class wants to write a reader's theater script that includes the information they have learned about the founding fathers to help others learn more about them too. They use Fritz's book as the basis of their script but add information from computer sources as well. When they perform their reader's theater for the entire eighth grade, the response is very enthusiastic.

Several eighth-grade social sciences teachers ask if they may borrow the scripts so their students can reread them. The reader's theater is a great hit, and, best of all, Mrs. Duncan's students achieve the highest scores they've ever had on an end-of-unit test. These students really understand the process the founders used to create the Constitution and the concerns they discussed during the process.

Conclusion

As the teachers in these classroom examples demonstrate, students benefit from exploring material and writing scripts. The repeated readings of familiar texts and the conversion of texts into scripts help English learners to become more confident and fluent in their English language production.

To present the material fluently, students must understand and internalize the meanings of the words they are speaking. To write a script, students must closely examine the texts on which they base the script. Working in groups provides opportunities for discussion and clarification of word meanings, the best way to express ideas, and the logical sequence in which to present events. All of these experiences work to increase reading comprehension and language acquisition.

Students from diverse backgrounds and age levels can experience repeated readings of text, explore characterization and expression, discover and illuminate new vocabulary, and participate in event sequencing through reader's theater presentations and script writing. These activities lead to and strengthen reading, oral fluency, and comprehension.

Rereading to clarify meaning can be used at every level even when you are not going to expand into script writing. Gibbons (2015) suggests encouraging students to use rereading whenever they encounter an unknown word. By reading to the end of the sentence then going back to reread the sentence, sometimes the context of the sentence supports understanding of the unknown word. Gibbons also recommends rereading the sentence before and after the one containing the unknown word (or phrase), looking for the word used elsewhere, and looking for familiar parts of the word such as prefixes and suffixes to help clarify meaning.

Examples of Approximation Behaviors Related to the TESOL Standards

PreK–3 students will:

- participate in retelling stories they have read.
- write dialogue based on stories they have read.

4–8 students will:

- rewrite narratives to include dialogue.
- expand and revise narratives to make stories more complex.

9–12 students will:

- use academic language to write scripts that convey complex concepts.
- relate academic knowledge in more than one discipline into scripts to demonstrate their connections.

References

Cannon, J. (1997). *Stellaluna*. New York, NY: Harcourt Brace.

Carrick, L. (2006). Reader's theater across the curriculum. In T. Rasinski, C. Brachowicz, and B. Lems (Eds.) *Fluency instruction: Research based on best practices* (pp. 209–250). New York, NY: Guilford Press.

Carrick, L. (2009) *The effects of reader's theater on fluency and comprehension: A study on fifth-grade students in a regular classroom*. Saarbruchen, Germany: VDM.

Cunningham, P., & Allington, R. (2010). *Classrooms that work: They can all read and write* (5th ed.). Boston, MA: Pearson Education.

Fritz, J. (1987). *Shh! We're writing the Constitution*. New York, NY: G. P. Putnam & Sons.

Gibbons, P. (2015). *Scaffolding Language, Scaffolding Learning; Teaching English Language Learners in the Mainstream Classroom.* Portsmouth, NH: Heinemann.

Hakim, J. (1993). *A history of US: From colonies to country* (Vol. 3). New York, NY: Oxford University Press.

Herrell, A., & Jordan, M. (2006). *50 strategies for improving vocabulary, comprehension, and fluency: An active learning approach.* Upper Saddle River, NJ: Pearson.

Jordan, M., & Herrell, A. (2000). Readers Theatre: A creative tool for strengthening skills of emergent readers. *Kindergarten education: Theory, research, and practice: A journal of the California kindergarten association.* 5(1) 11–31.

Tompkins, G. (2006). *Literacy for the 21st century: Teaching reading and writing in pre-kindergarten through grade 4* (2nd ed.). Upper Saddle River, NJ: Pearson.

Young, C. and Rasinski, T. (2009). Implementing reader's theater in an approach to classroom fluency instruction. *The Reading Teacher, 63*(1) 4–13.

13

Scaffolding English Writing
Matching Instruction to Language Development

One of the most challenging tasks for English language learners is acquiring English writing skills. In order to support students in this daunting endeavor, teachers must provide **scaffolding**, modeling, monitoring, and encouragement. Fortunately, recent innovative approaches now enable teachers to provide exactly the amount of support needed to move beginning English writers forward (Button, Johnson, & Furgerson, 1996; Tompkins & Collom, 2003). Providing scaffolding in writing instruction is vital because support in one language process (reading, writing, and speaking or listening) is highly supportive of all aspects of language learning (Hinkel, 2006). It is also important that English learners have opportunities to practice writing without having to worry about developing a final product for a grade (Evans, 2008).

As with any effective teaching approach, it is important to have an accurate understanding of what students already know about writing in English. This information is easily obtained through an **informal writing sample**. Simply ask students to draw a picture and write about that picture or read a brief story and ask them to respond to the story. For the earliest beginning English learners, you will have to demonstrate how to do this. The teacher can then select the stage of writing support appropriate for each student. This doesn't always require individual instruction; English learners can be grouped for this process because the teacher can adapt each student's expected involvement according to their language level and understanding of English writing. The examples of various approaches in this chapter are scaffolded in much the same manner as they would be in the classroom.

The Beginning Sequence

Modeled writing provides the beginning English student with a demonstration that shows how English sounds are represented by symbols. Teachers simply say the words while slowly writing them on a chalkboard, whiteboard, or a piece of paper. The writing should be simple at first. Knowing how much English students thoroughly comprehend is important to this process because you will want to write words that learners readily understand. You might start with statements like "Today is Monday. It is raining." If you are working individually with a student, you might write, "My name is Dr. Herrell."

Step-by-Step

The steps in modeled writing are the following:

- *Choose what to write*—Choose a simple sentence and write the words slowly, sounding out each word as you write it to demonstrate the sound-to-symbol correspondence.
- *Read and point to the words*—Read the sentence you have written, pointing to each word as you read it. Read the sentence slowly but fluently.
- *Reread the sentence with students*—Ask students to reread the sentence with you, pointing to each word as you read it.

Once you have modeled writing a few times, students will be ready to begin a daily writing journal (Díaz-Rico, 2018). Demonstrate to students how they can begin by drawing a picture and then writing about the picture. Even if a child is only capable of labeling parts of the picture, you want to model writing sentences just as you would talk to the child. Be supportive of children's efforts, whether they are letters indicating the initial sounds of the parts of the picture, complete sentences, or as much as the student is able to write in the beginning.

Step-by-Step

The steps in supporting students in beginning writing journals using modeled writing are the following:

- *Provide each student with a writing journal*—A **writing journal** can be a as simple as a few pages of unlined paper stapled together or a bound tablet.
- *Demonstrate the process*—Demonstrate how students can begin their journal by drawing a picture and then writing about the picture. Even if they are only capable of labeling parts of the picture, you want to model writing sentences just as you would talk to students.
- *Have students draw and write*—Have students draw a picture and then write about the picture. They can simply label parts of the picture or write sentences, depending on their ability.
- *Model writing based on a student's picture and writing*—Using a fairly large (3-by-5-inch, for example) sticky note, the teacher might write, "I see your cat has whiskers, a tail, and four paws." The teacher writes and speaks the sentence as the student observes. The teacher then places the sticky note on the student's journal page, providing both a writing model and a resource for the next day's journal entry.
- *Repeat the process daily*—This process needs to be repeated on a daily basis. Students draw and label a picture or write words, phrases, or a sentence, and the teacher responds with modeled writing.

This process is quite similar to what teachers do for a student in the early production stage of English speaking. They listen to what the student has to say and respond to the message with an English sentence that scaffolds the child's English production toward the next level of functioning. With modeled writing, the teacher responds to the student's attempts at English writing, building on what the student has written, and uses notes to provide a model of English writing and a resource for the student to use in future writing. Students can peel the teacher's note off the page and use both the structure and the spelling to construct a response on the next day's journal entry. See Figure 13.1 for an example of modeled writing.

Once students are beginning to respond in a daily writing journal, it is time to begin creating short written pieces using the **language experience approach (LEA)**. Language experience stories involve the teacher modeling the writing process, but in this format, students provide some input into what the teacher writes.

FIGURE 13.1 Example of Modeled Writing

The lesson looks something like this:

Teacher: Carlos, I notice that you and Maria got wet on the way to school this morning. Tell me what happened.

Carlos: It rain.

Teacher: Oh, it was raining. Was it raining when you started to school?

Maria: It rain when we walk.

Teacher: Let's write about what happened. Was it raining when you left home?

Maria: It no rain when we walk first.

Teacher: Can I write, "It wasn't raining when we started walking to school?"

Maria: Yes, no rain.

Teacher: (Writes, speaking the words as she writes them.)

It wasn't raining when we started walking to school.

Now, let's read this together.

The teacher and the students read the sentence together as the teacher points to the words.

Teacher:	What happened then?
Carlos:	Rain come hard.
Teacher:	Yes, it started to rain. Can we write, "Then it started to rain?"
	Let's say that together, "Then it started to rain." (Class repeats the sentence with her.) Carlos also said that it rained very hard, so we can write that also. (She writes the two sentences as she says them.)
	Let's read together. (Teacher points to the words as the class reads with her.)
	It wasn't raining when we started walking to school.
	Then it started to rain. It rained very hard.
Teacher:	What did you do?
Maria:	We run.
Teacher:	Why did you run?
Maria:	We no get wet.
Teacher:	Can we write, "We ran so we wouldn't get wet?"
Maria:	Yes, we no get wet.
Teacher:	We ran so we wouldn't get wet. (Writing the words slowly as she says them.)
	Let's read this sentence together. (They read the sentence as the teacher points to the words.)
Teacher:	Now let's read our whole story.
	It wasn't raining when we started walking to school.
	Then it started to rain. It rained very hard.
	We ran so we wouldn't get wet.
Teacher:	Carlos, would you and Maria like to draw a picture on our story?
Carlos:	Use markers?
Teacher:	Yes, you may use the markers.

Source: By courtesy of the authors.

The teacher displays the story on a bulletin board and she rereads it with Maria and Carlos several times during the day, always pointing to the words as they read them together. After school, the teacher types the story with one sentence per page and makes a little book for Maria and Carlos to illustrate and use for reading practice.

You will notice that the teacher writes sentences to express the ideas the students provide, modeling the correct English sentence structure while keeping the students' ideas intact. The teacher and students reread each sentence as it is written, giving the students oral practice in producing complete, grammatically correct English sentences. Because the teacher and students reread the sentences several times, the students are able to read and understand the sentences afterward.

Step-by-Step

The steps in conducting a language experience writing lesson are the following:

• *Select a topic*—Select a topic based on the students' experiences. If needed, provide an experience such as an art or science lesson to make sure the students have an experience to write about.

• *Ask the students to talk*—Ask students to tell you about the experience.

- *Model standard English*—If the students' responses are not stated in **standard English**, ask them if it's okay to restate the sentence, making sure that each student's idea is kept intact. (Note: This is different from the traditional approach to language experience lessons where students' words are written exactly the way they are stated. The purpose of restating their words in standard English is to support English language acquisition and development.)

- *Write the sentence*—Write the sentence, reading the words as you write them.

- *Have the students read with you*—Encourage the students to read the sentence with you, pointing to each word as you read it.

- *Have the students illustrate their stories*—Encourage the students to illustrate the story on the story chart.

- *Reread the story repeatedly*—Reread the story with the students several times during the day.

- *Provide follow-up activities (optional)*—Provide individual booklets of the story for the students to practice reading and illustrating the meaning of the words.

As students gain practice with language experience stories, the teacher begins to ask questions about when to use capital letters, what type of punctuation to use, and what sounds they hear in the words the teacher is writing (Mermelstein, 2006). This approach is called **shared writing**, which is similar to the language experience approach. The only difference is that the students begin to share in the decision-making process, although the teacher is still doing all of the writing. Once the students seem to understand the basic sound–symbol relationships, that is, which letters to use to represent sounds in words, it is time to progress to interactive writing.

Interactive writing (Button et al., 1996; Tompkins & Collom, 2003) is done in much the same way as shared writing, except the student is ready to do some of the actual writing. Building on an experience such as a story that has been read, an art project, or a science experiment, the teacher asks the students to tell about what they have done. The teacher leads the students through a sequence of steps to support their ability to write words and phrases as part of the interactive story. In this video, a kindergarten teacher demonstrates the use of interactive writing to support the students' understanding of sentence construction and sound–symbol representation. As you watch, ask yourself the following questions:

Enhanced eText
Video Example 13.1

What resources are available to the student who comes to the chart to write?

How does the teacher use scaffolding to support the student's use of writing conventions?

Step-by-Step

The steps in conducting an interactive writing lesson are the following:

- *Choose a topic*—Choose a topic based on the students' experiences. If needed, provide an experience as you did in language experience writing and shared writing.

- *Ask the students to talk*—Ask the students to talk about the experience and choose one of their sentences to write.

- *Restate the sentence to be written*—Restate the selected sentence and orally count the number of words in the sentence. Have the students repeat the sentence with you.

- *Say the word to be written*—Say the first word in the sentence and ask if anyone knows how the word begins. If you have a volunteer, ask the student to come to the chart or board and write the word. Before the student begins to write, ask the student to tell you the letter that begins the word. For the first word in the sentence, also ask, "Will you write a capital letter or a lowercase letter?"

- *Invite a student to write on the chart*—Encourage the student to write the word, supporting the choices of upper- and lowercase letters. If students make errors, help them make corrections. (You can use 1-inch correction tape to cover errors on the chart paper.)

- *Reread the word and state the rest of the sentence*—Reread the word, and then state the rest of the sentence. Repeat the process, word by word, until the sentence is complete.
- *Reread and repeat*—Reread the sentence with the group and ask for another sentence.
- *Complete the story*—Repeat the process until the students' ideas are represented.

Interactive writing provides **direct instruction** in writing English sentences related to a topic. It provides students with support as they discover the rules of punctuation, capitalization, and sentence structure. Multiple rereadings of sentences provide practice in oral English reading. Interactive writing can easily be done on a daily basis in a variety of situations. It can be used to summarize a story that has been read aloud, to summarize the steps in a class project, to write a thank-you note to a parent volunteer, or for almost any purpose, providing the students with a structured introduction to English writing. After students have experienced interactive writing and are comfortable with expressing themselves in writing, they are ready to move on to a writing workshop. The teacher may start writing instruction with modeled, shared, or interactive writing, depending on the students' understanding of English phonics and their English language development level. Figure 13.2 will help you match writing instruction to students' English language development level.

Adjusting the Task According to the Student's Levels and Needs

Each of the writing development approaches can be adapted to the levels and needs of individual students. Modeled writing can begin with teachers writing simple sentences as they slowly say the words they are writing. **Preproduction students** can be asked to point to one of the words. **Early production students** can be asked questions that give them a choice such as, "Is this word *red* or *green*?" Or, early production students can be asked questions that require a one- or two-word response. Additionally, early production students may begin writing journals in which they

FIGURE 13.2 Matching Writing Instruction to Students' English Language Development Level

Writing Format	What the Student Must Be Able to Do	Appropriate Language Development Level
Modeled Writing	Observe, point	Preproduction Early Production
Language Experience	Speak words and phrases related to an experience	Early Production Speech Emergence
Shared Writing	Speak words and phrases related to an experience Identify beginning sounds of words and verbally identify the letter to represent the sound	Early Production Speech Emergence
Interactive Writing	Speak words and phrases related to an experience Identify beginning sounds of words and write the letter to represent the sound Gradually be able to write more of the words with teacher support until they are writing whole words and phrases	Speech Emergence Intermediate Fluency

draw pictures and write words, phrases, or sentences. This gives the teacher an opportunity to use modeled writing with Post-it notes in response to the student's writing, as previously described.

With interactive writing, it is easy to adjust the task to the levels of individual students. As you write the story, you might ask one student to write an entire word, while another may come forward to write just the beginning sound with you writing the rest of the word. (That's why it's called interactive writing.) You may ask another student simply to add the period at the end of the sentence. In order to use the writing formats in this way, you must be acutely aware of the **language development levels** of your students and their knowledge of English phonics. By placing an **alphabet strip** close to the writing chart, you can provide another resource for students to use in choosing the letters to write and in forming them correctly. Some teachers use a small whiteboard to demonstrate the formation of letters to students. Using **correction tape** also provides teachers with a way to support students in correcting their own errors.

Basic Writer's Workshop

Writer's workshop (Graves, 1983) is an approach to teaching writing that supports students through the stages of creating a written product. The steps in the writing process (prewriting, drafting, conferring, revising, editing, and publishing) are each taught and demonstrated. The support each student needs to be successful is provided through **minilessons** and guided practice. This approach is especially powerful for English learners because they learn the steps, are given time to practice each step with feedback and guidance from the teacher, and they revise their own writing in sequential lessons based on their own levels of understanding (Herrell & Jordan, 2007).

Enhanced eText
Video Example 13.2

The teacher begins instruction in writer's workshop by demonstrating ways to formulate ideas. The teacher might demonstrate the drawing and labeling of a picture as one prewriting strategy. After drawing and labeling the picture with help from students, the teacher revisits the labeled picture to add descriptive words for each part of the picture. The teacher then supports the students in brainstorming other descriptive words that they can use to add interest to their pictures. Together the students and teacher create a chart of descriptive words they might use. The students are then given time to draw and label their own pictures. In this video, first-grade students work through the writing workshop with the help and support of their teacher. As you watch, consider the following questions:

- How does the teacher provide support for her English learners through the writing workshop process?
- How does the teacher make her expectations clear? How does she support students in meeting those expectations?

The purpose of this stage is to generate ideas and provide support in the form of English vocabulary the students can use in writing their stories. Older students might be taught ways to create webs for their stories or simply how to develop a list of writing topics with ideas and vocabulary. Journals can also be used as a prewriting strategy. Video Example 13.3 illustrates several ways in which journals can be used to encourage students' English writing development. As you watch, ask yourself the following questions:

Enhanced eText
Video Example 13.3

- How does journal writing help English learners develop confidence in their abilities to communicate in English?
- What role does daily journal writing play in English learners' progress in understanding English communication?

Once students have done their prewriting activity, the teacher uses their own labeled drawings to demonstrate how to use this piece of work to draft a story. The teacher involves the students in generating sentences related to their drawings and using the descriptive words they have added to the labels on the picture. Once the teacher has demonstrated how to draft stories, students talk about their own pictures and labels, and how they plan to start their stories. Talking about the story is an important step for English learners. Not only do they get to express their ideas verbally in English, but they also get to hear the ideas of their classmates. This often gives them some additional approaches to beginning their stories. Once again, the students are sent back to their seats to write based on the demonstration and discussion they have just experienced. If there are students who need extra support, they can sit with the teacher for additional help and supervision.

In the early stages of teaching writer's workshop, drafting the story may be as far as the instruction goes. The students may then read their stories to the teacher and receive feedback on areas to be corrected or added. Once the students are comfortable with these first two stages—prewriting and drafting—the teacher provides demonstrations in **conferring** (talking about the draft, giving and receiving suggestions), revising based on the suggestions, editing for spelling and mechanics, and publishing the written piece. For each new step introduced, the teacher uses a personal sample to walk the students through the process, then gives students opportunities to talk about their own piece of writing and how they will proceed. The teacher supports students who need it, while the others complete each step. Figure 13.3 highlights the steps of the writing process and important associated supports for English learners at each step.

Providing opportunities for oral practice is vital when using writer's workshop with English learners. Giving writers a chance to speak a sentence before writing helps them to formulate sentences in English and provides the teacher with an opportunity to correct grammar errors before they are written. In the beginning, some students may need to dictate their sentences. The teacher may choose to provide this service but will want to encourage students to take over gradually more and more of the writing task. In the writing conference, students should read their own work to the group. This gives them yet another opportunity for oral English practice as well as a chance to hear how their writing flows. Finally, students read their finished piece aloud from the **author's chair**. While this is a major time for celebration, English learners still need support in practicing this task with the teacher's help and guidance.

Involving English learners in writer's workshops gives teachers a unique opportunity to identify the types of errors that students are making as they write in English. Often, these errors include **irregular verbs**, incorrect vocabulary usage, and the overuse of common words. Teachers can then plan minilessons that involve authentic, active use of the English structures to provide experiences that help students understand proper usage and remember new vocabulary. Irregular verbs are especially difficult for English learners, and active learning lessons provide focused practice.

Since working on the computer is motivating for many students (Díaz-Rico, 2018), teachers have begun individual and classroom blogs to encourage their students to write. For a useful guide to setting up classroom blogs, see Dudeney and Hockley (2007).

In order to scaffold writing and provide instruction in each student's zone of proximal development (Vygotsky, 1962), students must be observed while they participate in writing activities. Teacher observation and the use of anecdotal records and checklists are valuable in documenting student progress (Gibbons, 2015). As you interact with students in modeled, shared, and interactive writing, observe the sounds students are able to represent and the language structures they use. Make notes as to which students need instruction in various areas and plan further instruction based on student need. Figure 13.4 is a checklist that can be used to observe beginning writing instruction.

Applications and Examples

Susan McCloskey teaches *kindergarten* in a richly diverse school in Fresno, California. She uses modeled writing each day in her classroom as she writes the daily agenda on the chalkboard. She says the words as she writes them and then has the students read along with her as she points to each word after she writes each sentence. Her students begin daily journals (Gibbons, 2015) from the first day of kindergarten. Susan staples unlined paper together and makes a journal for each month. She keeps these monthly journals in the students' portfolios to document their progress in writing for parent conferences.

FIGURE 13.3 Steps in the Writing Process

Steps in the Writing Process	Ways to Provide Support for English Learners
Prewriting Students draw, list, graph ideas for the piece to be written, and create a plan.	1. Have the students draw and label a picture. 2. Work collaboratively to create a chart of vocabulary that they might use. 3. Provide L1 lists to correspond with the vocabulary list. 4. Have students talk about their ideas and take dictation to create their writing plan.
Drafting Students write a rough draft based on the prewriting plan.	1. Demonstrate how to take ideas from the writing plan and generate sentences from those ideas. 2. Have students first tell what they will write and then have them write it down. 3. Provide guided practice with students who need extra help. This can even involve taking dictation from reluctant writers and gradually having them take over the writing task (individual interactive writing).
Conferring Students read their draft to others (students and teacher) who give compliments and suggestions.	1. The student who wrote the piece always reads it. (It's a draft, sometimes a sloppy copy.) 2. Teacher and other students first tell what they liked about the piece, then ask clarifying questions, and give suggestions. 3. Authors make notes on the draft and make decisions about what to keep and what to change. Teacher can take notes and help students make decisions, if needed.
Revising Students make changes to their written piece based on the comments and suggestions from the conference.	1. Teacher discusses the suggestions and helps students understand the suggestions and decide which suggestions to implement and which to ignore. 2. Teacher demonstrates how to rewrite the piece including the suggestions. 3. Students may be given the opportunity to word process the piece and include the changes as the piece is typed.
Editing Spelling, punctuation, capitalization errors are corrected.	1. Teacher may work with students to identify errors, use the dictionary. 2. Students may work with a partner to proofread each other's work. 3. If a word processor is used, students may use spell check and grammar check.
Publishing Writing is put into final form and published (word processed or recopied neatly), and put into a cover or onto a bulletin board.	1. Teacher demonstrates the publishing formats available and students choose from among them. 2. Teacher or peers walk students through the publishing process.
Celebrating Students take turns sitting in special chair designated as the "author's chair" and reading their writing.	1. Teacher serves as audience for students as they practice reading the piece. 2. Teacher makes suggestions and helps students practice fluency.

FIGURE 13.4 Checklist for Observing Beginning Writing

Name	Initial Sounds Represented	Final Sounds	Vowels	Comments

Susan also gathers her students in small groups to write about their daily activities. She groups the students based on which are ready for interactive writing, which are ready for shared writing, and which are able only to observe and have writing modeled for them. Because she observes her students carefully, she knows which students are ready to suggest letters to be used to represent words (shared writing), which are able to come to the chart to write letters and words (interactive writing), and which need to observe and help reread what is written (modeled writing).

Susan finds that this daily focus on writing in multiple formats supports her students' oral language development, their understanding of phonics and sentence structure, and their reading development. Although many of her students enter kindergarten with limited experience in English, her class consistently scores above the district average in the spring writing sample. They also enter first grade ready to move forward in their reading program.

* * * * *

Jody Salazar teaches remedial reading in a diverse *middle school* in Madera, California. Jody finds that her seventh- and *eighth-grade students* consistently misuse irregular English verbs. Because Jody knows that her students enjoy active group activities, she plans a series of activities to provide guided practice in using these verbs correctly.

As Jody plans these lessons, she wants to provide oral language experiences that support their use of irregular verbs in their writing. She devises ways to engage the students actively, practices the oral use of irregular verbs, and then follows up with a writing activity using the verbs. After each activity, she notes which of the students are correctly using the irregular verbs in their writing and oral speech and documents this growth using a checklist. She also notes which students need additional guided practice with irregular verbs and which verbs need to be revisited. Figure 13.5 is Jody's planning chart.

Conclusion

English learners can succeed in learning to write in English when their teachers provide the support they need to comprehend the complexities of writing. A gradual, sequential use of writing formats, which considers the language development levels of the students and their understanding of English sounds and how they are represented, is vital in providing the needed scaffolding. As with everything we present to English learners, we, as teachers, must assume responsibility for knowing the language, reading, and writing levels of our students and providing the scaffolding and support each student requires to be successful in the task at hand. Most importantly, as teachers of English learners, we must remember: "If we teach them, they will learn."

FIGURE 13.5 Jody's Planning Chart for Irregular Verb Instruction

Materials	Verbs	Activity
• Soft ball • Bubble mixture and wands	To throw To catch To blow	Teacher throws ball to a student; says, "José caught the ball." José throws ball; says, "I threw the ball. Maria caught it." Repeat. Teacher blows bubbles; students catch them. Teacher says, "I blew bubbles." Students take turns blowing bubbles and catching them.
• Individual whiteboards • Markers	To draw To write	Students draw an animal and then label it. They then tell the others what they drew and what they wrote.
• Snack-sized candy bars • Plastic knives	To choose To cut To eat	Students choose a candy bar, cut it, and eat it. They then tell, and write about, what they did.
• Miniature marshmallows • Spaghetti • Gummy bears	To build To bring To break	Students build a house for their gummy bear family using marshmallows and spaghetti. They then talk about the process they used.
• White construction paper • Markers	To fly To hold To let To draw	Students follow directions to fold a paper airplane. They then fly the planes and keep track of which ones go the farthest. They draw pictures on their planes. They then talk and write about the process.
• Various articles of clothing	To choose To wear To buy To find	Clothing is laid out on a table. Students choose an article of clothing and put it on. They then talk about what they did and write instructions for shopping for clothing.
• Cards for simple card game	To deal To begin To win To lose To cut	Students play a simple card game and then work together to write sentences that describe the sequence of events.
• Writing		Students write about each activity using irregular verbs.

Examples of Approximation Behaviors Related to the TESOL Standards

PreK–3 students will:

- participate in writing activities at their language development levels.
- express ideas in writing.

4–8 students will:

- use writing to express their understanding of sentences and paragraphs in English.

- write paragraphs on specific topics.

9–12 students will:

- use academic language to write reports.

- demonstrate understanding of different genres of writing.

References

Button, K., Johnson, M., & Furgerson, P. (1996). Interactive writing in a primary classroom. *The Reading Teacher, 49*, 446–454.

Díaz-Rico, L. (2018). *The crosscultural, language, and academic development handbook: A complete K–12 reference guide* (6th ed.). Boston, MA: Pearson Education.

Dudeney, G., & Hockley, N. (2007). *How to . . . teach English with technology*. Harlow, England: Pearson Longman.

Evans, L. (2008). Literacy issues for English learners: Making connections. In J. Govoni (Ed.), *Perspectives on teaching K–12 English language learners* (2nd ed.). Upper Saddle River, NJ: Pearson Education.

Gibbons, P. (2015). *Scaffolding language, scaffolding learning. Teaching English language learners in the mainstream classroom* (2nd ed.). Portsmouth, NH: Heinemann.

Graves, D. (1983). *Writing: Teachers and children at work*. Portsmouth, NH: Heinemann.

Herrell, A., & Jordan, M. (2007). *50 strategies for teaching English language learners* (3rd ed.). Upper Saddle River, NJ: Merrill/Prentice Hall/Pearson.

Hinkel, E. (2006). Current perspectives on teaching the four skills. *TESOL Quarterly, 40*(1), 109–131.

Mermelstein, L. (2006). *Reading/writing connections in the K–2 classroom*. Boston, MA: Pearson.

Tompkins, G., & Collom, S. (2003). *Sharing the pen: Interactive writing with young children*. Upper Saddle River, NJ: Merrill/Prentice Hall/Pearson.

Vygotsky, L. (1962). *Thought and language*. Cambridge, MA: MIT Press.

14

Reporting Back
Verbal Practice in Curriculum Connections

Reporting back is a strategy that supports students in bridging the gap between spoken and written language (Díaz-Rico, 2018; Gibbons, 2015). Gibbons (2015) also calls this strategy teacher-guided reporting. This strategy can be used as a follow-up after any active-learning experience. The students describe their experience using vocabulary that is connected with the experience so that classmates have a clear understanding of the materials and sequence of actions that were used. If they are able, the students then write their reporting-back summary to be included in the class daily news or their daily learning log. Figure 14.1 suggests activities appropriate for reporting back.

Step-by-Step

The steps in using the reporting-back strategy are the following:

- *Prepare the students for action*—Prepare the students for an active-learning experience by giving directions for the activity and modeling what is expected. Follow up your demonstration by saying, "After you finish your activity, you will report back to the class describing what happened. For example, if you were reporting back to the class on the experience just demonstrated, you would say, "Tell me what I did first." As the students relate the process, write the steps on the whiteboard:

    'I opened the jar of red paint.

    Then I opened the jar of blue paint.

    I took an eyedropper and used it to draw up some of the red paint.

    I dropped two drops of red paint into the plastic cup.

    Next, I used the eyedropper to draw up some blue paint.

    I put two drops of blue paint into the plastic cup.

    I took a toothpick and swirled the two colors together in the cup.

    When they mixed together they turned into purple paint.

    I learned that red and blue paint mix together to make purple paint.'

    "After you finish your activity, you and your partner need to decide what to say when you report back to the class."

- *List and review the steps*—After explaining the procedure to the students, list the steps on the chalkboard or on a chart. The steps might be:

FIGURE 14.1 Suggested Activities for Reporting Back

Area		
Art	Create an art activity book for younger students by trying out art projects and then writing step-by-step instructions of how they were done.	Computer use; photos or drawings to accompany text.
Dance	Create a dance to demonstrate the connections between movement and content area study, research dance in various cultures and historical periods, present an oral summary of the research along with the dance created.	Record the presentations; create a book describing the research done and the connections found.
Theater	Research and write a play related to a period of history, such as the American Revolution, Civil War, World War II, or the Roaring Twenties.	Publish the scripts along with the reports on the research done.
Language arts	Research and write informational books. Require the students to report back on their research along with the steps they used in writing and illustrating the book.	Publish the books along with pages from their learning logs describing the process used to research, write, and illustrate them, including any collaboration they did.
Science	Use experiments as a topic for writing a children's science activity book for younger students to use as summer science activities.	Add diagrams, photos, and learning log examples to the book.
Social sciences	Teach the students to write anecdotal records as they observe interactions among people in public places such as the school cafeteria or the local mall. Focus on describing body language and facial expressions as well as clothing and physical attributes.	Add drawings of the situations.

1. Mix your two colors together in the cup.
2. Make a list of the steps you used.
3. Practice reporting back with your partner.
4. Ask for help if you need it.

• *Verbalize the action*—During the activity, circulate throughout the classroom, reinforcing the vocabulary being used and scaffolding language by verbalizing what you observe. For example, as one pair is dropping paint into the cup, you might say, "You are dropping the paint into the cup. I see you dropping one, two, three drops of yellow into the cup."

• *Allow for verbal practice*—After the activity, give the pairs time to practice their reporting-back dialogues. Then, ask each pair of students to report back to the group. This works best if each pair has a slightly different task. In the color-mixing activity, each pair might have different colors or different numbers of drops to use so that the reporting back stays interesting and nonrepetitive.

• *Celebrate the achievements*—After each pair reports back, list important words that each one used on the chalkboard and celebrate students' use of interesting and important vocabulary. Emphasize the role the vocabulary plays in helping the audience to visualize exactly what the pair did.

• *Review the vocabulary used*—Discuss the verbal reports, asking the students which words they heard a lot. As new words are mentioned, have students write them on the interactive whiteboard or on a chart so they can use them as they write their reports.

• *Write the reports*—After completing the reporting back, have students write their verbal reports and use them either as news items for the class daily news or as daily entries in their learning logs. If needed, you can use interactive writing to support them in the writing phase or stop after the verbal reporting.

• *Assess student progress and understanding*—While the students report back, use the time to take brief notes to include in anecdotal records. Using a laptop computer or a tablet will enable you to quickly and easily enter the comments directly into individual student records, eliminating the need for copying them into the record at a later time. This saves you time and energy and helps you organize student records efficiently. Anecdotal records taken periodically over time serve as rich descriptions of students' verbal communication progress. They also make important additions to individual student portfolios.

• *Evaluate your use of reporting back*—Use the teacher self-evaluation rubric in Figure 14.2 to evaluate the ways in which you use reporting back in your classroom. Think of additional ways to use this powerful strategy to improve English speaking and writing over time.

FIGURE 14.2 Reporting-Back Teacher Self-Evaluation Rubric

Beginning	Developing	Accomplished	Exemplary
Provide an opportunity for occasional verbal reporting back.	Provide a daily opportunity for verbal reporting back.	Provide daily opportunities for verbal reporting back with several activities.	Provide opportunities for verbal reporting back for at least one student with every daily activity.
Use activities to display new vocabulary and occasionally discuss word meaning.	Use activities to display new vocabulary and discuss word meaning daily.	Use activities to display new vocabulary and discuss word meaning several times a day.	Use activities to display new vocabulary and discuss word meaning with almost every daily activity.
Provide rare or limited opportunities for English writing as a follow-up to activities.	Provide daily opportunities for English writing as a follow-up to activities.	Provide opportunities for English writing as a follow-up to activities several times a day.	Provide opportunities for English writing as a follow-up to activities several times a day. Find ways to share this writing through a class blog or classroom displays.

Applications and Examples

Ms. Christensen's sixth-grade students are creating a class "Rosetta stone" and then using the alphabet they inscribe on the stone to write messages in hieroglyphics as a part of their study of ancient Egypt. The Rosetta stone is created as a class project, but the individual messages are transcribed by pairs of students writing in clay using sticks as styluses.

Ms. Christensen has modeled the use of the Rosetta stone to create her message and how the stone must also be used to decipher other messages. She has left the instructions for the activity on a chart in the room, but the instructions are also written in hieroglyphics. She models her reporting back to the class with the directions, "Tell us what you did, step-by-step. Be sure to use words like *first*, *second*, and *next* so we can follow the sequence of what you did."

After the pairs complete their messages and report back orally, they write their messages in their social science learning logs, along with their translations and step-by-step descriptions of what they did.

Ms. Christensen has provided an activity that emphasizes the differences among casual spoken language between working partners, more formal spoken language used for class reports, and written language. As a closing activity, she engages the students in a discussion in which they compare the types of things they said to each other while they were working on the messages, the kinds of sentences they used when they reported back orally, and the sentences they wrote in their learning logs. They also discuss the vocabulary they used in the more formal reporting back and writing. The students decide that the language used in the formal oral presentations was more like the language used in the writing in the learning logs than the language they used while talking to their partners.

One student says, "When I was working with Jonathan, I used a lot of words like *this* and *that* because we were pointing to objects and talking about them. When I talked about the objects in the reporting back, I had to use the names for them and say what I was doing instead of just doing it."

* * * * *

Ms. Carlson is an art teacher at Johnson Junior High. Johnson has an extremely diverse student population, and the school has established a schoolwide goal of developing students' oral and written language. Ms. Carlson has decided to use reporting back as a strategy after each project, requiring the students to write descriptions of their projects and how they were made. This month, the classes are using clay to create three-dimensional figures showing their favorite recreational activities.

Ms. Carlson demonstrates the use of clay to make a tennis player in position to serve the ball. She then reports back to the students, modeling the use of sequence words to describe her step-by-step procedures. She uses the reporting-back sequence to model the **problem solving** she had to engage in to create a sculpture that showed the arm and racket extended into the air. Using the overhead projector, Ms. Carlson then demonstrates how she will transcribe her oral reporting into her art learning log. She also includes a photo of her sculpture in her learning log.

The students spend about a week completing their sculptures. They work on their reporting-back assignments and practice in pairs while the slower sculptors are finishing their projects. Ms. Carlson invites Mr. Gobel, the principal, to come in to hear the reporting-back presentations and view the sculptures. Mr. Gobel is very impressed with the art, the descriptive ways the students found to describe the steps they used, and the problem solving they were required to do. He suggests they repeat the process for their parents the night of parent conferences.

Conclusion

Reporting back is a frequently overlooked step in the learning process. It requires the students to use lesson-related vocabulary to review the steps they used in completing an assignment. The strategy provides a direct connection between instruction and language.

FIGURE 14.3 Supporting Students in Reporting Back

Preproduction	Early Production	Speech Emergence	Intermediate Fluency	Fluent
Encourage students to show what they did. Ask questions using the vocabulary you want students to develop. Create a model sentence (very short) and ask if that's what they did.	Follow the preproduction format but add a step. Repeat the sentence, telling what they did and pause to let them supply key words.	Create a cloze format and encourage students to add key words telling what they did. For example: "First, I __ took a __. Second, I added a __. Next, I added a __."	Encourage the students to report what they did. Create a word chart with key words. Have them write their report with support from you or a peer, using the word chart.	Students at this level may still need support in both oral reporting and writing. Be sure they understand that they can ask for help, saying "What is that word?" or "How do I say this?" (referring to the word chart).

English language learners are supported, when necessary, by being encouraged to use visuals that illustrate the steps and to supply the vocabulary so that they have a scaffold when they report back to the teacher or the class. Using interactive writing to support students who are not yet fluent in English enables everyone to participate. Figure 14.3 lists additional strategies for supporting English language learners in reporting back.

Examples of Approximation Behaviors Related to the TESOL Standards

Pre-K–3 students will:
- verbally describe the steps taken to complete an assignment.
- listen and add to a peer's report of an activity.

4–8 students will:
- use academic language to describe content knowledge gained from a class assignment.

- verbally describe the actions and contributions of each member of a group following a group activity.

9–12 students will:
- write a written report describing a long-range assignment.
- analyze and evaluate personal contributions to a group task.

References

Díaz-Rico, L. (2018). *The crosscultural, language, and academic development handbook* (6th ed.). Boston, MA: Allyn & Bacon.

Gibbons, P. (2015) *Scaffolding language, scaffolding learning: Teaching English language learners in the mainstream classroom*. Portsmouth, NH: Heinemann.

15

Leveled Questions

Adjusting Questioning Strategies to the Language Levels of Students

Leveled questions are used when teachers adapt the way they ask questions so that students can respond to them according to their language acquisition stage (Haley & Austin, 2004; Krashen & Terrell, 1983). This strategy is also called *differentiated questioning* (Díaz-Rico, 2018). To level questions, a teacher must observe students and note how they interact in English. Once the teacher knows the level at which a student interacts in English, the questions the teacher poses can be adjusted to ensure the student's success in providing answers. This may involve teachers using gestures or visuals or slowing their speech slightly while asking questions. Questions should be asked in a way that encourages the student to answer. They can feel comfortable answering by pointing to a visual, giving a one-word or complete sentence response, or sharing a full explanation. It is all dependent on the student's level of language acquisition. To use this strategy effectively, the teacher must know the student's level of English acquisition and provide enough context in the question so that the student can respond, either verbally or nonverbally, with understanding and confidence.

Step-by-Step

The steps in using leveled questions are the following:

- *Observe and document students' language levels*—Observe your students to determine their current levels of interaction in English. On a class list, indicate whether each student is at the preproduction stage, early production stage, speech emergent stage, or **intermediate fluency** stage. See Figure 15.1 for a description of students' English proficiency at each of these stages. You will need to keep your list updated as you work with the students and observe their responses.
- *Choose and gather materials*—Determine which visuals, **artifacts**, or gestures you will need to make your meaning clear to the students whose understanding of English is limited. Gather these support materials to use during the presentation of the lesson and your questioning. Remember, English language learners feel more comfortable participating when they have ways to demonstrate their understanding with visuals and support materials.
- *Plan a hierarchy of questions*—Plan a series of questions that will help you in involving your students and in determining their levels of understanding of the material you will be teaching. In the beginning, it is helpful to plan a series of questions at different levels so that you can move around the room and use appropriately leveled questions for individual students without too much hesitation or confusion. See Figure 15.2 for suggestions.

FIGURE 15.1 Appropriate Expectations for Students at Different Speech Stages

Stage	Appropriate Expectations
Preproduction	Nodding, pointing, physically demonstrating
Early production	One- or two-word responses, making choices from given language samples (Is it a whale or a dolphin?)
Speech emergence	Phrase or short sentences (expect grammar errors)
Intermediate fluency	Longer sentences, fewer grammar errors

Sources: Krashen and Terrell (1983); and Díaz-Rico (2013).

FIGURE 15.2 Appropriate Questions for Speech Stages

Stage	Question or Cue
Preproduction	"Show me . . . " "Which of these . . . ? "
Early production	"Is it the _____ one or the _____ one?" Questions that can be answered with one or two words.
Speech emergence	"Did this happen at the beginning or at the end? " "What happened next?" "Where did you find the answer?"
Intermediate fluency	"How did you . . . ? " "What was the character trying to do?"

Sources: Krashen and Terrell (1983) and Díaz-Rico (2013).

Watch a teacher adjusting her questions to the level of her students' language in Video Example 15.1 and note how she actively involves every child and adjusts her directions to their language levels. In Video Example 15.2, the teacher also assists a student by adjusting questions to the appropriate language development level. As you watch these videos, consider the following questions:

Enhanced eText
Video Example 15.1

- Why is it important to know the **English language development levels** of your students when planning a lesson?
- How does this teacher make sure that all her students can be successful?

- What scaffolding does this teacher provide for her students during this lesson?
- Think about a lesson you are planning and write some leveled questions for it. How does this activity help you to consider the language development levels of your students?

Enhanced eText
Video Example 15.2

- *Involve all students*—Use the list of students and their related speech levels as a checklist to make sure that you are involving all students in discussion and questioning. This also serves as a reminder that you need to adapt the levels of your questions to students' changing language acquisition levels.
- *Assess student progress and understanding*—Use the checklist you have created for observation purposes. Observe a few students each day until you have examples of the verbal responses typical for each student. Compile these responses into anecdotal records for student portfolios to document their expanding ability to respond to questions in class. These documentation strategies provide indicators of the students' progress in meeting TESOL and Common Core standards related to classroom interactions and academic language.
- *Add technology*—Copy and save related visuals from the Internet. These may then be provided to students as hard copies or as digital files. Providing students with laptops or tablets affords them great opportunities to improve during lessons and when working at home. They develop skills in using technology to research and respond to questions.
- *Use a teacher self-evaluation rubric to monitor your own progress in leveling questions*—Reflect on how and when you use leveled questions in your classroom. Use the self-evaluation rubric in Figure 15.3 to determine your level of implementation. Work on improving your leveling of questions as well as how frequently you use leveled questions in your classroom.

FIGURE 15.3 Leveled Questions Teacher Self-Evaluation Rubric

Beginning	Developing	Accomplished	Exemplary
Leveled questions are used whenever a child doesn't seem to understand a question asked of him or her.	Questions are leveled for preproduction and early production students.	Questions are often leveled for all ELL students.	Leveled questions are used daily for all ELL students.
Questions are leveled on the spot whenever a child doesn't understand.	Leveled questions are developed ahead of time as the lessons are planned.	Leveled questions are developed ahead of time for all lessons planned, and follow-up questions are also developed to determine students' depth of knowledge.	Leveled questions are developed ahead of time for all lessons planned, and follow-up questions are also developed to determine students' depth of knowledge. New vocabulary is incorporated into questions.
No record is kept of student answers and/ or confusions.	Assessment of student responses is kept on a casual basis.	A structured format of assessment (anecdotal records, checklists, etc.) is kept to document student growth.	A structured format of assessment (anecdotal records, checklists, etc.) is kept to document student growth. This growth is shared with parents and celebrated with students.

Applications and Examples

Leveled questions can be used at all grade levels and in all curricular areas. For example, in Ms. Chanis's first-grade class, the children are using manipulatives to join sets and build number sentences.

Ms. Chanis is addressing Common Core State Standards in mathematics. She wants her students to "use addition and subtraction within 20 to solve word problems involving situations of adding to, taking from, putting together, taking apart, and comparing, with unknowns in all positions, e.g., by using objects, drawings, and equations with a symbol for the unknown number to represent the problem" (CCSS.Math.Content.1.OA.A.1). As she does with all lessons, she is also addressing the development and acquisition of English vocabulary.

As Ms. Chanis moves around the room observing the students at work and asking questions, she varies the way she asks questions according to the language acquisition stages of her students. As she stops at Hnu's table, she asks Hnu to show her a set of six objects. Because Hnu is functioning at the preproduction stage in English, Ms. Chanis asks, "Show me 6." Hnu quickly counts out six blocks and lines them up on her desk. Ms. Chanis says, "Yes! 1, 2, 3, 4, 5, 6. You showed me 6." She points to the blocks as she counts them and smiles at Hnu. By keeping her sentences short and using sentence forms that have been modeled during the lesson introduction, Ms. Chanis is supporting Hnu's successful participation in the math lesson.

As Ms. Chanis moves to other students, she adjusts her questions to their language stage. She keeps track of the students with whom she interacts by checking their names off on a list, which also helps her to monitor the students' language stages.

Ms. Chanis asks an early production student to tell her how many objects are in the set on his desk. A speech emergent student is asked to give the number sentence for the set of two red blocks added to the set of four green blocks. An intermediate fluency student is asked to tell a story about a picture of a group of two pigs joining a group of four pigs wallowing in the mud.

Each leveled question is followed by a brief modeling of language to help support the students in incorporating more English speech into their verbal interactions. A student responds with one word and then listens as Ms. Chanis models the use of that one word in a short sentence. A student who responds with a short phrase will hear a confirmation that the phrase is correct, but then Ms. Chanis will scaffold that student's response by extending the phrase into a full sentence. Even in math, Ms. Chanis is aware of the need to continually scaffold language, academic language in particular, for her English language learners.

* * * * *

Leveled questions are appropriate at any grade level as long as there are students who need them to participate successfully in class interactions. In Mr. Burrows' ninth-grade class, there are a number of English language learners who need leveled questions to participate in class discussions and questioning periods.

As Mr. Burrows reviews the Cuban Missile Crisis with his students, he wants to discuss the reasons for concern at the time. Mr. Burrows structures a series of questions to help students locate Cuba on the map and recognize its geographic proximity to the United States, which was certainly a major reason for concern.

To encourage participation by his English language learners, Mr. Burrows interfaces his laptop with the classroom interactive whiteboard and displays a map of North America, including the Caribbean islands. He asks one of his preproduction stage students to go to the board and place his hand on the country of Cuba on the map. The student follows Mr. Burrows' instructions and proudly points to Cuba on the map.

Mr. Burrows asks an early production student to go to the map and look at it carefully. He then asks, "What is the name of the ocean or sea in which Cuba is located? Show me where you found that information on the map."

For a speech emergent student, he asks, "How far is Cuba from the United States?" He follows up that question with a request to "put one hand on Cuba and one hand on Florida on the map."

For an intermediate fluency student, Mr. Burrows asks, "Why was President Kennedy so concerned about the buildup of missiles in Cuba in the early 1960s?"

The discussion and questions continue, and the map is used to ensure that the students are able to understand the main points of the discussion. Mr. Burrows models English sentences as he points out the countries on the map and makes it clear that President Kennedy was concerned because the Soviet Union was putting missiles very close to U.S. shores. Mr. Burrows then uses small ship pictures placed on the map to illustrate how the United States blockaded the approaches to Cuba and caused the Soviet ships carrying missiles to return home. Mr. Burrows is aware of the need to provide visuals to support his English language learners' comprehension of English, but he is also aware that their understanding of spoken English is better than their ability to produce English sentences. He finds ways to make himself understood and to actively involve all students.

Conclusion

The use of leveled questions in the classroom requires that teachers know the stage of language development at which each student in their class is functioning. It also requires that teachers understand appropriate expectations for students at each stage of language development. This knowledge is vital, but it is not difficult to obtain if teachers are willing to observe students carefully.

After gathering this information and establishing a method for regularly updating the information, the teacher is ready to use leveled questions to ensure that each student in the class has opportunities to participate fully. Recent research in the use of leveled questions in high school science classes (Guilford et al., 2017) demonstrates how gradually increasing the levels of questions related to content reading can be effective with English learners in mainstream classes.

The need for leveling questions at the secondary level can be based on the students' English language development as well as on the type of content information the students are looking for in the text. Guilford et al. (2017) level content-reading questions in the following way:

Level 1 – Identifying factual information from the text
Level 2 – Inferring, interpreting, or analyzing information from the text
Level 3 – Going beyond the text, reading additional texts, exploring related issues, using outside knowledge and experiences to relate to the text.

The effectiveness of this strategy stems from several sources. Students become more fully engaged in lessons when their anxiety levels are reduced, their participation supports their understanding, and their self-confidence and language use increases. All of these factors contribute to the reduction of classroom management challenges as well.

Examples of Approximation Behaviors Related to the TESOL Standards

PreK–3 students will:

- respond to questions appropriate to their level of English language development.
- demonstrate understanding by physical and oral responses.

4–8 students will:

- ask clarification questions.

- demonstrate understanding through physical, verbal, and written replies.

9–12 students will:

- select, connect, and explain information.
- represent information visually and interpret the visual representation orally.

References

Díaz-Rico, L. (2018). *The crosscultural, language, and academic development handbook: A complete K–12 reference guide* (6th ed.). Boston, MA: Pearson Education.

Haley, M., & Austin, T. (2004). *Content-based second language teaching and learning.* Boston, MA: Pearson Education.

Guilford, J., Bustamante, A., Mackura, K., Hirsch, S., Lyon, E., & Estrada, K. (2017) Text savvy: Planning rich reading experiences that support language development and science learning. *The Science Teacher, 84*(1), 49–55.

Krashen, S., & Terrell, T. (1983). *The natural approach: Language acquisition in the classroom.* Oxford, England: Pergamon Press.

Bilingual Books and Labels
Supporting Biliteracy Awareness

Books and labels written in two or more languages, including English, are appropriate for use in bilingual or multilingual classes for several reasons. First, they validate students' home languages and allow them to use their L1 knowledge to support their understanding of texts. Valuing students' native language supports them in developing positive attitudes toward school and learning (Díaz-Rico, 2018). Another strategy that supports students in acquiring English while valuing their home languages is the construction of a classroom bilingual (trilingual) dictionary to which students contribute words in their home languages. This process also helps students identify cognates (Díaz-Rico, 2018).

In classrooms with children whose families speak indigenous languages, it is vitally important that books and labels from their home languages be included in the classroom environment. It is estimated that 50% of today's spoken languages will be extinct or seriously endangered in this century (Hadaway & Young, 2014).

Enhanced eText
Video Example 16.1

Video Example 16.1 explains the importance of affirming students' home languages. After viewing the video, ask yourself the following questions:

- How does providing bilingual books to take home help to involve parents as part of educational team?
- How does the placement of bilingual books in the classroom help English speakers?

Books and labels written in the home languages of students introduce some of the students' native culture to the classroom. They also provide opportunities for all students in a class to be exposed to multiple ways of expressing thoughts and value systems. In classrooms where students have learned to read and write in their first languages, labels and books in those languages provide access to information. Some books contain an entire text, written in two languages, and support the transfer of reading ability from the home language into English.

In classrooms where the students do not read and write in their native languages, bilingual books and labels in the students' home languages provide some exposure to the written systems of the native languages and to the customs and traditions of multiple cultures. Some books may encourage parents to read and discuss the books with their children. There are now many books available in which the cultures are depicted by stories, in English, with some samples of common expressions in the first language added for a taste of the language. For example, in "I Am Cucaracha" (Johnston, 1996), the Spanish words *señora*, *señor*, and *por favor* are integrated into the English text to add a Spanish lilt to the rhyme and rhythm of the poem. Such texts, while not truly bilingual, are written by authors familiar with the cultures about which they are writing, and they provide useful supports to multicultural studies in the classroom (Tomlinson & Lynch-Brown, 1996). There are several websites where these books are available.

Step-by-Step

The steps for implementing the use of bilingual books and labels are the following:

• *Identify the languages represented in the classroom*—Determine the home languages represented in your classroom and the stages of English development achieved by each student.

• *Pronounce and label common objects*—Provide opportunities for students to verbalize the words for common items in the classroom using their home language. Involve students in writing and placing labels for items around the classroom. For example, the words *door, la puerta*; *window, la ventana*; and *chalk, la tiza* would be displayed in a Spanish–English first-grade classroom. In classrooms with older students, the labels can be complete sentences such as, *Pon tu tarea aquí (Put your homework here)*.

• *Provide bilingual books*—Provide bilingual books, with the text written in both English and the home languages of the students, for use in read-aloud or independent reading according to the abilities of students to read in their home language. If the students do not read in their home language, enlist the help of a bilingual parent or instructional assistant to read the text aloud in the home language(s) of the students before reading the English version. Take time to stop during the English reading to compare the words and sentences in the different languages. Draw attention to any similar words. Discuss the books and the similarities and differences in the customs and situations depicted in the books. Encourage students to discuss how their experiences and family customs are similar to or different from the situations described in the books. Help students understand that a range of customs and beliefs exists within any culture, and that people from many cultures share similar customs and beliefs. See Chapter 10, Moving into Reading; Chapter 22, Learning Centers; and Chapter 36, Culture Studies, for additional ways to use bilingual books and labels.

• *Provide translations*—Provide translations of important texts whenever possible. Students can often assist with these translations. Ask bilingual parents or instructional assistants to read these translations aloud to the class or record them for students to use in the listening center.

• *Explore key vocabulary in several languages*—Periodically engage all students in learning key vocabulary in multiple languages. They can learn to name colors, count numbers, and ask basic questions in multiple languages. In addition, engage students in discussions of the customs depicted in the multicultural literature that is being shared in the classroom.

• *Monitor and evaluate your use of bilingual books in the classroom*—Use the self-evaluation rubric in Figure 16.1 to identify ways in which you can increase and improve the use of bilingual books and labels in your classroom.

Applications and Examples

Ms. Torres teaches a fifth-grade class in a border town in California. A number of her students move across the border to Mexico for a few months each year. Some of the students attend school regularly while they are in Mexico, but some do not. Ms. Torres is determined that the students will learn to read and write in English while they are in her class. She has decided to make the most of the students' reading and writing abilities in Spanish to move them toward more fluent literacy in English.

Ms. Torres and her students label everything in her classroom in both English and Spanish. They provide bulletin board captions in both languages, and Ms. Torres encourages the children to write in the language with which they are most comfortable. If the students write in Spanish, she asks them to write a sentence or two in English giving the main gist of the page. By doing so, everyone in the class can read and enjoy the stories that have been written. She also encourages collaboration so that her students can publish bilingual books with both English and Spanish texts.

Ms. Torres regularly reads picture books in English after her instructional assistant has read the same book in Spanish. After the book has been read in both languages, the students help

FIGURE 16.1 Bilingual Books and Labels: Teacher Self-Evaluation Rubric

Beginning	Developing	Accomplished	Exemplary
Non-English words are used and explained only when a student asks for a definition or explanation.	Non-English words are introduced to clarify the meanings of unfamiliar English words. English and non-English words are displayed when they are brought up in relation to lessons.	Non-English words are displayed and referred to in relation to lessons in all curricular areas.	Non-English words are displayed and referred to, and nuances of meanings are discussed. Students are encouraged to write in home languages as well as English.
Only English books are read aloud. Non-English words in the books are explained, and students who speak the language are asked to pronounce the words so others can hear the correct pronunciations.	Some bilingual books are available in the classroom, and native speakers are brought in to read them aloud to the class and discuss the similarities and differences in the languages.	Bilingual books are used to help students understand the differences in languages and cultures. Parents are invited to share cultural customs and bring in cultural artifacts.	Bilingual books and labels are displayed throughout the classroom. Native English speakers are encouraged to learn expressions, numbers, colors, etc., in several languages.
Teacher knows very few words in the home languages of the students.	Teacher is adding new words in the students' home languages by having students translate. The value of bilingualism is clear to the students.	Teacher and English-only students are adding new words in the students' home languages by having students translate. The value of bilingualism is clear to the students.	Bilingual books, labels, and posters are evident throughout the classroom, and students are encouraged to use a variety of languages in reading and writing. English-only students are encouraged to learn another language and add to their new vocabularies just as non-English speakers are acquiring new English vocabulary.

her to add words to the word wall—matching the English and Spanish words and cross-listing them alphabetically. This activity encourages the Spanish-speaking students to build their English vocabularies and the English-speaking students to build their Spanish vocabularies. With longer texts like chapter books, Ms. Torres reads one chapter in English and the next in Spanish. She then asks a student to summarize each chapter in the language that was not used. She finds that both her English and Spanish speakers are learning to listen carefully and are understanding both languages well.

One day, Juan, a Spanish speaker who regularly spends a few weeks in Mexico each year, comes to her with a special request. "My grandmother is very sick. I am afraid she is going to die. My mother would like for me to write the story of her life so that we will all remember her. Will you help me to translate it from Spanish to English so that my parents can read it and also my brothers and sisters, who don't read Spanish?"

Ms. Torres is excited about the project and shares the idea with the whole class. "I think we all have relatives who have interesting stories. Why don't we each choose someone to interview? We can write biographies for our class library and learn more about our family history at the same time."

The students are interested in the idea of conducting interviews, although they are not sure about the writing part of the project until Ms. Torres suggests that they can publish their biographies using the computer.

The next step in the project is to formulate interview questions. The students work in small groups to brainstorm the questions that will help them learn more about the life stories of their relatives. The groups share their lists of questions, and then the students go home to conduct their interviews.

Each day, the students return with more of their questions answered, and they begin to write the biographies. They work in pairs most of the time to help each other with vocabulary and sentence structure. Some of the more fluent Spanish writers finish their Spanish versions very quickly and then struggle over the English translations. Some of the English-speaking students are able to help with the translations because of the bilingual word wall and the Spanish–English dictionaries in the classroom. The English-speaking students use the same approach to writing in Spanish that Ms. Torres requires of the beginning English speakers. They write a sentence or two in Spanish to convey the gist of the story to the Spanish readers. The Spanish-speaking students assist the English speakers when they need help with this process.

Toward the end of the school year, all the biographies are written, illustrated, and bound, and the class decides to have a celebration to share the books with their families. They sit in groups and read their favorite parts of the biographies to the visitors. Ms. Torres is touched by the attendance and the enthusiasm for the project. One grandmother shares, "I never thought I would have a book written about me. And my relatives in Mexico can read it. So can my grandchildren who speak only English."

* * * * *

Students of all ages benefit from the use of bilingual literature and labeling and sharing. Mr. Fong's 10th-grade class is preparing a Thanksgiving assembly for the nearby elementary school. They want to help the younger students understand the concept of the various groups of pilgrims who have come to America from all over the world. To begin their research, they read books about emigrant groups that have come to America to escape war and oppression. The students decide to focus on several different pilgrim stories to illustrate how America is still receiving pilgrims today.

They begin with a brief reenactment of *Molly's Pilgrim* (Cohen, 1983) and then create a timeline of all the major immigrations to America. As they unroll the timeline across the stage, each 10th grader reenacts a scene from the life of one of the pilgrims they have researched. They begin with Juan de Oñate and the group of Mexican pilgrims who escaped to Texas 23 years before the Mayflower arrived, and they continue the reenactments all the way to present-day Bosnian pilgrims. To make their presentations authentic, each student has researched the language of the pilgrim groups and learned to say, "Thank God! We have arrived in America and now we are free!" in the language appropriate to the group they represent.

Mr. Fong is so impressed with their research and dedication to the project that he makes a videotape of their production to motivate next year's social science group. When he interviews the students about the project, he is surprised by some of their comments.

"I never knew there was more than one group of pilgrims."

"The hardest part of the research was learning to speak in Armenian—and it was only two sentences."

"I found out that my grandmother was a pilgrim. I never knew that."

"I never knew how hard the pilgrims had to work to survive."

Conclusion

The use of bilingual books and labels in the classroom encourages students to value other cultures and languages. English language learners are validated by the use of their home languages in the classroom and the study of their literature and culture. Native English speakers have an opportunity to experience the challenge of remembering vocabulary in a second language. The comparison and celebration of a variety of approaches and beliefs helps to build a cohesive community in the classroom.

Examples of Approximation Behaviors Related to the TESOL Standards

PreK–3 students will:

- respond appropriately to nonverbal cues.
- use acceptable tone, volume, and intonation in a variety of settings.

4–8 students will:

- use knowledge from L1 to inform L2 reading.

- use cultural knowledge to interpret literature.

9–12 students will:

- use L1 to enhance oral storytelling and writing.
- integrate cultural knowledge into oral and written reports.

References

Cohen, B. (1983). *Molly's pilgrim.* New York, NY: Bantam Books.

Díaz-Rico, L. (2018). *The crosscultural, language, and academic development handbook: A complete K–12 reference guide* (6th ed.). Boston, MA: Pearson Education.

Hadaway, N., & Young, T. (2014) Preserving languages in the new millennium: Indigenous bilingual children's books. *Childhood Education, 90*(5)27–31.

Johnston, T. (1996). *My Mexico—Mexico mío.* New York, NY: G. P. Putnam's Sons.

Tomlinson, C., & Lynch-Brown, C. (1996). *Essentials of children's literature* (2nd ed.). Needham Heights, MA: Allyn & Bacon.

17

Sorting Activities
Organizing Information into Categories

Sorting activities (Helman, Bear, Templeton, & Invernizzi, 2011) are activities that require students to sort objects, words, phrases, and sentences according to set **parameters**. Sorting activities are appropriate for use with English language learners because they provide a way for students to manipulate objects and written symbols to show their understanding of concepts, while acquiring the vocabulary and structures needed for verbal interaction (Echevarria, Vogt, & Short, 2010).

Sorting activities can be used in a wide range of curricular areas and, with careful planning and adaptations, are appropriate for kindergarten through 12th-grade students. Figure 17.1 provides suggestions for using sorting activities.

Word walls (Tompkins, 2013) are alphabetical lists of words created in the classroom for the purpose of word study and vocabulary development. They can be as simple as words written on individual cards and placed on a bulletin board or a list of words written on a large sheet of butcher paper. In classrooms where students are learning English as a second language, bilingual (or multilingual) word walls with the words written in several languages and illustrated can serve as a reference for students as they write or interact verbally. Some teachers create a number of different word walls in their classrooms, one wall containing **high-frequency words** for students to reference when writing, and other word walls containing words relevant to a literature or a content-area unit. When the class moves on to another literature focus, the teacher might collect the words written on cards, punch a hole in the corner of each card, and place them on a "word ring" to keep for the students' reference. Placing a copy of the cover of the book to which the words are related helps students to locate the appropriate word rings by simply recalling the context in which the words were studied.

Word sorts (Allen, 1999; Helman et al., 2011) are a good way to give students additional opportunities to interact with words. Teachers can sort the words from the word wall by beginning, ending, or vowel sounds; by parts of speech; by meaning; or by the number of syllables. Sorting encourages students to look at words more carefully and to think about ways in which words are similar or different. See Figure 17.2 for sample word sorts.

Word sorts can be used effectively in content-area classes to support student understanding of concepts. In science, for example, students can sort words related to plants and animals into a closed sort (teacher predetermined sort) by putting picture or word cards into either PLANTS or ANIMALS. They can then continue to do an open-sort with the same cards to choose their sort classifications such as 2-legged/ 4-legged or mammal/ egg laying. They can even continue into higher level sorts by using scientific classifications (DeLuca, 2010). To view a video showing how to use *Smart Notebook* to create an electronic sorting board, see Video Example 17.1.

Sorts of all kinds can be created using this program.

Enhanced eText
Video Example 17.1
https://www.youtube.com/
watch?v=NB7pRe1CYJk

FIGURE 17.1 Sorting Activities

Grade Level	Curricular Area	Description of Sorting Activity
Kindergarten	Phonemic awareness	Using small objects or pictures, students sort by matching sounds.
	Phonics	Using small objects or pictures, students sort by initial sound–letter representation.
	Math	Using small objects or math manipulatives, students sort by size, shape, or number.
	Science	Using animal pictures, children sort by attributes such as fur, feathers, and scales. Using pictures depicting weather conditions, students sort by season.
Primary	Phonics	Using small objects, pictures, or words, students sort by ending sound or vowel sounds.
	Math	Using number sentences, students sort by sum or difference.
	Writing	Using short sentences written on sentence strips, students sort by type of sentence (declarative, question, exclamation).
	English	Using word cards, students sort by parts of speech (nouns, verbs, adjectives, etc.).
	Science	Using leaves, students sort by leaf shape. Using animal pictures, students sort by classification (mammal, reptile, amphibian, bird).
Upper Elementary	Reading	Using sentence strips with sentences written on them, students sequence them to form a topic sentence and supporting details.
	Math	Using cards with word problems written on them, students sort them into stacks representing the four operations (addition, subtraction, multiplication, and division).
		Using cards with word problems written on them, students sort them into stacks estimating their correct solutions (1–5, 6–10, 11–15, 16–20, etc.).
	Vocabulary	Using word cards, students sort words into categories such as synonyms, antonyms, etc.
Secondary	Science	Students sort rock samples into classifications. Students match description cards with scientific samples, slides, experiments.
	Literature	Students sort plot summaries into genre classifications. Students match main character description with literature titles.
	Learning strategies	Students sequence cards with learning strategy step descriptions.
	Life skills	Students sequence cards with job application procedure descriptions. Students sort descriptions of job application and interview behaviors into piles marked Positive Behavior and Negative Behavior.
	Social sciences	Students sequence the steps in the legislative process. Students match attributes of nations to the names of the nations.

FIGURE 17.2 Sample Word Sorts

run	red	dog
jump	green	cat
hop	yellow	cow
tiptoe	blue	horse
stomp	purple	Hippo

Step-by-Step

The steps in implementing sorting activities are the following:

 • *Identify skills to practice in sorting mode*—Identify a skill that can be practiced or demonstrated using sorting. (See Figure 17.1 for suggestions.) Prepare the materials to be sorted, including containers or **pocket charts** in which to place the sorts.

 • *Explain the activity*—Explain the activity, model what the students will do, and provide some guided practice before asking the students to sort independently. Decide whether you want the students to undertake the activity individually, in pairs, or in small groups. If practice of the concept is the purpose of the sort, individual sorts are effective. If you want the sort to include practice in using English vocabulary and communication, paired or small-group sorts are more effective.

 • *Set up the routine and requirements*—Establish a routine for the students to use when they complete their sort. Some teachers encourage the students to take a digital picture of the sort and turn the picture in, others require a written response that explains the sort, and others simply have a peer check the sort.

 • *Assess the students' progress and understanding*—Any independent activity is only as powerful as the value given to it by the teacher. Take the time to have students explain their sorts and how they made their choices. This doesn't have to be done daily, but students must believe that the teacher values their efforts. Individual conferences also give the teacher an additional opportunity for verbal interactions and a chance to document growth not only in students' sorting skills but also in verbal English communication.

Applications and Examples

The students in Mr. Avedesian's kindergarten class are learning how to sort objects by listening to the beginning sounds of the words. Each student has an empty milk carton with the top cut off. On the table in the sorting center is a tray full of small objects such as balls, pencils, erasers, bracelets, hearts, apples, baby bottles, crayons, and markers. The students are looking for objects that begin with the same sound as their names. Mr. Avedesian reminds them to say their names and then say the name of the object to see if the sound matches. Because many of his students are English learners, Mr. Avedesian has the students work in pairs so that one member is an English speaker and can help supply the names of the objects.

Michael says, "Michael, ball," then shakes his head and returns the ball to the table and picks up the marker.

"Michael, marker," he says and smiles as he places the marker into his milk carton.

After the students have found the items that begin with the same sound as their names, they bring their milk cartons to Mr. Avedesian and show him the items they have found. Mr. Avedesian asks them to say the names of the items and then return the items to the table. Mr. Avedesian keeps a list of the students who are successful with this initial sort and pairs them the next day to search for items for their partners' names. He plans to match Michael and Simon for the second day. Michael will be looking for items that begin like Simon's name, and Simon will be looking for things that match Michael's name.

Gradually through the year, Mr. Avedesian will move through the initial consonants and begin to have the students sort for items that match the letters of the alphabet.

* * * * *

The 12th graders in Ms. Tan's preemployment class are getting ready for practice job interviews. She has designed a series of picture and description sorts to help them make good decisions as they practice interviewing and begin to apply for jobs. The first sort involves pictures of people in various forms of dress. The students sort the pictures into piles according to the job interviews for which the dress is appropriate.

This first sort is a picture-to-picture sort. The students simply match the pictures of the people with pictures of places of employment. After the students complete the sort, they fill out a form that lists the places of employment by entering the number of a picture of a person they selected who would be working at that place of employment using clues such as their dress to help them make the matches. After all the students have completed the sort, the class discusses the responses and why certain dress is appropriate for certain jobs.

The second sort involves reading a series of employment advertisements and matching pictures of people with the education and experience listed on the back with the jobs for which they are most qualified. Again, the students fill out a brief form that matches the letters identifying the job ads with the numbers identifying the applicants. The class discusses the meanings of the ads and the qualifications necessary for each.

The third sort involves placing a series of job application forms into piles marked Definite No, File, Interview, and Top Candidate. The students place the names of the applicants on a list with the same indicant at the top. For the list marked Definite No they are asked to state why they placed the applicant on this list. They are asked the same question for the names on the Top Candidate list. The class discusses the sort after everyone has completed the "paper screen."

"You mean you would get placed on the Definite No list just because of a few misspelled words on the application?" Jerome asks with indignation in his voice.

"For this particular job, spelling is a major requirement," Karen replies. "You are painting signs and decorating windows for sales. Besides, why would you hire someone who isn't careful enough to double-check his spelling on something as important as a job application?"

"Exactly," Ms. Tan confirms. "Remember, you are probably not the only applicant for the job. The employers are looking for the best candidates. They don't want to waste time interviewing people who are probably not qualified to do a good job."

Conclusion

Sorting activities provide hands-on experiences with manipulating pictures, letters, words, and longer texts. Sorting activities not only provide practice in making decisions and differentiating among concepts but also illustrate a technique for studying and organizing materials. Although sorting activities have a wide range of applications, they are highly effective for use with English language learners because they allow students to demonstrate their understanding with reduced reliance on language skills. Asking students to justify their sorts creates an opportunity for verbal interaction based on visual cues, which is supportive of emergent English speakers. Figure 17.3 lists some considerations to keep in mind to ensure that the sorting activities you plan are appropriate for students at varying levels of English language development.

FIGURE 17.3 Considerations for Sorting Activities for English Language Learners

Preproduction	Early Production	Speech Emergence	Intermediate Fluency	Fluent
Use real objects or photographs. Pair students with a fluent English speaker. Focus on the English names of objects at first and then on one attribute, such as categories (food, animals, etc.).	Pair students with fluent English speakers. Review the names of objects in photographs. Focus on one attribute of a word, such as the beginning sound.	Pair students with fluent English speakers. Review the names of objects and have the students pronounce the words several times. Sort by one attribute, such as the beginning sound or the category and then change and re-sort by another attribute.	English learners can begin to sort without a partner. Sorts can be extended to include attributes being studied, such as the number of syllables or vowel sounds or attributes related to science, math, or social sciences.	Keep in mind that fluent speakers of English who are not native speakers will still need support in areas such as pronunciation or definitions. Assign a native English speaker to help as needed. Also provide an answer key for use when the sorts are completed so students can self-correct.

Examples of Approximation Behaviors Related to the TESOL Standards

PreK–3 students will:

- sort pictures into categories.
- use phonics knowledge to sort words and pictures.

4–8 students will:

- sort words into categories, such as parts of speech, tenses, number of syllables, and so on.

- sort curricular knowledge into appropriate categories.

9–12 students will:

- use categories to organize curricular materials.
- sort information and materials and verbally explain the rules used for the sorting.

References

Allen, J. (1999). *Words, words, words: Teaching vocabulary in grades 4–12*. Portland, ME: Stenhouse.

DeLuca, E. (2010, March). Unlocking academic vocabulary. *The Science Teacher, 77*(3), 27–32.

Echevarria, J., Vogt, M., & Short, D. (2010). *Making content comprehensible for elementary English learners: The SIOP model*. Boston, MA: Allyn & Bacon.

Helman, L., Bear, D. R., Templeton, S., & Invernizzi, M. A. (2011). *Words their way with English learners: Word study for phonics, vocabulary, and spelling instruction* (2nd ed.). Upper Saddle River, NJ: Merrill/Prentice Hall.

Tompkins, G. (2013). *Literacy for the 21st century* (6th ed.). Upper Saddle River, NJ: Pearson Education.

18

Cloze
Using Context to Create Meaning

Cloze activities are based on written text in which some words are left out and blanks are inserted. Cloze paragraphs are often used to assess reading comprehension because the word choices students make allow teachers to evaluate students' understanding of the meaning of a text (Gibbons, 2015). Cloze activities provide a meaningful context in which to teach English vocabulary and reading decoding skills to English language learners (Hinkel, 2006). When done in pairs or small groups, these activities also provide an opportunity for students to discuss their choices and justify their selection of words.

Listening comprehension is a difficult skill to test, but Cheng (2004) found the use of a cloze format, where students choose a word from several choices to complete a sentence from the passage read, provided the best responses when compared to traditional multiple choice or open-ended questions.

Teacher-designed cloze activities are especially valuable because they can be adapted to the specific needs and language levels of students. By observing students' oral reading or running records, a teacher is able to identify students who are not cross-checking phonological and meaning cues. Creating paragraphs with words left out requires students to use multiple sources of information, such as context, to predict words that make sense in the paragraph. Cloze sentences can also demonstrate to students that they don't have to be able to read every word of a paragraph to understand its meaning. Cloze activities can be constructed so that students work in pairs to select words to fill in blanks in sentences within a paragraph, and to discuss the variety of words that might be appropriate. This activity introduces a verbal component to the exercise and gives students a chance to use background knowledge to guide their choices while defending their decisions (Zwiers, 2004).

The context of the sentence, in combination with **phonic cues** and **syntax cues**, helps readers to identify unknown words. Figure 18.1 shows the variety of ways one paragraph can be used to provide practice adapted to individual student needs.

Step-by-Step

The steps in using cloze activities are the following:

• *Observe student reading behaviors*—Observe your students as they read, and note their use of phonological, meaning, and syntax cues as well as their **self-monitoring**. Also note the categories of the words that seem to be giving them difficulty. A **running record** is an easy way to do this. (See Figure 32.2 for an example of a running record.)

FIGURE 18.1 Cloze Activities to Support Reading and Language Acquisition

Type of Cloze	Definition	Example
Traditional	Leave out words selected randomly.	I went for a walk to the _____. I wanted to _____ a _____. I watched carefully but I was to be _____.
Syntactic	Structure words are deleted.	I went _____ a _____ to the sea. ____ wanted ____ see ____ dolphin. I watched carefully ____ I was _____ be disappointed.
Semantic	Content words are deleted.	I went for a walk to the _____. I wanted to _____ a _____. I _____ carefully but I was to ____ disappointed.
Graphophonic	Some letters are deleted.	I w _____ for a w _____ to the s _____. I wanted to see a d _____. I watched c _____ but I was to be d _____.

Source: Gibbons (1993) and Zwiers (2004).

- *Group students for instruction*—Examine students' running records to determine which students are experiencing similar difficulties. Then, group these students together to provide a greater opportunity to focus on their language challenges.
- *Introduce cloze with a chart sentence*—Display a simple sentence on a chart and use a Post-it© note to cover up a word or two. Have students read the sentence with you and talk about which word is missing. Ask the students how they knew which word was missing. Help them to see that the rest of the sentence gives information to help identify a word that will fit in the sentence. Uncover the initial letter of the covered word to see if it matches their guess. If it doesn't, have them decide if another word will solve the problem.
- *Prepare a cloze activity to meet student needs*—Prepare a cloze paragraph by choosing a selection from a reading assignment at the students' instructional reading level and deleting words using one of the following methods:

1. Copy the paragraph onto poster board or chart paper and cover selected words with wide correction tape. Be sure to use the type of tape that is easily removed.
2. Copy the paragraph onto transparency film, leaving blanks in the text.
3. Copy the sentences from the selection onto sentence strips. Cut the words apart and leave some out by placing them in a pocket chart.
4. Project the paragraph onto an interactive whiteboard, leaving blank spaces in the text. Using an input device (laptop, wireless keyboard, tablet, etc.), enter letters into the blank spaces to create the words that have been omitted. Students could also choose from a list of posted possibilities and then "drag" their choices to the blank spaces in the text.

- *Identify appropriate words to fill the blanks*—Work with the groups of students, asking them to read the selection silently. Have students write down the words they think would best complete the selection. Ask each student to read the selection orally and insert the words he or she believes are needed to make the selection make sense. After the students read the selection with their chosen words inserted, have them explain how they decided which words to insert. Have them point to or read the parts of the selection that gave them clues. If they selected different words, have them discuss which words seem to fit best and why.
- *Assess student growth and understanding*—Using cloze paragraphs to assess student comprehension is very effective. Giving cloze assessments periodically to document growth in the use of context cues is an interesting way of assessing students' abilities to make sense of text. Periodic cloze assessments can easily be included in individual student portfolios to document growth in reading comprehension.
- *Add technology*—Cloze paragraphs at various reading levels can be created and saved on the computer. Students can complete the cloze assignments and then print their work. The paragraphs can then be graded and included in the portfolio. For information regarding software for creating cloze passages, see Figure 18.2.

Applications and Examples

Ms. Mendez has noticed that some of her second-grade students, especially the English learners, tend to look at the first letter of a word and then guess. They don't seem to be monitoring to make sure the words they are reading make sense. She designs a cloze activity that will force them to think about the meaning of the words in the passage. It looks like this:

Jack and Jill ___ up the___. They wanted to ___ some___. On the way, Jack ___ and Jill helped him by ___.

After the students read the passage, guessing words that make sense, Ms. Mendez shows them the same passage but this time each blank has the first letter of the word displayed. The passage now looks like this:

Jack and Jill r ___ up the r___. They wanted to f ___ some bl___. On the way, Jack f ___ and Jill helped him by st ___.

The students read the passage again, using the phonic cues to help them to decide which words fit into the blanks. They discuss how their choices are different. The teacher displays the passage a third time, without any blanks, and the children read it again.

Jack and Jill ran up the road. They wanted to find some blossoms. On the way, Jack fell and Jill helped him by stopping.

Ms. Mendez and her students discuss how they have to think about what makes sense in the sentence; even when they know the first letter of the word, it is still possible to choose the wrong word. Ms. Mendez cautions them to be sure to look at the whole word. After this lesson, Ms. Mendez will remind her students frequently about the importance of thinking about the words they read and the sense they make.

Cloze activities can be used at any level. They force readers to think about the meaning of a passage and to choose words to insert in the blanks that fit the meaning, structure, and **genre** of the piece.

* * * * *

Mr. Tompson notices that his 11th-grade English language learners have difficulty making sense of poetic language in narratives. To assist them in making sense of what he calls "tough text," he prepares the following cloze passage:

E ___ for the moment at least from the t ___ of fantasy, Jose in a short time set up a s ___ of order and work which allowed for one bit of l___: The freeing of the birds, which since the time of their founding, had made m ___ with their fl ___, and installing in their place m ___ clocks in every house. (Marquez, 1970, p. 45)

FIGURE 18.2 Software for Creating Cloze Passages

Program Title	Focus of Program	Types of Available Activities	Video
Vocabulary Worksheet Factory	Create Cloze activities from any text	Variety of vocabulary exercises such as crossword puzzles, word searches, definitions, **cloze paragraphs**	https://youtu.be/a4YyMGLfO-E
MS Word	Creating a simple cloze activity using MS Word	Hiding and revealing words in text	https://youtu.be/pDb5St8z5d8
Easiteach Word Wallet	Top 10 tips for cloze activities. How to create a cloze activity in Easiteach	Using original text or cut and paste tools to create cloze activities, word sorts, etc. in a variety of curricular areas.	https://youtu.be/YJKFD-kxDM-I easiteach

The students read the passage and discuss what they think it means. Mr. Tompson leads them to the conclusion that, although they can't read every word, they can understand the main idea of the passage. They work as a group to sound out and discuss the words *emancipated*, *torment*, *system*, *license*, *merry*, *flutes*, and *musical*. The teacher's goal is met. The students believe they can understand this tough text even without knowing every word. They also learn some new vocabulary as a result of the lesson.

Conclusion

As shown by these two examples, cloze activities support English language learners by helping them to focus on meaning in reading. Although new vocabulary may be difficult for the readers, cloze activities help students to learn ways in which the context of a reading passage—in combination with their knowledge of phonics, syntax, and prior knowledge about the topic—can support their understanding of the text they read.

Examples of Approximation Behaviors Related to the TESOL Standards

PreK–3 students will:

- supply omitted words in a cloze sentence, based on context.
- suggest optional words for substitution in a sentence, based on context.

4–8 students will:

- supply omitted words in increasingly more complex text.

- identify words in context that change sentence meaning.

9–12 students will:

- identify unknown words using both sentence context and phonetic cues.
- supply words in context based on syntactic knowledge (word order and parts of speech).

References

Cheng, H. (2004). A comparison of multiple choice and open-ended response formats for the assessment of listening proficiency in English. *Foreign Language Annals, 37*(4). Pp ??

Gibbons, P. (2015). *Scaffolding language, scaffolding learning: Teaching English language learners in the mainstream classroom.* Portsmouth, NH: Heinemann.

Hinkel, E. (2006). Current perspectives on teaching the four skills. *TESOL Quarterly, 40*(1), 109–131.

Marquez, G. G. (1970). *One hundred years of solitude.* New York, NY: Avon.

Zwiers, J. (2004). *Building reading comprehension habits in grades 6–12: A toolkit of classroom activities.* Menlo Park, CA: IRA.

19

Verb Action

Teaching Irregular Verbs through Experience

Several researchers have validated the importance of providing experiences in contextualizing vocabulary to support students in connecting new vocabulary with their prior knowledge (Calderon, 2007; McIntyre, Kyle, Chen, Kraemer, & Parr, 2008; Gibbons, 2015). Marzano and Pickering (2006) found that repeated practice in the use of new vocabulary is vital to retention and use of new words by students. "Acting out" new vocabulary is also mentioned as exemplary practice in several of these studies (Kamil & Hiebert, 2005; Kamil, 2004; Nagy, 2005; Stahl, 2005). Teachers can easily identify vocabulary that students are misusing or misunderstanding by observing their verbal and written products. Based on that information, teachers can plan experiences to support students' correct usage.

Irregular verbs used in the past tense are often overgeneralized by young children simply by adding -ed to any verb. Instead of saying "He ran away," they add -ed to the base verb and say, "He runned away." English learners of all ages often make the same overgeneralizations.

As teachers observe the misuse of English words, they can provide experiences that support correct usage, along with repeated practice. Having students keep an "irregular verb journal" encourages the use of new vocabulary in writing. Posting irregular verbs and other new vocabulary on a bulletin board or chart in the classroom provides a place for students to go for self-help and reminds teachers to provide periodic review.

Step-by-Step

The steps in implementing verb action are the following:

- *Observe students and monitor written work to identify verbs that are being misused*—Keep an observation log where you can note verbs and other vocabulary that students misuse either orally or in writing. Simply note the date, student's name, and the verb that was misused. This will help you plan needed lessons as well as document the effectiveness of the lessons after they are taught.
- *Plan active experiences to practice the correct usage of identified words*—As you notice the repeated misuse of verbs, plan a lesson that includes some physical action to be performed by the students. Give the students repeated practice in using these verbs and then follow up with a written activity to give the students practice in writing the correct form of the verbs. Figure 19.1 provides suggestions for **active learning experiences** related to irregular verbs.

FIGURE 19.1 Active Experiences Related to Irregular Verbs

Verbs	Strategy	Reading/Writing/Verbal Connections
Throw and *catch* Write the words on the board and talk about how we show that we have already completed the action. Write: I <u>throw</u> the ball. I already <u>threw</u> the ball. I <u>catch</u> the ball. I have already <u>caught</u> the ball.	Use a tennis or soft foam ball. Have students toss the ball to one another. After they throw the ball, they say, "I threw the ball." After they catch the ball they say, "I caught the ball."	Have students start an irregular verb journal to record these activities. After each activity, have the students write some sentences telling what they did. For example: "I threw the ball to Joanne. She caught the ball and then threw it to José." Require a set number of sentences to be written depending on the students' abilities.
Cut and *eat*	Bring Hershey bars, apples, or a pan of brownies to class. Have each student cut the bar, apple, or brownies and then eat a piece. After they cut the food, have them say, "I cut the apple." Note that the past tense of the verb *cut* is irregular because it doesn't add *ed*. After the students eat the food have them say, "I ate the apple."	Have the students journal what they did with the food. Have them note the verb studied on the margin of the page and write what they did. For example: "I cut the candy bar, then I ate one of the pieces. José cut the candy bar, but he ate three pieces."
Write and *draw*	Have students draw a picture and write a sentence about the picture they draw.	Ask each student to tell what they did. For example, "I drew a picture of a cat. I wrote that the cat was named Kitty."
Blow and *burst*	Bring bubble soap and pipes or wands to class. Ask students to blow bubbles and then burst them. If you are working with students who are learning the names of parts of the body, you can give commands such as, "Burst the bubbles with your elbow." Then, change the body parts each time. You may want to put students into groups of two to four to help control the action.	After the activity, ask students to tell you what they did. They should tell you that they *blew* bubbles and then *burst* them. Encourage them to tell you who blew the bubbles and who burst them. After you discuss the activity, have students write about it, telling who blew the bubbles and who burst them.

Continued

Verbs	Strategy	Reading/Writing/Verbal Connections
Build and *break*	Provide students with spaghetti and mini-marshmallows. Ask them to build shapes using the spaghetti and sticking them together using the marshmallows. Encourage them to break the spaghetti whenever they need smaller pieces.	After the activity, ask students to discuss what they did, telling when they had to break the spaghetti and what they built. After the discussion, have them write several sentences in their irregular verb journal telling what they did. Provide an example such as, "Mary built two triangles. She broke one spaghetti piece into three pieces to make each triangle."
Drink, feed, and *bring*	Bring several hamsters to class and give one to each small group of students. Give them directions about feeding the animals and giving them water. After they feed and water the hamsters, discuss what they did.	Have the students write about their experience in their irregular verb journal. Ask them to start with telling about how the animals got to the classroom. Have students share what they wrote orally. Celebrate the responses and talk about the use of the past tense for, *drank, fed,* and *brought.*
Find, hang, and *hide*	Hide pictures of the students around the room. Ask students to find the pictures, label them, and hang them on a bulletin board that has been prepared with all the names of the students. After they find all the pictures, ask them to tell which pictures they found and where they hung the pictures.	Have students write in their irregular verb journals about the activity. Encourage them to tell how the pictures were hidden. After they write in their journals, have several students share what they wrote. Celebrate their responses and give extra praise to those who told who hid the pictures.
Continue to observe students and choose irregular verbs to study based on misuses that you observe.	Create a bulletin board or chart in the classroom where irregular verbs are posted as they are studied or discovered in books or writing in the classroom. Encourage students to be on the lookout for irregular verbs and post them on the bulletin board.	As additions are made to the bulletin board, take time to discuss the words and practice using them. When you hear repeated misuses of a verb, plan an active learning experience to practice using it correctly.

- *Document the activity by taking photos of students as they participate*—As the students participate in practicing the actions, take some pictures. These pictures can be used later to create a chart or bulletin board to remind students of the correct use of irregular verb forms.
- *Involve students in contributing to an irregular verb journal*—Have the students complete an irregular verb journal where they write about the experience they participated in, providing repeated use of the correct forms of the irregular verbs they practiced.
- *Create a chart, bulletin board, or word wall to provide a resource for students*—Create a bulletin board, chart, or word wall documenting the irregular verbs studied. Post the photographs of the activity to remind students of their experience. Keep the verb forms posted and encourage students to add irregular verbs to the display as they encounter them in reading or hear them in class verbalizations. Figure 19.2 is an example of this type of chart.
- *Continue to observe student oral and written usage to determine when reteaching or review is needed*—Continue to document your observations of verb and new vocabulary usage to help determine the effectiveness of the lessons. Note the dates of the activities and add examples of correct verb usage of the verbs studied as well as any continued misuse. Plan additional activities based on continued misuses. Keep a record of the lessons that provide positive results and words that need to be retaught. Base future lessons on this continued observation and documentation.

FIGURE 19.2 Irregular Verb Chart

Blow—blew	We blew bubbles.	
Draw—drew	We drew pictures.	
Cut—cut	We cut apples and candy bars.	
Eat—ate	We ate pieces of the food.	
Throw—threw	We threw the ball.	
Catch—caught	We caught the ball.	

- *Evaluate your approaches and the learning that takes place*—Use the teacher self-evaluation rubric in Figure 19.3 to evaluate your planning and implementation of verb activities. Plan new verb activities and add to your lessons to meet the higher expectations of the rubric.
- *Continue to observe and identify new verbs and other vocabulary to teach*—Continue to observe and document your students' verb and vocabulary usage and plan lessons based on verbs they still find challenging. Lists of common irregular verbs in English are available online.

Applications and Examples

Mrs. Samuels teaches kindergarten in a neighborhood where many students speak Spanish or Hmong at home. She wants her students to "actively engage in group reading activities with purpose and understanding" (CCSS.ELA-Literacy.RL.K.10), so she plans many activities to build background experiences and vocabulary with her students. To introduce words for colors and clothing, as well as *wore* and *chose*, the past tense forms of the irregular verbs *wear* and *choose*, Mrs. Samuels visits the local thrift store and purchases a variety of clothing items in sizes to fit

FIGURE 19.3 Verb Action Teacher Self-Evaluation Rubric

Beginning	Developing	Accomplished	Exemplary
Words to be studied are chosen randomly.	Words are chosen from random observations.	Words are chosen from periodic, planned observation.	Words are chosen from daily, planned observations.
Lessons include minimal active involvement of students.	Lessons include active involvement of students.	Lessons include active involvement of students, as well as opportunities for verbalization.	Lessons include active involvement, verbalization, and writing using the target words.
Lessons are done once or twice a week.	Lessons are done more than twice a week.	Lessons are done daily.	Lessons are done daily with opportunities for additional activities using the target words.
Lessons are rarely documented and little follow-up is done.	Lessons are documented.	Lessons and follow-up activities are documented.	Lessons, follow-up, and student progress are always documented.
Follow-up observation is random.	Follow-up observation and documentation are done weekly.	Follow-up observation and documentation are done daily.	Follow-up observation and documentation are done daily, and reteaching and review are done on a regular basis.

her students. She finds sweaters, scarves, jackets, and hats in several colors along with a bright red coat. She takes the clothing home, washes them, then takes them to school and piles them out on a table in the front of the classroom. Using the big book for *Mary Wore Her Red Dress* (Peek, 1988), Mrs. Samuels introduces the lesson. She reads the book aloud, points to each word as she reads it, and points to illustrations to help the students understand the story. Mrs. Samuels chooses one of the students to go to the front of the class and select an item of clothing from the pile and put it on. She then teaches a song to the tune of "London Bridge Is Falling Down" to review the name of the item that the student chose, the color of the item, and the past tense of *choose* and *wear*. The song goes, "Pablo chose a red coat, red coat, red coat. Pablo chose a red coat from the pile. Pablo wore the red coat, red coat, red coat. Pablo wore the red coat, with a smile." After teaching the song, Mrs. Samuels asks another student to come up and choose from the pile of clothing. As each student chooses an item and puts it on, Mrs. Samuels and the class sing with the student, practicing the names of the clothing pieces, the color words, and the correct form of the verb. Each student gets to choose an item of clothing and have the song sung about him or her.

During center time, Mrs. Samuels helps the students write about the experience. She has prepared large sheets of blank paper. On the bottom of each page Mrs. Samuels has written: _____ chose a _____ _____ from the pile. She helps students to write their names on the first blank, the color of the items chosen on the next line, and the name of the item of clothing on the last line. For example, Pablo's paper reads, "Pablo chose a red coat."

Some of the students know many of the letters to use to represent the first sound in the words. Those students can write the letter to represent the first sound. Others need more support. Using interactive writing (see Chapter 13), each student is able to complete a sentence in writing. After reading the sentence several times, the students go to their seats to illustrate the sentence they wrote. Each student in the class completes this activity.

Later in the day, Mrs. Samuels has each student come up to display the page he or she completed. The students read the sentence they wrote and then Mrs. Samuels comments on the picture, using the word *drew* several times. For example: "José *drew* a picture of himself wearing the red boots. Look, he *drew* a big smile on his face. He also *drew* the red boots so they look very big. He *drew* his blue shirt, and he *drew* his blue jeans, too. What a nice picture he *drew*." Mrs. Samuels binds the students' pages together to create a big book and places it in the reading corner. She sees her students constantly revisiting the experience while lying on the floor, reading the lines about what each student wore that day. They ask to repeat the process a few days later, and they all get to choose a new item of clothing to wear. There are many laughs and giggles as the others sing to them about what they are wearing. Mrs. Samuels is quite pleased with the results, saying, "The second time we did the activity the students *all* knew the names and colors for each item of clothing."

* * * * *

Mr. Michaels teaches middle school English/language arts in an economically challenged neighborhood. Most of his students speak English at home, but their vocabularies and experiences are limited. He has a few English learners in each of his classes. He observes that many students have trouble with the past tense of irregular verbs and all have limited vocabularies. He plans activities to build their vocabulary and provide practice in correctly using the past tense of irregular verbs, while also addressing the Common Core Anchor Standard to "demonstrate command of the conventions of standard English grammar and usage when writing or speaking" (CCSS.ELA-LITERACY .CCRA.L.1). He locates photos online for several items of clothing, kitchen utensils, furniture, and other everyday items that he has noticed his students cannot always name. He prints the photos and creates five identical decks of cards with the pictures on them. He also creates a folder on his computer with the pictures.

To begin the lesson, Mr. Michaels displays the deck of cards he has created, telling the students, "We are going to play a card game today. Before we play the game, we will review the names of the pictures on the cards. He uses the file of pictures from his computer to display them on the interactive whiteboard in his classroom. As he shows each picture, he asks students to name the object and tell how it is used. For example, when he shows a knife, a student might say, "That is a knife. We use it to cut our food." If no one knows the name of the item, Mr. Michaels talk about it. As the items are identified, their names are added to the pictures on the board. After the items are all identified, Mr. Michaels adds "headings" to the top of the board, and the class works together to sort them into categories: CLOTHING, FUR-NITURE, KITCHEN ITEMS, and OUTDOOR THINGS. He invites individual students to come up to the board and use their finger to drag a picture to its appropriate category. If a student has difficulty, he may ask the class where he should put it, or Mr. Michaels may ask another student to come up and assist.

After the categorizing is complete, Mr. Michaels then explains the rules for playing a card game called *Go Fish*. They must ask each other questions in order to get cards. "Do you have any furniture?" The other student must then answer, "Yes, I have a couch," or "No, I don't have any furniture." If they have a card in the category requested, they would pass that card to the student asking the question. The student who was asked the question then has the opportunity to ask a similar question to another student, using one of the categories. Mr. Michaels uses the whiteboard to review words they might need to play the game like *deal*, *pass*, *categories*, and so on. The students are divided into five groups, and each group plays a game of *Go Fish*. When they collect a set of four items in a category, they lay the set down, face up, and continue to play until someone has laid down all of his or her cards.

After the card game, the students write in their writing journals. Before they write, Mr. Michaels talks to them about words they should use in their journals and writes the required words on the whiteboard. He says, "You must tell how the cards got to the classroom. When you 'bring' something, we say you *brought* it." Then, he writes the word *brought* on the board.

"You must tell who *dealt* the cards. When you give everyone cards, we say you *deal* them. After you have done that, we say you *dealt* them." He writes the word *dealt* on the board.

"When the game is finished and someone wins, we say, 'Someone *won* the game.'" He writes the word *won* on the board.

"To help you remember each of these words, practice saying and using them as you play. After each game you need to write in your writing journals, so practice these words so you can use them when you write. After someone deals the cards, practice saying, 'Karen dealt the cards.' As you lay down sets in the game say, 'I laid down a set of furniture. The set is a couch, a chair, a table, and a lamp.' This will help the other people to make sure your set is really a set. At the end of the game say who won. After each game, write in your writing journals. If there is enough time, you can play another game."

The students enjoy the game, and most of the groups manage to complete three games within the 45-minute period. At the end of the period, Mr. Michaels has students from each group tell about what their group did using the required words. He has them come up to the board and draw circles around the words that their group used during the game and in their journals.

Conclusion

Building vocabulary, especially building a repertoire of irregular English verbs, requires multiple active approaches and much repetition. Using strategies that actively involve students provides them with experiences they can remember. This supports the retention of new vocabulary and irregular verbs. These activities require prior planning but need not consume an inordinate amount of classroom time. Having students process the words orally and in writing helps them to retain the vocabulary. Keeping a chart of irregular verbs displayed in the classroom helps students and the teacher to remember to use those verbs. The chart can also be used by the teacher to provide subtle corrections. If a student uses an incorrect verb form, the teacher can simply point to the word on the chart. Remember that keeping your voice, facial expression, and body language positive and friendly helps to reduce stress in students when they are corrected.

Examples of Approximation Behaviors Related to the TESOL Standards

PreK–3 students will:

- supply verbs in a sentence based on actions performed.
- suggest endings for verbs based on when the action occurred.

4–8 students will:

- supply correct irregular past tense verbs in increasingly more complex text.

- identify words in context that change sentence meaning related to when the action occurred.

9–12 students will:

- identify verbs that use irregular endings using both written and oral forms.
- correct their own errors when using irregular verbs in writing and oral speech.

References

Calderon, M. (2007). *Teaching reading to English language learners, grades 6–12. A framework for improving achievement in the content areas*. Thousand Oaks, CA: Corwin Press.

Gibbons, P. (2015). *Scaffolding language, scaffolding learning: Teaching English language learners in the mainstream classroom* (2nd ed.). Portsmouth, NH: Heinemann.

Marzano, R. J., & Pickering, D. J. (2006). *Building academic vocabulary: Teacher's manual.* Alexandria, VA: Association for Supervision and Curriculum Development.

McIntyre, E., Kyle, D. W., Chen, C.-T., Kraemer, J., & Parr, J. (2008). *Six principles for teaching English language learners in all classrooms*. Thousand Oaks, CA: Corwin Press.

Peek, M. (1988). *Mary wore her red dress and Henry wore his green sneakers*. Evanston, IL: HMH Books for Young Readers.

Grade	Center	Description
Upper elementary	Science Center	Students use materials in this center to replicate experiments demonstrated by the teacher.
	Observation Center	Students use this center to closely observe and write observations of nature and art, videotapes of performances in music, dance, and athletics.
	Theater Center	Students use this center to write scripts for scenes of their favorite books, enlist the help of peers to practice the scene, and then present it to the class.
	Editing Center	Students use this center to collaboratively edit student writing that is almost ready to be published. The center includes thesaurus, dictionaries, and English grammar texts.
Middle and high school	Logic Center	Student use this center to create "brainbenders," logic problems that can be solved by other students using props provided or made by the students.
	Video Center	Videocamera, tripod, and tapes are available in this center so students can videotape scenes from literature, vocabulary role-play, book commercials written by students, enactments of history, etc.
	Research Center	Encyclopedias, reference books, a computer with Internet access are all available at this center to encourage student research on topics under study in the classroom.
	Multiple Intelligences Center	Eight different ways of studying a topic are presented in centers corresponding to Gardner's Eight Intelligences (soon to be expanded to nine). Students are encouraged to: 1. write a song about the topic in the Musical Intelligence Center. 2. write a poem about the topic in the Linguistic Intelligence Center. 3. debate the topic with a peer in the Interpersonal Intelligence Center. 4. write in a personal journal about the topic in the Intrapersonal Intelligence Center. 5. write a logic or word problem about the topic in the Logical/Mathematical Intelligence Center. 6. draw a poster about the topic in the Visual/Spatial Intelligence Center. 7. choreograph a dance or mime in the Bodily/Kinesthetic Intelligence Center. 8. Use leaves or other natural objects to create props for the video center.

- How does she make her expectations clear?
- What does she do to help her English learners understand what to do?

- *Document the center work*—Introduce a method for students to document their participation in centers. This can be a simple list of names at the required centers, a contract form on which the students enter the names of the centers they will complete each day, or a work folder in which they place all center work completed each day. Students have to understand the requirements and the ways in which the center work will be assessed. Make sure your expectations are clear as to which centers are required and which are optional.

• *Bring students up-to-date*—Whenever centers are changed, repeat the explanation and model the steps so that students clearly understand what is required. Centers should be changed regularly so that students are challenged and provided with opportunities to practice new skills as they are taught.

• *Assess student progress and understanding*—It is vital that teachers validate and evaluate the work students do in learning centers or the students will not take their center work seriously. Teachers should set up a method for collecting and assessing the quality of center work. Celebration circles are one way of gathering students together to share their accomplishments during center time, and they provide the teacher with an opportunity to encourage students who are using their center time productively. Center products are good additions to the individual student portfolios as well.

Enhanced eText
Video Example 22.2

• *Add technology*—Computer centers are a powerful way of providing extra skill practice in a unique mode. Student-made PowerPoint presentations represent a good use of center time, as well. Some teachers have found the scripting and shooting of class videos to be fascinating and highly creative center activities. The students in this video are actively involved in the learning process. As you watch, consider the following questions:

• How is the use of technology enhancing the learning environment?
• Does the use of these learning centers enlarge student understanding of the functions of bar graphs?

Applications and Examples

The third graders in Mr. Martino's class are learning to write friendly letters. He has a number of students who are learning English as their second language, and he wants to make sure they have opportunities for extended practice with their newly acquired English writing skills. Mr. Martino decides that he will introduce a series of learning centers that will enable his students to practice writing letters and produce a class newsletter, which will give them **authentic practice** in writing in several domains. Using the computer to process and publish the newsletter will also ensure that students have an opportunity to "with guidance and support from adults, use technology to produce and publish writing (using keyboarding skills) as well as to interact and collaborate with others" (CCSS.ELA-LITERACY.W.3.5). The centers he sets up in his classroom will support the letter-writing project and expand it so that the students practice writing letters for different purposes.

Mr. Martino begins by creating a life-size mailbox out of a cardboard box that originally housed a washing machine. He sets up a Mail Processing Center in which students must cancel the student-designed stamps on the incoming letters and place them into alphabetized letter cubbies labeled with the third-grade students' names. Mr. Marino also creates a mail cubby for the kindergartners, so his students can also write to them. The instructions in the Mail Processing Center say, "Take the mail out of the mail collection box. Cancel the stamps using the mail cancellation stamp. If anyone mailed a letter without putting a stamp on it, stamp it 'Return to Sender' and place it in the mailbox of the person who sent it. Use the alphabetical sorting tray to sort the letters with canceled stamps alphabetically and then place them into the mail cubbies."

Mr. Martino recently taught proofreading to his class, so he also sets up a class project to create a newsletter using the computer. Students are encouraged to write articles for the class newsletter.

Mr. Martino sets up centers where the students will write articles and letters for the newsletter. These centers include:

- News Article Center—students write articles about class, school, and community news.
- Sports News Center—students write articles about sports activities in the school and community.
- Literary Review Center—students write reviews of books they've read.
- Letters to the Editor Center—students write letters related to problems or concerns they have.
- Dear Anna Center—students write and respond to letters to the advice columnist.
- Cartoons Center—students draw cartoons for the newsletter.
- Proofreading Center—students proofread all submitted articles and letters.
- Computer Center—students key in their corrected articles and letters and save them in the newsletter file.

Mr. Martino takes his students through the centers, carefully modeling what is expected at each center. He shows the students how they cross their name off the list at each center after they work in the center and how they list their center work on the daily work schedule each day. Figure 22.2 is the daily work schedule Mr. Martino uses to keep track of the centers the students are using and the quality of the work they are accomplishing.

The students in Mr. Tanaka's eighth-grade humanities class are discussing *The House on Mango Street* by Sandra Cisneros (1984). Esperanza, one of the characters in Sandra Cisneros's book, writes poetry. She shares her poetry with an aunt who later dies, leaving Esperanza no one with whom to share her poetry. Mr. Tanaka discusses this character and her poetry with his class one day. He wants to interest them in writing poetry but also support their understanding of the role of their home cultures in the types of poetry that is written.

"How many of you have ever tried to write poetry?" he asks. No one raises a hand. "Well," Mr. Tanaka says slowly, "I think it's time we tried."

A soft moan is heard in the class. "I want to introduce you to a variety of ways of writing poems," Mr. Tanaka says. "You might have noticed that the poems Esperanza writes don't rhyme. She tries to create a picture with words."

FIGURE 22.2 Mr. Martino's Daily Work Schedule

	Completed?	Self-Rating
Name _____ Date _____		
Work I accomplished today:	Completed?	Self-Rating
News article on _____	Yes No	1 2 3 4 5
Sports article on _____	Yes No	1 2 3 4 5
Letter to the editor on _____	Yes No	1 2 3 4 5
Letter to Dear Anna on _____	Yes No	1 2 3 4 5
Cartoon on _____	Yes No	1 2 3 4 5
Proofread _____ articles on _____	Yes No	1 2 3 4 5
Typed articles on _____	Yes No	1 2 3 4 5
Processed mail on _____	Yes No	1 2 3 4 5
Other reading or writing: _____	Yes No	1 2 3 4 5
Conference with teacher on _____		
Teacher comments: _____		
Plans for tomorrow: _____		

FIGURE 22.3 Cinquain and Diamonte Formula Poetry

A cinquain is a five-line poem with lines written in the following arrangement:

Line 1:   a one-word subject with two syllables
Line 2:   four syllables describing the subject
Line 3:   six syllables of action words relating to the subject
Line 4:   eight syllables expressing a feeling or a thought about the subject
Line 5:   two syllables describing or renaming the subject

An example of a cinquain written by a second grader:

Sneakers

smelly, dirty

jumping, turning, squeaking

They are so comfortable now!

grungy

A diamonte is a seven-line poem that is written in the shape of a diamond. This poetic form helps students demonstrate their understanding of opposites. A diamonte poem is written using this formula:

Line 1:   one noun as the subject
Line 2:   two adjectives describing the subject
Line 3:   three participles (ending in "ing") telling about the subject
Line 4:   four nouns; the first two tell about the subject, the second two tell about the opposite
Line 5:   three participles telling about the opposite
Line 6:   two adjectives describing the opposite
Line 7:   one noun that is the opposite of the subject

An example of a diamonte written by a seventh grader:

Winter

Cool and crisp

Rushing, reading, cramming

Books, papers, ball games, beaches

Sunning, swimming, playing

Hot and sweaty

Summer

Mr. Tanaka begins the study of poetry forms by teaching the eighth graders how to write concrete poems where they write a sentence or two creating a visual image with words and then arrange the words on the page to create a picture. He also teaches the class the formula for writing **cinquain** and **diamonte poems** (see Figure 22.3). Mr. Tanaka teaches formula poetry so that his students will "use precise words and phrases, relevant descriptive details, and sensory language to capture the action and convey experiences and events" (CCSS. ELA-LITERACY.W.8.3).

After he demonstrates and gives the class guided practice in writing poems in these three formats, Mr. Tanaka sets up a learning center where the students can gain extra experience in writing formula poems. He uses the word banks that the class has created in learning how to write formula poems, and he places the words in pocket charts so that the students can rearrange them into cinquain and diamonte poems. The forms of language in these poetry formats support the students' knowledge of English because they must use certain forms within the structure of the poems, nouns, verbs, and so on. Once the students have built poems in the center, Mr. Tanaka encourages them to recopy them on a single sheet of paper and leave them in the box at the learning center so that he can later bind the poems into a class poetry book. Mr. Tanaka reads the poems in the box each day and frequently asks permission to read them aloud in class. Sometimes the author asks him not to tell who wrote the poem and sometimes the poem is written in the student's home language. Mr. Tanaka shows appreciation for the students' efforts and gives

FIGURE 22.4 Mr. Tanaka's Poetry Center

them feedback on ways in which they can improve their poetry. He asks students to read and translate the poems for him if he can't read the language. Figure 22.4 shows how Mr. Tanaka's Poetry Center is arranged.

As the study of writing and culture continues, Mr. Tanaka gradually teaches a number of skills and strategies to his students. As the lessons are taught, Mr. Tanaka sets up additional learning centers in the classroom to provide additional practice for the students. Before long, the students are all working in centers while Mr. Tanaka works with small groups of students on the projects they are creating. The classroom centers provide Mr. Tanaka with time to give small-group instruction while his students are working on strengthening their writing and researching skills. Mr. Tanaka created the following centers in the classroom:

- Poetry Center—students create formula poems.
- Internet Research Center—students can search for information related to the culture project on which they are working.
- Webbing and Clustering Center—students create prewriting webs or clusters to get them started in writing.
- Art Center—students create visuals to enhance the writing and presentations being prepared.
- Unforgettable Character Center—a different character from *The House on Mango Street* is highlighted each day. The students read the short chapter about a character and either create an illustration for the chapter read, or they write a description of a character who is brought to mind by the Cisneros character and create an illustration for the new character. This center was added after a lesson on characterization and the four ways in which authors create characters: what they say, what they do, what they think, and how they look (Tompkins, 1998).
- Video Center—students create a short video to be used as a part of their project presentation. This video should represent a part of their culture that is difficult to depict without a visual image, such as typical verbal interactions, body language, personal space, or important artifacts. The video created in this center may be a simulation or a series of video clips made in the community or home, edited together using the simple editing equipment in the center.

- Elements of Culture Center—Mr. Tanaka selects a quote from Edward T. Hall's book *Beyond Culture* (1981) and posts it each day. The students are instructed to read the quote and record their response to it on a small voice recorder he has placed in the center. They may work alone or in pairs, and they may respond in English or their home language. After they have reflected on the quote of the day, students are to include the quote and their reflection in their culture report in some way—as a visual, a part of a video clip, or in writing. The quotes Mr. Tanaka uses include thoughts like the following:

> It [time] is also tangible; they speak of it as being saved, spent, wasted, lost, made up, accelerated, slowed down, crawling, and running out. (p. 19)

At the end of the month-long study, Mr. Tanaka's students have a new vision of culture and its place in shaping their beliefs and priorities. They discuss differences in cultures with peers of their same ethnic background and discover that their assumptions are not identical. The learning centers have given them opportunities to expand their skills with practice over time. The students have had extensive experience in using the Internet for research, and they have all read and discussed two pieces of literature that have helped them to broaden their understanding of literature, poetry, and culture: *The House on Mango Street* and *Beyond Culture*.

Conclusion

The use of learning centers in the classroom is a powerful way to encourage students to practice the new skills they are gaining. Centers should be thoroughly explained to students so that they understand what is expected of them as they use the center. Both behavior and learning expectations must be made clear for the centers to support learning.

Well-planned centers enable students to refine their skills, expand their uses of newly acquired skills, and create new and different ways to demonstrate their learning. They are especially effective for English learners because they provide additional practice in newly developed skills and allow students to demonstrate their learning in a variety of ways. To harness the power of learning centers in the classroom, students must be encouraged to go beyond basic skills practice and find ways to be creative. Students should see their efforts recognized, valued, and celebrated if they are to expend maximum effort in learning center work.

Examples of Approximation Behaviors Related to the TESOL Standards

PreK–3 students will:

- follow modeled oral directions to participate successfully in learning centers.
- ask for assistance from peers to succeed at the learning center task.

4–8 students will:

- use materials in a structured way to construct or discover a specific learning objective.

- extend skills through independent practice based on classroom instruction.

9–12 students will:

- build on skills and information taught in class to solve real-life problems.
- use writing skills to create an innovative composition.

References

Bunch, G., Lotan, R., Valdes, G., & Cohen, E. (2005) Keeping content at the heart of content-based instruction: Access and support for transitional English learners. In D. Kaufman & J. Crandall (Eds.), *Content-based instruction in primary and secondary school settings* (pp. 11–25). Alexandria, VA: TESOL

Cisneros, S. (1984). *The house on Mango Stree*t. New York, NY: Vintage Books.

Freeman, Y., & Freeman, D. (2003) Struggling English learners: Keys for academic success. *TESOL Journal 12*(3), 5–10.

Haley, M., & Austin, T. (2004). *Content-based second language teaching and learning.* Boston, MA: Pearson Education.

Hall, E. (1981). *Beyond culture.* New York, NY: Doubleday.

Martin, S., & Green, A. (2012) Striking a balance: Advancing English language learners' linguistic fluency through learning centers. *The Science Teacher, 79*(4), 40–43.

Tompkins, G. (2012). *Language arts: Patterns of learning* (8th ed.). Upper Saddle River, NJ: Merrill/Prentice Hall.

23

Communication Games
Creating Opportunities for Verbal Interaction

Communication games (Ferlazzo & Sypnieski, 2012; Gibbons, 2015) are classroom activities that create opportunities and purposes for listening and verbal communication practice. Many times, the purpose of the communication in these games is to convey information or cause something to occur as a result of the activity. Some games provide practice in the use of a particular language function such as giving directions or asking questions. Other games require students to work together and communicate to solve a problem. Games are sometimes used in classrooms to develop and reinforce concepts, to add interest to the regular activities, and even to break the ice. Perhaps their most important function, however, is to give practice in communication skills (Richard-Amato, 1996). Suggested communication games are shown in Figure 23.1.

Step-by-Step

The steps in teaching communication games are the following:

- *Identify a language need*—Identify a language function in which your students need practice. Following directions, asking questions, and conveying academic information are among some of the most commonly used in communication games. Choose a communication game category from Figure 23.1.
- *Model the game*—Model the way the game is played by involving one or more students in demonstrating the game. Review the rules carefully, and post them in the room so that students can refer to them during the activity.
- *Organize the pairs or groups*—Organize the students in pairs or small groups, making sure you have a fairly fluent English speaker in each pair or group. Give the pairs or groups their tasks and get them started.
- *Guide the practice*—Move around the room providing support and encouragement.
- *Talk about the experience*—After the game, ask students to share their experiences, any problems they had, and the solutions they devised. Make a list of the vocabulary they found helpful, and discuss how it was used.
- *Assess the students' abilities to communicate orally*—As you observe their interactions, note which students need more practice with these types of activities. Provide small-group

FIGURE 23.1 Suggested Communication Games

Activity	Description	Example
Barrier games	Two students sit back-to-back or behind a screen (barrier). One student is given a complete set of instructions that must be conveyed verbally to the second student, who completes the task.	One student has a set of small colored blocks that must be arranged in a certain configuration. The other student, working from a diagram, gives oral directions to the student with the blocks so that the blocks end up in the proper configuration.
Information sharing	Each student has part of the information necessary to complete a task or solve a problem. They must share their information to accomplish the task.	Students are given materials to fold an origami flower. Each student has one section of the directions. Using the sequence words as a guide, the students take turns reading the directions silently and then conveying them orally so the members of the group can complete the folding task.
Inquiry and elimination	A small group of students works together. One student has a set of information that must be obtained by the others through questioning and elimination of irrelevant items. The group then decides the solution based upon their inquiry.	The class has been studying insects. The child designated as the expert in the group is given the name of an insect and a set of facts about that insect. By asking questions, the students must gather enough information about the insect so that they can determine which insect is described. When they have guessed the correct insect, they have also reviewed their knowledge of that insect.
Rank ordering	Students work together in a small group to suggest solutions to a problem and then reach consensus as to the rank order of the usefulness of each of the solutions.	The groups are asked to make a shopping list of important supplies to purchase for a camping trip. They are to brainstorm items and then rank order the importance of the items so that they could survive if they could take only the top five items. Food and water don't have to be listed; the groups are assured of having them.

Source: Ferlazzo and Sypnieski (2012) and Gibbons (1993).

▶ Enhanced eText
Video Example 23.1
Ehttps://www.youtube.com/
watch?v=8yGhNwDMT-g

guided practice to teach vocabulary, such as directional words or size and texture words, that will enable students to be more successful in future communication games. Enjoy this video on organizing and executing a basic communication game that will encourage students to listen and communicate to accomplish a simple task.

Applications and Examples

Ms. Darling's kindergartners are learning colors and shapes. She wants them to practice using the new vocabulary they are learning, so she designs a barrier game using attribute blocks—blocks in various geometric shapes and colors (construction paper shapes in a variety of colors will also work). She finds that games requiring lots of verbal interaction provide a strong incentive for English learners to practice their language skills. She explains to the students that they will be playing a game. She asks Tony to help her teach the game. Tony comes to the front of the room and uses the shapes designed for the overhead projector to follow Ms. Darling's oral directions. Ms. Darling shows the class the drawing she is holding and tells them, "This is the design that I want Tony to make. I will give him directions. He can't see the design. I have to tell him how to make it."

"The design is in a straight line," she tells Tony. "I will tell you the shapes to put in the line. Start at the left and move across the glass from left to right, like you do when you read. First, find the large red circle, and put it at the top of the projector."

Tony places the large red circle at the top of the glass on the left side. Ms. Darling is standing with her back to him, so she waits until he tells her he is ready for the next direction. "You will be sitting behind a screen, so you won't be able to see what your partner is doing. You have to talk to each other in order to build the design," Ms. Darling reminds the students. "Next, find the small green circle, and put it next to the large red circle," Ms. Darling says. Tony follows her directions.

Once the demonstration is complete, Ms. Darling arranges the students in pairs and places small science project boards between the pairs as barriers. She starts each pair with a simple design. They come to her for a new design when they finish the first one, and they take turns giving instructions. Ms. Darling moves around the room giving encouragement and language scaffolding as needed. After the activity, the class discusses the words that they used. Lara says, "It was hard. You had to remember a lot of things to say. The shape and the color and the size—a lot!"

Ms. Darling acknowledges Lara's comment, "Yes, it was hard. You had to use a lot of math language. You did a good job!"

* * * * *

Mr. Standford's 10th-grade English class is completing a study of *The Canterbury Tales* (Chaucer, 1365/1934). Because Chaucer's language is so difficult, Mr. Standford reads the Geraldine McCaughrean (1984) version of the stories aloud, comparing the simplified, illustrated version with the language in the older, more traditional version. Occasionally, Mr. Standford even reads the Middle English words to give the students a feel for the original. To provide a review of the work before the unit exam, Mr. Standford gives the students practice in discussing the tales and reviewing the information they have about each of them. He begins the lesson with an explanation, "Today we will be reviewing *The Canterbury Tales* so that you will all do well on the exam on Monday. You will be working in small groups to identify the main characters in the tales, their characteristics, and their stories. Let me show you how this will work."

Mr. Standford asks three students to come to the front of the class and ask him questions about the tales. He sets the stage for them. "You can ask me questions, which I must answer truthfully. You cannot ask me to name the character or tell you things directly about the character, but you can ask questions that can be answered with 'Yes' or 'No.' The person who is being questioned will have the character's name and the information about the character and tale so that the answers given will be accurate."

One student asks Mr. Standford if the character is a man. He answers, "No."

The next student asks if the character had animals. Mr. Standford answers, "No."

The third student asks if she was married several times. Mr. Standford answers, "Yes."

The first student then asks, "Is it the Wife of Bath?" Mr. Standford answers, "Yes."

The group then discusses how they eliminated characters as the questions were answered. They agreed that eliminating the men really narrowed the possibilities. They then reviewed the information about the Wife of Bath and her tale on the review sheet.

Mr. Standford divides the class into groups of four students and gives one student in each group a review sheet so that they are ready to field questions. He makes sure that there are strong students in each group. Each group has a copy of both the simplified, illustrated version and the more traditional version of the tales so they can check the accuracy of their answers.

Mr. Standford moves around the room as the questioning takes place. As each group reviews the characters, they take turns fielding questions. Mr. Standford saves the more easily recognizable characters for the English language learners and supports the students in returning to the texts whenever anyone needs help in answering questions. The students find they know a lot about the characters and the tales.

Conclusion

Communication games can be used at many grade levels and across all curricular areas as shown by the vignettes. Providing students with authentic reasons to communicate in English gives them opportunities to practice their English communication skills in a low-stress environment. Students are more likely to be successful because the situations are explained in advance, the vocabulary is practiced, and the context is built into the exercises. By lowering the stress level, making the activities game-like, and providing examples of vocabulary and sentence structure, the teacher reduces the affective filter for all students involved in the activity (Gibbons, 2002).

Examples of Approximation Behaviors Related to the TESOL Standards

PreK–3 students will:

- use listening skills in playing games.
- use verbal directions in playing games.

4–8 students will:

- use verbal descriptions to cause actions in others.

- follow a sequence of verbal directions to create a product.

9–12 students will:

- combine information in verbal directions to solve problems.
- give a sequence of directions and information to help another create a product.

References

Chaucer, G. (1934). *The Canterbury tales* (J. Nicolson, Trans.). New York, NY: Crown. (Original work published 1365)

Ferlazzo, L., & Sypnieski, K. (2012). *The ESL/ELL teacher's survival guide.* San Francisco, CA: Jossey-Bass.

Gibbons, P. (1993). *Learning to learn in a second language.* Portsmouth, NH: Heinemann.

Gibbons, P. (2015). *Scaffolding language, scaffolding learning: Teaching second language learners in the mainstream classroom* (2^{online} ed.). Portsmouth, NH: Heinemann.

McCaughrean, G. (1984). *The Canterbury tales.* Chicago, IL: Rand McNally.

Richard-Amato, P. (1996). *Making it happen.* White Plains, NY: Longman.

Cognate Strategies

Using the Home Language to Support English Acquisition

Words in two languages that share a similar meaning, spelling, and pronunciation are called **cognates**. While English may share few cognates with a language like Chinese, many of the world's languages share a linguistic base that produces cognates with English words. For instance, 30–40 percent of all words in English have a related word in Spanish. As teachers working with Spanish-speaking English language learners, cognates are an obvious bridge to the English language (¡Colorín Colorado!, 2007). For the purpose of suggesting strategies for using cognates with English language learners, in this chapter we will provide examples using Spanish–English cognates. Obviously many or most of the "romance languages" have cognates.

"Teaching English vocabulary is effective, but progress may be most rapid when this instruction is connected to the students' home language, such as providing a home-language equivalent or synonym for new words or focusing on shared cognates when available" (August et al., 2008). To appreciate the power of using students' first language to help them acquire English vocabulary, view Video Example 24.1 and think about how the students' backgrounds and home languages are used to foster learning. Consider the following questions:

Enhanced eText
Video Example 24.1

- In what ways is being bilingual a help in understanding vocabulary?
- How does the teacher's attitude toward second-language learners make an impact on learning?

Language acquisition researchers have found that students benefit from being aware of cognates (August, Carlo, Dressler, & Snow, 2005). Cognate awareness enables students to use words in their home language to help understand English words. Children can be taught to use cognates as early as preschool. Read-aloud strategies using quality picture books such as Charlotte Zolotow Award books have been found to support comprehension in English due to the high number of cognates used in these books (Montelongo, Hernandez & Herter, 2016). Using quality picture books with primary students and beginning English learners provides them with an asset as they continue their English acquisition. The knowledge that cognates support their English understanding facilitates the acquisition of academic vocabulary as more than 70% of the 570 words on the Academic Word List (AWL) are English-Spanish cognates (Lubliner & Heibert 2011).

As students progress through the grades, they can be introduced to more sophisticated cognates. They can also be introduced to cognates that have multiple meanings in both languages, although those multiple meanings don't always apply to both languages. One example of a cognate with multiple meanings is *asistir*, which means to *assist* (same meaning in English) but also to *attend* (different meaning). Using cognate study integrated throughout the curriculum provides another asset to the bilingual student giving the knowledge of two languages a positive attribute in a world that often views second language learners as having a deficit.

Knowing a word implies several things: its literal meaning, its various connotations, the sorts of sentences it fits, and semantic associations such as synonyms and antonyms (August et al., 2005). Second-language learners often have limited depth-of-word knowledge, even for frequently used words. Studies have found cognate instruction to be extremely beneficial in supporting cognate transfer in English learners (Dressler, 2000; Montelongo, Hernandez, & Herter, 2016).

Step-by-Step

(Note: For the purpose of giving examples of cognate instruction, we will use Spanish-English cognates. However, cognates exist in many other languages.)
The steps in using cognate instruction are the following:

- *Identify cognates for words being taught in English*—Before introducing a text to your students, identify words in the text that have cognates. You may find a large number of cognates, in which case you should select the ones most important for students to understand the meaning of the text. Lists of cognates in many languages are available online.

- *Provide instruction in the meanings of English and Spanish cognates*—Before reading the text, introduce students to the cognates important for understanding the meaning of the reading. Write the Spanish word and ask a Spanish speaker to pronounce the word. Then write the English word next to the Spanish word. Identify the parts of the words that are the same and note any differences in the spellings. Ask a student to explain the meaning of the words. Provide visuals if available. Use the words in several sentences to demonstrate how they are used. Provide students with other forms of each word. For example, for *centro/center* you may explain that the word *center* is sometimes used in a sentence like "Understanding the meanings of words is *central* to understanding the story. It still means 'in the middle' or important, in this case. Another example might be, 'He was the center of attention.' In this case the word means that all the attention was on him. He was important."

- *Focus on spelling differences between the two languages*—Note that the main cores of cognates are spelled the same, but the endings are different. As you identify more cognates, help the students to notice the familiar patterns to the Spanish endings.

- *Post cognates as they are studied*—Continue to post new cognates as they are discovered. Encourage students to find cognates to add to a class cognate chart. Use the chart to help support the understanding of word meanings whenever you are reading or writing. If a student struggles with verbalizations in English, locate a cognate on the chart to help the student make a word choice in English. Stress the number of words that are similar in the two languages. Video Example 24.2 has suggestions for additional ways to use cognates to enhance the learning of English.

Enhanced eText
Video Example 24.2

- *Adapt your cognate strategies to meet the English language development levels of your students*—Use Figure 24.1 to plan adaptations for your students at various levels of English language development.

- *Vary your cognate instruction approaches*—Include cognate study across the curriculum and vary the ways you identify cognates. Continue to stress the ways in which knowing cognates supports your understanding of English. Encourage English-only students to identify Spanish cognates as well. Figure 24.2 offers suggestion for varying cognate study.

- *Observe students to determine the need for reteaching or additional guided practice*—Continue to observe your students, document their progress, and reteach the use of cognates when they struggle with English vocabulary if there are cognates that support understanding.

FIGURE 24.1 Adapting Cognate Instruction for Different English Language Development Levels

Preproduction	Early Production	Early Intermediate	Later Intermediate Fluency	Early Fluency
Provide visuals or gestures to support understanding.	Provide choices of words to let students show their understanding. Say a word in English that has a Spanish cognate. Ask the students to identify a picture of the word.	Choose challenging words from a text that students are reading. Write a word on the board and have students identify the cognate in Spanish. Then have students read the English sentence from the text. Write the English and Spanish cognates next to one another on the board.	Choose challenging words and words that have similar meanings. Explore the nuances of meaning in words similar to those that have Spanish cognates. For example, *admitir* in Spanish means "admit to" in English. Discuss other words such as *confess* and how it has a similar meaning.	Continue to explore nuances of meaning. Have Spanish speakers read Spanish definitions aloud when needed to clarify meaning.
Teacher models using a simple Spanish–English dictionary with pictures and uses the pictures to support understanding.	Teacher models using a Spanish–English dictionary.	Teacher begins guided practice in using a Spanish–English dictionary.	Teacher continues to provide guided practice in dictionary use.	Teacher provides support for students to use Spanish–English dictionaries independently.

- *Encourage students to post cognates in their writing journals*—As students write in their writing journals, encourage them to keep a running list of the cognates they identify to help them broaden their writing vocabularies.
- *Stop frequently to ask students to verbalize word meanings*—When discussing text meaning in language arts, science, social sciences, or any content, stop to discuss the meanings of words. Accept a Spanish cognate as a definition when it's appropriate, and then have the student or another student give the meaning in English.
- *Evaluate your own use of cognate strategies*—Use the teacher self-evaluation rubric in Figure 24.3 to evaluate periodically and improve your use of cognate strategies. Continue to work to improve your cognate strategy use and develop more supportive approaches in your classroom.

Applications and Examples

Mr. Marshall teaches third grade in a school where the student population is about 40 percent native Spanish speakers. His students are making good progress in both reading and mathematics but find the vocabulary in science challenging. He often uses a science-based book for oral reading so that he can reinforce science concepts and vocabulary as well as expressive reading. He has

FIGURE 24.2 Activities for Cognate Study

Raise your hand!	Students raise their hands whenever they hear or read a word that has a Spanish cognate. This can be used during read-aloud, text reading, or classroom discussions.
Highlight words that have Spanish cognates	Provide written texts that have been copied so that students can mark on them. Encourage them to highlight words that have Spanish cognates. These texts can also be used to document reading strategies used or note questions students have about meanings.
Use sticky notes	Have students write English words on sticky notes when they find one that has a Spanish cognate. Use the sticky notes to add to the cognate chart in the classroom and identify false cognates as you discuss meanings of the words. Post the false cognates on a separate chart in the classroom.
Expand meanings	Have students expand cognate meaning by identifying the word in Spanish and English and then finding as many different expansions of the word as they can. Have them write a sentence for each expanded word they identify. Example using *assist/assistir*: I can assist you. I am assisting my brother. I assisted my teacher by erasing the board. My father has an assistant. Poor people often need public assistance.
Sort cognates	Give students cards with English and Spanish words on them. Some of the words are cognates, others are false cognates. Have the students work in pairs to identify the cognates and false cognates. Have each pair of students present one or two of the pairs they identify and explain how the words are used.
Identify multiple meanings	Have students identify English and Spanish words that have multiple meanings. Identify when one of the meanings makes the word a cognate but which definition does not match the English meaning. Have the students keep a page in their writing journal to identify multiple meaning words.

discovered a series of books that present science concepts and show everyday applications of the science content. The series he uses is called *Seeds of Science/Roots of Reading* published by the Regents of the University of California (Regents of the University of California, 2014).

Since his students have been studying the water cycle, Mr. Marshall chooses *Drinking Cleopatra's Tears*, a book that provides humorous examples of how the Earth's water is recycled over time. Because Mr. Marshall knows that his English learners will need support in understanding the science terms in the book, he looks through the text to find words that have Spanish cognates. As he reads the book aloud, he asks his Spanish speakers to identify words that seem similar to Spanish words. As they encounter words, Mr. Marshall lists the words on the board in both English and Spanish. He asks his Spanish speakers to pronounce each word as it is listed. He then asks his English-only students to pronounce the Spanish words as well. If his Spanish speakers don't suggest a word, Mr. Marshall suggests one and asks if they can think of a similar Spanish word.

FIGURE 24.3 Cognate Strategies: Teacher Self-Evaluation Rubric

Beginning	Developing	Accomplished	Exemplary
Choose high-frequency words.	Choose challenging words from texts students are reading.	Choose challenging words and provide additional words that could be substituted to add meaning or to clarify.	Choose challenging words, words that have similar meanings. Explore nuances of meanings.
Cognate chart is posted but not used regularly.	Cognate chart is posted and words added as they are studied.	Cognate chart is posted and words are added as they are studied. Students add words that they find in their reading.	Cognate chart is posted and words are added as they are studied. Students add words they read or hear in conversation. Students keep a cognate chart in their writing journal as well.
Cognates are mentioned periodically.	Finding cognates is done daily in various subject areas.	Cognate study is done across the curriculum every day. Spanish–English dictionaries are used by the students if needed to clarify meaning.	Students show evidence of their understanding of cognate use in their reading and writing. They utilize Spanish–English dictionaries if needed to clarify meaning.

One of Mr. Marshall's goals is to give his English-only students opportunities to acquire some Spanish vocabulary since they live in an area where they will often have to communicate with Spanish speakers. He also wants them to understand the challenge of learning a new language to help them build empathy for their Spanish-speaking peers.

As they read the book together, Mr. Marshall and his students discuss the concepts and vocabulary presented in the book. After the reading of the book, students add the words addressed during the discussion to the vocabulary list. They copy the list of Spanish–English cognates into their reading journals and write summary sentences about the book using some of the new vocabulary in their journal entries.

Mr. Marshall uses the growing list of Spanish–English cognates in the classroom to support his students' understanding of English vocabulary. He uses a list of cognates he found online to help him decide which words to add to the classroom list. He also has a small bulletin board labeled Cognate Jail. Students put false cognates in the Cognate Jail whenever they are discovered. His students identified the English word *pie* as being the same as a Spanish word, only to discover that the Spanish word means *foot* while the English word means something good to eat. After a good laugh about the problems they would have substituting English *pie*, for Spanish *pie*, they posted the word in the Cognate Jail.

Mr. Marshall documents the strategies he uses to differentiate instruction for his English learners, their progress, and the need for reteaching. He uses assessments such as reading running records and anecdotal records, and he saves copies of the students' journal entries that show their growing competence.

* * * * *

FIGURE 24.4 Example of Spanish–English Cognate List for Declaration of Independence

course/curso	human/humanos	dissolve/dissolver
political/politicos	assume/asumir	separate/separado
equal/igual	decent/descente	respect/respeto
opinions/pinion	requires/requiere	declare/declare
causes/causas	impel/impelen	separation/separacion

Miss Miller teaches 10th-grade social studies in a school where about 30 percent of the students speak Spanish at home. Before she introduces a text to be read, she identifies words that have Spanish cognates and prepares a PowerPoint slide (or slides, if needed) to highlight the cognates the students will encounter in the text. When she introduces a reading, she always provides background information and includes the vocabulary they will need to understand the passage to be read. She discusses the word meanings, and even uses Spanish–English dictionaries to read the word definitions in Spanish. She finds that many of the students are unfamiliar with the words, even in Spanish.

As Miss Miller prepares her lesson on the Declaration of Independence, she goes to chnm.gmu.edu/declaration/ to find a Spanish translation. She prints out both the English and Spanish translations and highlights the cognates. She prepares a PowerPoint presentation listing all the cognates. See Figure 24.4 for an example of a cognate list for the first paragraph of the Declaration of Independence.

To begin the lesson, Miss Miller reviews what the class has been studying about the Revolutionary War and discusses the word *declaration*. As she mentions a word that has a Spanish cognate, she simply points to the cognate displayed on the screen. When she discusses more difficult word meanings, she asks one of her Spanish speakers to read the definition in Spanish from the English–Spanish dictionary. She can often tell which words need to be defined in Spanish because she sees her Spanish speakers looking in their dictionaries.

The class works through the first paragraph of the Declaration together, stopping to explore word meanings and define words in both English and Spanish. Miss Miller works with the class to produce a summary sentence for the first paragraph, and the students write the summary sentence in their notes. Here is the summary sentence that the class negotiates for the first paragraph:

When a group of people finds it necessary to separate themselves politically from another group, it is a decent thing to tell the reasons for the separation.

She divides the class into small groups to complete the reading and discuss the meaning of the text. Each group is asked to read and discuss the paragraph, find cognates, and then write a summary sentence. Because Miss Miller has many students who are enrolled in Spanish class and many native Spanish speakers, most of the students are interested in Spanish pronunciations and definitions. She often asks a native Spanish speaker to write the summary sentence in Spanish and then read it aloud to see how many of her students studying Spanish can understand the translation. Miss Miller attempts the Spanish reading as well. Her students understand that she values bilingualism.

Miss Miller documents the cognate strategies that she uses in her classroom and the progress her students are making both in social studies and in reading and writing English. She wants to make sure that she varies the instruction enough to keep it interesting while supporting the needs of all her students.

Conclusion

Making students aware of cognates in English and Spanish can greatly increase their understanding of English text as well as improve their English writing. Although there are cognates in other languages, they are often not sufficient in number to be of major assistance. If you have students who speak languages other than English or Spanish in your classroom, they may be able to identify some cognates with the use of bilingual dictionaries, and this activity should be encouraged. Latin and Greek roots can also be of great help in unlocking the meanings of English words and can be introduced as a part of lessons to help students understand the meanings of vocabulary important to content-area lessons.

Examples of Approximation Behaviors Related to the TESOL Standards

PreK–3 students will:

- identify words that are similar in more than one language.
- use vocabulary discovered in oral production.

4–8 students will:

- edit writing to include varied vocabulary using cognate knowledge.

- increase the complexity of written and oral sentences by including cognates.

9–12 students will:

- include academic language in written reports based on cognate knowledge.
- recognize false cognates.

References

August D., Beck, I. L., Calderon, M., Francis, D. J., Lesaux, N. K., Shanahan, P., Erickson, F., & Siegel, L. S. (2008). Instruction and professional development. In D. August & T. Shanahan (Eds.), *Developing reading and writing in second language learners: Lessons from the Report of the National Literacy Panel on Language Minority Children and Use* (pp. 131–250). New York, NY: Routledge.

August, D., Carlo, M., Dressler, C., & Snow, C. (2005). The critical role of vocabulary development for English language learners. *Learning Disabilities Research & Practice, 20*(1), 50–57.

¡Colorín Colorado! (2007). Using cognates to develop comprehension in English. Retrieved January, 11, 2014 from www.colorincolorado.org/educators/background/cognates

Dressler, C. (2000). The word-inferencing strategies of bilingual and monolingual fifth graders: A case study approach. Unpublished qualifying paper, Harvard School of Education, Harvard University, Cambridge, MA.

Lubliner, S., & Hiebert, E. (2011). An analysis of English-Spanish cognates as a source of General Academic Language. *Bilingual Research Journal, 34*: 76–93.

Montelongo, J., Hernandez, A., & Herter, R. (2016). English-Spanish cognates in the Charlotte Zolotow Award picture books: Vocabulary, morphology, and orthography lessons for Latino ELLs. *Reading Horizon, 55*(1). 27–33.

Regents of the University of California. *Drinking Cleopatra's Tears.* Seeds of Science/Roots of Reading (2007). Retrieved January 11, 2014, from http://scienceandliteracy.org/sites/scienceandliteracy.org/files/strategyguides/SG_Drinking%20Cleopatra.pdf

25

RTI for English Language Learners

Documenting and Monitoring Student Progress and the Effectiveness of Intervention

Response to intervention (RTI) is an instructional delivery model that is designed to ensure early identification of at-risk learners and the provision of appropriate services for those learners. RTI strategies support teachers in documenting, analyzing, and adjusting instruction to ensure that English language learners (ELLs) are supported in acquiring English and content-area knowledge and learning strategies.

RTI may be viewed as an overarching conceptual framework that guides school improvement progress for all students. The specific purpose of RTI is to ensure that students are provided the **differentiated instruction** needed to avoid placing students into exceptional education programs unnecessarily. RTI shifts the focus away from the notion of the student as having a problem to the learning conditions and instructional strategies that are needed to support student achievement and success (Echevarria & Vogt, 2011).

According to Alba Ortiz (2008), an expert in the field of bilingual special education, "RTI may help us more quickly identify other factors contributing to low performance. It's important to respond early. . . . The more time passes, the harder it is to tell ESL issues from learning disabilities" (p. 2).

Heibert, Stewart, and Uzicanin (2010) suggest that RTI should be called "responsiveness of instruction" because the focus and intent of the model is to provide and document the use of appropriate methods, materials, grouping, pace, and support in language acquisition. The emphasis of RTI with ELLs is identifying what students *can* do and implementing instructional modifications or accommodations that support their success. The strength of the RTI model when used with ELLs is that the strategies used are documented. Periodic progress checks are also made so that ELLs are given the support they need to move forward in both language and content development. RTI with ELLs is NOT necessarily meant to move them into special education but to document what has helped them and what has not been successful. It also will help identify learning concerns apart from language development (Haager, 2007).

Although RTI is often described as a three-tiered program, it is more accurate to call it a multi-tiered program because there may be more than three tiers in an RTI process (Vaughn & Klinger, 2007). The basic RTI tiers are as follows:

Tier 1 is the general education classroom and core curriculum that all students receive.
Tier 2 provides qualified students with interventions that supplement the core curriculum and classroom practice.
Tier 3 involves more intensive, individualized intervention and may or may not include students with identified disabilities who have an Individualized Educational Plan (IEP) (Díaz-Rico, 2014). In some models, students with IEPs receive special education services in Tier 4.

Individual school districts require different documentation of the formal RTI process, but all teachers of ELLs must document the assessments, accommodations, modifications, and interventions that are given to ELLs. If and when the accommodations and modifications initiated at Tiers 1 and 2 do not provide the support a student needs to make satisfactory progress, the RTI process requires the school's student study team to make an official decision to place the student on Tier 3 for possible interventions and/or special education placement. In general, **accommodations and modifications** are defined as strategies teachers use to differentiate instruction. Interventions are generally more formal approaches, based on research, that are used after accommodations and modifications have not provided enough support to ensure the student's success. Interventions may take place for ELLs at Tiers 1 and 2 but must be provided at Tier 3. Figure 25.1 highlights RTI accommodations, modifications, and interventions.

One key element of RTI is using assessments to measure student progress and employing the results to inform the type of intervention needed. It also includes directing the focus of

FIGURE 25.1 RTI Accommodations, Modifications, and Interventions

Accommodations	Additional help given to a student in a general education classroom to support success Examples: Computer programs to support the mastery of basic skills Giving a test orally so student can respond verbally instead of in writing Moving a student's seat to reduce distraction
Modifications	Adjusting the expectations for a student in a general education classroom Examples: Giving an outline for an assignment (in the home language if needed) Reducing the number of problems assigned Providing pictures for new vocabulary
Interventions	Providing a research-based approach to support success in a core curriculum class or special class Examples: Small group instruction using sheltered English Developing vocabulary instruction to teach words needed for success in an assignment based on the student's English language development level Providing special instructional materials based on the student's English language development level

Note: All three approaches must be documented by (1) the assessment or observation used to identify the need, (2) the date the approach was begun, (3) periodic progress reports based on assessment and/or observation, and (4) the date and reason the approach was stopped.

instruction in the general education program (Fuchs & Fuchs, 2007). Assessments used include such measurements as:

- end-of-unit assessments;
- leveled running records;
- spelling tests; and
- anecdotal records documenting specific behaviors. (Echevarria & Vogt, 2011)

Parent involvement is another major element of RTI. Parents should be involved with key decisions and kept apprised of the accommodations, modifications, and interventions being used with their child. Teachers must also clearly document parent involvement and concerns at every stage of the process (Echevarria & Vogt, 2011). Video Example 25.1 will assist you in gaining a broad understanding of the process and what it looks like in the classroom setting.

Enhanced eText
Video Example 25.1
https://youtu.be/pJCBW1V8ufs

Step-by-Step

The steps in implementing RTI are the following:

- *Identify students' English language development levels, strengths, and learning levels through assessment*—All students identified as English language learners are required to be tested to determine their English language development levels. Students in second grade and above are required to be tested for their levels in English reading and writing as well. Teacher observations also provide information about a student's ability to participate in English interactions in the classroom as well as his or her strengths in other areas such as art, music, or physical activities. These assessments are documented and used to determine the appropriate instructional approaches and differentiation needed to support the student's success. Figure 25.2 shows one documentation form.

- *Use assessment results to identify areas to be addressed by differentiated instruction and possible approaches to use*—Assessment results and teacher observations are used to identify possible accommodations, modifications, and interventions appropriate for each student. See Figure 25.3 for a list of possible accommodations and modifications.

- *Document the assessment results and RTI plan, including length of intervention, plans for updating assessments, and parent involvement*—Document the accommodations, modifications, and interventions used, noting the date begun, periodic progress checks, observations, and ending date. Also, document parent conferences and any concerns they have. Be sure to allow sufficient time for approaches to be successful. At the same time, maintain ongoing reports of student progress, including assessments such as reading running records, writing samples, anecdotal records, and tests given.

- *Observe and document student responses to intervention as well as academic and language development progress*—In addition to response to interventions, document academic progress and progress in English language development. Provide language samples for changes in English language development levels. As the English language development levels change, be sure to document the changes in the modifications you use.

- *Adjust interventions when student progress slows or when students meet standards*—Observe students closely, note progress made, and note the adjustments you make in instructional approaches based on student progress and periodic assessments. Be sure to note when lack of progress is evident as well.

- *Ask for assistance from the school student study team when student progress is slow or lacking*—When a student does not make progress, or progress is very slow, ask the school student study team to look at the accommodations, modifications, and documentation you have collected. They may be able to offer suggestions for additional instructional approaches and

FIGURE 25.2 Accommodation/Modification Documentation

Student Name _____ Birth Date _____
Teacher Name _____ Grade Level _____

Accommodation/ Modification	Start Date	Progress	End Date

possible interventions or special education support. Include parents in your decision to take this step and in the educational planning process.

• *Continue to use assessment and documentation to support the instructional approaches used*—Follow the suggestions made by the school student study team and document all instructional approaches, further assessments, and student progress as required. Use these supporting actions to make any further needed changes.

Applications and Examples

Mrs. Elmore teaches first grade in a school where 50 percent of the students speak a language other than English at home. Since 11 of her 23 students are just learning English, Mrs. Elmore maintains a variety of documentation that confirms the observations and assessments she does on each of her students, as well as the accommodations and modifications she uses to support their progress. She does reading running records with each of her students once a week and

FIGURE 25.3 Possible Accommodations and Modifications

Requesting a health screening for vision and hearing
Providing a seat in the front of the room or in a study carrel to reduce distractions
Instituting a behavior or academic contract
Providing extend time for assignment completion
Adjusting the level of difficulty for an assignment
Reducing the number of math problems or sentences required
Providing the student with computer programs for needed practice
Allowing another student to translate for an ELL
Permitting a student to complete an assignment in his or her home language
Using cross-age tutoring

observes and writes anecdotal records periodically during sharing circle time, learning center time, and reading circle. Mrs. Elmore uses this information to record the changing English language development levels of her students along with the changes she makes in instructional approaches. She uses a number of strategies to support learning in her classroom and finds that many of them are as successful with her English-only students as they are with her ELLs. She uses many visuals and acts out new vocabulary. She finds that posting new words in the classroom helps her remember to use them repeatedly, and the students can use them in their writing. She sees that this is supporting both their reading and writing vocabulary. Mrs. Elmore confers with parents on a regular basis. She shares the documentation she has compiled and discusses student progress. She often employs the assistance of a bilingual aide to make sure parents fully understand their child's progress and any concerns she has. She also invites them to share any concerns they have.

In spite of all her efforts and the fact that most of her students are making impressive progress after three months in first grade, Mrs. Elmore is concerned about one of her students, Antonio, who is still not producing verbal or written English words. She takes her documentation to the school student study team, and the team (which includes Antonio's parents and a bilingual interpreter) decides to have further testing done by the school psychologist to see if he qualifies for any special education programs. The school study team recommends that an additional modification be used in the classroom. A bilingual aide is assigned to Antonio to work with him for 30 minutes a day, providing home language support to make sure that Antonio understands what is expected of him. Mrs. Elmore works with the bilingual aide to learn key words in Spanish in order to follow up on instruction with Antonio. She incorporates the modification and documents Antonio's progress. The school psychologist confers with Mrs. Elmore following a month of the suggested modification. She reports that Antonio is beginning to produce verbal and written English words and showing more understanding of classroom procedures. The school psychologist suggests continuing the modification and postponing the assessment for several months to observe Antonio's progress further. It looks as if this modification is beginning to work.

* * * * *

Shortly after author Adrienne Herrell retired from teaching at Florida State University, she received a phone call from one of her former college students who taught French at a local high school. This teacher had been in several English for Speakers of Other Languages (ESOL) classes that Adrienne taught, and she had some concerns about her new teaching position. Miss James, the teacher, had been assigned a class of ESOL students in addition to her French classes. Her high school had recently moved to a block schedule, which meant that classes met for 90 minutes a day instead of the traditional 55-minute periods. Her ESOL class met from 7:30 to 9:00 a.m. each day and then the students went to regular high school classes. Miss James had been assigned 16 students. The students spoke four different languages. Five of them spoke no English at all because they had very recently moved to Florida from Central America and had not studied English before coming to the U.S. Dr. Herrell agreed to visit Miss James's classroom to assist in testing the students' English abilities and to help Miss James with instructional planning.

After the students were assessed, 11 of them were identified as functioning at the intermediate fluency level of English, although several of them were reading and writing below grade level. The students ranged from freshmen to seniors. The five students functioning at preproduction and early production levels all spoke Spanish at home. Two of the students were siblings: a freshman boy and a junior girl. The other three were sophomores. Dr. Herrell and Miss James identified accommodations and modifications for the 11 students who were functioning at intermediate fluency. The students' other teachers were asked to share their assignments and expectations with Miss James so that she could build academic vocabulary with the students and provide support for the students during first period so that they could function more successfully in their regular classes for the rest of the day. One of the math teachers spoke fluent Spanish, and he agreed to translate assignments for the five students just beginning to learn English.

The students' assessment results and plans for accommodations and modifications were documented, and Dr. Herrell and Miss James updated the student profiles on a regular basis. Dr. Herrell agreed to work with the five preproduction and early production students on a daily basis, building English vocabulary, supporting the students as they began to produce verbal English, working on content they were encountering in their regular classes, and practicing asking and answering English questions they would hear in their classroom. Four of the five students made progress as they learned that they would not be asked to participate without support. One student, the freshman boy, never uttered a word of English, even with modeling and encouragement. His sister told Dr. Herrell that he never spoke much, even in Spanish, at home. She said that he was very shy.

At the end of the first nine-week grading period, 4 of the 11 students in Miss James' group tested out of the ESOL program. All of these students were from Eastern Europe and had studied English before moving to the U.S.

Dr. Herrell helped Miss James set up learning centers in her classroom that supported the students in acquiring new vocabulary. At the centers, they read some of the literature they were studying in their home languages, practiced English questioning and answering questions daily, reviewed their homework to make sure they understood the vocabulary and concepts, and kept English writing journals. Because the sophomore English classes were studying *Animal Farm*, one of the learning centers was a computer station where the students could watch the film of the book with Spanish translations. Miss James developed a bilingual dictionary on the computer. When students needed to have words translated, they added those words to the dictionary. Several of the students learned to search for visuals to add to the dictionary.

The five students who worked with Dr. Herrell began to participate in the learning centers with some success. The one student who was not producing much English either verbally or in writing was referred to the school student study team, and the district found a volunteer to work with him in his regular English class, providing Spanish translation for him. He continued to make slow progress.

Miss James continues to teach the ESOL class each semester. The class is always scheduled for the first period because the students themselves say that speaking English for an hour and a half each morning, with support, gets them in "English mode."

RTI assessments, accommodations, and modifications are used throughout this process. Decisions about what to include in the curriculum and how to structure it are made based on observations of the students, classroom testing shared by the regular classroom teachers, and periodic assessments such as reading running records, writing samples, timed assessments on the computer, and almost continuous anecdotal records shared with students for purposes of confidence building and celebration.

Conclusion

Although RTI was instituted to make sure that all students receive differentiated instruction to support their success in the general education program before being referred for exceptional education programs, the process is extremely helpful in supporting English language learners. RTI's emphasis on assessment and documentation is helpful to teachers because it provides an accurate picture of a student's functioning levels over time and documents student progress. The records that are kept as RTI is implemented are extremely valuable for teachers, student study teams, and parents in making decisions and suggestions for future instruction.

Examples of Approximation Behaviors Related to the TESOL Standards

PreK–3 students will:

- form and ask questions related to assignments.
- respond appropriately to assignments designed to meet needs identified by teacher observation.

4–8 students will:

- find and use information from several sources to complete assignments.

- edit and revise written assignments.

9–12 students will:

- take and support a position on an assigned topic.
- prepare for and participate in an oral report or debate.

References

Díaz-Rico, L. (2014). *The crosscultural, language, and academic development handbook: A complete K–12 reference guide* (5th ed.). Boston, MA: Pearson Education.

Echevarria, J., & Vogt, M. E. (2011). *Response to intervention (RTI) and English learners: Making it happen.* Boston, MA: Pearson Education.

Fuchs, L., & Fuchs, D. (2007). The role of assessment in the three-tier approach to reading intervention. In D. Haager, J. Klinger, & S. Vaughn (Eds.). *Evidence-based reading practices for response to intervention.* Baltimore, MD: Paul H. Brookes.

Haager, D. (2007). Promises and cautions regarding response to intervention with English language learners. *Learning Disabilities Quarterly 30(3).*79–86.

Heibert, E., Stewart, J., & Uzicanin, M. (2010). *A comparison of word features affecting word recognition of at-risk beginning readers and their peers.* Paper presented at the annual meeting of the Society for the Scientific Study of Reading on July 10, 2010, Berlin, Germany.

Ortiz, A. (2008). English-language learners with special needs: Effective instructional strategies. Retrieved October 13, 2014, from http://www.colorincolorado.org/research/keywords/intervention

Vaughn, S., & Klinger, J. (2007). Overview of the three–tier model of reading intervention. In D. Haager, J. Klinger, & S. Vaughn (Eds.). *Evidence-based reading practices for response to intervention* (pp. 3–10). Baltimore, MD: Paul H. Brookes.

26

Preview/Review

Building Vocabulary and Concepts to Support Understanding

Preview/review (Lessow-Hurley, 1990) is a teaching strategy usually associated with bilingual classrooms where a teacher or an instructional aide gives a preview of the lesson in the students' home language(s). The lesson is then taught in English, and the material is reviewed in the home language(s) to ensure content understanding. This same strategy can be adapted to an English-only classroom by using realia, visuals, gestures, and vocabulary instruction as part of the preview—making reference to the support materials during the actual lesson, and then reviewing and explaining the content of the lesson to the students using the support materials.

Preview/review is especially effective in facilitating content knowledge acquisition because of the contextualization of the academic language through the use of realia and visuals. Active involvement with key vocabulary before the lesson and reviewing after the lesson provide English learners with multiple opportunities for understanding (Nation, 2005). Reviewing vocabulary and main concepts after each lesson is an effective strategy and particularly vital for English learners. ELLs often are concentrating on making sense of the language during the lesson, so a review of information after the lesson helps them to identify and remember the most important points (Friend & Bursuck, 2006). Use of the preview/review lesson format also provides all students an introduction to the concepts and vocabulary of the lesson. Follow-up with a planned review gives students multiple chances to establish the vocabulary and concepts in English. Adding support with visuals and practice in verbal response helps to cement the concepts being taught. (Nguyen & Cortes, 2013).

Figure 26.1 offers suggestions of appropriate support materials and activities for preview/review lessons. Chapter 31, Advance Organizers, contains additional suggestions.

Step-by-Step

The steps in a preview/review lesson are the following:

• *Plan and gather materials*—Plan your lesson, identifying key concepts and vocabulary. Gather any realia, visuals, or support materials that will help students understand the concepts and vocabulary needed to comprehend the lesson.

• *Introduce key vocabulary and concepts*—Use the support materials you have gathered to introduce the important vocabulary and key concepts during the preview section of the lesson.

FIGURE 26.1 Support Materials and Activities for Preview/Review Lessons

Realia	Visuals	Activities
Foods Household objects Animals Costumes of the period Music of the period	Transparencies made from photos Magazine pictures Line drawings Art prints Maps	Role-playing Illustrating Sorting and labeling Lesson word walls Reader's theater Creating display boards Creating board games

The focus in this section of the lesson is *not* on actually teaching the lesson but on familiarizing students with key vocabulary and concepts.

  • ***Teach the lesson***—Teach the actual lesson, referring to the support materials and key vocabulary already introduced during the preview whenever possible.

  • ***Review vocabulary and concepts***—Review the key vocabulary and concepts, encouraging the students to demonstrate understanding by referring to the support materials.

  • ***Provide additional practice***—Create a bulletin board or learning center that allows the students to practice the key concepts further through use of the support materials used in the lesson.

  • ***Assess and document students' interactions***—Observe and document students' interactions with the materials and follow-up activities by completing written anecdotal records. Conduct individual conferences with students to give them an opportunity to demonstrate what they learned in the lesson. The anecdotal records can be included in individual student portfolios. See Figure 26.2 for an example of an anecdotal record. Video Example 26.1 provides an example of a teacher using preview/review to ensure student understanding of a read-aloud lesson.

Enhanced eText
Video Example 26.1
https://youtu.be/
hzG_dBhabn4

FIGURE 26.2 Example of a Preview/Review Anecdotal Record

10/16/15
Preview of Lesson on Zoo Animals:
Antonio was able to point to picture of a lion and an elephant. All other animals were unfamiliar to him. He did know the Spanish word for *snake*.
During the lesson, Antonio was attentive and volunteered to identify the picture of the lion. During the sorting activity, he was able to identify pictures of birds and reptiles.
In the review section of the lesson, Antonio repeated all the English names of animals and was able to point to each one when asked to identify them. He was able to recall the English names for *lion, elephant, snake, bear,* and *tiger*.

Applications and Examples

To prepare her second graders for a field trip to the zoo, Ms. Allen brings in photographs of zoo animals. She introduces the animals to the students using the photographs and creates a chart by displaying the photographs and listing key information about each animal, such as the names used for the baby animals, the type of food eaten by the animal, and the animal's natural habitat.

A map of the zoo is displayed in the classroom, and Ms. Allen teaches a lesson on asking questions and gathering information during the zoo trip. Each student is given a clipboard with information sheets about each animal the group will see. The students brainstorm questions they will ask the zoo guides about the animals, and the students practice taking notes on their information sheets.

As a review of the lesson, the students refer to the photographs of the animals and practice asking questions about them. The students are given individual zoo maps, and they place the names of the animals they will see in the proper places on the maps. As they note the locations on the maps, they refer to the photographs and key information on the charts they have made.

On the day of the zoo trip, the students ask questions and note the answers on their information sheets. When they return to the classroom the next day, they use their zoo maps and information sheets to add new information to the charts about the animals.

The students learned a lot about the zoo and the animals because they were prepared to ask questions during the field trip. By having the students practice asking questions, determining where they will locate the different animals at the zoo, and preparing them to take notes about the animals, Ms. Allen gave them an opportunity to benefit fully from their field trip. The students learned the vocabulary, language structures, and key concepts they would encounter on their trip.

* * * * *

Ms. Warren uses a preview/review approach to introduce vocabulary and historical settings to her high school English students prior to studying literary works. Before studying *The Great Gatsby* (Fitzgerald, 1925), Ms. Warren familiarizes her students with the music and art of the Roaring Twenties. She uses transparencies of great art to familiarize her students with costumes of the period, plays music of the period, shows clips from newsreels of the day, and engages the students in role-playing to act out the vocabulary they will encounter in their reading.

During the reading of the literature, Ms. Warren stops whenever necessary to refer to the transparencies or the students' role-playing to make connections between the preview activities and the passage being read.

As a review, the students are asked to refer to the support materials or role-playing to answer questions related to the literature being studied. The students are also asked to role-play certain passages from the work to share their understanding of the motivations and emotions of the characters. Small groups of students are assigned short passages of the work to reenact and then that passage and key vocabulary are discussed.

Conclusion

Preview/review is an especially effective strategy for English learners because it helps motivate students to learn. The preview part of the lesson not only prepares them by introducing vocabulary but, when done well, also generates interest in the topic to be studied. The review section of the lesson gives the teacher an opportunity to make connections, correct misconceptions, and engage students in a celebration of their accomplishments. See Figure 26.3 to learn how to differentiate preview/review lessons for students at varying language development levels.

FIGURE 26.3 Adapting Preview/Review Lessons for Varying Language Development Levels

Preproduction	Early Production	Speech Emergence	Intermediate Fluency	Fluent
Provide visuals for key vocabulary. Provide home language vocabulary as needed. Act out key concepts when possible. Use visuals throughout lesson and review. Keep visuals posted throughout lesson and refer to them frequently.	Use visuals as described for preproduction but add repetition of key words and phrases throughout the lesson. Pronounce the words and phrases and have students repeat them.	Introduce questioning in English. Encourage students to use visuals whenever needed and provide English models to support their English production.	Mispronunciations are still expected. Accept responses and practice correct pronunciations. Review vocabulary and concepts frequently.	Encourage full participation. Be sure to include students in discussions. Encourage all students to provide sufficient wait time.

Examples of Approximation Behaviors Related to the TESOL Standards

PreK–3 students will:

- respond appropriately to gestures.
- rehearse appropriate language related to the formality of the setting.

4–8 students will:

- interact appropriately with adults in formal and informal settings.

- use English and their first language (L1) appropriately in a multilingual setting.

9–12 students will:

- preview assigned reading and ask questions appropriately.
- seek more knowledgeable peers or teachers who can answer questions related to assignments.

References

Fitzgerald, F. S. (1925). *The great Gatsby*. New York, NY: Scribner/Simon & Schuster.

Friend, M., & Bursuck, W. (2006). *Including students with special needs: A practical guide for classroom teachers* (4th ed.). Boston, MA: Allyn & Bacon.

Lessow-Hurley, J. (1990). *The foundations of dual language instruction*. White Plains, NY: Longman.

Nation, I. S. P. (2005). Teaching and learning vocabulary. In E. Hinkel (ed.), *Handbook of research on second language teaching and learning* (pp. 581–596). Mahwah, NJ: Erlbaum.

Nguyen, H. and Cortes, M. (2013). Teaching mathematics to English language learners: Practical research-based methods, strategies. *Childhood Education, 89*(6).

27

Story Reenactment

Making Stories Come to Life!

Story reenactment is a strategy that encourages students to act out stories after they have read them or have heard them read. This strategy involves creating props for the students to use in reenacting stories so that they can use the language from a book they have heard or read and better comprehend the text by acting it out in sequence. Story reenactment can be done even with young children in their play centers. One study with preschool children encouraged them to use blocks and props in the block center to retell stories that had been read aloud to them. The teacher observed several examples of "book language and vocabulary" being included in the children's play and often included by both students and teacher in classroom talk after the reenactments (Heisner, 2005). Some teachers have extended the use of total physical response to using gestures in story reenactment (Seely & Romijn, 2006); see Chapter 2 for more information about this approach. Story reenactment provides opportunities for multiple rereadings, discussion, clarification, and oral and physical story recreation. All of this combines to deepen comprehension and build spoken and reading fluency using context-embedded language (Cummins, 1981; Reig & Paquette, 2009).

Props for story reenactment may consist of costumes for the students to wear or prop boxes containing items made of clay, flannel, or laminated photos that have been scanned from magazines or downloaded from the Internet. Part of the effectiveness of this strategy involves planning for active involvement of the students in discussing the stories and creating the needed props.

Step-by-Step

The steps in story reenactment are the following:

- *Read the story*—Read a story to the students or have them read the story independently.
- *Retell the story*—Have the students retell the story in sequence and list the props they will need to reenact the story accurately.
- *Gather or make the props*—Provide materials for the students to use in creating the props for the prop box. The materials might be clay, dough for baked-dough art, felt, or drawing materials. Encourage the students to sign up for the props they will make. See Figure 27.1 for instructions for making dough-art props. Overhead transparencies can be created that can be projected onto the wall as backdrops for the retelling. These backgrounds may also be digitized from the book itself or from other specific electronic sources and projected onto an available interactive whiteboard. Individual objects from the story can also be added to the whiteboard and may even be moved around on the "backdrop" by the children to reinforce their active use of the vocabulary further.

FIGURE 27.1 Baked Dough Recipe

4 cups flour (*not* self-rising)
I cup salt
I½ cups water

Mix ingredients together. Mixture will be stiff.
Knead for 10 minutes.

Make shapes desired, separate by thickness (poke holes in thick pieces).
Bake at 325–350 degrees (½ hour per ¼-inch thickness)
Cool.

Paint to resemble figures in the storybook.
Use acrylic paints or tempera mixed with Elmer's glue (half and half).

Other suggestions for prop boxes: Paper doll figures, flannel board figures, magnetic tape on the back of pictures, overhead transparency pictures, actual dress-up clothes, and larger props.

- *Store the props*—After the physical props are made, painted, and sealed, decorate a shoe box in which to store the props. The box can be labeled with a photograph of the cover of the book so the students can easily find the collection of story props they need.
- *Use the props for retelling*—Encourage students, working in pairs or small groups, to use the prop boxes to retell and reenact the stories.
- *Assess the retellings*—Listen to the story retellings and encourage the students who are using the "book language" and vocabulary. This is a good opportunity to document language usage and take anecdotal records. Note the completeness of the students' retellings and their inclusion of main events, characters, and inference. Take particular note when they begin to use more and more of the vocabulary as a result of multiple retellings. After the group reenactment, ask individual students to retell the story. Using a retelling rubric to score individual student retellings is a good way to document their growth and comprehension over time. See Figure 27.2 for an example of a retelling rubric.

FIGURE 27.2 Story Retelling Rubric

Novice (1)	Beginning (2)	Developing (3)	Capable (4)
Retelling shows little or no evidence of beginning, middle, or end.	Retelling shows inconsistent evidence of beginning, middle, and end.	Retelling has a beginning, middle, and end.	Retelling has a complete beginning, middle, and end.
Details are sketchy.	Some details provided but may be inaccurate.	Retelling describes the setting.	Setting is described in detail.
Very limited understanding of the story shown in the retelling.	Limited understanding of story elements is shown (setting, characters, problem/solution).	Elements of story are included in retelling (characters, problem/solution).	Retelling provides proper sequencing and details of story elements.
Note: Totaling the scores provides an overall assessment score, which can then be compared to future retellings in order to document student progress.			

Applications and Examples

Ms. Brown's kindergarten students are making dough-art props for the "Gingerbread Man" story. They are rolling out the dough and using cookie cutters to make the props. After the props are baked and cooled, the students paint them using a mixture of tempera paint and white glue. When the props are dry, they enjoy retelling the story, loudly proclaiming, "Run and run as fast as you can. You can't catch me. I'm the Gingerbread Man!"

Ms. Brown engages the students in identifying the props needed to tell the story, making those props, asking and answering questions about the sequence of the story, and retelling it with expression so they will be able to "confirm understanding of a text read aloud or information presented orally or through other media by asking and answering questions about key details and requesting clarification if something is not understood" (CCSS.ELA-LITERACY.SLK.2).

After the "Gingerbread Man" props are made, the students ask Ms. Brown, "Can we make props for 'The Little Red Hen' now?" Ms. Brown decides to have an ongoing center where the students can make story retelling props. They are enjoying the props, and she sees a lot of language practice going on as they use the props to retell the stories they have read.

Story reenactment is a strategy that seems to be made for English language learners. It provides a script for them to follow as they retell favorite storybooks. The props or costumes give them support in remembering the sequence of events. They gain confidence in their oral English abilities with each new retelling.

* * * * *

Mr. Zarras's sixth-grade English language learners are making props for the story *Where the Wild Things Are* (Sendak, 1963). The students read and reread the story so many times that they can tell it by heart. Mr. Zarras wants the students to "include multimedia components (e.g., graphics, images, music, sound) and visual displays in presentations to clarify information" (CCSS.ELA-LITERACY.SL.6.5). He is also hoping to build their confidence in speaking English. After the props are complete, the students will retell the story with props to their first-grade book buddies. The day finally comes when all the props are complete.

The sixth graders enter the first-grade classroom with broad smiles on their faces. The first graders sit enthralled as they listen to their sixth-grade friends reenact one of their favorite stories with the small clay props they have created. As soon as the sixth graders finish their production, Janey, one of the quieter first graders, shyly raises her hand. "Can I do it?" she asks. Soon, all the first graders are clamoring for a turn to retell the story using the props. The lesson is a great success.

The first graders are very excited when the sixth graders announce that they will leave the prop box in the first-grade class for them to use. The book and the prop box are presented solemnly to the first-grade class as a gift from their book buddies. The sixth graders are very proud of their ability to present the story so well and of their handmade gifts. Mr. Zarras is even prouder of his wonderful idea. It has boosted the self-confidence of his English language learners immensely.

Conclusion

Story reenactment, an extremely powerful strategy for English language development, can be used at any grade level. High school students enjoy the reenactment of literature they have read by using minimal costumes and props and by acting out the parts. Students can create overhead transparency props or computer graphics to reenact stories in the form of a slide show as an alternative to actual role-playing.

Enhanced eText
Video Example 27.1
https://www.youtube.com/
watch?v=aRvlGdU007g

Story reenactment provides a unique opportunity for teachers to observe and evaluate their students' comprehension of the stories reenacted and the students' use of unique vocabulary and sentence structures. No matter which type of prop is used in story reenactment, students benefit by increased interaction with story plot, language, and structure. Watch the students in the Video Example 27.1 reenact one of their favorite stories, which was written and produced in their class. As you watch, consider the following questions:

- What is the students' level of comprehension of the story?
- How does the construction and use of props add to their understanding?
- How does the re-enactment process benefit your ELLs?

Examples of Approximation Behaviors Related to the TESOL Standards

PreK–3 students will:

- use props and book language to retell a story.
- generate a list and make props to support story reenactment.

4–8 students will:

- write new versions of familiar stories.

- sequence and reenact complex story plots.

9–12 students will:

- create dramatic reenactments of historic scenes.
- create scenes demonstrating a variety of points of view centering on an issue.

References

Cummins, J. (1981). *Schooling and language minority students: A theoretical framework.* Los Angeles, CA: Evaluation, Dissemination, and Assessment Center, California State University.

Heisner, J. (2005). Telling stories with blocks: Encouraging language in the block center. *Early Childhood Research and Practice, 7*(2), 8–15.

Reig, S., & Paquette, K. (2009). Using drama and movement to enhance English language learners' literacy development. *Journal of Instructional Psychology 38*(2), 138–154.

Seely, C., & Romijn, E. K. (2006). *TPR is more than commands—at all levels* (3rd ed.). Berkeley, CA: Command Performance Language Institute.

Sendak, M. (1963). Where the wild things are. New York, NY: HarperCollins Juvenile Books.

28 Repetition and Innovation
Exploring a Book to Deepen Comprehension

Repetition and innovation involves using a piece of text in several different ways to reinforce understanding and the gradual integration of the text's vocabulary and concepts into the speaking and writing vocabulary of the students (Tompkins, 2012). The text is introduced and explored in multiple modes, with the students finally rewriting the text to create an innovation on the original. This approach is especially effective for English language learners because they have multiple opportunities to revisit both the text and the vocabulary in multiple learning modes. After students are familiar with a text extension and innovation activities, provide an opportunity to:

1. Focus on a particular part of grammar, vocabulary, or idiom
2. Respond creatively to what they have read through art or drama activities
3. Focus individuals more deeply on the information in the text by (for example) representing the content of the text in a new format (diagram, time line, story revision). (Gibbons, 2015)

Using new vocabulary in multiple ways supports the students in understanding meaning and integrating the words into their spoken and written vocabularies (Beck, McKeown, & Kucan, 2002). Figure 28.1 provides suggestions for innovations that can be used with this strategy.

Step-by-Step

The steps in implementing repetition and innovation are the following:

- *Choose a book that will sustain interest over time*—Choose a book that you and your students will enjoy reading a number of times. With repetition and innovation, you will be revisiting the same text several times, so the book should have some interesting vocabulary and action or it will become boring. A book with a pattern or obvious structure makes a good choice for this kind of activity. If necessary, have the book read in the students' first language(s) before reading it in English.
- *Explore the story structure*—Explore the structure of the story. If it is a **circular story**, focus on the fact that one thing leads to another and stress that as you read. If the story has a beginning, middle, and end, emphasize that as the book is read. Try to help the students understand the structure and the relationship of the events to the structure.
- *Play with words*—Explore the pattern or structure of the book by having the students do some substitution of words using word cards in a pocket chart. Have them change words within

FIGURE 28.1 Suggestions for Innovations

Format	Description
Pocket chart stories	Build stories using the pattern or structure from the focus book. A sentence frame is used with word cards and key vocabulary from the focus book.
Wall stories	The students retell the story, and individual pages are written on large pieces of construction paper. The pages are hung from a clothesline across the room or attached to the wall in sequence so the students can read the story using a pointer. When the wall story is taken down, it is made into a class big book.
Shape books	A cover and pieces of paper are cut into the shape of an animal or object that corresponds to the topic of the writing. The innovation is written and published as a shape book.
Circular stories	A story that begins and ends in the same place is published in a circular shape (see Figure 28.2).
Three-part books	Stories that have a distinct beginning, middle, and end are published in a three-part book format (see Figure 28.2).
Story quilts	Stories are written on individual pieces of paper that are decorated as quilt squares and tied together with yarn (see Figure 28.2).
Formula poems	Students publish poems in different formats.
Videos	Students write scripts as innovations on their focus book, and the enactments of the scripts are videotaped.
Puppet plays	Students write scripts as innovations, and the scripts are performed as puppet plays.

the pattern or structure of the book until they can substitute words and make meaningful patterns on their own.

• *Create an alternate text*—Using the pattern that you and the students have practiced on the pocket chart, have students write and illustrate a sentence on a single sheet of paper and then sequence the pages to make a class book. Read the book together, practicing the vocabulary and the pattern orally.

• *Create an innovation on the text*—Depending on the structure of the book, write an innovation such as a circular chart (for circular stories); a three-part book for beginning, middle, and end stories; or an accordion book for cumulative stories. (See Figure 28.2 for illustrations of these book forms.) Involve the children in supplying the key vocabulary for the innovation either

FIGURE 28.2 Publishing Formats

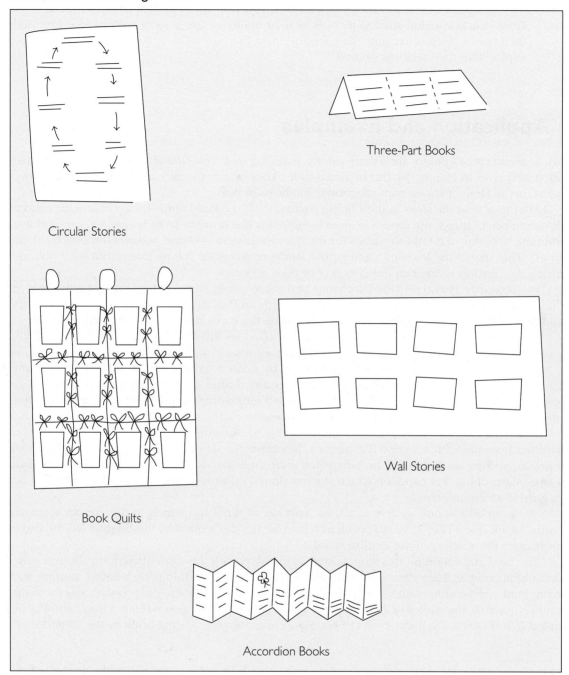

Circular Stories

Three-Part Books

Book Quilts

Wall Stories

Accordion Books

by doing the writing interactively (see Chapter 13, Scaffolding English Writing), or by taking their dictation.

• ***Create another innovation or version***—Create another innovation or new version of the same book in another format using the same pattern or structure. This time, you could create a wall story using large sheets of construction paper, or a story quilt with individual pages of the book tied together with yarn to form a large quilt. By this time, the students should be thoroughly familiar with the pattern, structure, and vocabulary.

• ***Assess to document vocabulary and comprehension***—Observe students to determine whether they understand the concepts being taught by setting up a learning center with materials for the students to create new versions of the story pattern you've introduced. As they complete new innovations or versions, you can evaluate their understanding of the story structure being studied as well as their ability to use a story pattern to create their own books. As you examine their writing, note their use of new vocabulary that has been explored in the literature studied.

Application and Examples

Ms. Leonard's first graders are sitting quietly, listening to *If You Give a Mouse a Cookie* (Numeroff, 1985) read in Hmong by the bilingual aide. They watch the pictures carefully and answer questions in Hmong about what the mouse might want next.

After they hear the story in their home language, Ms. Leonard helps them construct a chart of the sequence of things the mouse wanted using realia she brought from home. Ms. Leonard uses this time to review the English names for the household items—straw, scissors, broom, tape, and so on. That day at the learning centers, the students sequence the pictures from the book and match the pictures to the real items as one of their activities.

Ms. Leonard has also provided drawings of the household items on Language Master cards for the students. They can practice sequencing the cards so they are in the same order as the story, and they get to hear the English words as they slide the cards through the Language Master.

The next day, Ms. Leonard uses the pocket chart to display the sentence frame, "If you give a(n) (*animal*) a (*noun*), he or she will want a (*noun*)." Using the words from *If You Give a Mouse a Cookie*, the students build sentences by adding word cards to the sentence frame. Ms. Leonard and the students read the sentences aloud after they are built. At the end of the lesson, Ms. Leonard and each of the students write their favorite sentence interactively on a sheet of paper, and the students illustrate their sentences.

The third day, Ms. Leonard starts the morning by showing the students the book she put together from the sentences and illustrations they made the day before. They read the class book together, and the students smile broadly when their pages are read. Ms. Leonard then shows them a large sheet of butcher paper on which she has drawn the mouse from the story with blank lines in a circle all around him.

Ms. Leonard has one student at a time help her to write the words in the correct sequence on the blank lines. They have no problem remembering the sequence, the English words, and in most cases the spelling of the English words.

The final innovation on this story is started that day, with the students writing about another demanding animal. They decide to write about a pig and all the things he wanted, starting with some mud—and ending with some mud. They are very excited when Ms. Leonard tells them that Laura Numeroff, the author of *If You Give a Mouse a Cookie*, has also written a book about a pig called *If You Give a Pig a Pancake* (1998). Ms. Leonard then reads the book to the students.

* * * * *

The word wall in Ms. Avelar's fourth-grade classroom is covered with words the students have learned in their literature studies during the past few months. The students often use the word wall to find a word to make the stories they write more interesting. Ms. Avelar is planning an in-depth study of the parts of speech with the students based on Ruth Heller's series of books, each of which focuses on a part of speech in an innovative way.

Ms. Avelar begins the study by reading *A Cache of Jewels and Other Collective Nouns* by Ruth Heller (1987), which focuses on nouns. The students join Ms. Avelar in finding all the nouns on the word wall and then review the meanings of the nouns as they move the word cards from the word wall to the pocket chart.

As the students arrange the nouns on the pocket chart, Ms. Avelar asks, "How can we arrange the words so that we will be able to find them easily?"

"In alphabetical order!" the students answer in chorus.

"Of course. That's the easiest way to find them. But suppose I want you to do something different with the words this week?" Mrs. Avelar asks. "Suppose I want you to make different groups of nouns. One group would be nouns with only one syllable. The next group would be nouns with two syllables. The next with three syllables. Could you do that?"

"Of course we can," the students say.

"You can still put them in alphabetical order within each group," Ms. Avelar adds. "Then you will be able to find them more easily."

Once students have finished sorting the nouns into syllable groups, Ms. Avelar says, "Let's just look at the two-syllable nouns that we found." She reads down the list: *apple, auto, baby, bottle, butcher, candle, candy,* and so on.

"Let's see if we can think of some more two-syllable nouns for our list. We will want to have a nice variety of them for the project we are going to do this week."

The students add *taco, pizza, sneakers, jacket, pumpkin,* and *catsup* to the list.

"Now, I want you each to take one of these little booklets and write one of the two-syllable nouns at the top of each page. After lunch, we will work on a new category of words," Ms. Avelar says as she passes out booklets to each of the students.

After lunch, Ms. Avelar reads the Ruth Heller book on adjectives, *Many Luscious Lollipops* (1989). After practicing as one group, the students work in cooperative groups, adding a list of adjectives to each noun in their booklets. They are able to add some unusual adjectives working in the group setting. Some of the students have asked Ms. Avelar if they can prepare a second booklet in Spanish, and she has given them permission to do that. Several of the students who have asked permission to prepare the Spanish booklets are not native Spanish speakers, a fact that pleases Ms. Avelar.

On the third day of the project, Ms. Avelar introduces verbs, and the students practice the actions of the verbs they find on the word wall. Ms. Avelar reads *Kites Fly High* (1988), Ruth Heller's book about verbs, and the class brainstorms additional verbs to add to the word wall.

"I now have a hard job for you," Ms. Avelar says. "I want you to think of verbs for each of the nouns in your word booklets. For instance, the first noun in your booklet is *apple.* What can an apple do?"

"That's really hard, Ms. Avelar," Tino says. "An apple just sits there."

"That's good, Tino. Write *sits,*" Ms. Avelar says, smiling.

"Oh! I get it," Tino says with a grin.

After the students work in cooperative groups to write verbs for each of their nouns, Ms. Avelar introduces them to the pyramid poetry format. "We are now going to use the words we have been collecting to create a poem that looks like a pyramid," she says. "The title of the poem is a noun. Let's pick one of our nouns to use as an example."

"Pizza!" Gretchen exclaims.

"Good one," Ms. Avelar confirms, and she writes *pizza* on the chalkboard. "Now we need two words that describe the word *pizza.*"

"Hot and spicy," Tomas says as he licks his lips.

"Great!" Ms. Avelar says as she adds the line to the poem. "The next line has three words and uses verbs that tell about what the noun does. This is a hard one."

The students all turn to the page in their booklets with the word *pizza* at the top and start reading action words.

"I've got it!" Nikki says, beaming. "Steaming, bubbling, tempting."

"That's good," Ms. Avelar says as she adds the line to the poem. "So far we have:

Pizza
Hot, spicy.
Steaming, bubbling, tempting.

"Now we need a complete five- or six-word sentence about pizza," Ms. Avelar says.

"How about, 'I like pepperoni, mushrooms, and cheese'?" Tyrone suggests.

"That sounds great," Ms. Avelar says as she adds the line to the poem. "Now, we need one more complete sentence using 6 to 10 words about the pizza."

"Oh, I know!" Nikki suggests. "'Let's call Pizza Hut on the telephone right now!'"

"That's it," Ms. Avelar says and she writes Nikki's sentence on the board under the other lines. "Let's read our poem." The whole class reads together.

Pizza

Hot, spicy.

Steaming, bubbling, tempting.

I like pepperoni, mushrooms, and cheese.

Let's call Pizza Hut on the telephone right now!

"Can you guess why it's called a **pyramid poem**?" Ms. Avelar asks.

"It looks like a pyramid," Tyrone responds.

"That's true," says Ms. Avelar. "That's why you have some lines with 4 or 5 words and some with 6 to 10 words. You choose the number of words you need to make each line a little longer than the one before it. It has to form a pyramid shape. Now, you know what I want you to do next." Ms. Avelar smiles.

"Write poems!" the class shouts.

"Yes, I want you to write pyramid poems," Ms. Avelar says. "You may write by yourself or with a partner. You may write in English or in Spanish. You may write with paper and pencil or on the computer. Use the word booklets to help you. Does anyone need a partner?"

The students move close to their partners and some go to the computers to write. Several students go to tables away from the others to write by themselves, but everyone is busily engaged in writing poems using their word booklets.

Conclusion

Repetition and innovation strategies provide students with multiple opportunities to learn new concepts. The choice of repetition and innovation should be based on observation of the students' understanding of the concepts being presented. Each repetition or innovation should build on the last so that the students are experiencing gradually more difficult applications of the concepts. These activities are especially supportive of English language learners because they see multiple definitions and uses of the new concepts and vocabulary they are using. Video Example 28.1 will demonstrate how the implementation of a "repetition and innovation" lesson can be carried out.

Enhanced eText
Video Example 28.1
https://www.youtube.com/
watch?v=ypzhS0lziKE

Examples of Approximation Behaviors Related to the TESOL Standards

PreK–3 students will:

- illustrate the main events in the story.
- write an alternate ending to a familiar story.

4–8 students will:

- write a sequel for a familiar story.

- write a formula poem based on a familiar story.

9–12 students will:

- write a new version of a familiar plot.
- rewrite a story from an alternate point of view.

References

Beck, I., McKeown, M., & Kucan, L. (2002). *Bringing words to life: Robust vocabulary instruction.* New York, NY: Guilford Press.

Gibbons, P. (2015). *Scaffolding language, scaffolding learning: Teaching English language learners in the mainstream classroom.* Portsmouth, NH: Heinemann.

Heller, R. (1987). *A cache of jewels and other collective nouns.* New York, NY: Grosset & Dunlap.

Heller, R. (1988). *Kites fly high.* New York, NY: Grosset & Dunlap.

Heller, R. (1989). *Many luscious lollipops.* New York, NY: Grosset & Dunlap.

Numeroff, L. (1985). *If you give a mouse a cookie.* New York, NY: Macmillan/McGraw-Hill.

Numeroff, L. (1998). *If you give a pig a pancake.* New York, NY: Macmillan/McGraw-Hill.

Tompkins, G. E. (2012). *Language arts: Patterns of practice.* Upper Saddle River, NJ: Macmillan/Prentice Hall.

Language Focus Lessons
Supporting English Vocabulary and Structure Acquisition

Language focus lessons (Gibbons, 1993; Goldenberg, 2008) emphasize English vocabulary and usage rather than the curricular content. These lessons may explore content such as math, science, or social sciences, but the focus of the lesson is on the language being used rather than the content itself. The language selected for language focus lessons is based on a teacher's observation and knowledge of the language forms and functions that give language learners difficulty, such as presenting opinions, stating comparisons, or summarizing information (Echevarria, Vogt, & Short, 2010; Gibbons, 2015). Focused instruction enables English learners to progress more rapidly and achieve higher levels of language proficiency (Ellis, 2006). Examples of appropriate language for language focus lessons are shown in Figure 29.1.

Step-by-Step

The steps in teaching a language focus lesson are the following:

- *Observe and note language errors*—Observe your students and take notes on the types of language that they tend to misuse. Plan time to work with small groups of students who have the same needs for direct instruction in language usage.
- *Gather materials*—Gather realia, visuals, and ideas for hands-on demonstrations of the language usage to be taught.
- *Explain and model language usage*—Introduce the vocabulary and model its use, simultaneously using the language as you model. Give several examples for each term so that students can see when and how the language is used.
- *Practice in active mode*—Give students an opportunity to perform or model a hands-on movement or activity as they use the focus language.
- *Practice for mastery*—Design an activity that allows you to observe the students' mastery of the focus language. If they do not connect the language to the actions correctly, repeat the third and fourth steps.
- *Assess using observation*—Performance tasks can be planned to determine each student's mastery of the language focus lesson. Provide an opportunity for each student to use the focus language in context and use an anecdotal record or checklist to keep a record of the student's performance. See Figure 29.2 for examples of an anecdotal record and checklist to document a performance task.

FIGURE 29.1 Suggested Language Forms and Functions for Language Focus Lessons

Language Form	Curricular Connections	Examples
Articles *a, an, one, the, this, these*	Words that indicate plurals, singular forms	Cloze activities, narratives with articles and numerical indicator left out, which might relate to any subject area
Prepositional phrases, position words *in, on, under, beside, in back of*	Language arts, science, social sciences	Using literature that shows position, such as *Rosie's Walk* Math activities such as placing a certain number of things *beside* others or stacking things *on top of* others using number and position words
Degrees of obligation *must, may, might, could, should*	Predictions in science, literature, class rules	Discussion of class rules in which situations are discussed, and student choices are compared with rules that *must* be followed Science experiments where hypotheses are being tested, students discuss what *might* happen Problem-solving activities in which things that *could* be tried are listed and compared with things that *must* be done
Comparison words *smaller, larger, fewer, less, wider, narrower, taller, shorter, greater than, less than, equal to*	Mathematics, describing in any subject area	Discussion of size of groups or objects, attributes of anything being compared
Content-related words	Mathematics, science, social sciences, reading	Use of content words in context. Scientific terms such as *experiment, liquid, solid, gas* presented with realia, multiple examples

Applications and Examples

Mr. Lee is concerned because his first graders often leave off endings of words, both orally and in writing. He observes and notes the students who are doing this and plans a language focus lesson for these students. During math the next day, Mr. Lee gathers six students to do an activity with joining sets and writing story problems. Each student is given a laminated picture of a lake with large lily pads and small green and brown frogs. He instructs the students to pick out 15 green

FIGURE 29.2 Sample Anecdotal Record and Checklist to Document a Performance Task

4/30/15 Claudio was given six plastic frogs. Teacher asked, "How many frogs do you have?"
Claudio – Six.
Teacher – Tell me in a whole sentence.
Claudio – I have six frog.
Teacher – Remember to add the "s."
Claudio – I have six frogs.
Teacher moves one of the frogs in a jumping motion to a lily pad.
Teacher – What did the frog do?
Claudio – He jumped.
Teacher – YES! He jumped. How many frogs do you have now.
Claudio – I have five frogs.

Checklist Format

Name _____ Date _____			
Context: **Performance task to test plurals and *ed* endings**			
Task	**Date**	**Date**	**Date**
Uses plural *s* spontaneously			
Uses plural *s* when reminded			
Uses *ed* ending spontaneously			
Uses *ed* ending when reminded			
Comments:			

frogs and put them on the lily pads. He then says the following sentence, emphasizing the plural /s/ each time he says it, "There are 15 brown frogs on the lily pads in the lake. Six of them jump into the water to cool off. How many frogs are left on the lily pads?" As the students count out the six frogs, he asks, "How many frogs jump into the water?"

The students answer, "Six."

"Yes," Mr. Lee says, "Six frogs jump into the water."

Mr. Lee then asks each student to repeat the words, "Six frogs," emphasizing the final /s/.

"When you add /s/ to the word *frog*, it lets you know there is more than one frog," Mr. Lee explains. "It is very important to pronounce the /s/. One thing you will notice is that when you add the /s/ to the end of the word *frog*, it sounds like a /z/. The *s* at the end of the words sometimes sounds like a /z/, but we still spell it with an *s*. We will make a chart of the words that sound like a /z/ at the end when we add *s* to them."

"We will put the word *frogs* in jail because the *s* doesn't follow the rules and sound like an *s* should sound," Mr. Lee says as he writes the word *frogs* on a 3-by-5 card and puts it on a bulletin board that has bars on it like a jail cell. "We will put other words in jail whenever we find that they are not following the rules. If you find any more words that are spelled with an *s* at the end but sound like /z/, be sure to tell me so we can put those words in jail."

Next, Mr. Lee has the students write story problem about the frogs, emphasizing the writing of the *s* on the words *frogs* and *lily pads*.

"Mr. Lee, Mr. Lee!" calls Gustov. "We have to put *pads* in jail too! It sounds like a /z/, just like *frogs*."

"Good for you, Gustov! You're a great word detective," Mr. Lee says as he hands Gustov a blank card and a marker. "Put that word in jail."

"Now, I want you to think of other word problems you can write using the frogs and the lily pads," Mr. Lee says.

After the students have a chance to write some problems, Mr. Lee has them read the problems aloud and the other students work them out using the frogs and the lily pad pictures. Once Mr. Lee sees that the students are adding the *s*, both in speaking and in writing, he changes the focus of the lesson to the /ed/ ending, using the same materials but emphasizing that the frogs already jumped into the water. Because the /ed/ at the end of the word *jumped* sounds like a /t/ instead of /ed/, the children decide that *jumped* must also go to jail.

José says, "English is hard, Mr. Lee. There are a lot of rule breakers."

"This is very true," Mr. Lee says with a sigh. "But you are very smart, and you will learn to speak English. Just look at the word jail if you need help with a rule breaker. Maybe we need to write the rule that each of the words breaks so we can remember. What should we say about *frogs* and *pads*?"

"They sound like /z/ when they should sound like /s/," Arturo suggests.

"What about *jumped*?" asks Mr. Lee.

"It sounds like /t/ when it should sound like /ed/," Tomas says.

"Let's put them in different cells!" Katey adds.

At the end of the lesson, Mr. Lee teaches the students a signal he will use to remind them when they are leaving off endings in their oral speech and in their written work. The signal he and the students agree on is a pinkie finger touched to the end of the nose. The students and Mr. Lee practice giving this signal to each other to help them to remember to pronounce ending sounds carefully.

Mr. Lee knows that one lesson will not solve the problem of the dropped endings on words, but he will use the pinkie to the nose signal to remind the students to pronounce /s/ and /ed/ clearly when they are speaking, and to add them in writing. He also signals toward the word jail board to help the students remember how to pronounce the endings.

As the year progresses, Mr. Lee plans to teach more language focus lessons and add the other sounds for the /ed/ ending as he sees the need. The children, in the meantime, are looking for more words to put in jail.

* * * * *

Ms. Karras plans to teach a language focus lesson with her sixth-grade English language learners who are having difficulty understanding words that describe the classroom rules. She plans a lesson in which they will review the rules and use examples to help the students understand the meanings of the words *must, may, might, should,* and *could.* To teach this lesson, Ms. Karras will refer to the rules and procedures chart shown in Figure 29.3.

Ms. Karras poses questions based on the statements printed on the chart. As Ms. Karras and the students discuss each item, they make a "requirement line" on the chalkboard, placing

FIGURE 29.3 Mr. Karras' Rules and Procedures

1. You must speak to classmates and teachers with respect.
2. You should raise your hand before speaking.
3. You may get materials and books without asking permission.
4. You may get drinks as needed.
5. You should keep your books and materials in good order.

each of the "requirement words" from the chart along the line according to its strength. The students decide that *must* is a very strong word that means "every time, no question about it," and they place *must* at the far right of the "requirement line." They place *may* to the far left and discuss the word *could* in relation to *may*. They decide that *could* and *may* are about the same in strength. *Should* is discussed next. The students decide that *should* is not really as strong as *must*, but in the classroom, both words are often used to mean "It's required. You have to do it."

The lesson continues this way until all the words are placed along the line according to their strength. Ms. Karras then asks the students to think of laws and rules from home and the community that would be examples of each of the words on the chart. Cher suggests, "My dad got a ticket because he didn't stop at a stop sign. Stopping at stop signs goes under *must*."

"Great example!" Ms. Karras says. "The laws are musts. Can you tell me why?"

"Because you can kill someone if you drive a car and don't follow the laws," Cher states solemnly.

"That's true, Cher," Ms. Karras says. "Can you think of an example for *might*?"

"If my mother has time after dinner, she *might* bake a cake," Tina suggests.

"Good example, Tina," Ms. Karras says. "She doesn't have to do it; it's just a possibility. Is there another word you can use in place of *might* in that same sentence?"

"If my mother has time after dinner, she *could* bake a cake," Tina replies.

"Does that mean the same thing?" Ms. Karras asks.

"Not really," Juan comments. "*Might* means she's thinking about it. *Could* means it's something she can do but maybe she's not even thinking about it."

"I think you've got it," Ms. Karras says. "Let's practice some more."

Ms. Karras gives the students cloze sentences written on sentence strips and asks them to take turns reading the sentences and decide which word from the chart completes the sentence best. After they decide on the best word, they have to explain their choice. When they finish this exercise, the chart looks like the one in Figure 29.4.

Conclusion

Language focus lessons are appropriate whenever a teacher identifies a mispronunciation or misuse of language that occurs consistently. The lessons can be used with individual students, small groups, or the whole class. However, it is important with young students, or those just beginning to risk oral communication, that the lesson not be allowed to interfere with communication. If a student mispronounces or misuses language but the message is clear, it is always important to respond to the request or message. The teacher should note the misuse and the speaker or speakers who misuse the language, and then plan a language focus lesson to support English

FIGURE 29.4 The Requirement Line and Sample Sentences

may	can might	should	must

< - >

I _____ go to the movies.   I _____ do my homework.
    I _____ have some candy.   I _____ follow rules.
I _____ go to bed early.   I _____ pick up the trash.
    I _____ give you a pen.   I _____ obey my dad.
I _____ ask my sister.   I _____ copy this over.
    I _____ do that.   I _____ be polite.

learners in refining their use of English. Language focus lessons are most effective when they are presented in a positive way and the students are encouraged to practice the newly acquired skills in an authentic context. There are many new programs being developed to assist teachers with language focus lessons. To view an overview of one of these packaged programs see the Video Example 29.1.

Enhanced eText
Video Example 29.1

Examples of Approximation Behaviors Related to the TESOL Standards

PreK–3 students will:

- form and ask questions related to assignments.
- gather and organize materials needed to complete assigned work.

4–8 students will:

- find and use information from several sources to complete assignments.
- edit and revise written assignments.

9–12 students will:

- take and support a position on an assigned topic.
- prepare for and participate in an oral report or debate.

References

Echevarria, J., Vogt, M., & Short, D. (2010). *Making content comprehensible for elementary English learners: The SIOP model.* Boston, MA: Allyn & Bacon.

Ellis, R. (2006). Current issues in the teaching of grammar: An SLA perspective. *TESOL Quarterly, 40*(1), 83–107.

Gibbons, P. (1993). *Learning to learn in a second language.* Portsmouth, NH: Heinemann.

Gibbons, P. (2015). Scaffolding language, scaffolding learning: Teaching English language learners in the mainstream classroom. Portsmouth, NH: Heinemann.

Goldenberg, G. (2008). Teaching English language learners: What the research does—and does not—say. *American Educator, 32*(2), 8–44.

30

Graphic Organizers

Visually Representing Ideas, Text, and Connections

Graphic organizers are visuals or pictures created to represent ideas, text, or connections between texts. Graphic organizers aid comprehension by enabling readers to label aspects of a text, using language from that text, to visually illustrate the connections between events and characters. Graphic organizers also support English learners by taking a lot of potentially confusing English vocabulary and concepts and presenting them in an organized, visual format (Echevarria, Vogt, & Short, 2010). There are a number of graphic organizers that can be used to support students in reading and comprehending text (Bromley, Irwin-DeVitis, & Modlo, 1995). **Venn diagrams** are used to compare different texts or a reader's experiences with text in the form of overlapping circles. **Flow charts** are used to represent the sequence of events in text visually.

The number of different ways in which graphic organizers can be used to support understanding in readers is endless. Matching the graphic organizer to the purpose of the lesson is vital. Visit the TeacherVision website (https://www.teachervision.com/lesson-planning/graphic-organizer) to obtain a list of printable graphic organizers.

As students create the graphic representation of a text, they are required to reread, discuss, and explore relationships within the text. Graphic organizers are also effective ways to brainstorm, plan, and organize writing. In addition, teachers can use conceptual organizers to make ideas within informational text more accessible to students. Students are required to think more analytically to place individual characteristics and ideas in their proper position within the diagram (Tompkins, 2013). These diagrams may also be used to assess student learning. Watch this teacher complete a graphic organizer with her 6th, 7th, and 8th graders in a "Newcomer Class" (see Video Example 30.1).

Enhanced eText
Video Example 30.1
https://youtu.be/
ecw3oaH6ZAQ

Research in the use of graphic organizers in teaching English language learners to read and write in English clearly demonstrates how their use benefits ELLs. They show growth in both organizing their thoughts to write (Borjalizadeh et al., 2015) and in comprehending English reading material (Hanjoni & Shafiel, 2017).

Step-by-Step

The steps in implementing graphic organizers are the following:

• *Identify the teaching purposes*—Identify text to be used that can be supported with a graphic organizer. Refer to Figure 30.1 to find a graphic organizer that can be used to support student understanding of the text and your teaching objective.

FIGURE 30.1 Comparing and Contrasting *Frederick* and *Rodents: From Mice to Muskrats*

Frederick   **Rodents: From Mice to Muskrats**

live in a stone wall
talk like humans
write poetry
gather words, sun rays,
and colors

eat corn, straw, wheat
and nuts; store food for
winter, burrow for cold
weather; don't hibernate

eat caterpillars,
berries, and insects
live in hollow logs
don't talk

- *Explain the purpose*—Explain the graphic organizer and its purpose to your students, and model how the organizer works. Construct an example, talking through the construction as it is built.

- *Involve students in constructing a graphic*—Walk students through the building of a graphic, asking questions that lead them to place components in the proper places on the graphic.

- *Discuss the connections*—Support students in discussing the connections shown on the graphic while using the vocabulary included in the text in the discussion.

- *Provide additional practice in using graphic organizers*—As students become familiar with a variety of graphic organizers, encourage them to use the graphics to represent their understanding in a variety of contexts.

Applications and Examples

Mr. Flores and his second-grade class are studying a unit on rodents. As part of the unit, Mr. Flores sets up a cage containing a couple of field mice for the students to observe. They observe the mice for a few days, and then Mr. Flores reads the book *Rodents: From Mice to Muskrats* (Miller, 1998) to the students. Mr. Flores asks the students, "What do our mice need to live here in the classroom?"

Roberto says, "They need something to eat and water to drink."

"And how will they get that here in the room?" Mr. Flores asks.

Lucy responds, "We have to give it to them."

"Yes, that's right, Lucy," says Mr. Flores. "And, what does this book tell us they would eat if they were living out in the field?" asks Mr. Flores. Several students name different foods that Mr. Flores read from the book, and he writes the list on the chalkboard. He then asks students to tell him something about where the mice live when they live outside the classroom. "Do they have nice warm cages out there?" he asks.

"No," says Quan, "they have to find like an old log to live in or something."

"Yes," replies Mr. Flores, "and what if they can't find a hollow log?"

"Well," Jenny says thoughtfully, "they could dig a hole in the ground and sleep there."

"Exactly, Jenny," says Mr. Flores, "and that is what we call a burrow. They can make their home under the ground and live there safe and warm." Mr. Flores then adds a statement that mice live in hollow logs or burrows to the list on the chalkboard. "Now I would like to read one of my favorite stories about mice to you. Listen carefully and see how many of the things we just talked about are in this story too," says Mr. Flores.

He reads the book *Frederick* by Leo Lionni (1967) to the students. After reading the story, Mr. Flores asks the students, "What are some of the things that Frederick and his family can do that the field mice in the first book can't do?"

"Frederick can talk!" exclaims José.

"Sí, José," replies Mr. Flores. "In the story I just read, Frederick and his family can talk. Do you think real field mice can talk like Frederick can?"

"Nooooo," the students all reply in unison.

"But sometimes they make little noises, kinda like they're talking, Mr. Flores," says Lavina.

"Yes, they do," replies Mr. Flores. "But is that the same kind of talking that Frederick does?"

"Nooooo," intone the students.

"So," Mr. Flores says, "then there are some things in the book about Frederick that are different than some of the things we heard about field mice in the first book I read. Tell me some of the other things that are different in the book about Frederick."

The students share that Frederick gathers words, sun rays, and colors instead of storing food for the winter. They also note that he writes poetry, which they think highly unusual for a mouse.

"How do you think Frederick can do all those silly things?" Mr. Flores asks the students. "None of the mice do those kinds of things in the first book I read to you."

"Because the mice in the first book are real mice, and Frederick is just a make-believe mouse," Toby answers.

"That's right, Toby," says Mr. Flores. "The first book is a book of facts—we call it an informational book—and the book about Frederick is make-believe, or fiction."

"So, today, boys and girls, we are going to compare some of the facts and ideas from both books and see if we can decide which ones are facts and which ones are fiction. Let's start by seeing if we can name some things that are the same in both books," states Mr. Flores. As students suggest things that are the same in both books, Mr. Flores lists them vertically on the chalkboard. They decide that in both books, the mice eat corn, straw, wheat, and nuts. They agree that both books are about field mice. In both books, the mice store food for winter and dig burrows for protection against cold weather. They see in both books that the mice don't hibernate but do find a place where they can be safe and warm for the winter.

After they create the list of things that are the same, Mr. Flores draws a pair of overlapping circles around the list (see Figure 30.1). Once Mr. Flores draws and introduces the Venn diagram, he then leads the children in a discussion about what things are different in each story and lists those items in the appropriate section of the Venn diagram. He then reminds the students to notice that the things that are the same are in the parts of the circles that overlap and that the things that are different are in a part of the circle all by themselves.

Mr. Flores then uses the Venn diagram in a short discussion with the children, leading them to the conclusion that even though one of the books is factual and the other is make-believe, there can be some factual information even in a make-believe book. Mr. Flores reviews the concept of fact versus fiction by asking students to come to the board and point to a fact in the diagram and then to point to something that is fiction in the diagram.

* * * * *

Ms. Vang's 10th-grade class is beginning the production of a school newspaper. Before they begin to write news stories, Ms. Vang explains the necessity of including basic facts in their news stories. She presents the students with a graphic organizer to remind them to proofread for the basic facts before they submit stories for the paper. Using a news story from that morning's paper, she walks the students through the graphic, looking for the basic facts in the news story to answer the questions who, what, when, why, and how. See Figure 30.2 for the graphic Ms. Vang uses with her journalism class.

Conclusion

Using graphic organizers in reading analysis encourages and enables students to examine text from a variety of perspectives. The graphics presented here are examples of organizers that support readers in making sense of text, relating it to past experiences, and understanding connections made in text. Students can work in cooperative groups to create graphic organizers and discuss the meaning of materials they are reading. Seeing the structure of text represented visually

FIGURE 30.2 News Release

Minnesota Magicians Win Series Against the Russians

In a three-game matchup between a 16-and-under hockey team visiting from Russia and the Minnesota Magic, the local boys won two of three games. The Russians, visiting in a series entitled "Hockey Crossing Borders," are staying in Minnesota for the month of September 2018 playing hockey every day against local 16-and-under teams.

The Magic, an invitational all-star team, is composed of skaters from several local high school hockey teams including Northfield, Greater Prairie, Medina, Post Lake, and Shelby. Goals for the Magic were made by Kurt Jacobs, Post Lake; Mike Hertzfield, Shelby; Connor Batman, Northfield; and Jack Arthur, Greater Prairie.

Although the Russian team included several skaters over six feet tall and outweighing the Magic skaters, the Minnesota defense kept them to a total of four goals for the three-game series. The Russians won the first game 2–1, and the Magic won the next two games holding the Russians to one goal per game.

The Russians were hosted by the Greater Prairie hockey team, and all games were played in Medina and Greater Prairie. The Magic has been invited to travel to Russia to resume the competition.

Graphic Organizer for the News Story

Who? _____

What? _____

When? _____

Where? _____

Why? _____

How? _____

---

supports students who are having difficulty with comprehension and helps them to work through vocabulary and concepts that are unclear to them. Using graphic organizers has been shown to encourage students to become more analytic in their reading and to reflect more deeply on the meaning and contextual clues found in text (Bromley et al., 1995).

Examples of Approximation Behaviors Related to the TESOL Standards

PreK–3 students will:
- represent text structures with graphic organizers.
- interpret simple graphic organizers.

4–8 students will:
- use graphic organizers to compare and contrast texts and concepts.

- read graphic organizers and use them to explain concepts.

9–12 students will:
- design graphic organizers to represent academic text.
- read and explain graphic organizers of academic text.

References

Borjalizadeh, M., Shabani, M., Sorahi, M. (2015). The effect of graphic organizers on EFL learners' writing skills. *Modern Journal of Language Teaching Methods 5*(4). 132–137.

Bromley, K., Irwin-DeVitis, L., & Modlo, M. (1995). *Graphic organizers.* New York, NY: Scholastic Books.

Echevarria, J., Vogt, M., & Short, D. (2010). *Making content comprehensible for elementary English students.* Boston, MA: Allyn & Bacon.

Hanjoni, A., and Shafiel, E. (2017). The effect of graphic organizers on reading comprehension of Iranian EFL learners with a focus on gender. *Modern Journal of Language Teaching Methods, 7*(3). 256–263.

Lionni, L. (1967). *Frederick.* New York, NY: Trumpet.

Miller, S. (1998). *Rodents: From mice to muskrats.* New York, NY: Franklin Watts/Grolier.

Tompkins, G. (2013). *Literacy in the early grades: A successful start for pre-K through grade 4 readers and writers.* Upper Saddle River, NJ: Pearson.

31

Advance Organizers
Getting the Mind in Gear for Instruction

Advance organizers (Ausubel, 1963) are brief presentations of abstract concepts given before a lesson to help learners make connections between their existing knowledge and the new information to be presented. The form these organizers take depends on the age, developmental level, and existing knowledge of the learner. Two forms of advance organizers can be used, based on the nature of the material to be presented. An **expository organizer** is designed to present concepts and principles to the learner by creating a bridge between what is already known and the new material to be learned. This form of organizer is used when the new material is quite unfamiliar. When the material to be learned is somewhat more familiar, a **comparative organizer** can be used. This form of organizer serves to integrate new material with similar material already understood by the learner and focuses on how the new and known material differs. This is particularly important when the new material may be confused with the previously known material.

Attention to the developmental levels and previous knowledge of learners is important when designing advance organizers (Ausubel, 1963). The use of advance organizers with English language learners is particularly effective because their design builds on the past experiences of the learner and provides bridges to the new material being taught (Cummins, 1986; Diaz-Rico, 2018). Because the developmental levels of the learners are critical to the design of advance organizers, appropriate formats for organizers are shown in Figure 31.1.

Recent research (Bagheri & Bhadori, 2014) has also validated the effectiveness of using advance organizers when English learners are asked to listen to materials presented orally. The value of reviewing known information or introducing new concepts and vocabulary is an important use of advance organizers.

Step-by-Step

The steps in designing and using advance organizers are the following:

• *Identify the main concepts in a lesson to be taught*—Identify the main concepts or understandings the students must master in the lesson. Consider the previous knowledge and experiences of students and develop a way to connect this previous knowledge to the new information. Notice how the teacher connects an appropriate activity to the concept she is introducing in this lesson: Authors "playing with words." (See Video Example 31.1)

Enhanced eText
Video Example 31.1
https://youtu.be/
OX50SoCj4OI

FIGURE 31.1 Appropriate Formats for Advance Organizers

Developmental Levels	Attributes of Learners and Suggested Formats for Advance Organizers
Preoperational preschool/ kindergarten	Need concrete experiences like field trips, hands-on activities, role-plays, Venn diagrams with pictures, realia, photographs
Concrete-operational elementary grades	Depend less upon concrete props as they get older; English learners will still need some of the supports named for preoperational students for language development; activities like 20 questions, debate, oral readings, Venn diagrams with words can now be used
Abstract-logical middle and high school	Learners' dependence on concrete props decreases, they are able to go beyond the "here and now"; English learners will still need concrete props to demonstrate new vocabulary; activities like debates, use of biographies, current events, interviews are now appropriate

• *Design a way to connect prior knowledge to the new concepts*—Design a visual, hands-on learning experience or discussion topic that will encourage the use of known vocabulary and relate new vocabulary to what is already understood. As you design the advance organizer, examine Figure 31.1 for suggestions as to appropriate formats for the developmental levels of your students.

• *Present the advance organizer*—Present the organizer you have designed, encouraging discussion and questions. Relate the new vocabulary to known experiences and vocabulary using gestures, visuals, and restated explanations.

• *Teach the new information*—Teach the new information, relating it back to the advance organizer when appropriate.

• *Add technology*—There are many ways in which technology is helpful in creating effective advance organizers. Videos related to the topic to be presented and PowerPoint presentations that incorporate visuals downloaded from the Internet or scanned from book illustrations are particularly effective ways to integrate technology into advance organizers. Visit the TeacherVision website (www.teachervision.com/lesson-planning/graphic-organizer) to obtain a list of printable graphic organizers.

• *Assess the students' understanding*—Use the advance organizer to assess the students' understanding before moving on to the main lesson. It is vital to assess the connections made by the students. This can be done during the presentation of the advance organizer and the teaching of the lesson through observations, anecdotal notes related to student interactions, responses, participation, and questions. It can also be done by asking the students to create a visual or graphic relating prior experiences explored in the first part of the lesson to those concepts introduced in the latter part of the lesson. These graphics can then be examined for conceptual connections and placed in individual student portfolios. See Figure 31.2 for an example of ways to differentiate assessment for students of different English language development levels.

Applications and Examples

Ms. Flores has noticed that the only shape her kindergarten students recognize as triangles are isosceles triangles. She wants to help her students "correctly name shapes regardless of their

FIGURE 31.2 Differentiating Assessment for Levels of English Development

Preproduction	Ask the student to point to aspects of the advance organizer. Example: Point to the tomato.
Early Production	Ask the student to name aspects of the advance organizer. Example: Show me the leaf and the stem of the tomato.
Speech Emergence	Ask the student to tell you about aspects of the advance organizer. Example: What is this part of the tomato called? What is it used for?
Intermediate Fluency	Ask the student to compare two aspects of the advance organizer. Example: Tell me the differences between this tomato and this other one.
Fluent	Ask the student to explain how aspects of the advance organizer are related to one another. Example: How are these two tomatoes the same? How do you know that they are both tomatoes?

orientations or overall size" (CCSS.MATH.CONTENT.K.G.A.2) and to understand that all three-sided figures are triangles, so she designs an advance organizer to introduce a lesson on triangles. Because her students are only five years old and have limited English language ability, Ms. Flores knows that she must present the advance organizer in a concrete, hands-on form.

To build on the students' prior knowledge, Ms. Flores brings in five tomatoes she has selected because they all have different shapes.

She begins by showing the tomatoes and asking, "What are these?"

The students answer, "Tomatoes."

"How do you know they are tomatoes?" Ms. Flores asks. "What makes them tomatoes?"

"Red," Xiong answers.

"Round," Tina suggests.

"Yes," Ms. Flores agrees. "They are red and round. But they don't all look alike. How do you know they are tomatoes?"

"They smell like tomatoes," Nico says. "We could cut them open."

"Good suggestion," Ms. Flores says as she cuts two tomatoes in half.

"They have seeds inside," Michael says.

"Yes," Ms. Flores agrees. "We know they are tomatoes because they are red, they are round, they smell like tomatoes, and they have seeds inside."

Ms. Flores then takes out a green tomato, puts it on the table, and asks, "Is this a tomato?"

The students giggle and say, "Yes! But it's green."

"It will get red when it's ready," Nico says. "It's still a tomato. It's just not red yet."

"You are too smart for me," Ms. Flores says. "I want to show you something about triangles."

Ms. Flores takes out large cardboard examples of right-angle, isosceles, and obtuse triangles and places them on the chalk tray. "These are all triangles. They don't look exactly alike but they each have three sides." She runs her finger along the sides of each triangle as she counts, "One, two, three."

She then passes the cardboard triangles to the students and encourages them to run their fingers along the three sides of each example, counting the sides. She brings out enough examples for each student, and they pass them around while touching and counting the three sides. Ms. Flores then introduces a sorting game using the cardboard triangles and other cardboard shapes. The students place the shapes together, categorizing them as circles, squares, triangles, and rectangles even though the shapes within the categories are not all the same size. The students place the various types of triangles together and categorize them all as triangles.

Even though the students in Ms. Flores's kindergarten had previously recognized only isosceles triangles, they were able to use the advance organizer to help them understand that just as all tomatoes did not look exactly the same, there were different kinds of triangles.

* * * * *

Ms. Burton teaches ninth-grade social sciences in a highly diverse neighborhood. She is planning a unit about pluralistic society in the United States. She wants her students to recognize the value of diversity in society instead of focusing on rigid allegiance to their own cultural groups and to "determine the meaning of words and phrases as they are used in a text, including vocabulary describing political, social, or economic aspects of history/social science" (CCSS.ELA-LITERACY. RH.9–10.4). As she reads the information to present to the students, she decides to use an advance organizer to prepare the students to incorporate the new information with their existing knowledge.

Building on the old ideal of the United States as a "melting pot" of cultures and the pluralistic view of America as a "salad bowl" of cultures, concepts that are explored in the text the class will be reading, she feels her students will need help to understand these concepts. Ms. Burton decides that an eating activity may help the students better understand the concept of valuing both differences and similarities in a pluralistic society.

Ms. Burton brings in a slow cooker and a salad bowl to class. She takes some cheese, salsa, and chopped vegetables and combines them in the pot as she explains, "Years ago in America when people moved here from other countries, they were all expected to blend in together. America was called the melting pot of cultures. We're using this pot, or melting pot, today to demonstrate what happens when the cultures melt together."

After the ingredients melt together, Ms. Burton asks each student to take a tortilla chip and scoop some of the mixture onto their chip and taste it. After they have taken a taste, she asks them questions about the exact ingredients they had eaten.

"I think I got some peppers and salsa in my scoop," Angel says. "I definitely tasted something hot."

"Because the ingredients were all melted together, it was hard to identify exactly what you ate," Ms. Burton agrees. "This is exactly what happened to the new immigrants as they came to America. They learned to melt into American society, and in many cases, their languages and cultures were lost."

"My grandmother never lost her language," José says. "She stayed at home and took care of the children and only speaks Spanish to them."

"This is true," Ms. Burton says. "The older members of the families often stayed at home and did not melt into the American society."

"But now let's look at what happens in a society where the differences among people are appreciated," Ms. Burton says as she takes out the salad bowl and the salad ingredients. "In a salad bowl, which is the description of what happens in American society now, all the ingredients are mixed together. Instead of melting their flavors together as they did in the melting pot, each ingredient retains its own identity and flavor. The salad is better because of the variety of ingredients—lettuce, tomatoes, cucumbers, cheese, dressing, and even onions. As you eat the salad, you can enjoy the unique flavors of each of the ingredients."

As the students enjoy small cups of salad, they talk about each of the ingredients they are tasting. "I like the tomatoes best because they taste sweet," Jesse says.

"I think tomatoes are best in a salad," Moua says. "I don't like tomatoes by themselves."

"A bowl of salad is like American society today," Ms. Burton says. "America is strong because of all the different groups that have come here. The groups are trying to keep their identities and teach their children about their heritages."

Ms. Burton pauses to make this next important point, "In order for the different groups to keep their cultures and traditions and still be able to fit into American society and be accepted, we must learn to value and celebrate the contributions of each individual and group. This is called a *pluralistic* society. It means that there is not just one right way to live but that we can all participate in jobs and school and still celebrate our religions and cultures and even keep speaking our languages in business and within our family groups. For this to happen though, we must appreciate the ways people are different and the ways they are the same. Let's talk about these differences and similarities."

Enhanced eText
Video Example 31.2
https://youtu.be/
qPT-LRqQE_Y?t=343

Ms. Burton then moves the students into a discussion of their cultures, languages, and traditions as the students help her make a list of these things on the board. She continues to use the terms *melting pot* and *salad bowl* to support the students' understanding of the importance of maintaining the value of diversity if a pluralistic society is to be peaceful. Watch Video Example 31.2 for yet another example of using advance organizers with secondary students.

Conclusion

Ms. Burton and Ms. Flores have found ways to use advance organizers to help students build on their background knowledge to understand unfamiliar concepts. By presenting an advance organizer before moving into instruction, teachers activate prior knowledge in their students, explore unfamiliar vocabulary, and support students in seeing similarities between familiar knowledge and new applications or concepts. The bridges formed by advance organizers are especially supportive of English language learners because they tend to reduce the students' anxiety levels and make English instruction more comprehensible.

Examples of Approximation Behaviors Related to the TESOL Standards

PreK–3 students will:

- draw pictures representing their past experiences related to the topic being discussed.
- ask questions to make connections between their past experiences and the topic being discussed.

4–8 students will:

- verbalize relationships between new information and prior knowledge.

- take notes about new information and relate it to prior knowledge.

9–12 students will:

- skim the table of contents to determine key points related to the topic being studied.
- evaluate information and its relationship to prior knowledge.

References

Ausubel, D. (1963). *The psychology of meaningful verbal learning*. New York, NY: Grune and Stratton.

Bagheri, M. S., & Bahadori, M. M. (2014). The effect of providing background knowledge and previewing questions on improving listening comprehension of EFL learners. *Modern Journal of Language Teaching 4*(1). 97–103.

Cummins, J. (1986). Empowering minority students: A framework for interaction. *Harvard Review, 56*, 18–36.

Diaz-Rico, L. (2018). *The crosscultural, language, and academic development handbook: A complete K–12 reference guide* (6th ed.). Boston, MA: Pearson Education.

32

Guided Reading
Providing Individual Support within a Group Setting

Guided reading (Fountas & Pinnell, 1996) is an approach to teaching reading in a small-group setting while providing individual coaching. The students are taught in groups of four to six, all reading at approximately the same level. Teachers use **running records** to determine the students' reading levels and their use of **cueing systems** (attention to phonics, meaning, word order, sentence structure, and the relation of the text to the students' prior experiences). Running records also determine if the students are self-correcting and **self-monitoring** to ensure reading comprehension. Reading for meaning is an important factor in teaching English learners because they can become strong "word-callers" and must be taught to focus on meaning (Vacca et al., 2011). Guided reading is a powerful tool because it provides frequent opportunities for students to read challenging material in small groups with the support and guidance of the teacher. It provides a scaffolding routine because it is predictable, and the students know they will be supported in understanding the text (Peregoy & Boyle, 2013).

A guided reading lesson begins with a **book walk** in which the students and teacher look through the book and predict what will happen. It then progresses through multiple readings of the book, with students reading to themselves at their own pace. During this time, the teacher moves from child to child in the group, listening to each one read and coaching him or her on decoding, self-monitoring, and comprehension strategies. This coaching is done by asking each student questions like, "Does that word start with a *d*?" or "Does that make sense?" The students continue to read until each child has been coached.

Teachers then conduct minilessons based on the needs of the students identified during the coaching sessions. Teachers use this opportunity to discuss the story and determine whether students need support in understanding what they have read. Vocabulary is discussed, clarifying and relating it to the story, the illustrations, and the students' background experiences. The group may then engage in writing, phonics, or other skills activities.

Enhanced eText
Video Example 32.1
www.youtube.com/
watch?v=3AHxqggc-yl

The guided reading approach is appropriate for English language learners because of the focus on vocabulary development, individual instruction, and opportunities for verbal interactions. Because the English language learners participate in a group discussion of the story and the vocabulary encountered, they benefit from the language interactions of the small-group setting. Since their needs may be different from the native English speakers, the individual coaching provides the teacher with an opportunity to support their understanding, correct pronunciation, and clarify word meaning and misconceptions caused by reading in their second language. Watch Video Example 32.1, a second-grade teacher takes her students through a guided reading lesson in this video and notice how she skillfully keeps them on task and actively participating. As you watch, consider the following questions:

- How does this approach help the teacher to individualize instruction?
- Why does this approach to teaching reading benefit English language learners?

Step-by-Step

The steps in teaching a guided reading lesson are the following:

- ***Group the students for instruction***—Place students in groups of four to six, based on information from running records. Choose a book at the appropriate reading level for the students in the group, based on their interests whenever possible. Although guided reading can be used with any text, it is most effective when used with authentic texts that interest the students.
- ***Begin the process***—Gather the group at a table and take a book walk through the book to be read. A book walk involves looking at the illustrations on each page, predicting what will happen on that page, discussing and modeling the meaning of vocabulary that will be needed to read the page, and building background knowledge. Sometimes it will be necessary to use visuals, gestures, or realia—real objects—to support the students' understanding of the vocabulary. It is also very helpful to relate vocabulary words to words in the child's home language whenever possible.
- ***Read aloud but not in unison***—Give the students copies of the book and encourage them to read aloud at their own pace. Move from student to student, listening to each student's oral reading and giving instruction as needed in **decoding**, reading fluently, or self-monitoring. Ask questions to help students learn to self-monitor. Encourage students to reread the story if they finish before you have listened to and coached each child. See Figure 32.1 for suggested questions and prompts to use.

FIGURE 32.1 Questions and Prompts to Promote Self-Monitoring and Comprehension in Guided Reading

Student's Behavior	Sample Questions or Prompts to Use
Guessing words	Does that make sense?
Skipping words	Point to each word as you read it. Did it match?
Inserting extra words	Point to each word as you say it. Were there enough words?
Substituting words that start with the same letter	Does that make sense? Look at the whole word.
Appealing for help from the teacher	Give it a try. How does it begin?
Incorrect reading of a word	Try that again. You made a mistake. Can you find it?

• *Pair students for additional practice*—Pair up students to read to each other, and listen to their oral readings one more time, coaching and celebrating their successes.

• *Teach minilessons based on student needs*—Introduce a minilesson based on the needs you see as you coach individuals. Focus on self-monitoring and problem-solving strategies. Conclude the lesson with a discussion of the story, writing the students' words down in the form of a dictated story or interactive writing lesson. Encourage all the students to participate in an oral rereading of the story written. Join a second-grade teacher as she takes her students through a guided reading exercise in this video (see Video Example 32.2), and stay tuned at the end for an interesting series of questions and answers, perhaps some of the very questions that occurred to you as you watched the exercise.

Enhanced eText
Video Example 32.2
www.youtube.com/
watch?v=GdGZON3rigY

• *Assess on a regular basis*—Assessment plays a very important role in effective guided reading instruction. Students must be taught using books at their instruction level (Tompkins, 2009). To identify the student's instructional reading level, the teacher must find books that the student can read with 90–94 percent accuracy and at a 75 percent comprehension level. Coaching students in books at their instructional level allows them to be successful while making enough errors so that coaching can take place. If the book is too hard, students can become frustrated and may give up trying. If the book is too easy, the teacher has no opportunity to teach strategies that students can use when encountering difficult text.

Teachers use a variety of strategies, including running records, to determine students' instructional reading levels. For a simplified version of the running record, have a student read a section of text to see how many errors are made. Count the number of words in the section read and note the number of errors. If the errors equal 6–10 percent of the total number of words in the section read and the student can retell the story with some general understanding of the events, the book is probably at the student's instructional reading level. For an example of a more formal running record, see Figure 32.2. It is important to know the level of the book being read in order to make adjustments up and down if the current book is too easy or too difficult. Many

FIGURE 32.2 Example of a Formal Running Record

Passage	Errors	Self-Correct	Errors MSV	Self-Correct MSV
✓ ✓ ✓ ran ✓to✓ ✓ Jack and Jill went up the hill	2		Ⓜ Ⓢ V	
✓ find ✓ ✓ ✓ ✓ to fetch a pail of water.	1		Ⓜ Ⓢ V	
✓ ✓ ✓ ✓ ✓ ✓ head Jack fell down and broke his crown,	1		Ⓜ S V	
✓ ✓ ✓ ⌠ falling too ^{SC} and Jill came tumbling after. ⌡R		2	Ⓜ Ⓢ V Ⓜ Ⓢ V	ⓂⓈⓋ ⓂⓈⓋ

resources are available for determining the levels of books. For a list of leveled books, visit the Arbook Find (www.arbookfind.com) or the Scholastic website (teacher.scholastic.com/products/guidedreading/leveling_chart.htm.)

In addition to determining a student's instructional reading level, the teacher must also observe the types of errors the student makes to determine how best to provide effective coaching. See Figure 32.3 for suggestions for effective coaching based on the types of errors being made.

Applications and Examples

First and second grade teachers use guided reading with all students. Although guided reading as described in this chapter is usually done in primary grade classrooms, it is appropriate for English language learners of all ages because of the comprehension instruction and language development it supports. It is particularly valuable for English language learners because of the repeated reading it encourages and the vocabulary that is introduced, modeled, and connected to illustrations.

For example, Ms. Garcia is using the little softback book *Where's Tim?* (Cowley, 1996) with a group of Southeast Asian students. The book tells of a child looking for his pet cat. He looks in many places, including the kitchen cupboard, and finally finds the cat under the bedspread.

FIGURE 32.3 Guided Reading Strategies

Problem	Suggested Strategies
Insufficient background	Use realia, visuals, or videos to build background. Read aloud picture books that relate to the same topic .
Unfamiliar vocabulary	Use realia, illustrations, or skits to act out meanings. Provide translation to home language for unknown words.
Word-by-word reading	Provide a fluent model by using echo reading. In echo reading, the teacher reads the sentence fluently and the student rereads it using expression and intonation echoing the teacher's model. Provide a model of reading with correct phrasing and ask the child to repeat the reading, phrase by phrase.
Reading past miscues without self-correcting	Stop the reader and focus on the miscue if it changes the meaning of the sentence. Support the reader in the use of phonics, meaning, syntax, and context so that the use of multiple cues is modeled and stressed.
Inability to answer questions after reading	Support the reader in looking back at the text to find the answers. Focus on the meaning as the text is reread. If the question is inferential, support the reader in finding clues that may help him or her to make guesses related to the question. Discuss the possibilities and agree on a likely response. Try to find ways to connect the questions and answers to the reader's background knowledge.

Ms. Garcia does a book walk with her second-grade students, showing the pictures and asking the students to predict where the boy might look next. When Ms. Garcia reaches the page where the boy is looking in the kitchen cupboard, she shows them the cupboard behind her, under the classroom sink.

She says, "This is a cupboard. It's like a closet, but it's usually found in a kitchen or bathroom. It's not as tall as a closet." She gestures toward the coat closet as she says the word *closet*. She repeats *cupboard*, pointing to the cupboard. She repeats *closet*, pointing to the coat closet.

When the boy discovers the lump under the bedspread, Ms. Garcia demonstrates a lump by covering a stuffed cat with a towel. She says, "The boy saw a lump. The cat made a lump under the bedspread." She has the students pull their hands up under their sleeves to show her how their hands make lumps under their sleeves. They then read the story.

Conclusion

Guided reading can help English learners in the upper grades understand content reading such as science and social sciences where the vocabulary is often unfamiliar to students. Using this approach; walking students through the reading material; examining illustrations, charts, and graphs; and discussing each activity serves to support students as they are building comprehension. Reading in pairs and encouraging summary and discussion is also appropriate with older students.

Good organization is essential to successful implementation of guided reading strategies.

Examples of Approximation Behaviors Related to the TESOL Standards

PreK–3 students will:

- respond to teacher questions to make sense of text.
- use a balance of cueing systems to unlock unknown words.

4–8 students will:

- use self-questioning to make sense of text.

- monitor self-reading to evaluate personal comprehension.

9–12 students will:

- periodically stop and self-evaluate for metacognition while reading.
- use active fix-up strategies when reading comprehension breaks down.

References

Cowley, J. (1996). *Where's Tim?* Auckland, New Zealand: Wright Group.

Fountas, I., & Pinnell, G. (1996). *Guided reading: Good first teaching for all children.* Portsmouth, NH: Heinemann.

Peregoy, S., & Boyle, O. (2013). *Reading, writing, and learning in ESL* (6th ed.). Boston, MA: Longman.

Tompkins, G. (2009). *Literacy for the 21st century: Teaching reading and writing in prekindergarten through grade 4.* Upper Saddle River, NJ: Pearson Education.

Vacca, J. A. L., Vacca, R. T., Gove, M. K., Burkey, L. C., Lenhart, I. A., & McKeon, C. A. (2011). *Reading and learning to read* (8th ed.). Boston, MA: Allyn & Bacon.

33

Cohesion Links

Understanding the Glue That Holds Paragraphs Together

Cohesion links are the important parts of written and spoken paragraphs that connect sentences so that they form a cohesive whole. These links often appear in the form of pronouns that refer back to a person, place, or thing in a previous sentence or references that require the reader to recall a previously stated fact or condition. Cohesion links that are frequently used in spoken and written English are often confusing to English language learners. This is because the use of pronouns or use of ellipses where words are understood—but not spoken or written—are not always easy to connect to words used in previous sentences (Herrell & Jordan, 2006). Other cohesion links such as words that indicate sequence (e.g., *first, second, third*) can be taught. They serve well to support students' understanding of the text structure. Links that negate or minimize a previous statement such as *nevertheless, moreover,* and *nonetheless* are especially confusing to English learners and must be addressed, modeled, and practiced (Peregoy & Boyle, 2013). The forms of English writing and speaking that English language learners find most confusing are shown in Figure 33.1. Good examples of the use of cohesion links, which are sometimes called cohesive devices, can be seen in the Video Example 33.1.

Enhanced eText
Video Example 33.1
https://www.youtube.com/watch?v=i8bvEOMdX_w

Lessons in this strategy make cohesion links more visible and understandable to English language learners and support their understanding of both spoken and written material. Discussing cohesion links helps English learners improve both their oral and written English production. A lesson in revision supports all learners in understanding the process (Swain, 1993).

Step-by-Step

The steps in teaching a lesson on cohesion links are the following:

• *Use a sample paragraph*—Prepare a paragraph at the students' reading level that contains pronouns, conjunctions, substitutions, or ellipses. You may want to use a **document camera** or smartboard to project the paragraph so the whole group can see it. Start with a fairly simple paragraph and then gradually add complexity in future lessons. Write the paragraph so that you can uncover one sentence at a time.

• *Read one sentence at a time*—Cover all but the first sentence of the paragraph and have the students read that sentence aloud with you. Discuss any words that substitute for others or refer the reader to another word in the sentence. Uncover the second sentence and repeat the

FIGURE 33.1 Cohesive Ties in Written and Spoken English and the Difficulty They Cause ELLs

Cohesive Tie	Example	Problem
Reference	A tall figure was standing outside the door. <u>The</u> figure turned quickly toward <u>her</u> as Sally stepped onto the porch. As <u>she</u> regained <u>her</u> composure <u>she</u> watched as <u>he</u> turned without a word and walked away toward the bus stop in the rain.	These underlined reference words often refer back to something already mentioned in the text. English language learners often do not recognize the relationship between the sentences and words used to refer back to a previous sentence.
Conjunctions	He worked all day <u>although</u> he was tired. <u>Finally</u> he laid down his hammer. He wasn't finished, <u>but</u> his work was getting sloppy. <u>So</u> he was afraid of ruining his work <u>unless</u> he got some rest.	Conjunctions are key words in helping the reader determine the connections between ideas and the sequencing of events. English language learners do not always understand the connections that conjunctions demonstrate and so they often misunderstand the text being read or heard.
Substitution	He was given a new pair of shoes for Christmas. His old <u>ones</u> were too small.	When one word is substituted for another, English language learners often do not recognize that both words are referring to the same thing.
Ellipses	He sat down, ✓ stood up, and then ✓ sat down again. He said, "Some people like to dance and others don't ✓."	The checks in the example show places where words are left out but the reader or listener assumes meaning as if the words were present. English language learners may not recognize what is missing or may not be able to supply the meaning because of the omitted words.
Lexical cohesion	The giant was now in a land of tall *trees* and flowing *rivers*. He was still <u>running</u> hard, although he was <u>slowing</u> down considerably. He went <u>galloping</u> over an enormous *forest* and on into a huge *range of mountains*.	If an English language learner does not see the connections between the underlined words or the words in italics, this selection will not make as much sense as it should.

Source: Adapted from Gibbons (1991) and Halliday and Hasan (1966).

process, supporting the students in making connections between words in the first sentence and references in the first sentence. If you are using an overhead projector, you can cover the paragraph with a clear transparency and use a dry erase marker to draw an arrow back to the proper noun or any other word that has been replaced by a pronoun. Using a smartboard you can simply add the arrow to indicate the words the pronouns are replacing. This process will help make the connections visible to the students. You might also choose to use an erasable highlighter directly on the text being projected when using a document camera.

• *Read the rest of the paragraph one sentence at a time*—Work your way through the entire paragraph this way. Make connections among pronouns and nouns, sequence words, conjunctions, and multiple ways of referring to the same thing.

• *Practice in pairs*—Follow up this lesson by dividing the students into pairs and giving each pair a paragraph written on plain paper if you are using a document camera or on a transparency if you are using an overhead projector. Encourage the pairs to work together to draw arrows from pronouns to the words in other sentences to which the pronouns refer. Have them label the conjunctions and circle words that describe the same things.

• *Review the connections*—Have the paired students display their paragraphs on the document camera, overhead projector, or smartboard and discuss their conclusions after they have completed their work. Have the entire group discuss the connections in the paragraphs that help build meaning as the paragraph is read.

• *Continue to review over time*—Regularly review the connections found in future reading assignments by asking questions such as, "To what word in the first sentence does the word *he* in this sentence refer to?"

• *Assess on a regular basis*—Periodically ask students to demonstrate their understanding of cohesion links by giving them paragraphs to mark. Ask them to draw lines between the connections, as you have demonstrated and they have practiced. After these paragraphs are evaluated, they can be dated and included in individual student portfolios to document student growth over time.

Applications and Examples

Ms. Collom's kindergarten class is writing a language experience story about their trip to the pumpkin patch. The first sentence they dictate is "We went to the pumpkin patch." She stops and asks, "Who went to the pumpkin patch?"

The students respond, "We did!"

Ms. Collom asks, "Who is *we*?"

Philip answers, "Ms. Collom's class—all of us!"

"You are right, Philip. We use the word *we* because it is shorter and easier to say than 'Ms. Collom's class went to the pumpkin patch.' When we say 'we,' we mean Ms. Collom's class."

The class then dictates, "We saw a scarecrow. He was funny." Ms. Collom asks the students, "Who was funny?"

The students laugh, "The scarecrow!"

"Yes," Ms. Collom says. "We don't have to say, 'We saw a scarecrow. The scarecrow was funny.' We can say 'he' was funny because we already said we were talking about the scarecrow."

Ms. Collom knows that pronouns are sometimes difficult for English language learners to understand. She is providing support that will aid their listening and reading comprehension in the future.

* * * * *

Ms. Barnes is teaching a lesson on revising with her eighth-grade writing class. This tends to be rather difficult for English learners, and she finds "showing" more effective than just "telling" for these students. She displays a paragraph on the computer screen, projected on a large monitor so that all the students can see it. The paragraph says:

I was walking down the garden path when I met a small, round man. The small round man was dressed all in green with pointed shoes and a round bowler hat. The small round man's face was round and his cheeks were red. I felt as if I had seen the small round man somewhere before.

Ms. Barnes reads the paragraph aloud to the students and asks them if there is anything that bothers them about the paragraph. The students reply that the phrase "the small round man" is repeated too many times. Ms. Barnes asks for suggestions as to how that could be fixed. The students help her replace "the small round man" with pronouns so that the paragraph sounds better. After the students help her replace the noun phrase with pronouns, Ms. Barnes questions the students about the pronouns and to whom they refer. The students have no problems understanding the paragraph, although many of the English language learners do not know anything about leprechauns.

The students work together to make the paragraph more interesting. One of the challenges Ms. Barnes issues is, "Can you think of some more interesting words to use so that this paragraph isn't so boring?"

Gradually, using suggestions from various students and discussing the meanings of the words added, the class revises the paragraph so that it finally reads:

I was walking slowly down a winding garden path lined with a wild variety of blossoms in every possible color when I met a squat, rotund man with a shiny red face. He was dressed all in green: emerald jacket and trousers, brilliant green velvet shoes with glittering gold buckles, and a round green satin bowler hat. His face was so round that he looked like a caricature of every leprechaun I had ever seen in a book. Even though I knew that leprechauns are usually found in the imaginations of Irishmen and fools who have consumed too much malt, I couldn't wait to get home to describe him to my family. He was the happiest vision one could possibly see on the seventeenth day of March!

As Ms. Barnes and her class revise the paragraph, they discuss the uses of pronouns, the meanings of the words they use, and the images they portray. They connect the sentence "He was dressed all in green" with the phrase that follows, "emerald jacket and trousers," and arrive at the conclusion that the phrase illustrates the reference to "dressed all in green" because emerald is a shade of green.

The students discuss the importance of varying the words so that the readers can envision the sight of the leprechaun and his vivid clothing surrounded by the spring flowers along the garden path. They also have learned that using pronouns helps the narrative sound more natural, but it is important to know to whom the pronouns refer or the narrative doesn't make sense. The students also add a number of new words to their personal writing dictionaries that day.

Conclusion

Lessons on cohesion links support students in making sense of both spoken and written English. Teachers help students to understand the formats by explaining the meaning of pronouns, ellipses, conjunctions, substitutions, and other abstract references in text and spoken language by giving examples and by providing students with guided practice in analyzing English text. They also encourage students to take time to analyze the reasons for their own misunderstanding. Demonstrating the connections by writing the sentences and drawing arrows to the words that are needed to make sense of the sentences makes the cohesion links more comprehensible to the reader or listener.

Examples of Approximation Behaviors Related to the TESOL Standards

PreK–3 students will:
- identify pronoun referents in written text.
- combine sentences with appropriate conjunctions.

4–8 students will:
- substitute descriptive phrases for nouns in written products.

- identify the difference in meaning when conjunctions are changed in a sentence.

9–12 students will:
- use ellipses appropriately in written and spoken text.
- identify similar lexical connectives in text to build comprehension.

References

Gibbons, P. (1991). *Learning to learn in a second language.* Portsmouth, NH: Heinemann.

Halliday, M., & Hasan, R. (1966). *Cohesion in English.* New York, NY: Longman.

Herrell, A., & Jordan, M. (2006). *50 strategies for improving vocabulary, comprehension, and fluency: An active learning approach.* Upper Saddle River, NJ: Pearson.

Peregoy, S., & Boyle, O. (2013). *Reading, writing, and learning in ESL: A resource book for teaching K–12 English learners* (6th ed.). Boston, MA: Pearson.

Swain, M. (1993). The output hypothesis: Just speaking and writing aren't enough. *The Canadian Modern Language Review, 50,* 158–164.

34

Language Framework Planning
Supporting Academic Language and Content Acquisition

Language framework planning (Gibbons, 2015; Hinkel, 2006) is a strategy in which a teacher identifies the academic language necessary for students to be successful in a lesson and plans activities that support the use of the language in multiple functions. It is called language framework planning because the teacher creates a framework prior to the lesson that identifies the topic, activities, language functions, language structures, and vocabulary that will be part of the lesson. The framework is shown in Figure 34.1.

Planning for language instruction varies by content area. For example, a literature lesson may involve describing; a science lesson, classifying; a mathematics lesson, justifying. All of these functions of language require explanation, modeling, and guided practice (Díaz-Rico, 2018). In this

FIGURE 34.1 Language Framework Planning for a Kindergarten Sorting Lesson

Topic	Activities	Language Functions	Language Structures	Vocabulary
Shape	Sorting attribute blocks by shape	Classifying Describing	They are all [shapes].	Triangle Circle Square Rectangle
Size	Sorting attribute blocks by size	Classifying Describing Comparing Contrasting	These [shapes] are all [size]. This one is [smaller, larger].	Large Small Medium Smaller Larger Bigger Littler

way, language and content acquisition are both supported. Integrated and contextualized teaching of multiple language skills are critical factors in supporting effective learning and language development for English learners (Hinkel, 2006).

Step-by-Step

The steps in language framework planning are the following:

• *Identify language objectives*—Identify the language objectives of the lesson to be taught. These objectives should relate to the functions of language and the sentence patterns and structures to be practiced as part of the lesson. To identify these objectives, ask yourself the following two questions:

1. What are the language demands of this particular lesson?
2. What are the language levels of the students?

It is helpful to create a checklist on which you can record the functions the students use regularly so that you can structure lessons to give them practice in using new functions of language in a variety of content areas. A language function checklist is shown in Figure 34.2.

• *Identify and model problematic structures*—Identify the language structures that are likely to give students problems and plan to model their use early in the lesson. If you are keeping regular samples of the students' language, these records are extremely helpful in planning language lessons based on the kind of documentation shown in Figure 34.3.

• *Plan an instructional sequence*—Plan the sequence of the lesson by creating a chart, like the one in Figure 34.4, in which the language functions, structures, and vocabulary are modeled and then practiced by the students as part of the activity.

• *Assess and document student progress*—Plan a way to document the students' success in using the language in the context of the lesson and ways to build on this lesson to give them additional practice in the use of the language functions and structures gained. Anecdotal records and checklists are both helpful in documenting this type of learning.

• *Add technology*—Use the computer to create and print out game pieces or cards that the students can use to practice the structures that have been taught in the lesson.

Applications and Examples

Language framework planning can be used at all grade levels and in all curricular areas to support language and content acquisition. For example, Mr. Gomez is planning a project using interviews to introduce his third-grade students to the ways in which information is gathered from primary sources or from people who experienced the events being studied. He wants his third graders to learn to conduct interviews, practice their oral language skills, and find ways to confirm information gathered in this format. He also wants his students to "determine the meaning of words and phrases as they are used in a text, including vocabulary describing political, social, or economic aspects of history/social science" (CCSS.ELA-LITERACY.SL.3.1.C) as he prepares them to ask questions, clarify meaning, and summarize their findings. He begins by having his students read several articles from the local paper concerning some recent decisions made by the city council, which will greatly restrict the amount of money being allocated to summer youth programs. The articles name the city council members who voted to lower the city's investment in summer programs. Mr. Gomez and the students list the names of the people who should be interviewed, including some of the people who lobbied for the continued allocation of funds for the summer programs. Mr. Gomez then begins to plan the language lessons that will help prepare his students to conduct worthwhile interviews. His language framework plan is shown in Figure 34.4.

FIGURE 34.2 Functions of Language in the Classroom

Student's Name _____ School Year _____								
Social Functions Observed (date)								
Asking permission								
Asking assistance								
Asking directions								
Denying								
Promising								
Requesting								
Suggesting								
Wishing/hoping								
Academic Functions								
Classifying								
Comparing								
Giving/following directions								
Describing								
Questioning								
Evaluating								
Expressing position								
Explaining								
Hypothesizing								
Planning/predicting								
Reporting								
Sequencing								

Sources: Gibbons (1993) and Díaz-Rico (2013).

FIGURE 34.3 Sample of an Anecdotal Record That Documents Language Needs

Roberto	**January 23**	**Giving directions to Joey**

Roberto and Joey are moving pieces around a game board. Roberto is telling Joey how to move his game piece. "No, put it by. . . put it by the tree." Joey places his piece beside the tree on the board. Roberto says, "No, not there . . . put it on the. . . . " He reaches over and moves the game piece under the tree. Joey says, "Oh, you meant UNDER the tree." Roberto nods.

FIGURE 34.4 Mr. Gomez's Language Framework Plan for Primary Source Projects

Topic	Activities	Language Functions	Language Structures	Vocabulary
History	Read article from the newspaper	Describing Reporting Sequencing	First the council . . . then	Council sequence words
Research	Brainstorming	Following directions Questioning Planning Reporting	When did you . . . ? Why did you . . . ?	Prioritize Allocate
Visuals	Planning/ creating a visual	Expressing needs Expressing plans Asking for feedback	I will need . . . . I plan to . . . . Do you think . . . ?	Labels for materials
Oral reports	Presenting research	Explaining Summarizing Asking questions	First, I . . . . I found . . . . Do you . . . ?	Interviewed Documenting

By planning ahead, Mr. Gomez is prepared to provide the support the students need to participate successfully in the primary source project. He knows that many of his students have difficulty coping with academic language, particularly in production. As a result of this, their participation in class is severely restricted. To counter this, Mr. Gomez plans to model the language structures and allow the students to work together in small heterogeneous groups so that they can support each other in preparing their questions and interviews. Mr. Gomez also plans to encourage the students to work in pairs to conduct the interviews, requiring each of the students to ask some of the questions.

Mr. Gomez is aware that several of his English language learners are talented in art, and he will encourage other students to enlist their help in preparing visuals to accompany their reports. He has high hopes for the success of this project, and his hopes are rewarded.

Language framework planning is especially helpful with older English language learners. Planning to provide language models for meeting needs specific to academic assignments supports the participation and success of all students.

* * * * *

FIGURE 34.5 Ms. Brock's Language Framework Plan

Topic	Activities	Language Functions	Language Structures	Vocabulary
History	Show video of last year's event	Describing Evaluating Explaining	This student is . . . How could this be . . . ? How could you . . . ?	Simulate Display Research
Research	Demonstrate the planning process	Sequencing Describing Explaining Planning Reporting Sequencing	First, you . . . Next, you . . . You must plan and document . . .	Sequence words Describe Reenact
Practice	Students walk through a simple simulation	Describing Explaining Enacting Reporting Sequencing	I think that . . . This happened first. This happened because . . .	Predict Confirm Cause/effect Document

Ms. Brock is preparing a lesson for her middle school social studies students to demonstrate how to prepare a project for History Day. Because her classes contain many English language learners, she decides to prepare a language framework for the lesson. Her framework plan is shown in Figure 34.5.

As the students participate in planning their History Day presentations, Ms. Brock is able to observe and keep records of their use of the planning process and the language associated with the lesson. She also makes sure they are able to "determine the meaning of words and phrases as they are used in a text, including vocabulary specific to domains related to history/social sciences" (CCSS.ELA-LITERACY.RH.6–8.4). She can then plan subsequent lessons in which the students will have opportunities to use the history language that they are acquiring in connection with hands-on lessons.

Because Ms. Brock frequently plans complete language framework lessons, she decides that a simpler planning form is in order and adds a language planning section to her basic lesson plan format. She finds that this saves her time, but it also helps her to remember to consider vocabulary, language functions, and structures in all her lesson planning. Her basic lesson plan format is shown in Figure 34.6.

Conclusion

Although language framework planning is time-consuming, it provides a vital link to the difficulties many English language learners experience in content-area classrooms. When teachers observe English language learners who are not participating fully in classroom activities or are finding little success in their classroom interactions, attention to the language framework of the lessons may provide valuable clues for ways to support these students better in the classroom.

FIGURE 34.6 Language Framework Planning Added to a Basic Lesson Plan Format

Lesson Title _____ Date _____

Objective:

Language Objective:
Vocabulary Focus:
Language Functions to Model:
Language Structures to Model:
Materials:
Motivation:

Procedure:

Closure:
Evaluation:
Provisions for Individual Differences:
Target Students: Needs:

Lesson Reflection:

Examples of Approximation Behaviors Related to the TESOL Standards

PreK–3 students will:
- use appropriate language structures to ask and answer questions.
- imitate language and actions of others in interacting verbally.

4–8 students will:
- use context of reading materials to construct meaning.

- plan cognitive strategies to complete reading and writing assignments.

9–12 students will:
- use self-monitoring and self-correction to build a vocabulary.
- evaluate own success and set academic goals.

References

Díaz-Rico, L. (2018). *The crosscultural, language, and academic development handbook: A complete K–12 reference guide* (6th ed.). Boston, MA: Pearson Education.

Gibbons, P. (2015). *Scaffolding language, scaffolding learning: Teaching English language learners in the mainstream classroom.* Portsmouth, NH: Heinemann.

Hinkel, E. (2006). Current perspectives on teaching the four skills. *TESOL Quarterly, 40*(1), 109–131.

Free Voluntary Reading
Nothing Helps Reading Like Reading

Free voluntary reading (Freeman & Freeman, 2009; Krashen, 1993; Krashen, 2004; Krashen, 2011) is a powerful tool for involving students in the reading of English text. Free voluntary reading (FVR), is a system for encouraging silent, self-selected reading of enjoyable books written at the students' independent levels. It has been found to support reading comprehension, writing, grammar, spelling, and vocabulary development even though the texts read are written at an easy reading level. Series of books in which the reader becomes familiar with the structure, main characters, and setting in the first book and then reads sequels are especially appropriate for building vocabulary and comprehension in readers with limited English vocabularies. To spark interest in reading for pleasure, many teachers are introducing the graphic novel, which uses a comic book format with many illustrations that also support comprehension in ELL readers (Nilsen & Donelson, 2009).

In *The Read-Aloud Handbook*, Jim Trelease (2013) cites research that correlates the number of books to which students have access with their reading progress. He also points out the disparity between the numbers of book in classrooms and school libraries in poor neighborhoods versus more affluent ones. He notes some aspects of free reading that seem to make a difference in students' interest in free reading, namely, (1) access to books, (2) personal ownership of the books, and (3) self-selection of the books.

Although free voluntary reading has been criticized (Hernandez, 1997) as difficult to implement because of the large numbers of books required, it has been shown to be effective for English language learners because of the power in exposing them to a large volume of English reading and the anxiety-reducing power of easy reading (Freeman & Freeman, 2009). Figure 35.1 suggests sources of reading materials for free voluntary reading.

FIGURE 35.1 Sources of Materials for Free Voluntary Reading

Visit the following websites:	
Bantam Books	Randonhousebooks.com
Class Libraries	booksource.com
Harper Collins	https://www.harpercollins.com/childrens
Scholas-tic	teacher.scholastic.com/products/guidedreading/leveling_chart.htm

Step-by-Step

The steps in implementing free voluntary reading are the following:

- *Identify the independent reading levels of students*—Identify the independent reading levels of the students in your class and gather a number of books at their levels. Organize the books in a way that identifies the reading levels and provides easy student access to the books. To identify other sources of easy reading materials for your students, enlist the help of the school media specialist.

- *Explain the program to the students*—Introduce the free voluntary reading program to the students, explaining that reading widely helps them learn new English vocabulary and improves their writing, spelling, and grammar, even when the reading material is not difficult. Set up a system so they can check out books freely, taking them home to read or reading them during **drop everything and read (DEAR) time** or **sustained silent reading (SSR)** time in the classroom. Provide a celebration system so that the class keeps track of the numbers of books being read by class members. Arrange for celebrations as the class reads 100, 500, and 1,000 books. Focus on the number of books being read rather than the difficulty of the books chosen. The object is to get students reading more.

- *Discuss the books in groups*—Schedule informal literature discussions so students can share their favorite books and talk about favorite authors. Use these discussions to provide positive feedback to the students who are reading a lot of books. Encourage wide reading by introducing new authors of easy reading books and giving book talks about new books as they are added to the classroom collection. Keep these introductions informal, for example, "This is a new book by Mary Grace. If you enjoyed her other books, you'll probably like this one. It's about an ice-skating competition."

- *Add motivation over time*—Keep the momentum going by adding new celebrations during the year. Add such activities as creating video commercials for favorite books, keeping track of the number of students who read a certain title to determine the class's favorite books, and scheduling guest appearances by favorite authors. Holding read-a-thons in which students read for a given number of hours per night until they reach self-set goals (10 hours, 50 hours), and then presenting awards, such as a 10-hour reader button or a 50-hour reader button, add incentives as well.

- *Assess to monitor progress and plan instruction*—Have students keep a log of the books they've read to help them see the progress they are making in the volume of reading they're doing. Using a computer to create and update the log can greatly simplify the process, provide additional motivation, and give teachers easy access for reviewing students' progress. Some teachers have found that simply adding a starting and completion date for each book in the reading log helps students see that their reading rate is increasing. Having students keep a log of new words they're learning from the books they read has also proved successful for some teachers. All of these methods of documentation should be done as a form of celebration of students' progress as readers. Taking notes and writing anecdotal records of the students' involvement in group discussions of books often reveals increased verbal communication and comprehension of reading material as well.

Applications and Examples

Ms. Gerrard's third-grade class shows little interest in leisure reading until she introduces free voluntary reading. Ms. Gerrard brings in a series of new paperback books to the class, reads the first book in the series aloud, and sets up a system for keeping track of the number of students who read each book. Students in the class are given a new composition book in which to record the titles of the books they are reading—in school and at home.

There is a tally sheet in the class library on which students record the books they are reading to keep track of the number of times each book is read by a student. One of the students is appointed class record keeper, and he keeps track of the reading being done each week in two ways. First, he posts a list of the week's most popular books, and then he totals the number of books read by the entire class each week.

Ms. Gerrard provides time each day for free reading. At the end of the free reading period, she encourages students to share comments about the books they are reading, such as an especially funny part or a reading recommendation. As the cumulative count of books read by class members mounts, Ms. Gerrard gives periodic celebrations. For the 100-book milestone, the class has a cookie party with chocolate chip cookies made and eaten in class. For the 500-book milestone, the students are given free time to sit under the playground trees and read for 30 minutes after lunch. Ms. Gerrard can see that her English learners are reading more now that they have the option of choosing their books.

* * * * *

Mr. Tibbs's eighth graders are enjoying the introductory day of their free voluntary reading program. Mr. Tibbs begins the program by bringing in a number of comic books to the class because

FIGURE 35.2 The Books We've Read

Category	Place a sticker in a box for each book read.										TOTAL
Adventure											
Biography											
Comic books											
Folktale											
Horror											
Information											
Mystery											
Poetry											
Science fiction											
										Class Grand Total ____	

FIGURE 35.3 Mr. Tibbs's Notice to Parents

Dear Parents,

     Your children may be bringing home some new reading material this week. We will be encouraging the students to read books—even comic books—to increase their reading enjoyment, fluency, and vocabulary. This program is called free voluntary reading (FVR) and has been shown to benefit students in the following ways:

- It promotes reading comprehension.
- It supports vocabulary development.
- It supports writing, spelling, and grammar knowledge.

We know that *nothing helps reading like more reading*. You can help by:

- Providing time for your child to read each day.
- Providing a quiet place for reading.
- Talking to your child about the books being read.
- Modeling the enjoyment of reading yourself.

Thank you for your support!

Mr. Tibbs

he realizes that his English learners enjoy illustrated text but are embarrassed to read lower-level "picture books." At first, the students don't believe that they are being allowed to read comic books in school. Mr. Tibbs makes it clear that it doesn't matter what they read because reading improves reading. He shares his goal—for each student to read every day. On the second day of the program, Mr. Tibbs brings in a collection of easy books that can be checked out for free reading at home, and he also makes the comics available for checkout. The students are encouraged to keep a list of the books and comics they are reading. Mr. Tibbs posts a chart on which the students place a sticker for each book they read beside the category of the book. The chart he uses is shown in Figure 35.2.

Because Mr. Tibbs realizes that the support of the parents is vital to the success of this new reading program, he prepares a notice for the parents so that they understand the purpose of the free voluntary reading program. He encourages their participation and their assistance in providing time to read, providing a quiet place to read, and encouraging their children to meet their reading goals. His parent notice is shown in Figure 35.3.

The eighth graders are a little wary of the intent of this new reading program, but they like the reading materials that are available to them. Slowly they relax and begin to enjoy their free reading. Mr. Tibbs gives them a free reading period every now and then as a reward for good work or to celebrate reading milestones, such as when the class reads 200 books. The free reading done by the class is showing a steady growth each week.

Conclusion

Free voluntary reading is an important strategy in helping both fluent English students and English language learners develop a love for reading, and it provides a valuable shared literary experience. There are a number of children's and young adult writers producing series of books that build on a common theme or familiar characters. These books are especially appropriate for free voluntary reading by English language learners because the sequels are set in familiar contexts. The authors of these series have created texts that are interesting to readers at certain age levels and yet are easy to read and understand. In addition, a number of the classics have been rewritten in simplified language so that teachers can provide understandable versions of these books as class

FIGURE 35.4 Titles Available in the Classics Series

Published by HarperCollins: Each book in this series has sections that tell about the author, the book, the main characters, and the setting. The books also contain notes to aid comprehension and a complete glossary.

The Adventures of Robin Hood	*A Journey to the Center of the Earth*
The Adventures of Tom Sawyer	*The Odyssey*
Don Quixote	*Oliver Twist*
Frankenstein	*The Red Badge of Courage*
Ivanhoe	*Romeo and Juliet*
Joan of Arc	*The Strange Case of Dr Jekyll and Mr Hyde*

Puffin Classics published by Penguin Books

The Adventures of Robin Hood	*The Lost World*
Around the World in Eighty Days	*The Luck of Troy*
The Call of the Wild	*Moonfleet*
The Extraordinary Cases of Sherlock Holmes	*Myths of the Norsemen*
The Great Adventures of Sherlock Holmes	*Oliver Twist*
Great Expectations	*The Red Badge of Courage*
The Hound of the Baskervilles	*A Tale of Two Cities*
Journey to the Center of the Earth	*Tales of Ancient Egypt*
Kidnapped	*The Three Musketeers*
King Arthur and His Knights of the Round Table	*Treasure Island*
	Twenty Thousand Leagues Under the Sea

Enhanced eText
Video Example 35.1
https://www.youtube.com/
watch?v=DSW7gmvDLag

literature studies are conducted. Figure 35.4 provides a list of some classic titles available in series form. Although access to a large number of books is necessary for this strategy to be successful, a number of the book series are available in paperback at reasonable prices. Please enjoy the Video Example 35.1 featuring Dr. Stephen Krashen speaking on the Power of Reading as it relates to the success of students in our schools today.

Examples of Approximation Behaviors Related to the TESOL Standards

PreK–3 students will:

- read and discuss books read at the recreational reading level.
- relate events and characters in series books.

4–8 students will:

- express personal likes and opinions of books read for pleasure.

- read increasingly more difficult books for pleasure.

9–12 students will:

- use vocabulary gained from independent reading in speech and writing.
- support opinions about character motivation by locating and sharing text that illustrates their opinions.

References

Freeman, Y., & Freeman, D. (2009). *Academic language for English language learners and struggling readers*. Portsmouth, NH: Heinemann.

Hernandez, H. (1997). *Teaching in multicultural classrooms*. Upper Saddle River, NJ: Merrill/ Prentice Hall.

Krashen, S. (1993). *The power of reading*. Englewood, CO: Libraries Unlimited.

Krashen, S. (2004, April). *Free volunteer reading: New research, applications, and controversies*. Paper presented at the RELC conference, Singapore.

Krashen, S. (2011). *Free volunteer reading*. Santa Barbara, CA: Libraries Unlimited.

Nilsen, A. P., & Donelson, K. E. (2009). *Literature for today's young adults* (8th ed.). Boston, MA: Pearson.

Trelease, J. (2013). *The read-aloud handbook* (7th ed.). Boston, MA: Penguin Books

36

Culture Studies

Learning Research Skills and Valuing Home Cultures in One Project

Culture studies (Freeman & Freeman, 1994, 2009) are studies in which students research and share information about their own cultural history. These studies will vary greatly depending on the ages of the students in the class. Generally, these studies fit in well with the Common Core State Standards, which integrate the study of history and social sciences with the study of reading, writing, speaking, and listening.

Many different language arts skills can be supported by culture studies. Students are required to use reading, writing, speaking, listening, viewing, and visual representation of ideas to interview their parents, grandparents, and other members of their culture. The key to making this strategy work is the way the word *culture* is defined. Any culture study should begin with a discussion of culture and what makes up a culture. This can be done effectively by examining the culture of the classroom and what makes it unique. The use of time, the attitude toward learning, the expectations for participation, the rules about how to get along with each other, the structure that is in place regarding the use of materials, verbal and nonverbal interactions, and notions of personal space all contribute to the culture of the classroom (Díaz-Rico, 2018). These aspects of culture should be listed on a chart or whiteboard in the classroom to remind students to examine them in the cultures they are documenting.

Once students understand the broad definition of *culture,* they can begin to organize the study of their own culture. Some teachers have found it profitable to encourage students to work in pairs or small groups so that they can begin to compare and contrast cultural norms as an ongoing part of the study. For possible approaches to culture studies see Figure 36.1.

Step-by-Step

The steps in implementing culture studies are the following:

• *Find an age-appropriate project*—Decide on a project that is appropriate for the ages of your students and that supports the objectives for your grade level. Examine the objectives in both social sciences and language arts to determine ways to integrate both curricular areas. (See Figure 36.1 for suggestions.)

• *Set up the goals and parameters*—Identify the purpose of the projects to be done and determine whether the research and activities should be done individually, in pairs, or in small

FIGURE 36.1 Culture Studies Appropriate for Different Grade Levels

Group	Projects	Activities
Kindergarten	Family portraits Working together	• Draw a picture of your family. • Tell about what your family likes to do together. • Draw a picture of some work that your family does together. • Tell about how the work is divided and who does each part. • Tell about the things each family member can do to help the work get done. • Is there anyone in your family who teaches other people in the family how to do things? What things?
Primary grades	People are different, people are the same The way we do things changes from generation to generation	• Group investigation of basic ways in which cultural groups are the same and different. Choosing one aspect at a time, have the students interview people of their own cultural groups about how the particular aspect is regarded (for example, the use of time, the importance of education, the regard for animals, the significance of different colors, the role of food in celebrations, the division of work, etc.). • Individual students interview and research family photo albums for examples of how things have changed from generation to generation. Questions asked of family members should also examine how these changes have affected the use of time and the value system of the family.
Upper elementary grades	Our state and nation	Each student researches the impact of her or his own cultural group on the history of the state and nation. The child's own family history should be examined first to determine the reason for immigration, if any, or the family work history and how the occupations of generations fit in with the history of the state and nation. The changes in value systems, occupations, and places where the family moved should be compared to the general trends in the state, nation, and world history when applicable.
Middle school	Values and history	Students examine their family's values in relation to how time is spent, the priorities for the expenditure of money, the differences in expectations for male and female children, any inequalities in the past or present in the division of work or responsibilities within the family. The celebrations and rituals that have continued over time and the use of language and interactions in solving problems or disputes should also be examined.
High school	Nation building	Students examine the movements in history that affect the building of nations and how their culture has followed or differed from the general trend. The contributions of women, minorities, and the effect of world events are all considered in light of the building of nations around the world. The changes that have taken place in the students' own families and cultures as a result of or in response to these events should also be considered. The construction of time lines and personal family histories in relation to world events is appropriate.

Note: The suggestions provided here relate to the broad themes recommended in the California History/Social Sciences Framework (California State Department of Education, 1988).

groups. If a main goal is to get students to interact and share the information they are gathering, then pairs or small groups should be used. Make a visual with the students that clearly identifies the steps they should take in their research and the products they will be expected to create. For an example of this visual, see Figure 36.2.

• *Make expectations clear*—Encourage students to identify the main elements of a good project and create a rubric or checklist based on their suggestions. It is important that they know what is expected of them and how their report will be evaluated. See Figure 36.3 for a sample of a cultural study checklist.

• *Plan the culminating activity*—Plan a celebration involving school administrators and families so the students can share their research and results.

• *Assess student growth and progress*—As students work in groups, the teacher has a unique opportunity to observe; record anecdotal notes; and document the students' language interactions, social language skills, and research strategies. The self-evaluation checklist in Figure 36.3 provides a good format for individual conferences, the results of which make an informative anecdotal record. Anecdotal records and results of the culture study project should be included in individual student portfolios along with the student self-evaluation forms.

• *Add technology*—Culture studies are perfect for integrating technology. Students can complete a lot of their research using the Internet. Using a word processor to write the actual reports can motivate students as well. Using other computer formats to create charts and visuals makes the reports more interesting, as does the creation of PowerPoint slide shows for the

FIGURE 36.2 The Steps You Will Take to Create Your Family Time Line

1. Introduce yourself to your group, telling your name and the cultural group with which you identify yourself. If you do not identify yourself with an ethnic group, try to identify your broad cultural affiliation such as Mexican American, German American, European American, or White Anglo-Saxon Protestant. You may even have to identify the cultural group from your mother's side and your father's side.

2. As a group use your social sciences book to research the history of the world from 1900 until today and create a time line of major events. (Hint: Several of these time lines are included in your textbook.) Each member of your group should make a copy of the general time line and place his or her own birth on the time line.

3. The group should brainstorm questions they will ask as they interview members of their family about the events on the time line that they remember. The purpose is to learn as much as you can about how the world events since 1900 affected your family. Did any members of your family fight in any of the wars? Did the family move to another city or country because of world or economic events? (See number 5 for other ideas.)

4. Each member of the group should arrange to interview members of her or his own family or other members of her or his cultural group and report back each day to share the interviews that have been conducted and the information that has been revealed. Events shared by the interviewees should be charted on the time line and written in narrative form.

5. At the conclusion of the week, groups should meet together to plan a presentation format for sharing the information they have gathered with the whole class. Be creative and include visuals or reenactments! Each member of the group should have a speaking part in the presentation. The following information that should be highlighted in the presentation:
   • In what ways were the family events affected or family histories altered by world and economic events?
   • In what ways were the different cultural groups affected by these events?
   • Which cultural groups seemed to be least affected by the world and economic events?
   • How did the world and economic events affect the basic values and priorities of the different cultural groups?

FIGURE 36.3 Checklist for Culture Study Reports

Before you present your culture study, check to make sure you have all the following:

_____ I made a visual to help me show what I learned.

_____ My visual is large enough to see easily.

_____ I have checked the spelling and grammar.

_____ I have note cards prepared, which will help me remember the main points I want to make.

_____ I have included information in my report from interviews of people in my generation, my parents' generation, and my grandparents' generation.

_____ I have included information in my report about the main historical events that affected my family history.

_____ I have included information in my report about the changes in values and priorities from generation to generation.

_____ I have included interesting family stories in my report so that "the flavor" of my cultural heritage is evident.

_____ My visual and note cards will be submitted to my teacher at the conclusion of my report.

final presentations. Researching websites like Yahoo!, Google, Dogpile, or Ask Jeeves for Kids can provide valuable information for these projects. Just ensure that your students are accessing "kid-friendly" sites and that parents are informed of any research tools your students are using. Any use of technology in the process should be documented in the portfolio and celebrated as an additional format of effective communication.

Applications and Examples

Mr. Watanabe's fourth graders have been studying California history all year. They have explored the history of the state from the pre-Columbian settlements and people through modern-day immigrations and rapid population growth. They have created a time line of the history of the state with major events prominently noted. As Mr. Watanabe introduces the final segment of the study of California history, he shows some pictures of his family. "This is a picture of my family. This is my grandfather and my grandmother. This is my father and this is my mother. And this is me," he says as he points to the small child in the picture. "I am going to tell you about how my family's history fits on the time line of California history we have created."

"My grandfather was a fisherman in the San Francisco area in the 1930s. When the Japanese bombed Pearl Harbor in 1941, the American people became very suspicious of all Japanese people. The American government moved all the Japanese families from the West Coast into camps so that they could not conspire with the Japanese government to attack the West Coast of America. The picture I showed you was taken at the Manzanar War Relocation Camp here in California where my family lived for four years. My whole family lived behind barbed wire like criminals simply because they were of Japanese heritage.

"You would think that my mother and father would be very bitter about this part of history and how they were treated. My parents, however, see it as something that was natural. They say that people get frightened in time of war and do unreasonable things. Part of my Japanese culture is the value of serenity. I think that an important part of my culture is thinking serene thoughts so that the aggravations of life do not upset the higher thoughts of the mind. My grandfather wrote some beautiful music while he was in the relocation camp. He used the time he was given to create something of beauty."

Mr. Watanabe placed a card along the class time line under January 1942 that said, "Mr. Watanabe's family goes to Manzanar War Relocation Camp." He then talks about what he wants each member of the class to do as a part of his or her final study of California history.

"As your final study of California history, I want you to interview the members of your family, your clan elders, your priests, or older people you know who belong to your culture. I want you to find out how long your family or people have been in California, what caused them to come, and what part they played in any of the California events that we have been studying. If your parents do not know the answers to your questions, ask your grandparents or other elderly people in your families. What other ways can you think of to get information about this study?"

"We could look in old photograph albums," Juanita answers.

"My grandmother has a family Bible that has the whole history of our family in it!" Jerrod exclaims.

"That will be very helpful," Mr. Watanabe says with a smile. By the end of the week the time line is bulging with 3-by-5 cards noting events in the families of the students. Some of the students are amazed at how long some of the Mexican and Native American families have lived in California.

"I thought the Mexican families were all new immigrants," Melissa said. "My family only moved to California in 1980. Maria's family has been here for generations. Compared with her family, we are the new immigrants."

* * * * *

Mrs. Jeffreys teaches 12th-grade English in a high school where most of the students are from white Protestant families. Her husband teaches the same grade level and subject in a highly multicultural school, and they often discuss how different the students at the two schools are in their views of the world. One night over dinner, Mr. and Mrs. Jeffreys decide that they want to do a project that will help the students from the two schools get to know each other and their differing viewpoints.

The Jeffreys choose the book *Plain and Simple: A Woman's Journey to the Amish* by Sue Bender (1989) because the book tells the story of one woman's visit to another culture and how the things she learns about that culture cause her to reflect on her own. Each student is asked to reflect on the incidents discussed in the book and how he or she relates to the customs, values, and interactions in his or her own families and cultural groups.

The Jeffreys assign conversation partners from their fourth-period classes. They intend to start small and see how well the project is accepted. They agree to read and discuss the first chapter of the book on Monday and have their students reflect on the chapter, talk to their families on Monday night, and post their first e-mail conversations on Tuesday.

The first chapter of the book talks about how the author falls in love with Amish quilts—their simple designs and bold colors—and begins to think about the Amish people. She compares her lifestyle and values with those of the Amish people and wants to create an area of calm peace in her life. As the Jeffreys read the first chapter, they stop periodically and discuss their own lives, values, and cultures and how their family heritages contribute to their beliefs. They ask the students to think about the values Ms. Bender lists in the first chapter and how they equate their own personal and family's values to those the author discusses. The students are then given a list of things to discuss with their families that evening and told that they will be discussing their self-reflections and information gained from their families via e-mail with a student at the "other high school" the next day. The students all chuckle, knowing exactly how they are connected to the "other high school."

The next day in the computer lab, the students are all busily writing to their new conversation partners. The Jeffreys ask the students to save the correspondence each day so that the information they share and gather from their conversation partners can be used in the future.

On Wednesday, the discussion begins with what has been learned through the conversations. Many of the students are amazed to discover the differences in the use of time and the priorities expressed by their conversation partner.

"My partner has lessons every day after school. He's taking trumpet lessons and French lessons, and he's being tutored in calculus. He has no time for fun. He goes from school to lessons to homework to bed," says Mikel.

"What does that tell you about his values?" asks Mr. Jeffreys.

"I think it tells more about his family's values because he doesn't seem to want to take all those lessons," replies Mikel.

"That may be so—but he's doing it," says Mr. Jeffreys.

"Oh, I see your point," Mikel replies. "His values involve going along with his parents' expectations of him—improving himself in the areas of music and languages. He did say he was expecting to go to college on a music scholarship."

After their discussion of the first day's conversations, the Jeffreys read and discuss each chapter of *Plain and Simple*—where the author examines things that affect the culture of the Amish. The Jeffreys give the students their next assignment, which is to reflect on the chapter and their own family values related to the issues mentioned in the book.

The study continues in this pattern over the next two weeks. After the book has been read and the conversation partners have discussed a number of issues related to culture, they are assigned a report to be written that represents the values they have discovered as they reflect on the book. The partners are to share the things they discovered about their own cultures and how their belief systems were formed, including the influence of their families, their religion, their interests, their school, and their friends. Each student is invited to contribute a paper to a journal he or she will compile collaboratively, titled "Our Stories, Cultural Conversations." The Jeffreys are pleased to see that almost everyone contributes a story to the journal. The stories contributed show a respect for the students' own cultures and the new information they have gained about their partner's culture.

Conclusion

Culture studies provide a way for teachers to build the classroom community while engaging their students in an in-depth social sciences project that requires research. Language arts skills such as interviewing, note-taking, using the steps in the writing process, and oral and visual presentations must be taught. The classroom community is greatly enhanced when teachers share their own culture study and discuss the multiple ways the study was conducted. Appreciation of the values, customs, and unique contributions of the different cultures is heightened through the process of investigating multiple cultures through firsthand accounts of personal experiences.

Examples of Approximation Behaviors Related to the TESOL Standards

PreK–3 students will:

- represent family culture orally and in pictures.
- verbally explain ways that people are the same and different.

4–8 students will:

- explain the role of different cultures in U.S. and state histories.

- explore the values associated with different cultures.

9–12 students will:

- explain and explore the different roles and expectations of people from a perspective of gender in a variety of cultures.
- research and construct family histories and time lines in relation to world history.

References

Bender, S. (1989). *Plain and simple: A woman's journey to the Amish*. New York, NY: HarperCollins.
California Department of Education (1988). California History/Social Sciences Framework. Sacramento, CA: California State Department of Education.

Díaz-Rico, L. (2018). *The crosscultural, language, and academic development handbook: A complete K–12 reference guide* (6th ed.). Boston, MA: Pearson Education.

Freeman, D., & Freeman, Y. (1994). *Between worlds: Access to second language acquisition.* Portsmouth, NH: Heinemann.

Freeman, D., & Freeman, Y. (2009). *Academic language for English learners and struggling readers: How to help your students succeed across content areas.* Portsmouth, NH: Heinemann.

37

Microselection

Finding Key Words and Main Ideas

The ability to find the key words in individual sentences, also called **microselection**, is a prerequisite for students in understanding how to find the main idea in longer reading passages (Baumann, 1982). By beginning with individual sentences, students find success and gradually transfer this ability to longer text passages. The ability to locate key words in sentences and main ideas in passages is a critical skill for several reasons. Students are better able to retain the meaning of a reading when they can locate and recall main ideas rather than trying to remember each detail because they haven't been able to prioritize the information read. Once they can identify the main idea, they are more likely to be able to paraphrase the meaning of a sentence rather than having to memorize it as written (Echevarria, Vogt, & Short, 2016).

Microselection is done at the sentence level and practiced in several ways before it is expanded into finding the main idea in paragraphs and whole passages. Students are taught first to identify important key words and then to paraphrase the meaning of a sentence. They are taught to identify and find meanings for words with which they have limited or no understanding. The use of resources like dictionaries, the Internet, peers, and teachers is part of the instruction as well. Starting with finding key words and main ideas in short passages or paragraphs is vital for English learners and can then be used to support comprehension in longer passages (Herrell & Jordan, 2006). Although microselection (Irwin, 2006) involves the understanding of individual words, phrases, and sentences, the skills of identifying key words and paraphrasing are important to comprehension at the paragraph and whole-selection level as well. This is especially valuable for English learners.

Step-by-Step

The steps in teaching microselection are the following:

• *Introduce the concept of microselection*—Explain that understanding the meanings of important words in a sentence is key to understanding the whole sentence. No one can be expected to remember every word heard or read, but identifying the important words in a sentence makes it easier to understand and talk about the meaning of the sentence. Being able to focus on and talk about the important concepts in a sentence is more valuable, and easier, than having to memorize the complete sentence.

• *Model the identification of key words*—Read a sentence from a reading selection required of the students. For example, using the social sciences text, you might read, "The role of women in industry changed dramatically due to their widespread participation in traditional male jobs during World War II." Model the selection of important words in the sentence by writing the words *women*, *industry*, and *World War II* on the board. Demonstrate how, by remembering the key words, you can restate the sentence, keeping the meaning without saying it exactly as it was written. You might say, "I can restate the main idea in my own words by saying, 'During World War II, women proved they could work in any job in industry by performing tasks usually done by men.'"

• *Guide students in practicing microselection*—Begin guided practice by asking students to read a sentence and identify the most important words to remember. Then ask students to tell what the sentence was about without repeating the original sentence. Repeat this exercise several times until the majority of students understand. Plan additional guided practice for students who need more instruction.

• *Pair students for additional practice*—Put the students into practice pairs, making sure that you don't pair two students who are weak readers or both struggling English learners. Give students a reading assignment and ask each pair to read the passage one sentence at a time, identify key words, and restate the sentence in their own words. Have students read the sentence silently. Follow that with having one student identify the key words and the second student restate the sentence. When the key words are identified, they can be written on a list or highlighted in the text using highlighting tape. The partners take turns identifying key words and restating the sentence. The teacher may use this time to provide guided practice for those who need additional support. Additional suggestions for providing support for English language learners is included in Figure 37.1.

• *Discuss the procedure*—Bring the group back together and ask the students in each pair to share the key words they identified. If they disagree about key words, encourage them to defend their choices.

• *Assess to identify the need for additional instruction or guided practice*—Observe students during the initial lesson, guided practice, and sharing process to identify those who may need more instruction. Place reading passages in a learning center and ask students to list key words for each passage, sentence by sentence. Use the results of this activity to determine needs for further instruction. Because this is such a vital skill, continue to practice with students until they understand the process.

Applications and Examples

Mrs. Dowling's second graders are having difficulty with word problems in math. She plans a series of lessons in microselection to sharpen their skills in recognizing the key elements in these problems that are necessary for reaching appropriate solutions. She wants her students to

FIGURE 37.1 Suggestions for Supporting English Learners in Microselection

Preproduction	Early Production	Speech Emergence	Intermediate Fluency	Fluent
Pair students with a student who can provide first language support.	Pair students with another who can help with pronunciation of English main ideas.	Have students repeat the sentences that contain the main ideas as well as the summary sentences.	Pair students with a strong English student.	Fluent English learners can serve as partners for student less proficient in English. They can be helpful in providing first language interpretations as well.

be able to "use addition and subtraction within 100 to solve one- and two-step word problems involving situations of adding to, taking from, putting together, taking apart, and comparing, with unknowns in all positions, e.g., by using drawings and equations with a symbol for the unknown number to represent the problem" (CCSS.MATH-CONTENT.2.OA.A.1). Mrs. Dowling decides that microselection is an essential skill in helping students identify the elements in word problems that give them information as to which math operations to use in solving the problems. Mrs. Dowling writes the following word problem on the overhead projector:

> John and Susan each have three cookies. Their friend Sara comes to play with them. They want to share the cookies with their friend, but they want to make it fair. How many cookies will each child get to eat?

Mrs. Dowling asks the students to read the first sentence. "What are the important words in this sentence?" she asks the class.

"I think the word *each* is important. It tells you that John has cookies and so does Susan," replies Juan.

"Very good. The word *each* is important. You know there are more than three cookies," responds Mrs. Dowling.

The students go on to identify *three*. They then practice restating the first sentence as "There are two children who *each* have *three* cookies."

Mrs. Dowling leads the class through the exercise sentence by sentence, and they identify more key words: *friend, share, fair*. Mrs. Dowling asks them what John and Susan have to do to solve the problem. The students decide each of the two children should give the friend one cookie. They would *share* to make it *fair*. *Each* child would have two cookies.

Mrs. Dowling pairs the students and gives them more word problems to solve. They read each sentence, identify the key words, and then restate the sentence. As the students are working, Mrs. Dowling moves around the room. She observes the students as they choose the important words and talk about them. Every now and then, she asks students to restate a sentence to make sure they understand. She is quite pleased with the results exhibited by the children.

* * * * *

Mr. Guerrero wants to have his ninth-grade remedial reading class read *The Adventures of Robin Hood* (Green, 1994). Because his students are having great difficulty retelling anything they read, Mr. Guerrero thinks he needs to provide them with direct instruction in microselection. He knows that *Robin Hood* will be difficult reading for his class, especially his English learners, but they are motivated to read the book and Mr. G. is determined to help them find success.

Mr. G. starts by reading the prologue aloud to provide background for the story and to model how he selects important words from individual sentences so that he will be able to comprehend and enjoy the book. The prologue is written in "olde" English and begins with two stanzas from "The Birth of Robin Hood", which Mr. G. reads aloud. The older English is not easy for his students to understand at first, but by reading the poem with expression and fluency, Mr. G. helps the students to understand the poem. The poem simply tells that Robin Hood was born in the woods among the lilies.

"Now," begins Mr. G., "I will read one sentence at a time. I want you to listen carefully, and we will choose the important words in the sentence. The first sentence is 'Although it was a hundred years since the Battle of Hastings, there was no real peace in England.' Can you tell me which of the words in that sentence are important?"

Joseph raises his hand. "Yes, Joseph?" says Mr. G.

"*Hundred years* are important words. They tell you when this is happening."

"Yes, it's a hundred years after the Battle of Hastings. That battle took place in 1066. But that's not the important point," says Mr. G. "Who can tell me what is important?"

"*No peace* are important words," says Tino. "The battle was a hundred years ago, but there's still no peace," he adds.

"Very good!" says Mr. G. "Do we know why there's still no peace?"

"No," the class says slowly.

"Maybe the next sentence will tell us," suggests Mr. G.

"The next sentence says, 'William the Conqueror had divided the country amongst his followers, only in special cases leaving the old Saxon Thanes the ownership of even a small part of what had once been their properties,'" reads Mr. G.

"Whoa," says Nicki. "That's a long sentence."

"Yes, it is," replies Mr. G. "Let's break it up. 'William the Conqueror had divided the country amongst his followers' is the first part. What are the important words in that part?"

"*William the Conqueror* tells who did it, so I guess that's important," says Nicki.

"That's a good way to choose the words," says Mr. G. "What was it William did?"

"*Divided* and *country* are important. They tell why there's no peace," adds Tino. "*Amongst* and *followers* tells who he gave the land to."

"Yes, you are right," says Mr. G. "Now, Tino, can you tell me in your own words what the first part of this sentence means?"

"William the Conqueror gave some pieces of land to people who supported him," says Tino with a smile. "Hey, this isn't so hard."

Mr. Guerrero walks the class through the prologue, identifying important words and clarifying meaning. He teaches the meaning directly for the first page and then switches to guided practice, with the students working in pairs for the next page. Once they have completed the prologue and he is assured that his students can identify important words and paraphrase sentences, he introduces the first chapter. "I want you to continue to read silently through this chapter. You can stop every now and then and discuss what you have read with your partner," he tells them. "If you find that you disagree on the meaning or importance of any of the sections, I want you to go back and read that section one sentence at a time and select the important words and try to restate the sentence in your own words. If you don't know the meaning of a word, discuss it with your partner first. If you can't figure it out, use the dictionary to look it up." This part of the activity helps the students practice microselection and "cite strong and thorough textual evidence to support analysis of what the text says explicitly as well as inferences drawn from the text" (CCSS.ELA-LITERACY.RL.9–10.1).

"Don't go on reading unless you understand what you are reading. When you are finished reading the first chapter, I want you to write a paragraph about what happened in the chapter or draw a picture to show what happened. Once everyone has finished reading the chapter, we will talk about it."

The students complete their reading, and Mr. G. gathers them together to discuss it. "Did you have to look up any words?" he asks.

"Joel and I looked up *perilously*," replied Mario. "It means 'with great danger.'"

"Who would like to share their drawings or writing?" asks Mr. Guerrero. Several students volunteer. The lesson concludes with the sharing of written summaries and illustrations, which serve as a review of the chapter. Mr. G. is encouraged with the first day's lesson and plans to expand on it the next day with a lesson on periodic paraphrasing to monitor understanding.

His English learners found this lesson particularly helpful because it gave them an opportunity to discuss and explore words and their meanings within the context of the sentences.

Conclusion

Teachers have long recognized the difficulty students have in identifying the main idea of a passage. Teaching students to identify important words in the selection—microselection—is an important step in helping them to master the task of identifying main ideas. English language learners often have even more difficulty because of their more limited vocabularies. Giving instruction, demonstration, and guided practice in identifying important vocabulary and discussing the meanings of the words supports all students but is especially vital in instruction for English language learners.

Examples of Approximation Behaviors Related to the TESOL Standards

PreK–3 students will:

- identify key words in oral readings.
- state the main idea of a simple paragraph.

4–8 students will:

- identify key words in paragraphs they've read.

- use the key words to write a main idea statement for a paragraph they've read.

9–12 students will:

- use key words to take notes in academic classes.
- state main ideas for academic text.

References

Baumann, J. (1982, December). *Teaching children to understand main ideas.* Paper presented at the annual meeting of the National Reading Conference, Clearwater, FL.

Echevarria, J., Vogt, M., & Short, D. (2016). *Making content comprehensible for English learners: The SIOP model.* Boston, MA: Pearson.

Green, R. (1994). *The adventures of Robin Hood.* New York, NY: Puffin Books.

Herrell, A., & Jordan, G. (2006). *50 strategies for improving vocabulary, comprehension, and fluency* (2nd ed.). Upper Saddle River, NJ: Pearson.

Irwin, J. (2006). *Teaching reading comprehension processes* (3rd ed.). Needham Heights, MA: Allyn & Bacon.

38

Read, Pair, Share

Working with a Partner to Negotiate Meaning

Read, pair, share is an adaptation of a partner activity called think, pair, share (Herrell & Jordan, 2006; McTighe & Lyman, 1988). In this activity, partners read together, stopping after each paragraph or appropriate section of text to answer the traditional "who, what, where, when, and how" questions related to the text they have just read. Whenever the partners cannot answer a question, they return together to the selected text to find the answer. Figure 38.1 shows the questioning format used with this strategy.

This approach is a strong reinforcing activity for English learners, giving them the opportunity to read and reread tough text while receiving encouragement and support from a partner. Pairing an English learner with a strong English speaker gives both students an opportunity to explore the language at a relaxed pace in a less stressful environment. The social element introduced in this activity offers a positive opportunity for verbal and social interaction, reinforcing language acquisition and development. Malinka (2006) offers another suggestion called cued story retelling in which the partners create pictures of important events so that they can retell the story with the picture cues to support them. This is a perfect way to help English learners begin to recount orally what they've read.

Step-by-Step

The steps for implementing read, pair, share are the following:

- *Introduce the question words*—Begin the activity by introducing and explaining the questions words *who*, *what*, *when*, *where*, and *how*. Talk about newspaper reporters and the fact that they must include answers to all five of these questions in a newspaper article to make sure they tell the entire story. Explain that some paragraphs don't include information in response to all five question words.

- *Model each step of the strategy*—Ask one student to act as your partner and give the class a paragraph and questioning format page for use in practicing the strategy. Introduce the title of the strategy and say, "This page tells you exactly what we will do. First, we will read the paragraph silently. Let's do that now." Model silent reading while the whole class does the same.

- *Model how to work with a partner*—Explain that students will work together to try to answer the questions. The share step also involves going back to the paragraph to share the

FIGURE 38.1 Questioning Format for Read, Pair, Share

Narrative Format

Title _____ Paragraph Number _____

Answer each question with information from the paragraph read.

1. *Who* are the people mentioned in the paragraph?
2. *What* are the people doing in the paragraph?
3. *When* does this activity take place? (year or time of day)
4. *Where* are the people in the paragraph? (country or location in building)
5. *How* does the action take place?

Informational Format

Answer each question with information from the paragraph read.

1. *Who* are the people mentioned in the paragraph?
2. *What* information is shared in the paragraph?
3. *When* does this activity take place? (year or time of day) Is the timing of the information important?
4. *Where* does the action or activity take place? (country or location in building) Is the location important?
5. *How* do all the pieces fit together?

Note: If any questions are inappropriate for the paragraph being read, the partners are encouraged to rephrase the question using the question word to make it appropriate.

Source: 50 strategies for improving vocabulary, comprehension, and fluency: An active learning approach. 2nd ed. Used with permission.

location of the answers to the questions or share the responsibility of rewording the questions to fit the paragraph. The teacher and his or her partner then model this step as the class observes. They model finding the answers and writing words, phrases, or sentences on the questioning format page. Remind the class that they will share their answers with the whole class after the entire reading assignment has been completed in read, pair, share.

• *Model the modifying of questions*—Because students often have difficulty understanding how to modify questions to fit a paragraph, it is important to model this process. Using an interactive whiteboard or similar projection system, show some sample paragraphs and model modifying questions to make them appropriate for the paragraph. For example, the text may not identify exactly whom the story is about in each paragraph. Instead of asking "Who?" for each question, the question might be modified to read, "What information does this paragraph tell you about who is doing the action?" If the question "Where?" cannot be answered, the question could be modified to ask, "Does the paragraph give you any hints about where this took place?" Teach the students to look for hints such as the weather conditions or maybe some description of what the people are wearing that might indicate whether a place is particularly hot or cold. Sometimes the answer may just have to be, "There's nothing in the paragraph to give a hint about this." When you select paragraphs to use as examples, choose some that will provide students with ideas about how to reword questions.

• *Pair the students*—Assign each student a partner, being careful not to pair two weak students together. Try to pair English learners with strong English models to encourage language development. Give the students a reading assignment and questioning format pages with enough format pages for each paragraph in the reading assignment. You can copy about four formatting pages on each sheet of paper. Give the students time to work on their assignment as you move around the room providing assistance as needed.

- *Discuss the assignment*—Once the students have completed the assignment using the read, pair, share method, bring the class back together to discuss the process. Encourage them to share the answers they found to the questions and any questions they modified.
- *Assess to identify the need for additional instruction or guided practice*—As you circulate during the practice session, note students who will need more guided practice. Also note students who use the strategy easily. Use this information to create future pairs as well as provide extra practice for those who need it. If necessary, provide practice with less challenging reading material for those who need it.

Applications and Examples

Because Miss Garabedian's third grade students are exploring a semester-long theme of "celebrating our uniqueness," she decides to use the book *Chrysanthemum* (Henkes, 1991) when she introduces the read, pair, share strategy to her class.

She begins, "Girls and boys, I have a very special book to share with you today. It's about a little girl who has a unique name. Her name is Chrysanthemum. Have any of you ever known anyone named after a flower?"

"Oh, Miss G., I have two aunts named Violeta and Rosa," states Orchid enthusiastically. "And, of course, I'm a flower, too."

"Well, how do you think Chrysanthemum feels about having such an unusual name?" asks Miss G.

"I think it's great," answers Orchid.

"Well, today we're going to find out how Chrysanthemum felt about it, but we're also going to learn to do something called read, pair, share," continues Miss G. She focuses the students' attention to the projection on the interactive whiteboard and displays a paragraph on which she has written "Who? What? When? Where? How?"

"These question words are the words that we use when we want to make sure we gather all the information we can about a topic," says Miss G. "Newspaper reporters use these questions to make sure they report all the facts about a story they are writing. We will use these question words to make sure we understand everything about what's happening in the story." She then replaces the first projection with a second one on which she has listed the questioning format they will use for the read, pair, share activity.

Who is the paragraph about?
What is the character doing?
When does this action take place?
Where does the action take place?
How does the character perform the action?

"These are the questions we will ask ourselves as we read each paragraph in the story," explains Miss G. "Now, I need a partner to help me demonstrate how we do read, pair, share. Orchid, why don't you be my partner?"

"Yes, ma'am!" says Orchid with a smile as she nods her head vigorously and comes to the front of the room to sit by Miss Garabedian.

"Now, the first thing we do is read," says Miss G. "Just read the first paragraph to yourself and then look up so I'll know you are finished." Miss G. and Orchid read the first paragraph silently.

"Now, let's see if Orchid and I can answer the first question. 'Who is the paragraph about?'" Miss G. says, "Well, Orchid, what do you think?"

"I think it's about Chrysanthemum, but we don't know that yet. I guess we can say it's about a little baby girl."

"OK, so I'll write 'a little baby girl' under the first question," says Miss G. "The next question is, 'What is the character doing?' Well, she's not doing much yet, is she, Orchid?"

"No," answers Orchid. "She's just getting born."

"Good thought," says Miss G. with a smile as she writes "she's just getting born" under the second question. "Now, I want you all to know that you won't need to write down all the answers to the questions once you learn how to use this strategy. You'll just be using it to make sure you understand the story, but for today we're going to write down the answers to make sure we remember to do all the steps."

"Now, the next two questions are not really appropriate for this paragraph, and you will find that to be true for some paragraphs," says Miss G. "When does this action take place? Where does the action take place? All we can say is that, in this case, we really don't know." Miss G. points to the final question on the list and says, "This 'how' question doesn't fit this paragraph either, but it's one we can reword. 'How did her parents feel about the baby?' is an important question for this paragraph so we want to ask that 'how' question instead of the one suggested."

Miss G. crosses out the "how" question and writes in, "How did her parents feel about the baby?"

Orchid says, "Let me write the answer, Miss G."

Miss G. gives Orchid the marker, and Orchid writes, "They thought she was absolutely perfect."

"Very good, Orchid," says Miss G. "Now we share the responsibility of going back to the paragraph and making sure we have answered the questions correctly and found the answers in the text. We also make sure that we didn't forget to answer any of the questions that fit the paragraph and that we can't reword any of the questions we left out."

"Let's talk about rewording the questions for a minute," suggests Miss G. "The only word you have to keep in each question is the question word. Notice, we changed 'How does the character perform the action?' to 'How did her parents feel about the baby?' because that question matched the paragraph better. We just needed to keep the question word *how*. Now you might at times change some of the other questions. Let's work with our partners to read the next page and then we'll practice changing the questions to fit the paragraphs."

Miss G. assigns partners to work together and then has them read the next page silently. She leaves the questions on the whiteboard and asks the partners to answer them or change them so they fit the paragraph better. Because the next paragraph describes how her parents named her, the students change several of the questions. They answer "Who is the paragraph about?" by saying "her parents."

They change "What is the character doing?" to "What are the characters doing?" and answer it, "They are naming their baby." They add another important "what" question by asking "What did they name her?" and answer "Chrysanthemum."

They agree to skip "When does this action take place?" and "Where does the action take place?" because they aren't that important to understanding the story. They change "How does the character perform the action?" to "How did they choose her name?" and answer, "They thought of the most perfect name they could because the baby was so perfect."

After the students finish reading the book, Miss G. leads a discussion of the story and finds that the students have a lot of interesting thoughts about the uniqueness of Chrysanthemum and the delightful Delphinium Twinkle, Chrysanthemum's music teacher. They also have some interesting comments about occasions when their classmates had teased them. They could really relate to that problem!

When they discuss the read, pair, share strategy, the students also have some insightful things to say:

"Changing the questions made us think about what was happening in the paragraph."
"We almost retold the paragraph when we answered the questions."

Miss Garabedian is pleased they were so successful in their use of read, pair, share, and she plans to use it with informational text the next day.

* * * * *

Mr. McMillan wants his 11th-grade U.S. history class to understand some of the prominent figures of the war years of the 1940s and to see some of their more personal characteristics. He wants to make some of these icons of history come alive for his students. He introduces them to reading biographies, which is a new experience for many of his students. Mr. McMillan uses read, pair, share to introduce this new genre.

He explains the procedure to his students and models it by bringing one of the students to the front of the class and actually going through the procedure as a demonstration for the class. During the demonstration, Mr. McMillan introduces the set of questions that students will be using during the process. For informational text, in particular, he feels that this is an extremely important part of the read, pair, share process.

Mr. McMillan reveals a chart he has prepared for the lesson that contains the questions the students will use with each other during the process:

> Who? Are there any people mentioned in the paragraph?
> What? What is the paragraph about?
> When? Is the time important in the paragraph? If so, when did it happen?
> Where? Is the location important in the paragraph? If so, where did it happen?
> How? How do the elements relate to the main idea of this paragraph?

He then asks his students to read chapter 20, "A Lonely Little Girl," in Joy Hakim's *A History of US: War, Peace, and All That Jazz* (1995). This chapter discusses some of the personal characteristics of Eleanor Roosevelt's early life and gives the students insights into her early struggles and what made her the person she ultimately became.

After the students read the text and share the question-and-answer process, they are surprised to find out about the struggles that this grand lady went through in the early years of her life. By sharing the information through questioning, they are also exposed to the point of view of other students and become more aware of the personal side of an individual that can be discovered through reading and interacting with biographies.

Conclusion

The interaction of students during reading and comprehension processing provides an excellent scaffold for developing these skills. For English learners, it also provides an opportunity for language development in a supportive and cooperative environment. They begin to see through the eyes of another and to understand more readily the processes that might be necessary to obtain a deeper understanding of reading material. They also begin to see that even informational text can include elements of personal interest and involvement. Encouraging students to think and share thoughts together can help them develop stronger tools for relating to and understanding text.

Examples of Approximation Behaviors Related to the TESOL Standards

PreK–3 students will:

- talk about a book they've read or heard.
- listen to another person's ideas about a book.

4–8 students will:

- compare characters in a narrative text.
- discuss the elements of text.

9–12 students will:

- discuss the author's purpose.
- demonstrate understanding of informational text structure.

References

Hakim, J. (1995). *A history of US: War, peace, and all that jazz*. New York, NY: Oxford University Press.

Henkes, K. (1991). *Chrysanthemum*. New York, NY: Scholastic.

Herrell, A., & Jordan, M. (2006). *50 strategies for improving vocabulary, comprehension, and fluency: An active learning approach*. Upper Saddle River, NJ: Pearson.

Malinka, N. (2006). Fun with storytelling. In V. Whiteson (Ed.), *New ways of using drama and literature in language teaching* (pp. 41–42). Alexandria, VA: TESOL.

McTighe, J., & Lyman, F. (1988). Cueing thinking in the classroom: The promise of theory- embedded tools. *Educational Leadership*, *45*, 18–24.

39

Attribute Charting
Organizing Information to Support Understanding

Attribute charting, also called **semantic feature analysis** (Peregoy & Boyle, 2016), is a way of visually organizing information to support students' understanding of the attributes of the concept being studied. For example, if students are engaged in the study of continents, they might construct an attribute chart by looking at maps and noting descriptive information such as which continents are found in the Northern Hemisphere; which are connected to other continents; which are surrounded by water; and which are mountainous, flat, or varietal in elevations.

This strategy supports English language learners because the chart they make clearly illustrates their understanding of the main attributes of a topic—in this case, continents. By making a chart of these attributes, students can more easily compare and contrast the continents. Students are involved in active research to determine which of the attributes are possessed by the individual continents, and they are given opportunities to interact verbally as they construct the chart. Attribute charting presents an opportunity for the teacher to reinforce many basic concepts as the chart is created. English spelling and pronunciation are reviewed as the students become active contributors to the chart. This approach is especially valuable in content areas such as mathematics, science, and social sciences where vocabulary is more discipline-specific (Díaz-Rico, 2018). All this attention to detail provides a scaffold that the student can then use in talking and writing (Gibbons, 2015). A sample students' attribute chart for the study of continents is shown in Figure 39.1.

Step-by-Step

The steps in teaching the use of an attribute chart are the following:

- *Choose a concept to chart*—Determine whether the concept you are teaching lends itself to charting its attributes. If it does, make a list of the attributes, traits, or characteristics that could be charted.
- *Discuss attributes or traits*—Involve students in a discussion of the traits or attributes of the examples that illustrate the concept being taught. Provide students with a set of clear instructions and encourage them to contribute to the completion of the attribute chart by examining the examples to see which attributes are present in each. Demonstrate how to use a

FIGURE 39.1 The Continents

Continent	Island	Connected	Mountains	Flat	Rivers	Desert	Forest	Ice
Africa	−	✓	✓	✓	✓	+	+	−
Antarctica	−	−	✓	✓	−	−	−	++
Asia	−	+	✓	✓	✓	✓	✓	−
Australia	+	−	✓	✓	✓	✓	✓	−
Europe	−	+	✓	−	✓	−	✓	−
North America	−	✓	✓	✓	✓	✓	✓	−
South America	−	✓	✓	✓	✓	−	✓	−

marking system for the task. For example, an attribute might simply be checked on the chart or marked with another symbol to show how closely it fits a given parameter. For the continent lesson, under the attribute of "connectedness," the continents of Europe and Asia would be marked with a plus sign because they are connected across a large area of land, while North and South America would be marked with a check mark because they are more minimally connected. Australia would be marked with a minus sign because it is not connected to any other continent.

• *Explore the materials*—Engage students in an exploration of resource materials available to support their understanding of the attributes being marked. When charting animals, students might look at pictures of animals. When charting continents, students would want to examine maps and photographs. Give multiple opportunities to search for and view realia, photographs, and video to ensure understanding of the concept and its attributes. Model the use of the academic language being learned and help the students make connections among the academic language, their background knowledge, and colloquial language (BICS).

• *Use the charted material*—Provide a follow-up activity that encourages students to use the information on the attribute chart. This might be a writing assignment in which they must use the chart to compare and contrast two of the examples. Or, it might be an activity in which the students illustrate and label the attributes of one of the examples from the chart.

• *Add technology*—These kinds of chart-based activities are often well suited to the use of computer spreadsheet programs. Such programs make it easy to create a chart, save it on the computer, fill in the appropriate completed activities, sort by attributes, and print out the results.

Applications and Examples

Mr. Villalobos and his first-grade English learners are looking at pictures of animals and discussing where the animals live in preparation for a unit on the zoo. Because the class will be visiting the zoo, Mr. Villalobos wants the children to understand that the habitats in which the animals are housed are not exactly the same as where the animals live in the wild. Because the class has just completed a study of farm animals, the discussion of the pictures also involves comparing and contrasting zoo and farm animals. As the discussion continues, Mr. Villalobos decides that the children will benefit from constructing an attribute chart. As he begins to draw the chart, he engages the children in a discussion of each animal, its natural habitat, and whether it is a farm or zoo animal. The chart they construct is shown in Figure 39.2.

Mr. Villalobos begins the discussion by activating the children's background knowledge of the farm animals they have recently studied and their visit to the farm. He shows the children a picture of a duck and asks the children to name the animal and tell if the animal has fur or feathers, two or four legs, lays eggs, or has live babies.

Next, Mr. Villalobos shows a picture of another animal and repeats the process.

As the children add information about the animals whose pictures they are examining, Mr. Villalobos models making an attribute chart. He demonstrates with the duck and says, "This word says *duck*. Now I will mark what you told me about the duck. The duck is a farm animal." Mr. Villalobos makes an X under the word *farm*. "He lives on land and in the water. I have to mark both of these words. He has two legs, and duck babies come from eggs."

Once Mr. Villalobos has modeled the marking of the chart for the duck, he involves the children in marking the chart for the horse's attributes. The children read and reread the attributes on the chart as they decide which traits should be marked for each animal. Once they have completed the chart they are shown what to do next.

FIGURE 39.2 Class Animal Attribute Chart

Animal	Farm	Zoo	Natural Habitat Land	Water	4 Legs	2 Legs	Wings	Hair	Babies Live	Eggs
Duck	✗		✗	✓		✗	✗			✗
Horse	✗		✗		✗			✗	✗	
Elephant		✗	✗	✓	✗			✗	✗	
Lion		✗	✗		✗			✗	✗	
Pig	✗		✗		✗			✗	✗	
Giraffe		✗	✗		✗			✗	✗	

Mr. Villalobos holds up a piece of construction paper as each child does the same. He models folding the paper in half and monitors as the children do the same. He models drawing two animals, one on each half of the paper. The children do the same, choosing the two animals they want to compare. Mr. Villalobos then models the writing of sentences about each animal, focusing on the attribute chart as the source of the words they will need. "The horse lives on a farm. He lives on land and has four legs. He has hair, and his babies are born live."

The children's language and concept acquisition is supported by the use of the attribute chart. Mr. Villalobos supports the construction of the chart with the use of modeling, both by writing and identifying the resources the students have. In doing this, Mr. Villalobos is able to enable the children to in successfully integrating their knowledge with the completion of a short writing assignment.

* * * * *

Just as young children benefit from seeing their ideas and assignments visualized, older students also gain insight when charts are used to support their learning and planning. Creating charts the students can use as resources provides support and scaffolding needed by English learners.

For example, Ms. Vue has noticed that her seventh-grade science students don't always use the strategies they have learned to support their understanding of the science concepts they are studying. The science fair is approaching, and all the students are supposed to be preparing projects for the fair. Ms. Vue decides that an attribute chart could be used to review the learning strategies involved in preparing a good science project.

"Today, I want to review the steps in the **scientific process** you are using to prepare your science project," Ms. Vue says as she projects a blank attribute chart on the interactive whiteboard in her classroom. The chart she displays is depicted in Figure 39.3

Ms. Vue points to the steps in the scientific process on the overhead chart and reviews what each step means. She then goes back to the top row of the chart to ask, "Why do you think I wrote these particular things across the top of this chart? What do they have to do with doing a science project?"

Rodney raises his hand and Ms. Vue acknowledges him. "I think those are the strategies that are needed to actually do the steps in the project."

"Exactly," Ms. Vue replies. "Each of the steps in the scientific process involves the use of some of the learning strategies listed—and maybe some I haven't listed. Let's talk about how they are related to the steps in the scientific process."

As she points to the first step in the scientific process, Ms. Vue asks, "What does asking a question involve? Do you need to have any prior knowledge of the subject to ask a question?"

Stefan answers, "I think you have to know something about the subject you are going to use for your project or you won't know what kinds of questions to ask."

"Yes," Ms. Vue replies. "That is true. So, having prior knowledge is important to being able to ask a question. We could say that using prior knowledge is a trait or attribute necessary to do this step in the scientific process well. What about resourcing? Who remembers what that term means?"

Adriana replies, "It means using resources like encyclopedias and textbooks. You'd have to use resourcing to do a good job of asking a scientific question. If you didn't, you may ask a question that has been answered many times."

"That's true," Ms. Vue says. "What about note-taking? Why is that listed?"

"You won't be able to remember everything you read," Josef says. "That's why you have to take notes. But I'm not sure you need to do it just to ask a question. That's more what you do later on in the process."

As Ms. Vue works through the steps in the scientific process and relates them to the learning strategies needed to do a thorough job of the science project, the students can see by the chart exactly what they will need to do to complete each step. The last item on the chart—communicating—elicits some spirited discussion.

"You'll be doing all this work for nothing if you can't communicate to others. You need to be able to make your steps and results clear," Alberto says.

"And how do you do that?" Ms. Vue asks.

FIGURE 39.3 Ms. Vue's Attribute Chart

Steps in the Scientific Process	Prior Knowledge	Resourcing	Note-Taking	Planning	Communicating
Ask a question					
Make a hypothesis					
Collect data					
Record data					
Analyze data					
Answer the question					
Prepare a display to share your processes and results					

Sources: Chamot and O'Malley (1994), Díaz-Rico (2013), and Peregoy and Boyle (2013).

"By drawing pictures and listing your methods and results in order. Oh, and you have to make sure that you define your terms well so everyone knows what you are taking about," Alberto answers.

"So being able to communicate also takes some planning. Some of these attributes are connected," Ms. Vue says. "That's why I wanted you to see them in chart form. Maybe a chart can help you to communicate your steps, methods, data gathering, and results."

Conclusion

By using an attribute chart, both Mr. Villalobos and Ms. Vue helped their English learners understand both organization and content. They helped their students to visualize what is required of them. In the process, they taught them an organizational strategy that might be helpful as they communicate their academic processes and results. The students have had an opportunity to see the fifth and sixth language arts, *viewing* and *visually representing*, in action. This lessens their dependence on *reading*, *writing*, *speaking*, and *listening*.

Watch this video showing how English language learners benefit from the use of an attribute chart to clarify their understanding and comprehension as they work with language structure and vocabulary.

Enhanced eText
Video Example 39.1
https://youtu.be/
aBAIAEoipYg

Examples of Approximation Behaviors Related to the TESOL Standards

PreK–3 students will:

- verbally identify attributes of realia.
- verbally identify attributes of common nouns.

4–8 students will:

- verbally identify attributes of content-related concepts.
- visually represent attributes of content-related concepts.

9–12 students will:

- analyze attribute charts to summarize similarities among concepts.
- write a compare-and-contrast paper using information from an attributes chart containing content-related concepts.

References

Chamot, A., & O'Malley, M. (1994). *The CALLA handbook: Implementing the cognitive academic language learning approach.* Reading, MA: Addison-Wesley.

Díaz-Rico, L. (2018). *The crosscultural, language, and academic development handbook: A complete K–12 reference guide* (6th ed.). Boston, MA: Pearson Education.

Gibbons, P. (2015). *Scaffolding language, scaffolding learning.* (2nd ed.) Portsmouth, NH: Heinemann.

Peregoy, S., & Boyle, O. (2016). *Reading, writing, and learning in ESL: A resource book for K–8 teachers* (7th ed.). White Plains, NY: Longman.

Integrated Curriculum Projects

Using Authentic Projects to Integrate Content Knowledge

Enhanced eText
Video Example 40.1

The **integrated curriculum project** (Helm & Katz, 2010; Meyers, 1993) is an approach to curriculum planning in which knowledge and skills in several curricular areas are combined to accomplish an authentic task. Learning by doing, a common shorthand for the idea that active participation helps students to understand ideas or acquire skills, is an established principle of progressive education (Kohn, 2004).

Integrated curriculum projects differ from thematic units in several ways. There is no attempt to bring all subject areas into the project. The studies are integrated, usually around an active-learning project, so that the students are learning vocabulary and having experiences that demonstrate the need to use knowledge in multiple disciplines to complete real-life work. An authentic project is accomplished using only those curricular areas necessary to complete the objective. The integrated project approach used with the first-grade class in this video documents how to integrate curriculum while addressing standards in multiple areas. Consider the following questions as you watch the the Video Example 40.1:

- How many areas of the curriculum are included in this activity?
- How does using an integrated project approach increase efficiency in terms of addressing subject matter requirements while meeting curricular standards?

This approach is appropriate for English language learners because of its focus on vocabulary in multiple contexts and authentic projects, which embed the language in real tasks. In addition, the work that is done in an integrated curriculum project is almost always accomplished in cooperative groups of students working together to create a project. This approach gives English language learners many opportunities to interact verbally within a supportive, small-group setting while engaging in activities that require communication (Kohn, 2004).

You can find support materials and planning guides for curriculum projects at the ELL Tool Box website (ell toolbox.com).

Watch these teachers working together to integrate curriculum by planning together and sharing their individual strengths:

Step-by-Step

The steps in implementing integrated curriculum projects are the following:

• *Identify an authentic project opportunity*—Be alert to curriculum possibilities related to science and social sciences curricula; national or local news events; and service project needs in the school, community, or your own classroom. If no ideas emerge from that approach, interview your students to determine their interests. Ask questions like, "If you could study anything at all, what would you like to learn about?" For further suggestions see Figure 40.1.

Involve students in project planning. This will enhance their intrinsic motivation. Present the project or possible projects and engage students in brainstorming ideas about what might be accomplished. It is very important for students to be enthusiastic about the project and perceive opportunities for real accomplishments.

FIGURE 40.1 Suggestions for Integrated Curriculum Projects

Grade Level	Projects
Kindergarten	• Making our playground cleaner (prettier, safer) • Eating healthful food • Our families
Primary	• Making our neighborhood cleaner (prettier, safer, more friendly) • Making our school safer • Who are our neighbors? (neighborhood study) • Where does our food come from?
Upper Elementary	• Our friends, our world (origins of the students and families) • Making our town (city, county) cleaner (safer, friendlier) • How our officials are elected • Lobbying for a cause • Manufacturing a product
Middle School	• Advocating for safe leisure activities • Adopting a group (peer tutoring, supporting the elderly, etc.) • Beautifying a public area • Publishing a magazine or newspaper • Integrating photography, art, spokesmanship into school
High School	• Uniting the community • Designing and implementing a homework center • Walking in their shoes (cross-cultural study or studies of the physically challenged) • Advocating for changes in the school system
All levels	• Studies based on a good piece of literature

- *Relate the project to grade-level Common Core State Standards and ESL standards*—While you plan the curricular connections, required vocabulary, and key lessons, keep in mind the concepts that students will need to accomplish grade-level and ESL objectives. Focus on the multiple uses of vocabulary and skills they will need to complete the project successfully. List other groups, organizations, teachers, and administrators who can be enlisted to support the project.
- *Identify the class goals*—Conduct a class problem-solving session in which you and the students identify the most important products or accomplishments they want to achieve, the problems they will need to overcome, and the people who will need to be involved.
- *Establish working groups and their assignments*—Form cooperative groups, making sure that the English language learners are paired with strong language models, and divide the labor so that each group is responsible for designated tasks. Provide each group with a list of their responsibilities and roles, and encourage them to work together to set a time line for accomplishments, as well as a checklist of tasks to be carried out.
- *Integrate learning*—Plan ways to involve the cooperative groups in studying, planning, implementing, and celebrating each step of the way.
- *Integrate assessment to ensure effective instruction*—It is important to recognize each student's contribution to group planning and project implementation. To do this, teachers must observe the process carefully and help students to evaluate their own and others' contributions. Projects help students to get to know one another and to recognize the different talents each possesses.

Some teachers like to have students do self-evaluations after a project is complete. It is also helpful to have the groups complete a group evaluation form where they list the contributions of each member of the group. It is easier for the group to do this type of evaluation if the teacher has publicly recognized students' contributions throughout the project.

Applications and Examples

When Ms. Frangelica's first graders hear that they are getting a new student, Serieta, from the same Caribbean island where their teacher grew up, they are very excited. Because her students are so interested in the island, Ms. Frangelica begins to plan a study of Serieta's native island. She realizes that she can put together an integrated curriculum project based on her students' interest in the new student and her native island. She plans to build the study on Frank Lessac's book *My Little Island* (1984), which has always been a favorite of hers. The book is rich in vocabulary related to new foods, geography, and activities that will be fascinating to the first graders but familiar to Serieta. Ms. Frangelica also plans a project in which her students will become pen pals with the students in Serieta's old class. Ms. Frangelica lists the curricular areas she can integrate:

Music: Caribbean music, dance, rhythm
Nutrition: new foods, food groups, diet
Geography: island, Caribbean Sea
Social sciences: effect of climate and natural resources on housing, food supplies, and activities; occupations; customs and celebrations and their origins; contrasting the use of time and resources with the way things are done in the United States
Language arts: writing to pen pals, reading books about life and customs of the Caribbean
Vocabulary: a wall of Caribbean words with pictures and realia to illustrate them, and native expressions
Parent involvement: bring other Caribbean parents in for interviews; demonstrations of music, dance, and cooking

Because Ms. Frangelica knows how poor the schools are on her island, she plans a service learning project in which the children will become involved in sending something of educational value to Serieta's old school. She will involve the children in making this decision once Serieta arrives and can tell them more about the needs of the school, but she envisions the students soliciting donations of, or raising money for, books for Serieta's old school. This will involve extensive research on her students' part, exchanges of letters between the schools, and decision making in the selection of books to send. As she thinks about the integrated curriculum project that is growing in her mind, she realizes the children will learn a great deal because they will be involved in each step of the project. She immediately gets to work choosing the music to play as the students arrive on Monday morning, and she gets out her old sun hat to wear to help set the mood. She gathers some artifacts from the island to label and place around the classroom. As she looks around her apartment, she finds a conch shell, photos of brightly painted houses on stilts, an artificial frangipani flower, a coconut, and a stuffed iguana. Her project is under way.

Ms. Frangelica hopes to begin an email exchange between students if the island school has Internet service. She plans to make Serieta the official interpreter so that Serieta and her classmates understand the value of being bilingual.

* * * * *

Ms. Boland teaches seventh-grade English in an inner-city middle school. Her students are from several cultural groups, some Hispanic and some Southeast Asian. The local neighborhood doesn't provide many opportunities for students to see much beauty as they walk to school each morning, but students usually come in smiling. One morning, Tia enters with an angry stomp. "I *hate* graffiti!" she states strongly. "My grandmother just painted her front fence yesterday, and it's already marked again."

Several of the other students join in the discussion, but no one seems to have a solution to the problem. The discussion gets Ms. Boland thinking about the neighborhood in which her students live. Several of the school service groups have painted murals on the outside walls of the school. The murals do help. No graffiti has been painted over them. But the walls without murals are still covered regularly, no matter how quickly the graffiti is painted over. Ms. Boland is not convinced that graffiti is the main problem. She is more worried about the general feeling of despair and discouragement that she often recognizes as she confers with parents.

That evening, as she attends her photography class at the local community college, Ms. Boland has an idea. After class, she approaches her photography instructor. "I want to do a photography project with my seventh graders. Do you have students who would be available to help them learn how to take pictures?" she asks.

"Yes, I think we could do that," replies Mr. Stephens, the instructor. "Better than that, though, we have a service club on campus that I sponsor. We just happen to be looking for a project."

"Great!" Ms. Boland replies. "Here's my idea. I want my students to begin to see some beauty and hope in their neighborhood. I thought if they could look through the lens of a camera, they could begin to see the beauty in their world and think about ways that they can contribute to their neighborhood. I plan to use the photography project to motivate their writing and their thinking about the control they have over their futures. Seventh graders are at such an important point in their education; I think maybe giving them some new interests might be helpful in inspiring them as readers, writers, and thinkers."

"Wow!" Mr. Stephens replies. "You're biting off a lot, but I think I see where you are going. But first things first. Do you have any cameras? Do they know how to take pictures?"

"No, I don't know, and no!" Ms. Boland says with a grin. "That's why I need help."

"Well, the service club meets Thursday night at the student union. Can you and a couple of your students come and present the idea?" Mr. Stephens asks.

"We can do that," Ms. Boland replies. "What time?"

The next day Ms. Boland presents her idea to her first-period class. She simply tells them that she thinks they will enjoy learning to take pictures as a **prewriting strategy** and asks if anyone is interested in the idea. Many hands go up. Tia's hand is one that is not raised.

"Tia, you don't want to learn to take pictures?" Ms. Boland asks.

"It's not that," Tia replies. "My grandmother still thinks that you steal people's souls when you take their pictures. She won't like this. And, also, I don't have a camera."

"What if we could get cameras to use and you can take pictures of scenery or buildings rather than people?" asks Ms. Boland.

"I think that will be all right," Tia replies slowly. "I'll have to ask."

"I'll be glad to talk to your grandmother, if that will help," Ms. Boland says.

The next few days are busy in Ms. Boland's class. She organizes cooperative groups to plan the photography projects. The groups plan their needs: digital cameras, release forms for people they will photograph, and permission forms for walking field trips around the neighborhood. One group plans a presentation to the principal for his support. Another prepares for the presentation to the community college service club. On Thursday evening, Ms. Boland and her group attend the meeting of the community college service club and get support for inexpensive cameras for the class. They also receive help from some of the photography students, who agree to come and give lessons in basic photography. The next week is spent in planning their photography projects and looking for possible pictures to meet the criteria set by Ms. Boland. The pictures are to illustrate one of the following themes:

- My culture
- My neighborhood
- Beauty in unexpected places
- Intergenerational interactions

Ms. Boland teaches the use of photography as a prewriting strategy by asking the students to think of a picture they could take and then drafting a short essay that might accompany the picture. In the meantime, students from the community college come to the first-period class and teach basic principles of photography. The second week, the students embark on a walking field trip and take pictures. Working as partners, the students each take six pictures. While one student uses the camera, the partner writes a brief description of the picture that is taken and jots down any notes the photographer dictates. Once the photos are downloaded, the students start working on their essays.

Ms. Boland is so impressed by the photos and the essays that she shares them with a professional photographer friend a few weeks later. "I would love to have a way to enlarge the photos, mount them, and display them," Ms. Boland says. "The students are very motivated by this project. They are learning a lot about photography and writing. But, more than that, they are developing a renewed interest in their neighborhood and the people who live there. I've created a monster. We simply do not have the money to continue this approach on an ongoing basis."

"Why don't you get the students involved in some problem solving?" her friend replies. "I'll work on some ideas through the local photo gallery group, but it would be wonderful if the students could help solve their own problem."

"I agree," Ms. Boland says.

The next morning, Ms. Boland presents the problem to her class. She reconvenes the cooperative groups for a brainstorming session, and the groups quickly formulate a list of ideas. By the end of the period, the groups each have a project they are willing to pursue to raise funds to continue their photography project. One group is going to approach the local newspaper to publish an article about the project with the hope of identifying possible donors. One group is going to approach the principal for help. One group is going to talk to the cafeteria manager to see if they can sell ice cream or snacks at the end of each lunch period to raise funds. One group is going to call the photography and education departments at the local university to see if there are any funds available to support university–community partnerships. Each group has a plan of action.

Six months later Ms. Boland can hardly believe how many of the plans have produced results. As she watches the parents circulating around the room looking at the beautifully mounted photos and essays, she notices the local television station filming the event for the evening news. The article and full-color spread that appeared in the local newspaper is displayed prominently on one wall. The university professors, community college instructors, and students who were all part of the project are beaming their approval. The students are getting many opportunities for oral language practice explaining how they got their ideas and how exciting the project has become. Ms. Boland is thinking about all the knowledge of grants and budgets and advocacy that the students have gained through this endeavor, and she is already planning her next integrated curriculum project.

Conclusion

Integrated curriculum projects are powerful because they go a step beyond the traditional thematic unit to completing an authentic task. Whether the task is providing books for students in a poor community, using photography to improve writing skills and community pride, or applying math and science skills to design a reading loft for the classroom, students begin to see the practical applications of school subjects through integrated curriculum projects. They also gain multiple opportunities to practice their spoken and written English as they gather information, make presentations to possible supporters of the project, and participate in the planning and implementation of the project.

Examples of Approximation Behaviors Related to the TESOL Standards

PreK–3 students will:

- verbally describe a classroom or school problem to solve.
- use appropriate language to suggest solutions.

4–8 students will:

- use beginning research skills to find solutions to real problems.

- use language skills to persuade others to support a project.

9–12 students will:

- verbally describe neighborhood, city, or state problems that need a solution.
- participate in planning and implementing problem-solving projects.

References

Helm, J., & Katz, L. (2010) *Young investigators: The project approach in the early years* (2nd ed.). New York, NY: Teachers College Press.

Kohn, A. (2004). Challenging students—and how to have more of them. *Phi Delta Kappan, 86*(3), 184–194.

Lessac, F. (1984). *My little island*. London, England: HarperTrophy (Macmillan).

Meyers, M. (1993). *Teaching to diversity: Teaching and learning in the multi-ethnic classroom.* Toronto, Canada: Irwin.

KWL and Data Charts
Researching and Organizing Information

KWL charts (Ogle, 1986) are three-section charts that students use to explore what they know (K), what they want to know (W), and what they learn (L) about a topic. Typically, the teacher prepares the three-part chart with the letters K, W, and L at the top of each section. Graphic organizers such as KWL charts make content and the relationships among concepts more visible and understandable for English learners (Goldenberg, 2008). See Figure 41.1 for a sample KWL chart.

The teacher introduces the topic and asks the students what they know about it. The teacher then lists the students' responses on the chart under the K. This is very much like brainstorming; the teacher doesn't edit the responses, just notes them under the K column. The teacher then asks the students what they would like to know about the topic and lists their responses under the W, for "want to know." The L column is left blank at this point; it is filled in only as the students find information related to the questions they have listed in the W column.

Enhanced eText
Video Example 41.1
www.youtube.com/
watch?v=oK6hi79OJns

Observe a class building a KWL graphic organizer in this video, and note how students use the chart to record and classify their learning. As you watch, consider the following questions:

1. How does the teacher activate their background knowledge?
2. How does she find out what interests the students?

An extended version of a KWL chart is called a KWL Plus. Two additional columns are added to follow both the K and L columns. In the additional columns, students cite their sources as they find new information for the L column. This allows them to verify or reject information listed in the K column by evaluating the accuracy of their sources. Figure 41.2 provides an example of a KWL Plus chart.

Using KWL charts to activate prior knowledge and document new learning while reading informational text has been shown to be an effective strategy for English learners (Riswanto, Risnawatti, & Lismayanto, 2014).

Data charts (Tompkins, 2007) are graphic organizers that give students an effective format for recording the knowledge they gain as they research a topic. Data charts are valuable in teaching students to organize the information they gain in a form suitable for studying for tests or preparing

FIGURE 41.1 Sample KWL Chart

K	W	L
(What we **KNOW**)	(What we **WANT** to know)	(What we **LEARNED**)

FIGURE 41.2 Using data and KWL Charts with English learners

Preproduction	Early Production	Speech Emergence	Intermediate Fluency	Fluent
Use data chart to introduce basic vocabulary. Add new words under L column.	Add new concepts to L column as taught.	Encourage sentence formation using new vocabulary.	Begin to encourage simple paragraph formation using facts and vocabulary. Introduce simple factual writing using concepts and vocabulary learned.	Use KWL and data charts as resources for writing reports.

oral and written reports. A data chart is a perfect companion to the KWL chart; students record their research and cite sources, providing a succinct, one-page summary of the information gained on a topic. See Figure 41.3 for a sample data chart.

FIGURE 41.3 A Sample Data Chart

Group Members _____
Topic _____

	Questions				
	How does it look?	What does it eat?	Where does it live?	What are its natural enemies?	Other important information?
Sources and Readers					
Book: Reader:					
Book: Reader:					
Book: Reader:					
Book: Reader:					
Book: Reader:					

Source: Herrell and Jordan (2006).

Step-by-Step

The steps in using KWL and data charts are the following:

• *Choose a topic to use in introducing basic research skills*—Based on your Common Core social sciences or science standards, decide on a grade-appropriate topic to use in teaching students how to gather basic information for the purpose of preparing oral or written reports.

• *Prepare a blank KWL or KWL Plus chart*—If this is your students' first experience with KWL charts and basic research, you will want to use a basic KWL chart. You can always note the corrections and cite the sources under the K column *after* the research is done and as the L column is completed.

FIGURE 41.4 KWL Plus Chart

K	Source	W	L	Source

Source: Based on Herrell, A., & Jordan, M. (2006). 50 strategies for improving vocabulary, comprehension, and fluency: An active learning approach (2nd ed.). Upper Saddle River, NJ: Pearson.

• *Introduce the KWL chart in a group lesson*—Explain that the class will be studying a topic and to begin the study, you, the teacher, need to know what they already know about the topic. As the students tell you things they know, write their responses in the K column. Do not edit at this point. Write all responses on the chart, even if some students refute certain statements. Explain that part of the study is to find sources to verify or reject information that we may believe to be true. After their "known" statements are exhausted, ask the students what they want to know about the topic and record their responses in the W column of the chart.

• *Provide students with books and resources to read about the topic*—Depending on the ages and stages of your students, you can plan a trip to the library, time to research online, and time to read age-appropriate books about the topic. Provide individual copies of the class KWL chart for them to use as they find information about the topic.

• *Demonstrate how to add new information to the L column of the KWL chart and make corrections to the K column*—As students find answers to the questions in the W column of the chart, have them place those answers on their individual KWL charts. Gather the group together each day to allow them to share the information they have gained about the topic. If they find information that verifies statements made and recorded under the K column, encourage them to share that information and their source. Add new information gathered under the L column and, again, share the source of the information. If you are using the KWL Plus format, cite the source in the source column.

• *Introduce the data chart as a way to organize the information they are gathering*—Use the questions generated under the W column to head the columns on the data chart. Demonstrate how the students' answers can be noted under the questions and the sources documented under the left column. See Figure 41.4 for an example.

• *Demonstrate how to use the data chart to organize and write a report on the topic*—Using the information on the data chart, model the writing of a report. Taking the information, create sentences and write them on a chart or overhead transparency to demonstrate how to use the information while creating sentences of your own. Stress the importance of *not* copying sentences directly from the original sources without using quotation marks and giving credit to the source. Figure 41.5 shows a sample report written from a data chart.

FIGURE 41.5 Organizing Information on a Data Chart

Topic: Bats					
Questions **Sources**	**How many different kinds of bats are there?**	**How do they see?**	**What do they eat?**	**Do they suck blood?**	**Other interesting facts?**
Zipping, Zapping, Zooming Bats, by Ann Earle	980	echolocation	bugs, fruit; different kinds of bats eat different things		
Bats by Gail Gibbons	almost a thousand	listening to echoes they send out	different things like bugs and fruit	vampire bats suck blood	60%–70% of bats are insectivores bats are the only true flying mammals 20% of all mammals are bats

- *Use assessment to ensure effective instruction*—Note student participation in the creation of the KWL chart by using a checklist or anecdotal records. If you notice English learners who are not contributing, schedule a time to talk with them privately to assess their background knowledge about the topic informally. A good way to do this with preproduction and early production students is to use a picture book on the topic to see which pictures they can identify. For example, if you are studying ocean life, show pictures and ask them to point to a shark, octopus, sea lion, and so on. If they are early production or speech emergent students, they can name the pictures or tell you simple things about the pictures. Figure 41.6 suggests some other ways to use KWL charts with English learners.

FIGURE 41.6 A Sample Report Written from a Data Chart

Bats
Many people believe that bats are blood-sucking carnivores. Those people are wrong! There are 980 different types of bats. Sixty to seventy percent of bats are insectivores. This means that they eat insects. Other bats eat fruit. Different kinds of bats eat different kinds of food. Bats fly at night, and they use echolocation to help them see. This means that they send out sonars that hit walls or trees to tell them where the objects are. Vampire bats are the only bats that actually suck blood. Most vampire bats live in Central America, so we don't have to worry about being bitten. Bats are the only true flying mammals, and bats make up twenty percent of all mammals.

Source: Connor Bateman, 7th grade, Falcon Ridge Middle School, Apple Valley, Minnesota. Used with permission.

When students are researching a topic, make sure you provide materials on a variety of reading levels. Even if you are teaching secondary students, provide books with good photos or illustrations. Students can work in groups to prepare their additions to the data and KWL charts. They can also work in pairs to prepare oral reports on the topic. Often English learners can support the group by producing visuals or charts to enhance the oral reports.

Applications and Examples

As Mrs. Trivet's kindergartners enter their classroom, they see small containers of frogs on every table. After they spend some time watching the frogs and talking excitedly about them, Mrs. Trivet gathers the children on the carpet. She begins the lesson by saying, "We are going to learn about frogs this week, but first I want to know what you already know about frogs." She starts a chart by heading it with a large capital K. She tells the students, "This is the list of things you know."

Mrs. Trivet starts a list of the things the children suggest. After about 20 minutes, she has a list that includes:

Frogs can hop.
Frogs are green.
Frogs say "ribbit."
Frogs eat bugs.
Frogs can swim.
Frogs have big eyes.
Frogs lay eggs.
People eat frogs' legs.
Mothers get mad when you leave frogs in your pockets.

After the children seem to run out of ideas for the list, Mrs. Trivet asks them what they would like to learn about frogs. She starts a second chart to the right of the first chart and writes a large capital W at the top saying, "These are the things we want to know." The list includes:

How can frogs jump so far?
How many bugs can they eat in a day?
How many different kinds of frogs are there?

The children exhaust ideas for this list quickly, and Mrs. Trivet sends them back to their seats to look through the books she has placed on each table. Half an hour later Mrs. Trivet asks the children to come back to the carpet, and they complete the Want to Know list they have started. After looking at the resource books, they add several things to the list:

How do frogs change from fish to frogs?
What's the difference between a frog and a toad?
Where do frogs live?
How old do frogs get before they die?

Each morning during the opening reading time, Mrs. Trivet reads a book to the children about frogs. After they hear a book, the children add things to the KWL chart they are building under the heading, L—What we have <u>learned</u>.

Mrs. Trivet uses the information they are gathering to create a simple book about frogs for the children to complete. The pages consist of facts they have learned about frogs and illustrations the children make and add themselves. Their frog books also provide practice in reading and writing now that they are very familiar with the words from the KWL chart and the books they've heard.

The children's completed frog books consist of these sentences. They fill in the blank on each page and draw a picture to illustrate the sentence.

My Frog Book by _____ (child writes name)
Frogs come in many <u>colors</u>.
Frogs lay <u>eggs</u>.
When the eggs hatch they start out as <u>tadpoles</u>.
The tadpoles swim and their bodies use the material in their <u>tails</u> to grow.
Their tails get smaller and smaller and they begin to grow <u>legs</u>.
When their tails disappear and they have grown four legs, their mouths come <u>open</u>.
When they can open their mouths, they begin to eat <u>bugs</u>.

Mrs. Trivet is very pleased with the children's learning. They are reading a number of new words and writing a lot about frogs when they are given free writing time. The children also enjoy reading the sentences on the KWL chart using a pointer Mrs. Trivet has made with a plastic frog glued onto a dowel. In the process of this interesting study, Mrs. Trivet ensures that her students are able to "use a combination of drawing, dictating, and writing to compose informative/explanatory texts in which they name what they are writing about and supply some information about the topic" (CCSS.RLA-LITERACY.W.K.2).

Because of the ages and developmental stages of her students, Mrs. Trivet uses the KWL chart without adding a data chart. These two charts are very versatile and can be used independently or in sequence.

* * * * *

Ms. Chan attends an in-service workshop entitled "Project Wild" where she experiences hands-on activities for teaching environmental studies. During the workshop, she learns ways to involve students in exploring the environment and is introduced to a number of books to support her environmental studies.

Because Ms. Chan teaches eighth grade in a school where the students spend two hours a day with her as a part of a block schedule, she decides to combine their language arts and environmental studies to involve the students in using a data chart to prepare for writing term papers.

Ms. Chan introduces the topic by engaging her students in the creation of a KWL Plus chart. She asks them what they know about the environment in California and why people are concerned about certain plants and animals. The students respond by suggesting things they know about environmental concerns as Ms. Chan writes their responses under the K of a KWL chart. The list they create looks like this:

K
Some plants and animals in California are becoming extinct.
Cities are being built in places where the plants and animals live.
Some building projects have been stopped because they endanger certain plants or animals.
Some builders have been very angry because they have not been allowed to build in certain areas.

Ms. Chan then asks the students what they would like to know about this topic, and she lists their responses under the W of the KWL chart. Their list looks like this:

W
Which plants and animals are endangered in our area of the state?
Has any building been stopped in our area due to endangered species?
Why is it important to keep endangered species alive when there are so many different species of plants and animals?

Ms. Chan introduces the study by talking about "Project Wild." She tells the students that she learned about many of the birds and animals in California that are in danger of becoming extinct due to population growth in the state. "The people of the state are building more and more homes, and these new homes are pushing the wildlife out of their natural habitats," Ms. Chan tells her class. "I want to share a wonderful book that I discovered. This book helps us to understand exactly what is happening to the wildlife in California. It also gives us specific information about certain endangered species, wildlife that is in danger of being lost forever."

"This book is what I call 'tough text.' I want to show you a way to read tough text and break it into understandable pieces so you can use it in your term papers. You will be writing term papers about endangered species, why they are endangered, and what we can do to reverse the problem."

Ms. Chan starts the lesson on data charting by displaying a transparency that lists the subheadings in the first chapter of the book *California's Wild Heritage: Threatened and Endangered Animals in the Golden State* (Steinhart, 1990). Ms. Chan explains the process they will use to study this text. "We will look at the headings for each section of this chapter first. I want you to think of questions that you think might be answered in each section before we read the section. You will be creating a chart where you can write the answers to the questions when we read. We will also be charting any other important information we find in each section as well, like the questions we listed on our KWL chart."

"The title of this chapter is 'Evolution and Biodiversity in California.' This first part is an introduction to the chapter. Can you think of any questions that might be answered in this section?" Johanna responds, "Maybe it will explain the meanings of biodiversity and maybe evolution. It will probably also tell us why it's important in California."

"Exactly," answers Ms. Chan as she writes the following questions: What is biodiversity? What is evolution? and Why are evolution and biodiversity important in California? Ms. Chan moves on to the next few sections of the text in the same way. She encourages the students to think about the subheadings and predict the questions that might be answered in each section, each time charting the questions on a blank data-chart transparency.

As Ms. Chan reads aloud, she stops periodically to ask if any of their questions have been answered. When the students locate an answer, Ms. Chan demonstrates how to chart the answers under the proper question on the chart. She also demonstrates the charting of other important concepts and facts that were not a part of the questions they predicted would be answered but may have been listed on their original KWL chart. As she is leading this activity, she is helping her students "determine the central ideas or conclusions of a text [and] provide an accurate summary of the text distinct from prior knowledge or opinions" (CCSS.ELA-LITERACY.RST.6–8.2).

After Ms. Chan models the charting process using the first section of the chapter, she guides the students through charting the second section. She then divides the students into four groups, making sure that each group includes several strong readers. She assigns a section of the text to each group, supplies each group with the transparency of questions generated for their section, and gets them started.

As the groups read, discuss, and chart the rest of the chapter sections, Ms. Chan circulates around the room, providing support. When the groups have completed their charting, Ms. Chan brings the class back together to discuss the answers they found and the process they used.

Once the sections of the first chapter are discussed, Ms. Chan demonstrates how to use the information they charted to create an introduction to a term paper on endangered species. See Figure 41.7 for examples from the data chart and Figure 41.8 for the draft introduction that Ms. Chan shares.

Ms. Chan then instructs the students to use the rest of the book and other books on endangered species that she has provided in the classroom to create data charts from which they may continue preparing their papers. "You have created an introduction for the whole idea of biological diversity and endangered species. Now, I want you to begin to focus on one particular species that is endangered and why that species is endangered. While most of your papers will contain this background information in the introductions, the rest of the paper will be very different, depending on the species you select to research."

FIGURE 41.7 Data Chart on Biodiversity in California

Topic: Evolution and Biodiversity (Teacher Models)			
Questions Sources	**What is biodiversity?**	**What is evolution?**	**Why are biodiversity and evolution important in California?**
California's Wild Heritage by Peter Steinhart	A variety of plants and animals needed to support one another in a community	When plants and animals change over time in order to survive	Plants and animals have to change because people move into their territory.
Guided Practice (Section II)			
Section II: The Nature of Biological Diversity	**Why is biodiversity important?**	**What species are endangered?**	**Why are some creatures more easily protected?**
California's Wild Heritage by Peter Steinhart	Every change in plants and animals in an area affects the others and causes them to have to change as well.	Plants and animals living in areas where people are building homes and businesses	Some plants and animals are appreciated and enjoyed by people.
Independent Practice (Students complete in groups)			
Section V: The Value of Species Diversity	**How do species disappear?**	**What does "survival of the fittest" mean?**	**Why is species diversity important?**
California's Wild Heritage by Peter Steinhart	The environment may change or they may be cross-pollinated or bred with other species.	The strongest plants and animals are the ones that survive.	Areas where the plants and animals are all alike are less likely to adapt to changes in the environment.

FIGURE 41.8 Ms. Chan's Draft Introduction Based on Data Chart Information

California is lucky because the state is home to a great variety of plants and animals. Another way to say this is "California is biologically diverse." Because of all the different plants and animals, California has many beautiful woods, mountains, and seashores. This presents a danger to the beautiful plants and animals because many people are moving to California. As the people build new homes and businesses, many of the plants and animals are being crowded out of their natural environments. People also bring such things as aerosol cans and gasoline fumes, which endanger plants and animals. To demonstrate the importance of saving the natural plants and animals of California, this report will focus on one species, the _____, and show how the survival of this species is important.

Conclusion

KWL and data charts are effective ways to engage students in exploring text and documenting the information they find. Both strategies provide opportunities for hands-on involvement of students and interactions with both teacher and peers. These charts offer support in teaching students to learn from written text, organize new knowledge, and use data to create oral and written reports.

Interaction with peers in selecting material to be added to the charts is valuable to English learners. Working with a partner or in a small group encourages interaction and provides opportunities for clarification in a low-stress situation. Of course, the teacher must carefully structure the partnerships and small groups to ensure that English learners will be supported.

Examples of Approximation Behaviors Related to the TESOL Standards

PreK–3 students will:

- tell what they know about a topic.
- verbalize questions they have about the topic.

4–8 students will:

- find resources to support or reject assumptions.

- use KWL and data charts to organize a report.

9–12 students will:

- use KWL Plus and data charts to write academic reports and cite resources.
- analyze information and evaluate the credibility of resources.

References

Earle, A. (1995). *Zipping, Zapping, Zooming Bats*. New York, NY: Harper Collins.

Gibbons, G. (2000). *Bats*. New York, NY: Holiday House.

Goldenberg, G. (2008). Teaching English language learners: What the research does—and does not—say. *American Educator, 32*(2), 8–44.

Herrell, A., & Jordan, M. (2006). *50 strategies for improving vocabulary, comprehension, and fluency: An active learning approach* (2nd ed.). Upper Saddle River, NJ: Pearson.

Ogle, D. (1986). KWL: A teaching model that develops active reading of expository text. *The Reading Teacher, 39*, 564–570.

Riswanto, Risnawatt, & Lismayanti, D. (2014). The effect of using KWL strategy on EFL students' reading comprehension achievement. *International Journal of Humanities and Social Science. 4*(7).

Steinhart, P. (1990). *California's wild heritage: Threatened and endangered animals in the Golden State*. Sacramento, CA: California Department of Fish and Game.

Tompkins, G. (2007). *Literacy for the 21st century: Teaching reading and writing in pre-kindergarten through grade 4* (2nd ed.). Upper Saddle River, NJ: Pearson.

42

Collaborative Reading

What to Do When They Can't Read the Textbook

Collaborative reading (Gibbons, 1993) is a strategy that assists English language learners when they are reading for information. This strategy also allows a teacher to support readers of various abilities in working collaboratively as they study a specific topic. Students use a variety of library and/or textbooks with information on a topic being studied. These books are selected to cover a range of reading levels and meet the needs of the class. Collections of books of varying reading levels on the same topic are frequently called text sets (Goodman, n.d.; Ivey, 2002; Tovani, 2004).

Collaborative reading provides a method for all students—regardless of reading ability—to participate in a group research activity (Tompkins, 2013). The groups have the advantage of reviewing information from four or five different sources, depending on the number of students in each group. Members of the group then discuss the information gathered so that everyone can become an expert on the topic. Because the teacher selects books appropriate for the reading levels within the group of students, each student can make a significant contribution to the collective task. English language learners are supported because, if necessary, they have texts with simpler language and illustrations. Each member of the group can contribute in unique ways.

English language learners may contribute to the collaborative effort by drawing a visual to represent the main points of the collaborative research. This allows them to provide a translation of the information orally to the group, which can be helpful if there are other students who share the same home language. They can also provide information related differences in way in which the concept is used in the students' home cultures. Collaborative reading has been shown to be effective in multiple research studies, including studies of the approach's effectiveness with English language learners (Klinger & Vaughn, 1999).

Step-by-Step

The steps in a collaborative reading lesson are the following:

- *Gather a range of books on a topic*—Gather books on the topics to be studied, making sure to include books at various reading levels so that all students will be successful in finding information.
- *Organize heterogeneous groups*—Carefully considering the strengths and needs of the students, organize your students into groups of four or five to explore topics. Make sure that each group contains a student with strong reading and writing skills. Have each group explore either a different topic or a different aspect of one topic. Instruct the groups to brainstorm questions

they want to answer about their topic. These questions can be included on a KWL chart, a chart on which the students note the things they know about the topic, the things they want to know about the topic, and (after the collaborative reading) the things they learned about the topic (see Chapter 41). These individual KWL charts can be created using a word processing program that includes a chart-creating function. Students may also simply brainstorm their questions and handwrite them on a list. Depending on the topics, it sometimes works to have the whole class brainstorm questions and then have each group answer the same group of questions on its topic. Provide each member of the group with a book on the group's topic. Be careful to match the books with the students' reading levels. Each member of the group then researches the group's questions using a different book on the topic.

• ***Provide research instruction***—Instruct the members of the groups to find the answers to the group's questions in their books and take notes about the information they will share with their group. You may have to teach a mini-lesson on how to read and take notes—jotting down important facts.

• ***Create a data chart***—After group members have completed their note-taking, have them discuss their findings, create a data chart (a form of information matrix) or other visual, and plan how they will share their research with the whole class. A data chart form is shown in Chapter 41.

• ***Practice and share information***—Have the groups work on their group presentation and then share their research and visuals with the whole class.

• ***Document the group process***—Document the group's success in working together, following instructions, gathering information, and presenting its information to the class. You can do this documentation through anecdotal records, checklists, or rubrics. See Figure 42.1 for an example of this type of checklist.

FIGURE 42.1 Collaborative Reading Group Participation Checklist

Student Names / Behaviors					
Works collaboratively					
Follows instructions					
Gathers information					
Finds resources					
Makes suggestions					
Presents information					

Applications and Examples

Ms. Frederick's third graders are studying insects. Because the students' reading abilities vary greatly and the science textbooks are too difficult for many of the students, Ms. Frederick decides to gather a number of library books for them to use in researching insects. The media specialist at her school is extremely helpful in locating books at varying reading levels, and Ms. Frederick locates four or five books or chapters in books for each of the insects the students have identified as interesting. Ms. Frederick arranges the books by topic: bees, ants, beetles, grasshoppers, and roaches. She labels the books with correction tape so that she will be able to give students books at their reading levels. The easiest books are marked with a 5, the next easiest with a 4, and so on—with the most difficult labeled as a 1.

The students sign up for groups depending on their interests, but Ms. Frederick makes sure that there are some able readers in each group. Before she lets them start their research, Ms. Frederick does a lesson on note-taking. Using an informational book on spiders, she reads aloud and models note-taking on her classroom document camera. She stops after a few examples and has the students help her decide what notes she should add. Before she has finished, the students understand how to select important information for their notes, and they also have learned why spiders were not included on their list of insects to be researched.

The next part of the mini-lesson involves finding research questions. Ms. Frederick leads the class in asking basic questions, which she writes on the transparency of the data chart. This enables the students to discover how to look for information, answer the research questions, and note the information in the proper box on the chart. She models the use of several books on spiders to demonstrate that the students will not find the answers to all the questions in the same book. She also points out some conflicting information in several of the books.

Ms. Frederick moves the students into their interest groups, and they begin to read their books and take notes. Toward the end of the period, she instructs the students to add their information to the group data chart. The students are then given a few minutes to discuss their findings within the group.

During science period the next day, the students get back into their groups and discuss how they will present their findings to the class. One group decides to make a fact book about bees and read it aloud to the class. Another group decides to make a poster about grasshoppers with a large labeled picture of a grasshopper and small posters surrounding the large one with facts about grasshoppers. The ant group wants to make a model of an ant with papier-mâché. Group members will write facts about the ant on large green paper shaped like blades of grass and place the ant in the grass. The beetle group decides to put its data chart on poster board and give an oral presentation using the data chart. The roach group has gathered real samples (no longer alive) to show how they differ in size and color. Each group is busy preparing its visual and presentation.

Ms. Frederick's class was able to learn many things through its collaborative reading projects. Every student contributed information to the group reports. All the students learned much more about the topics than they could have learned reading independently. They felt like researchers and were successful in presenting information orally.

* * * * *

Ms. Stacy is a fifth-grade teacher with a multicultural class ranging in reading ability from first-grade level to eighth-grade level. She decides to do a collaborative reading project on the human body. Ms. Stacy follows much the same procedure as Ms. Frederick did, but with one interesting twist. On the day of the presentations, Ms. Stacy moves all the desks in her classroom to one side. She sets the chairs up in a large semicircle, three chairs deep. At the door of the classroom that morning, Ms. Stacy has each child sign in and get a name tag, a folder with a yellow pad and pencil, and a paper robe that she purchased at a medical supply house. Her students are all presenters at a mock medical conference. She has invited the local television station to come and tape the conference, and she has set up a lectern, microphone, and sound system—transforming the students into medical professionals at a conference. They present their reports and visuals solemnly, smiling for the camera only when they're finished with their reports. After their reports, the groups must field questions. They handle the questions well. They have obviously done their research thoroughly. Each group seems to know which member of the group is likely to know the answer to the question. One student, when stumped for an answer, replies, "I'll have to get back to you on that one."

Conclusion

Collaborative reading can be used to provide students with knowledge from a variety of sources. It supports the forming and strengthening of a classroom community by providing students with an activity in which their unique gifts (such as speaking more than one language, drawing, or using a computer or other technology to create visuals) supply a valuable component to the group presentation. In the process of creating, practicing, and presenting the group report, students have several opportunities to acquire new vocabulary, to write and re-read English and home language summaries of the material, and to communicate in English for a meaningful purpose.

Examples of Approximation Behaviors Related to the TESOL Standards

PreK–3 students will:

- verbally explain information gained from book illustrations.
- use the table of contents to locate information in nonfiction books at appropriate reading levels.

4–8 students will:

- use indices to locate information in nonfiction books.

- contribute to a group topic study by reading and sharing information.

9–12 students will:

- participate in group studies by reading and organizing data in a useable way.
- verbally explain facts and connections between information read in nonfiction books.

References

Gibbons, P. (1993). *Learning to learn in a second language.* Portsmouth, NH: Heinemann.

Goodman, J. R. (n.d.). *Text sets: Providing possibilities for adolescent readers.* Retrieved September 24, 2014, from http://www.ed.sc.edu/raisse/pdf/handouts/iraGoodman.pdf

Ivey, G. (2002). Text sets: A supplementary alternative. *Educational Leadership, 60*(3), 20–23.

Klinger, J., & Vaughn, S. (1999). Promoting reading comprehension, content learning, and English acquisition through collaborative strategic reading (CSR). *The Reading Teacher, 52,* 738–747.

Tompkins, G. (2013). *Literacy for the 21st century: A balanced approach* (6th ed.). Upper Saddle River, NJ: Merrill/Prentice Hall.

Tovani, C. (2004). *Do I really have to teach them to read? Content Comprehension: Grades 6–12.* Portland, ME: Stenhouse.

43

Cooperative Learning
Group Interactions to Accomplish Goals

Cooperative learning (Johnson, Johnson, & Holubec, 2002) is a term used for a collection of strategies in which students work together to accomplish a group task.

> K–12 researchers have concluded that, to succeed, group work must be carefully structured; students must be thoroughly prepared through social skill–building activities; assignments must be open-ended rather than have preset answers; and the task must be such that a group, rather than an individual, is required to accomplish it. (Leki, 2001, p. 41)

The group task is structured so that each member of the group is expected to perform an assigned task. Because of the embedded structure of the unique tasks assigned to each member of the group, cooperative learning is much more effective than ordinary group work usually done in classroom situations. Appropriate training and structure are important to the success of the strategy.

Cooperative learning activities must be preceded by some team building for the members to understand the value of working together and so they can get to know each other's strengths. Suggestions for team-building activities are given in Figure 43.1.

In addition, teachers must make their expectations clear if cooperative learning activities are to be successful. Some of the principles of cooperative learning are explained in Figure 43.2.

One of the important duties of the teacher during cooperative learning is the use of intervention strategies to ensure the participation of all students involved in the group projects (Cohen, 1994). Cooperative learning activities are especially effective for English language learners because they have more opportunities for verbal interaction in small groups (Kagan, 1989). This opportunity for verbal interaction has been shown to support both content and English achievement (Gagnon & Abell, 2009; Wilson & Bradbury, 2016). The importance of providing tasks for cooperative learning that encourage verbal interactions is evident in this video. As you watch, think about the following questions:

Enhanced eText
Video Example 43.1

- What parts of cooperative learning are important to plan for English learners to be successful?
- What is the teacher's role in making sure the English learners are active participants?

English language learners working in cooperative groups must be given assignments according to their levels of English proficiency, which requires the teacher to be aware of their stages of language acquisition. See Chapter 15 for how to use leveled questions with children of different abilities in English reading and writing.

FIGURE 43.1 Common Team-Building Activities for Cooperative Learning Teams

Activity	Rules
Arts project	Team members work together to create an artistic display of the team members' names.
Assembly line	Using an arts or crafts project, team members assemble a product in assembly line fashion.
Brainstorm	Teams work against the clock to find three commonalities among the team members, following rules for brainstorming: all ideas accepted. One team member suggests a category and others quickly contribute ways in which they might be alike within that category.
Group task	Group works together to complete a puzzle, word search, or brain teaser.
Line up	Team members work quickly to assemble themselves according to a given stipulation such as height, age, birthday, or number of siblings.
Team identity	Team members work together to reach consensus on a team name, logo, and motto.

Sources: Cohen (1994), Díaz-Rico (2013), and Meyers (1993).

Step-by-Step

Steps in using cooperative learning strategies in the classroom are the following:

• *Assign groups and build a team*—Divide the class into cooperative groups. Provide a team-building activity as a warm-up to help students see the advantages of cooperation and so they can get to know each other. Each time a new team is formed, there should be a team-building activity to help members become familiar with each other's capabilities (see Figure 43.1).

• *Assign roles within the groups*—Give the team members cards that identify their assigned roles and list clear descriptions of their duties. These can be computer-generated and contain graphic images to aid in identifying the role and expectations. Usually one member is designated as the leader, one as note-taker, one as reporter, and one as timekeeper. It is also helpful to give members name tags that designate their roles so that all members of the group know what is expected of one another. Tasks especially appropriate for English language learners include artist, visual creator (drawing or computer-generated), mime, or translator—providing a physical reenactment or second-language translation of key points for other second-language learners in the classroom.

• *Assign the task*—Give each team a task to complete and remind each member of the roles they are expected to serve to assist the others in completing the task. The leader keeps everyone

FIGURE 43.2 Principles of Cooperative Learning

Principle	Example	Benefit to English Language Learners
Cooperative tasks are designed so that individuals must work together for the task to be accomplished.	Jigsaw activities involve each member of the team being given a piece of the information so that they must work together or no one will have all the necessary data.	English language learners must be encouraged to participate in the tasks or the whole team will fail to accomplish their assignment.
Positive interactions are developed and encouraged.	The group's evaluation is based on individual and group marks. Group members are rewarded for peer tutoring and supporting weaker students.	Because peer tutoring and group support of individuals are encouraged and rewarded, all students are supported to succeed.
Students have opportunities to work in different teams.	A variety of plans are used for grouping, such as interest groups, random groups, heterogeneous groups, etc.	English language learners have an opportunity to get to know other students in meaningful ways and to demonstrate their competence in a variety of ways.
Social, language, and content skills are all learned in the process of interacting with the group.	Social and academic language interactions in cooperative groups help the students to learn pro-social behaviors as well as content knowledge.	English language learners benefit from the verbal interactions, learning social norms and content-related language.

Sources: Cohen (1994), Díaz-Rico (2013), and Meyers (1993).

working and focused, the note-taker keeps records of the team activity, the reporter shares the information or results with the class at the completion of the activity, and the timekeeper makes sure they are on task and moving toward completion of the task within the time limit. Watch this video to see a middle school teacher clarify the task assigned to the groups in a cooperative learning activity.

• ***Intervene to ensure full participation***—The teacher's role is crucial in establishing a tone of cooperation and successful group interaction. Without appropriate team building, expectations, and validation of the contributions of all individuals within the group, cooperative learning exercises might actually be detrimental to the academic and linguistic development of English learners (Leki, 2001). Teachers must carefully monitor group participation and intervene whenever a student is being excluded from the group process or taking over the work of the group (Cohen, 1994). To monitor these behaviors, teachers must listen to make sure all members of every group are being given a chance to talk, watch for physical signs that students are being excluded from the group, and

Enhanced eText
Video Example 43.2

Enhanced eText
Video Example 43.3

use a variety of strategies to assign status to nonparticipating or excluded members of the groups. Teachers can do this by mentioning a personal skill or strength that excluded members can contribute to the task, or by asking questions such as "Is everyone getting a chance to talk?" If the teacher's interventions don't correct the problem, a student should be assigned to tally the number of times that each student talks and be responsible for asking each student his or her opinions in an organized way. If this continues to be a problem, the teacher should schedule more team-building activities before using cooperative learning again. Watch this video of a team-building exercise to see how a middle school teacher monitors participation and encourages cooperation. As you watch, consider the following questions:

- How does the teacher make her expectations clear?
- How does she provide support and encouragement for the English learners?
- Why do you think the teacher keeps up a running commentary?
- What do you think she would have done if one student was being excluded from the activity?

- **Report back to the class**—Provide an opportunity for the groups to report back to the class at the end of the assigned time. Each group should share their solutions.

FIGURE 43.3 A Cooperative Learning Group Report Form

| Group Name _____ |
| Task _____ Date _____ |

Group Member	Contributions	New skill practiced? (yes, no, or comment)

Comments

_____
_____
_____
_____

_____
Group Member's Signature

Note: Each group member must fill out a form. The group must agree on the new skill to be practiced. Suggestions: taking turns, sharing materials, staying on task, asking questions, summarizing ideas, encouraging others, restating suggestions, etc.

Sources: Cohen (1994), Díaz-Rico (2018), and Meyers (1993).

• *Debrief and examine the group process*—Give each group an opportunity to debrief, discussing the process and the roles each team member played in the success of the group. Have each group fill out a group report form that focuses on both product and process. A sample group report form is shown in Figure 43.3.

Applications and Examples

Ms. Truit's fourth graders are working in cooperative groups to use their math and problem-solving skills to plan a party for the end of the year. Each group of four has been given a budget of $25 to spend, and they are to decide on the refreshments, decorations, and games to be played. At the end of the planning period, each group will present its plan for the party, complete with a drawing of the decorations, a detailed refreshment list including costs figured from a grocery store price list, and a presentation detailing the process the group used to solve the problems and make decisions. The group with the best plan will actually get to do the shopping, make the decorations, and be in charge of leading the games. The winning group will have a full school day without other assignments to complete their party preparations.

The groups work diligently to complete their calculations and draw their decorations. The group leaders are encouraging everyone to work together, and Ms. Truit is monitoring closely and intervening when necessary to ensure full participation by her English learners. The note-takers are in charge of preparing the detailed plans, while the reporters are working along with the others to practice what they will say in their oral presentations. The timekeepers are keeping a close eye on the clock. Motivation and cooperation is high. Everyone wants to have a chance to give their party.

* * * * *

Ms. Hill's math students at Mountain High are using their calculators to solve problems related to the state budget. One of the gubernatorial candidates is promising a 12% reduction in the state income tax and a 6% increase in education spending. Ms. Hill has formed cooperative groups for the purpose of figuring out the answers to some weighty questions.

Each group leader is given a list of line items in the state budget. The group comptroller has been given a detailed list of state income from income taxes, the state education budget, and anticipated revenues for the coming year. Each group secretary has been given a list of bills currently being considered by the state legislature and their anticipated cost. The group calculator has been given the task of making calculations as requested by other members of the group.

The groups have been given the following seven tasks:

1. Figure the effect of a 12% reduction in state income taxes.
2. Figure the effect of a 6% increase in state education funding.
3. Figure the cost of new legislation if all of the bills currently being considered are passed or if only 50% of them are passed.
4. Figure by what percentage the state revenues must increase for it to be possible for the gubernatorial candidate to carry out his promises (listed in tasks 1 and 2).
5. Create a visual on transparency film showing your calculations and what combination of factors would make the candidate's promises possible. In this task, you may decide which bills could be passed and what the increase in revenues would have to be on any combination of factors.
6. Watch the clock to make sure the group will be able to complete the task within the time limit. You should be finished and ready to present in 45 minutes.
7. Group reporters will present the results at the end of the class period. They may enlist the help of any (or all) of the group members in making the presentation.

The groups are working hard to make professional presentation visuals, double-check their calculations, and make sure they haven't overlooked any bills that might make a big difference in their calculations. They are learning a lot about calculator math and state government, including vocabulary unfamiliar to a number of them. The teacher is circulating to monitor the group efforts, define unfamiliar words, or refer the students to resources within the room—including the online computer services. She wants to make sure that her English learners have the necessary scaffolding to participate in the activity.

Conclusion

Cooperative learning provides an opportunity for communication, planning, research, and oral and visual presentations in the classroom. However, quality group cooperation does not occur overnight. Taking the time to build teams, monitor group interactions, and debrief after the activity are all vital pieces of the cooperative learning process. The groups are not just learning content but also valuable interpersonal interaction skills. Because there is a definite task to accomplish and support is provided, English learners have a greater opportunity to access the learning. Videorecording the group interactions and having the group watch the video and examine their own behaviors, strengths, and weaknesses are supportive activities when creating the learning community (Herrell & Fowler, 1997). Varying the format for cooperative learning activities helps students learn different roles they can serve in being part of a group. Figure 43.4 shows some different formats that can be used.

FIGURE 43.4 Formats for Cooperative Learning

Three-step interview	Working in pairs, student number one interviews student number two, they switch roles, and then share what they've learned with the class.
Roundtable	In a small group, one student starts a story or review of a lesson, and each student contributes in turn. This can be done in writing or orally.
Think, pair, share	The teacher asks a question. The students work in pairs and go through the three-step interview process (mentioned previously) before they share their responses. They are encouraged to use parts of each response to make the pair's response.
Solve, pair, share	The teacher poses a problem. Students work individually at first and then in pairs or small groups to share answers using the three-step interview or roundtable approach.
Numbered heads	Each team member draws a number (1–4 for a four-member team). The teacher poses a question. The group works together to solve the problem or answer the question and makes sure everyone in the group knows the answer. The teacher calls a number and the student with that number in each group responds to the question.
Jigsaw	Each student participates in a home team and an expert team. Expert teams work together to gather information on their aspect of the problem and then members go back to their home teams to share what they've learned so that all home teams get information on all aspects of the problem or project.

Sources: Díaz-Rico (2018); Herrell and Jordan (2006); and Johnson, Johnson, and Holubec (2002).

Examples of Approximation Behaviors Related to the TESOL Standards

PreK–3 students will:
- use social language to request information.
- follow rules to interact in a small-group setting.

4–8 students will:
- actively participate in assigned cooperative learning tasks.

- understand and perform a defined cooperative learning group role.

9–12 students will:
- select, connect, and explain information through cooperative group interaction.
- assume a role in the presentation of group outcomes.

References

Cohen, E. (1994). *Designing groupwork* (2nd ed.). New York, NY: Teachers College Press.

Díaz-Rico, L. (2018). *The crosscultural, language, and academic development handbook: A complete K–12 reference guide* (6th ed.). Boston, MA: Pearson Education.

Gagnon, M., and Abell, S. (2009). ELLs and the language of school science. *Science and Children 46*(5) 50–51.

Herrell, A., & Fowler, J. (1997). *Camcorder in the classroom: Using a video camera to enrich curriculum.* Upper Saddle River, NJ: Merrill/Prentice Hall.

Herrell, A., & Jordan, M. (2006). *50 strategies for improving vocabulary, comprehension, and fluency: An active learning approach.* Upper Saddle River, NJ: Pearson.

Johnson, D. W., Johnson, R., & Holubec, E. (2002). *Circles of learning: Cooperation in the classroom* (5th ed.). Edina, MN: Interaction Book.

Kagan, S. (1989). *Cooperative learning: Resources for teachers.* San Juan Capistrano, CA: Resources for Teachers.

Leki, I. (2001). A narrow thinking system: Non-native English-speaking students in group projects across the curriculum. *TESOL Quarterly, 35*(1), 39–63.

Meyers, M. (1993). *Teaching to diversity.* Toronto, Canada: Irwin.

Wilson, R., & Bradbury, L. (2016). Stalk it up to integrated learning! Using foods we eat and informational texts to learn about plant parts and their functions. *Science and Children, 53*(9), 46–51.

Learning Strategy Instruction

Acquiring Self-Help Skills

Enhanced eText
Video Example 44.1

Learning strategy instruction (Gagne, 1985) is based on supporting students in understanding their own learning and in monitoring the methods and results of strategies they use in reading, writing, discussions, and research. Strategy instruction is a powerful student-centered approach to teaching that is backed by years of quality research. In fact, strategic approaches to learning new concepts and skills are often what separate good learners from poor ones (Luke, 2007). Learning strategy instruction helps support English language learners in employing self-monitoring and self-help approaches to succeed in school (Chamot & O'Malley, 2009; Echevarria, Vogt, & Short, 2010). To understand the difference between teaching and learning strategies, watch this video, (https://youtu.be/rhYI3w5I0EA) which focuses on learning strategies and their importance to English learners. As you watch, ask yourself the following questions:

1. How do teaching strategies affect a student's learning strategies?
2. Why do we tend to hesitate to focus on learning strategies with English learners?

Three areas of instruction are addressed in learning strategy instruction: metacognitive, cognitive, and **social/ affective**. All three areas are self-related. Learners focus on strategies they can use to improve their own success in school. **Metacognitive** strategies include having a plan for learning, monitoring the learning that is taking place, and evaluating how well content has been learned. **Cognitive strategies** include how to manipulate material mentally or physically to facilitate learning. **Social/affective strategies** include ways to interact with others or control your own emotions in ways that support your learning. See Figure 44.1 for descriptions of some of the strategies included in each category.

Step-by-Step

The steps in teaching learning strategies are the following:

- *Match strategies and curriculum*—Select the strategy to be taught by thinking about the curriculum and the demands it will make on learners. Plan to teach only a few strategies at first, giving students opportunities to practice the strategies well before introducing new ones.

FIGURE 44.1 Categories of Learning Strategy Instruction and Their Descriptions

Metacognitive Strategies	
Planning	Preview the material to plan a way to organize it for use.
Organizing	Plan the method of study to be used. Parts of the material to be studied and the sequence of study is determined.
Selective attention	Focus on key words or concepts to be learned.
Self-management	Organize a plan for studying, including time and place.
Monitoring comprehension	Check your comprehension during reading or listening.
Monitoring production	Focus on your speech or writing while it is happening.
Self-assessment	Plan ways to check on your learning through such things as learning logs, reflective journals, and checklists.
Cognitive Strategies	
Referring	Use research and resource materials such as dictionaries, encyclopedias, word walls, etc.
Classifying	Organize like materials together, grouping the knowledge or concepts to be learned.
Note-taking	Write down important information and key words to be learned.
Activating prior knowledge	Make connections between what is being studied and your experiences.
Summarizing	Review the main ideas either orally or in writing.
Deduction or induction	Look for patterns to formulate and use a rule.
Imagery	Use mental or drawn pictures to aid in memory or understanding.

• *Reflect on learning task approaches*—Develop students' self-awareness by having them reflect on how they approach a learning task. Remind them of the cooperative learning activities they have been involved with and what they have learned about their approaches to learning during the debriefing sessions. See Figure 44.2 for additional introductory activities.

• *Model strategy use*—Model the strategy you are teaching. Call the strategy by name each time you model it. Explain how the strategy works to support the students' learning. Give examples of instances in which the strategy will be helpful.

• *Practice the strategy*—Provide an opportunity for students to practice using the strategy while you are available to assist, if needed.

• *Discuss strategy use*—Hold an evaluation discussion. Ask students to demonstrate how they used the strategy and what was difficult for them. Provide a self-evaluation tool, or scoring rubric, for them to use in evaluating their strategy use. See Figure 44.3 for strategy self-evaluation tools.

• *Make visuals for self-help*—Have students make strategy posters to display in the classroom that explain the steps to take when using the strategy. Refer to those posters frequently when making assignments. Help the students see that they have choices in strategies to use and that strategies can be used in many different contexts and learning tasks.

• *Assess to document strategy usage*—As strategies are taught, make a checklist with the strategy names and student names to use as you observe them completing assignments. Watch for strategy use and ask students to explain their strategy usage. Notes on the checklist can be transferred to anecdotal records, documenting student growth in strategy usage over time.

FIGURE 44.2 Learning Strategy Introductory Activities

Activity	Description
Brainstorming	Students suggest ways they have used when studying material. No judgment is made. The list is made and then students can use the list to suggest learning tasks that would match well with the strategies suggested. The benefit of this activity is to introduce the idea that there are many learning strategies and students have choices in approaches.
Partner interviews	Students pair up and interview each other about the strategies they use for studying. After the interviews, each student describes one strategy shared by the partner.
Questionnaires	The teacher prepares a questionnaire about strategy usage, which the students fill out. The results are tabulated and used as a basis for a group discussion.
Task think-aloud	Students demonstrate a task, such as tying shoes and think aloud to demonstrate the strategies they use. After one student demonstrates the task think-aloud, a student who has a different approach is given an opportunity to demonstrate it.
Strategy list think	A list of strategies such as note cards, diagrams, webs, and oral review are listed on the board, and students give suggestions as to the learning tasks that would be appropriate for their use. Example: Note cards don't work for studying for a spelling test but do work for preparing an oral presentation.

FIGURE 44.3 Learning Strategy Self-Evaluation Tools

Strategy Use Rubric

Student's Name _____

Learning Strategy _____

Each time you use a learning strategy, place an **✗** on the continuum to show how well you think you used it.

< – >

Poorly	OK	Well
I did not follow the steps well.	I did follow the steps. I didn't give it my full attention.	I followed the steps and was successful.

Strategies used this week:	Subject area:	Effectiveness
_____	_____	1 2 3 4 5
_____	_____	1 2 3 4 5
_____	_____	1 2 3 4 5
_____	_____	1 2 3 4 5

Applications and Examples

Some of Ms. Hernandez's second-grade English learners consistently fail their weekly spelling tests. Ms. Hernandez realizes that some of the students don't have strategies for studying their words. She begins the learning strategy instruction by initiating a conversation with the students on Monday morning as she is getting ready to list the new words for the week.

"How are you studying the words for your spelling test?" Ms. Hernandez asks the class.

"I write the words on a big piece of paper and hang it on my bulletin board at home," Amanda replies. "I look at the words every day and spell them to myself."

"I make flash cards and use them to practice writing the words," Carlos says.

"Let's make a list of all the methods we use to study spelling words," Ms. Hernandez says. She writes *Make a poster* and *Make flash cards* on the chalkboard. As the students add suggestions, the list grows. When the students have exhausted their ideas for studying the words, Ms. Hernandez says, "I want to show you one way of studying the words that I used when I was in second grade. You may find it helpful."

Ms. Hernandez gives each student ten 3-by-5 cards. As she writes the new spelling words on the board, she spells them aloud, and the students write them on their 3-by-5 cards.

"Now, let me show you how to use the cards," Ms. Hernandez says. "You look at one card at a time. You spell the word aloud as you look at the card." She then demonstrates with one word. "These, t-h-e-s-e, these."

"Next, you look at the word again, turn the card over, and write the word." She demonstrates this step.

"You turn the card back over and check to make sure you spelled the word correctly. You repeat the spelling to yourself before you move on to the next card."

Ms. Hernandez then instructs the students to go through the procedure with their new words. While they are practicing, she walks around the room, stopping to give encouragement and to ask questions about the meanings of the words or to ask students to use a word in a sentence.

After their practice session, Ms. Hernandez gives the class a practice test. A number of the students get a perfect score on the test.

"How do you think this method works?" Ms. Hernandez asks the class.

"I think it works great!" Erma says. "I never got a hundred on Monday before."

"You will want to use this strategy several times this week to make sure you really know the words," Ms. Hernandez reminds the students. "I chose these words because they are words you often misspell in your writing, so be sure to double-check your spelling of them in your writing this week, too."

Ms. Hernandez is supporting her students' use of learning strategies in response to a concern she has about their study strategies. She introduces the new strategy by helping the students recognize that it is necessary to have a strategy for studying. She models one strategy and has the students practice using it. After an evaluation exercise—the spelling test—she gives the students an opportunity to discuss their use of the strategy and how it works. She also relates the strategy to their assignments and why they would want to use the strategy.

* * * * *

Ms. Teale has a number of students in her eighth-grade math class who do not regularly turn in homework. She devises the student questionnaire in Figure 44.4 to determine the students' approaches to doing homework.

Ms. Teale analyzes the results of her homework questionnaire, but before sharing the results with the class, she asks the students to predict what she found when she compared their responses on the questionnaire with their grades in the class. She puts the students into groups of three and asks them to discuss the questionnaire and which of the responses were most important in ensuring that homework was done regularly and grades were good. Each group shares predictions that are remarkably similar. The consensus is that doing homework regularly, at a set time and place, is most helpful.

Ms. Teale then asks the students to discuss the barriers they encounter in doing homework. They come up with this list of barriers:

No place to study
Younger brothers and sisters interfere
Television is always on
Lack of motivation
After-school jobs

The students brainstorm ways to overcome the barriers to doing homework. Their suggestions include talking to their parents and finding a place in the house for them to do homework, setting up a schedule, asking that the television be turned off for a set amount of time each evening, and setting up a homework club so their younger siblings are also doing homework.

Ms. Teale demonstrates a time management strategy in which she shows how she plans the ways she uses her time between the end of the school day and bedtime. She gives each student a daily planning paper that divides the hours from 3 p.m. until 11 p.m. into half-hour segments. She leads the students through a planning activity in which they examine the ways they use their time and helps them find an hour each evening in which they could do homework. Several of the students are surprised at the amount of time they spend watching television or talking on the telephone.

Ms. Teale organizes a role-play activity in which the students pair up and conduct a conversation as if they are talking to their family about the homework problem and giving suggestions as to how it can be solved. The students practice sharing their daily planning sheets with their families and enlisting their support in implementing a homework hour for the family. Ms. Teale emphasizes how helpful this family approach will be to the younger students in the family.

At the end of the next week, Ms. Teale asks each of her students to write a brief reflection on the homework issue and whether their planning and family discussions were helpful. Those students who carried through on the assignment are asked to share their reflections with the class. Although

FIGURE 44.4 Homework Questionnaire

Name _____

Please mark your answer to each question with an ✗ placed at the appropriate place on the continuum or checklist.

1. I do homework assignments

< – < – – – – – – – – – >
Never   Sometimes   About half   Most of   Always
                                         the time   the time

2. I do homework

___ while watching TV or listening to the radio

___ at the kitchen table

___ in my room ___ on my bed ___ at my desk

___ right after school ___ after dinner ___ right before I go to bed

3. My parents ask me if I have homework

< – < – – – – – – – – – >
Never   Sometimes   About half   Most of   Always
                                         the time   the time

4. I feel the practice I get doing homework is

< – >
A waste   Somewhat helpful   Helpful   Important   Very important
of time

5. I feel the weight given to homework assignments in this class is

< – >
Too much   About right   Too little

she still has a few students not completing homework, Ms. Teale thinks the exercise was successful for several of the students. The number of homework assignments being submitted has increased, and several of the students are sharing success stories involving their younger brothers and sisters.

Conclusion

Learning strategy instruction helps students become more responsible for their own success in school. Teaching students how to monitor their own understanding and identify, plan, and implement ways to help themselves understand and evaluate the effectiveness of the strategies being used supports their motivation to learn and their self-confidence. English learners need to develop their own self-monitoring support systems to enhance their English language development. Self-monitoring is commonly associated with the language arts but is equally important in mathematics. Instruction in metacognition in math, including rereading word problems, noting the important factors, estimating a possible range of answers, and so on, is especially vital in addressing the Common Core State Standards that require students to explain the processes they use (Díaz-Rico, 2018; Unrau, 2008).

Although study skills have been taught in school for a number of years, learning strategy instruction introduces the idea that students don't always learn in the same ways. The individual learning style and strong intelligences (see Chapter 45, Multiple Intelligences Strategies) are important in identifying strategies that work for each individual experiencing difficulty with tough text.

Examples of Approximation Behaviors Related to the TESOL Standards

PreK–3 students will:

- recognize and verbalize when they don't understand.
- employ self-help strategies to correct errors.

4–8 students will:

- use reading comprehension processes and "fix-up" strategies

when experiencing difficulty with tough text.
- identify the strategies used to make sense of text.

9–12 students will:

- employ study skills to enhance their own learning.
- recognize personal learning strengths and use them to increase academic progress.

References

Chamot, A., & O'Malley, J. (2009). *The CALLA handbook* (2nd ed.). Reading, MA: Addison-Wesley.

Díaz-Rico, L. (2018). *The crosscultural, language, and academic development handbook: A complete K–12 reference guide* (6th ed.). Boston, MA: Pearson Education.

Echeverria, J., Vogt, M., & Short, D. (2010). *Making content comprehensible for elementary English learners: The SIOP model*. Boston, MA: Allyn & Bacon.

Gagne, E. (1985). *The cognitive psychology of school learning*. Boston, MA: Little, Brown.

Luke, S. (2007). The power of strategy instruction. *Evidence for Education, 1*(1).

Unrau, N. (2008). *Content area reading and writing: Fostering literacies in middle and high school cultures*. Upper Saddle River, NJ: Merrill/Prentice Hall.

45

Multiple Intelligences Strategies

Teaching and Testing to Student-Preferred Learning Modes

Multiple intelligences (Gardner, 1993, 2006, 2011) are the ways people are smart—the modes in which they process information effectively. Though traditionally teachers have taught only two intelligences in the school setting (linguistic and logical/mathematical), at least seven *additional* intelligences are well researched and documented, and others are currently being documented (Gardner, 2006). See Figure 45.1 for an explanation of the nine intelligences currently documented.

Although all people possess all intelligences at varying levels, it is helpful for teachers to present content material through a variety of intelligences to make the information comprehensible to all learners.

It is equally important to encourage students to demonstrate their understanding of content in a format consistent with their strong intelligences. Using knowledge of multiple intelligences and being flexible in planning instruction and assessment is one way to help students be more successful in the classroom. Multiple intelligences strategies are especially beneficial to English language learners since allowing them to learn and demonstrate their understanding in the mode in which they are most confident serves to lower the affective filter and boost their self-esteem and motivation.

In a study to determine the effect of multiple intelligences on students' willingness to communicate in a second language (Mohammadeh & Jafarigohar, 2012), it was found that students strong in linguistic and interpersonal intelligences were more willing to attempt to communicate in a second language while students strong in musical intelligence were more inclined to attempt verbal sounds in a second language. Providing students practice in the use of different intelligences logically provides more confidence and practice in using these intelligences.

In addition to planning instruction for multiple intelligences, designing centers where students can practice new skills in multiple ways builds on their strengths while giving them multiple opportunities to experience new concepts and vocabulary (Armstrong, 2009). The teachers in this video recognize the importance of encouraging students to explore content through a range of multiple intelligences. As you watch, consider the following questions:

Enhanced eText
Video Example 45.1

1. What is the purpose of the group's planning process?
2. How does the group members' recognition of the need to create challenging centers serve the needs of the students?

FIGURE 45.1 Multiple Intelligences and Their Meanings

Intelligence	Definition
Bodily/ Kinesthetic	Body-smart, sports-smart, hand-smart—the person has the ability to move through space effectively, learns well with movement, and can imitate movements easily.
Intrapersonal	Self-smart—the person understands his or her own ways of knowing and learning; is in tune with his or her own needs.
Interpersonal	People-smart—the person reads others well, works well in groups, and interacts effectively with other people.
Linguistic	Word-smart—the person manipulates words and language easily, understands what is read, and enjoys verbal interactions.
Logical/ Mathematical	Number-smart, logic-smart—the person manipulates numbers and/or logic easily; understands the logical connections among concepts.
Musical	Music-smart—the person expresses him- or herself easily in rhythm and melody; sees patterns and music in all endeavors.
Visual/ Spatial	Picture-smart—the person sees pleasing visual/spatial arrangements around him- or herself; has the ability to learn and express with visual arrangements, art, and beauty.
Naturalistic	Nature-smart—the person senses patterns and makes connections to elements of nature; has a strong affinity for animals, the earth, and the environment.

Sources: Gardner (1993), Armstrong (2009), and McKenzie (2014).

Step-by-Step

The steps to implement the use of multiple intelligence approaches for teaching and assessing are the following:

• *Explain multiple intelligences*—Introduce the concept of multiple intelligences to your students. Depending on their ages you might use the actual labels for the intelligences, explain the definitions and examples, or simply talk about people being smart in different ways while using the "body-smart," "people-smart," and "self-smart" labels to help them understand the concept. Explain that knowing more about the way you learn is one way to help yourself to do better in school. Tell the class that you will be giving them some choices in the way they study and the way they show you that they are learning. In explaining the intelligences to students, you may want to use a book written for children by Thomas Armstrong (2011), *You're Smarter Than You Think*.

• *Adjust lessons and assessments to student intelligences*—Assume that the students in your classroom have a variety of intelligences and plan your lessons and assessments to allow students a choice in the way they study and the way they document their understandings. See Figure 45.2 for suggestions on how to allow this flexibility.

One way to encourage choices by your students is shown in this video, which highlights the use of multiple intelligences learning centers.

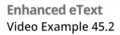

Enhanced eText
Video Example 45.2

• *Observe and document student choices*—Observe your students during the first few times that you allow them choices in their mode of studying and/or documenting their learning. Keep track of the choices they make and talk to them about their preferences and the ways they would choose to spend their time. You may also want to have them take the informal Multiple Intelligences Assessment Survey found in Appendix A. Build a system for your classroom in which the students have regular choices.

• *Provide self-evaluation opportunities*—Provide some ways for the students to evaluate their own work and the choices they make about the ways in which they do the work. A self-evaluation rubric is helpful in teaching students to self-monitor and evaluate their own comprehension and production in different learning and assessment modes. See Figure 45.3 for a suggested self-evaluation tool for students as they participate in multiple intelligences activities.

Applications and Examples

The students in Ms. Barry's second-grade class are reading and comparing different versions of Cinderella stories. Ms. Barry has chosen *Jouanah, a Hmong Cinderella* (Coburn & Lee, 1996) as the focus book of the week because so many of her students are from Hmong or Hispanic cultures and the book is available in Hmong, Spanish, and English. After she reads the book aloud to the class, Ms. Barry suggests that the students might want to do some activities focusing on the book in literacy centers this week. Because she has read so much about multiple intelligences, Ms. Barry has decided to set up eight centers, each allowing the children to interact in a way unique to one of the intelligences. Ms. Barry sets up the following centers:

• *Listening Center* (linguistic intelligence), where the children listen to the story in either Spanish, English, or Hmong and look at the pictures in a copy of the book written in the language of choice.

• *Music Center* (musical intelligence), where the children listen to a recording of Hmong music and dress up in traditional Hmong festival clothes. Older Hmong students are invited to teach traditional Hmong dances to Ms. Barry's children at this center.

• *Games Center* (bodily/kinesthetic intelligence), where the children play traditional Hmong games as they are played at Hmong festivals similar to the one attended by Jouanah in the Cinderella tale.

• *Audio Recording Center* (intrapersonal intelligence), where the children respond to the Hmong Cinderella story on a recording, telling about their favorite part of the story or what they would have done if they had been Jouanah.

• *Story Reenactment Center* (interpersonal intelligence), where the children work in groups and use props related to each of the Cinderella stories they have read to reenact the plots.

• *Pattern Center* (logical/mathematical intelligence), where the children complete pattern strips based on intricate traditional Hmong patterns similar to the ones shown in Jouanah's festival clothes in the Hmong Cinderella story. Once the patterns are completed, they are used as borders for the bulletin board where the products from the Art Center will be displayed.

• *Art Center* (visual/spatial intelligence), where the children draw the features and create costumes for male and female paper dolls, which will be added to the bulletin board depicting

FIGURE 45.2 Teaching and Assessing Through Multiple Intelligences

Intelligence	Teaching	Assessing
Bodily/ Kinesthetic	Introduce motions Encourage role-playing Allow movement	Have the students show, not tell Encourage the use of role-play to document learning Encourage the use of mime, dance, the invention of physical games to document learning
Intrapersonal	Give opportunity for self-teaching, computer tutorials, Internet, programmed learning	Use self-evaluation rubrics Allow the person choices in ways to best show the learning Encourage the use of self-made multimedia reports
Interpersonal	Encourage group work Celebrate group skills Teach process and encourage reciprocal teaching	Encourage group reports Use group evaluation reports Evaluate the products of the group, holding all members responsible
Linguistic	Give reading/follow-up Encourage additional reading/ writing	Use written response activities Oral reports Dialogue journals, learning logs
Logical/ Mathematical	Quantify instruction Relate instruction to logical constructs Relate instruction to math/ logic puzzles	Have student design a math or logic game that shows what has been learned Have student design "mind-benders"
Musical	Teach with rhythm, rap Relate instruction to songs, poetry	Have student demonstrate understanding by writing a rap or song
Visual/ Spatial	Teach with visuals, charts, drawings	Have student make posters, charts, illustrations, dioramas, constructions
Naturalistic	Teach with examples from nature	Ask student to connect the concept with examples from nature (in writing, in chart or diagrams, or orally)

Sources: Gardner (1993), Armstrong (2009), and McKenzie (2014).

FIGURE 45.3 Self-Evaluation Rubric for Multiple Intelligences

Name _____   Date _____

Activity _____   Intelligence _____

My understanding of the content of this activity is:

< – ->

Very   Slight   About average   Better   Outstanding
minimal   than normal

I think that my understanding was affected by:

_____ my background knowledge   _____ the way in which the material was
                                                       presented

To understand the material better, I will need:

_____ nothing, I understand   _____ more practice (in same mode, in
                                                       another mode)

_____ another presentation of the content (in same mode, in another mode)

My ability to convey my understanding in this activity was:

< – ->

Very   Slight   About average   Better   Outstanding
minimal   than normal

I think that my performance (demonstration of understanding) would have been improved by:

_____ a different choice of response   _____ more practice

I chose to demonstrate my understanding through:

_____ writing   _____ drawing/graphics   _____ music   _____ math

_____ role-play   _____ dialogue   _____ personal discussion

_____ group project   _____ other _____

A better choice for me might be:

_____ writing   _____ drawing/graphics   _____ music   _____ math

_____ role-play   _____ dialogue   _____ personal discussion

_____ group project   _____ other _____

the festival where Jouanah and Shee-Nang met in the story. The children are also encouraged to create other pictures to be added to the bulletin board.

• *Nature Center* (naturalistic intelligence), where the children plant pumpkin seeds and create a journal based on daily observations of the progress of the growth of the seeds.

• *Putting It Together Center* (existential intelligence), where students choose two or three characters from the book and paste pictures (provided in the center) on a piece of paper. They then copy a sentence from the book that shows how the characters related in the story. After that, they write a sentence of their own telling how the characters were related in the story *or* how they felt about each other and *why* they feel that way. For example, one student wrote, "The daughter didn't like Cinderella because she was pretty. I know because the daughter was mean when she talked to Cinderella."

Ms. Barry encourages the children to use the centers for the entire week. They must keep track of the centers they visit and rate their enjoyment and the work they do in each using a self-evaluation rubric similar to the one in Figure 45.3. At the end of the week, Ms. Barry reflects on the choices the children made in their center use and realizes that their choices tell her a lot about their learning preferences. She feels that they will benefit from additional opportunities to choose the ways in which they explore the curriculum.

****

Realizing that his English learners need simpler text with illustrations, Mr. Yoshino designs a project for his 11th-grade literature class encouraging students to read classic children's tales they missed reading in their childhood. Each student has identified the children's literature that he or she most enjoyed as a child. Mr. Yoshino has shared some of the classic tales from Japan, and others have brought in favorite tales they read or heard in their homes. If a written version of the story was not available, the students transcribed the oral tales for future generations. Mr. Yoshino is very pleased with the students' work and wants to plan a culminating activity to celebrate their explorations into cultural literature.

"I would like for you to share some of your work with the elementary students next door," Mr. Yoshino begins. "I think some of them have never heard some of the stories you have discovered, and I would like for us to find ways to get the younger students as excited about literature as you are."

"I have been reading about something called multiple intelligences, which talks about how people have multiple ways of knowing and learning, and I would like for you to think about a way that you could share your favorite story with the younger children. Let's brainstorm some of the things we might do," Mr. Yoshino says as he turns to the chalkboard.

"I think my story needs to be reenacted," Marin says. "But, I will need to have other people to help me do it."

"That's fine," Mr. Yoshino replies as he writes *Reenactment* on the board. In just 10 minutes the class has created a list that includes:

- Reenactment
- Mime
- Puppet show
- Interpretive dance
- Student involvement
- Read-aloud with finger puppets
- Rap
- Skit
- Storytelling with costumes
- Story told in song
- Show with children taking parts

"This looks wonderful," Mr. Yoshino says as the class appears to be running out of ideas. "If you think of anything you want to add to the list, feel free to add it. I want you to begin to work, either alone or in groups, to plan your presentations. I will talk to the principal at the elementary school and set up a date for our presentations. What shall we call them?"

"Why don't we call it a Literature Festival?" Frederick asks.

"Good idea. Any other suggestions?" Mr. Yoshino asks.

"I like Frederick's idea," Janine says. "We can set it up like a festival and have some booths where the children can be actively involved in dressing up and being a part of the action. Other places they can just sit and listen."

"That sounds like a good plan because we are trying to support the use of different intelligences and ways of learning," Mr. Yoshino says. "Who wants to form a cooperative group?"

"I need some players for my reenactment," Marin says. "But first I need to develop my script. May I work on that first?"

"Sounds like a good plan," Mr. Yoshino says. "Does anyone need a cooperative group to start work today?"

Soon the room is full of busy noise. Some of the students have begun to work in cooperative groups, dividing the responsibilities among the members. Others, like Marin, will need a group later but have to do some individual work first. A few have chosen to do a solo presentation and are busily planning how they will do it. Everyone is actively involved.

Conclusion

The use of multiple intelligences strategies supports students' learning of new materials because it allows them to use the processing systems in which they integrate knowledge most effectively. This has proven particularly important for English learners. Providing multiple ways for the students to demonstrate their understanding bolsters their confidence in their own abilities and reduces their anxiety.

Examples of Approximation Behaviors Related to the TESOL Standards

PreK–3 students will:
- use a variety of learning strategies to enhance understanding.
- verbalize understanding of various ways to learn.

4–8 students will:
- identify personal strengths of intelligence.

- choose preferred approaches to learning.

9–12 students will:
- analyze personal learning preferences.
- use study methods aligned with learning strengths.

References

Armstrong, T. (2009). *Multiple intelligences in the classroom.* Alexandria, VA: Association for Supervision and Curriculum Development.

Armstrong, T. (2011). *You're smarter than you think: A kid's guide to multiple intelligences.* New York, NY: Free Spirit Press.

Coburn, J., & Lee, T. (1996). *Jouanah, a Hmong Cinderella.* Arcadia, CA: Shen's Books.

Gardner, H. (1993). *Multiple intelligences: The theory in practice.* New York, NY: Basic Books.

Gardner, H. (2006). *Multiple intelligences: New horizons in theory and practice.* New York, NY: Basic Books.

Gardner, H. (2011). *Frames of mind: The theory of multiple intelligences.* New York, NY: Basic Books.

McKensie, W. (2014). *It's not how smart you are, it's how you're smart!* Retrieved from http://surfaquarium.com/MI/index.htm

Mohammadeh, A., & Jafarigohar, M (2012). The relationship between willingness to communicate and multiple intelligence among learners of English as a foreign language. *English Language Teaching 5*(7).

46

Multimedia Presentations
Oral Reports for the New Millennium

Multimedia presentations (Díaz-Rico, 2018) involve the use of media such as audio and video equipment (DVRs, video players, video cameras), computers and related software, and Internet sources to research, publish, and make classroom presentations. In recent years, the availability of computer multimedia technology, Internet access, and materials in multiple languages has greatly improved, making the use of these resources in the classroom more practical. The use of multimedia presentations with English language learners is especially important because the approach affords flexibility in both teaching and learning. When students are encouraged to share ideas through visuals, English learners are empowered because their contributions are no longer entirely language based (Cummins, 1994).

Students benefit when teachers use multimedia resources in presenting lessons because such media add context to the language and the lessons. Students using multimedia resources to gain access to information in multiple languages are supported in their learning. When students use multimedia resources to present their research, writings, and projects, they can document and present their growing capabilities without the constraints often encountered when making oral reports.

In the use of multimedia, it is not just the finished product—the report or presentation—but also the processes of exploring, synthesizing, and summarizing that technology creates. These opportunities allow meaningful learning to take place while also allowing the students to blend content learning with language acquisition.

The use of multimedia resources in the classroom presents some challenges for both teachers and students. In fact, teachers who lack experience in this approach are sometimes overwhelmed with both the possibilities and the potential barriers. However, there are many resources available to teachers for incorporating the use of multimedia resources in the classroom, some of which are presented in Figure 46.1.

Step-by-Step

The steps in implementing multimedia presentations are the following:

• *Model media use*—Model the use of multimedia resources by incorporating video clips, an overhead projector, video projector, audio recordings, interactive whiteboards, and other media as you teach. Emphasize how the use of the media allows you to demonstrate visually or orally as you teach. Before you ask students to use multimedia approaches, give them experience in seeing the effectiveness of different media in support of learning (Roblyer, 2006).

FIGURE 46.1 Multimedia Classroom Resources for Teachers

References

Bus, A. & Newman, S. (Eds.) (2008). *Multimedia and Literacy Development Achievement for Young Learners. New York:* Routledge.

Cheng, I. Safont, L. Basu, A. & Goebel, R. (2010). *Multimedia in Education: Adaptive Learning and Testing.* Singapore. World Scientific Publishing Company Pte. Ltd.

Harris, J. (series of articles). Mining the Internet. *The Computing Teacher.*

Herrell, A. & Fowler, J. (1997). *Camcorder in the Classroom: Using the Videocamera to Enrich Curriculum.* Upper Saddle River, NJ: McMillan/Prentice Hall.

International Society for Technology in Education. (2000). *National Educational Technology Standards for Students: Connecting Curriculum and Technology.* Washington, D.C. Author.

Lewis, C. (1997). *Exploring Multimedia.* New York:DK Publishing.

Pitler, H., Hubbell, E. & Kuhnm, M. (2012). *Using Technology with Classroom Instruction that Works.* Alexandria, VA: ASCD.

Rogers, A., Andres, Y., Jacks, M., & Clauset, T. (1990). Telecommunication in the Classroom: Keys to Successful Telecommunicating. *The Computing Teacher. 17, 25-28.*

Serim, F. & Koch, M. (1996). *NetLearning: Why Teachers Use the Internet* Sebastopol, CA: Songline Publications.

Smith, G. &Throne, S. (2009). *Differentiating Instruction with Technology in Middle School Classrooms.* Washington, DC. International Society for Technology in Education.

- *Introduce media slowly*—Introduce the different media slowly. Begin with one piece of equipment and encourage students to use it as they demonstrate learning. You might choose to begin with an overhead projector and transparency film by having cooperative groups work together to create a transparency that documents their work. Have the students practice standing in front of the class using the overhead to show their work. Give instructions as to where to stand and how to turn the projector on and off. Demonstrate how they can reveal one portion of the transparency at a time to show new information as it is discussed and how two or three transparencies can be placed on top of each other to create a graph or a more detailed visual.

- *Add new media as appropriate*—Repeat the demonstration and use of different media as it becomes appropriate. Always review the reasons that equipment is used so students can begin to make wise choices about the media they may want to use to support their presentations and determine whether the use of media actually enhances the quality of the demonstration.

- *Allow time for practice*—Allow yourself and the students time to practice with equipment before using it for more formal presentations. When computers and other presentation platforms are introduced, new users need time to explore them, their functions, and possibilities. When introducing the Internet, new users, teachers, and students alike will need to see the procedures for gaining access and the website addresses clearly displayed so they can practice logging on and searching for information until they are comfortable with the sequences.

• *Create working partners*—Pair technology users based on experience, with a more experienced user supporting a new user. Don't overlook the more experienced user as a classroom resource. Often students have a lot of expertise to share with teachers and other students. Be sure to include training for the more experienced users so that they are aware of the importance of "talking the new user through the procedure" and *not* jumping in to do it for him or her.

• *Make a media assignment*—Assign a presentation that requires a multimedia element and support the students in developing their presentations. Gradually require more sophisticated media use. Start by using media with which the students are comfortable, and then gradually add different possibilities as the students become more familiar with equipment, software, and usage. Encourage partner work in the beginning so that more experienced users of technology can provide support for new users. Figure 46.2 lists a number of suggestions for multimedia projects.

FIGURE 46.2 Suggestions for Multimedia Projects

Grade Level	Project	Equipment/Access
Kindergarten	Story retelling	Overhead projector Transparency pictures
	Math presentations	Math manipulatives Overhead projector
Primary	Book talks (video book reports)	Video camera, VCR, monitor
	Publishing books	Computer with software for word processing and illustrating (Children's Writing and Publishing Center)
	Research on the Internet	Computer with Internet access, listing of websites that the teacher has previewed
Above Third	The sky's the limit!	Computer with Internet access
		Writing and publishing software
		Hyperstudio
		Video productions
		Computer programmed presentations using professional presentation packages such as PowerPoint
	Classroom connections projects	Internet projects connecting classrooms across the nation (www.gsn.org)
	Space exploration projects	Internet projects related to space travel and exploration (www.nasa.gov)

Applications and Examples

Ms. Grundbrecher's second graders are busily engaged in a project titled "Farm to Market." Because their school is in an agricultural area, the district encourages the study of the production of food; how it is harvested and transported to market; and the interdependence of farmers, food processors, and distributors. This is appropriate for Ms. Grundbrecher's English learners because many of their parents work in the agricultural industries, giving the children a good background knowledge in this area.

The students are familiar with the Macintosh computer because they use it regularly to publish their writing. For this project Ms. Grundbrecher introduces them to Kid Pix, a computer program that allows them to create graphs and illustrate their research. The students are using a "stamp" option, which has a large library of pictures to illustrate their reports.

For this introductory unit using computer technology, the students will use the library and a few websites already selected by the teacher to gather their information. They start with the area of the country where they live and the foods they see growing in the fields. They widen their search to determine the different foods that are grown in the rest of the state and finally research agriculture in other states. They then create a graph using the stamps from the Kid Pix program to illustrate the variety of foods grown in the United States. After identifying the wide range of food grown across the country, the class begins to look at transporting the food from place to place. Again using the Kid Pix stamps, the students create a map that visually represents the journey of the crops and the many different people employed to make it possible for the food to be available.

Ms. Grundbrecher is lucky enough to live in an area where she can take the students to visit the fields, a processing plant, and a distribution center. After all the research the second graders have done, they are very knowledgeable visitors. They ask important questions about the types of transportation used to deliver the food, where it goes, and how long it takes to get there. This type of "hands-on" learning also gives them lots of opportunities to take pictures, interview participants, and integrate learning in a variety of ways. The foreman at the processing center is impressed and asks one of the students how they know so much about the processing and distribution of food.

* * * * *

Mr. Bateman's 10th-grade chemistry class is discussing possible uses for chemistry in real life. He particularly likes this type of activity to get his English learners involved in using their developing language skills in authentic learning. Yolanda is interested in becoming an astronaut and asks, "Why do I need to study chemistry if I want to be an astronaut? I can't see any use for it in space."

"That's an interesting question, Yolanda," Mr. Bateman replies. "I was just reading about a service provided by NASA where students can read articles about the space program and even have their questions answered by astronauts and engineers associated with the program. Let's start a list of questions that we would like to have answered."

Mr. Bateman creates a KWL chart on a large sheet of butcher paper. "Let's first talk about what we know about the space program and then we'll generate some questions we want to have answered. We'll use the textbooks and online resources to try to find answers first, and then create a list of questions for the engineers and astronauts at NASA."

The students list all the information they have about the space program and when they are finished, they realize that what they know is mostly related to the launch procedures that they view on television. They really have little knowledge about the actual experiments that are being done in space or what scientific knowledge is being gained through the launches.

Mr. Bateman has contacted NASA online and received a copy of the teacher's guide that accompanies the NASA *Live from . . .* series. Using this introduction to the NASA programs, the students interact with scientists through the NASA question–answer repository, where a number of their questions are answered. The students find that by reading information about research goals, viewing photos online, and searching for actual data gathered from shuttle flights and other NASA projects, they are gaining a much broader understanding of all the different types of research being conducted through the space programs.

As it becomes obvious that the NASA research connection will be an ongoing study, Mr. Bateman realizes that several of his students are spending a lot of time in the chemistry labs and computer stations working on projects that stem from the NASA teaching materials and the Internet connections. Yolanda is no longer the only student interested in the space program.

"Mr. Bateman, did you know that the space program uses engineers, chemists, biologists, data analyzers, doctors, veterinarians, and a whole lot of other types of scientists?" Joseph asks. "I never knew that so many different jobs were involved in the space industry."

"It's an exciting program," Mr. Bateman replies. "The American public knows very little about all the inventions and medical benefits we have gained from the research."

"Well, if they'd just get on the Internet, they'd know," Joseph says. "It's all on there at the NASA website."

Conclusion

Multimedia presentations in the classroom support students in conveying information to their peers. The use of audiovisuals helps students and teachers to connect vocabulary and meaning, particularly for English learners. The use of computers, DVDs, digital camcorders, phones, tablets, and other technology in the classroom appeals to students and motivates them to be more innovative in completing assignments. Using the Internet in the classroom introduces some challenges, however. Just as in researching from more traditional materials, students will need instruction in giving credit and citing sources. They may be tempted simply to download reports from the Internet; therefore, specific guidelines will need to be set and behavior monitored in the classroom setting.

Examples of Approximation Behaviors Related to the TESOL Standards

PreK–3 students will:

- use a drawing to illustrate a story read, told, or written.
- use classroom computers and the Internet to locate answers to questions.

4–8 students will:

- conduct research using a variety of resources (books and technology).

- orally present information aided by technology-created visuals.

9–12 students will:

- use multimedia software to enhance oral presentations.
- create innovative projects combining media.

References

Cummins, J. (1994). The acquisition of English as a second language. In M. Spangenberg-Urbschat & R. Pritchard (Eds.), *Reading instruction for ESL students*. Newark, DE: International Reading Association.

Díaz-Rico, L. (2018). *The crosscultural, language, and academic development handbook: A complete K–12 reference guide* (6th ed.). Boston, MA: Pearson Education.

Roblyer, M. D. (2006). *Integrating educational technology into teaching* (4th ed.). Upper Saddle River, NJ: Pearson.

Suggested Further Reading

Bus, A., & Neuman, S. (Eds.) (2008). *Multimedia and Literacy Development: Improving Achievement for Young Learners*. New York: Routledge.

Cheng, I., Safont, L., Basu, A., & Goebel, R. (2010). *Multimedia in education: Adaptive learning and testing*. Singapore: World Scientific Publishing Company Pte. Ltd.

Pitler, H., Hubbell, E., & Kuhn, M. (2012). *Using technology with classroom instruction that works*. Alexandria, VA: ASCD.

Smith, G., & Throne, S. (2009). *Differentiating instruction with technology in middle school classrooms*. Washington, DC: International Society for Technology in Education.

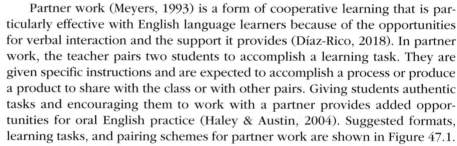

47

Small Groups and Partners

Interactions to Enhance Instruction

Skills grouping (Gibbons, 2015; Peregoy & Boyle, 2013) is the act of arranging students in groups based on their need for instruction in a specific skill. Skills grouping is done for a short period of time, usually for only a few lessons, and is effective only when the groups are based on the teacher's knowledge of the language and skill levels of the students. The criterion for grouping is based on teacher observation of a specific instructional need. This greatly enhances the delivery of comprehensible input because the lessons are planned to scaffold learning at the students' present level of functioning (Krashen, 1985).

Skills groups tend to be heterogeneous as far as reading levels and overall academic functioning are concerned. A skills group might have students reading on a range of levels. Skills groups consist of students with a specific instructional need, for instance, a group of students that is not using quotation marks correctly or a group of students that needs instruction in solving math problems involving fractions. Skills groups are used effectively in the teaching of language usage, reading, language arts, and mathematics skills. For additional ideas to make your small groups more effective, view this slide presentation and note the preparations necessary to teach an effective small-group lesson while keeping the rest of the class engaged in important tasks.

Enhanced eText
Video Example 47.1
https://www.youtube.com/
watch?v=AF3T2aZM3ko

Partner work (Meyers, 1993) is a form of cooperative learning that is particularly effective with English language learners because of the opportunities for verbal interaction and the support it provides (Díaz-Rico, 2018). In partner work, the teacher pairs two students to accomplish a learning task. They are given specific instructions and are expected to accomplish a process or produce a product to share with the class or with other pairs. Giving students authentic tasks and encouraging them to work with a partner provides added opportunities for oral English practice (Haley & Austin, 2004). Suggested formats, learning tasks, and pairing schemes for partner work are shown in Figure 47.1.

Watch this video to see the power of partner work in a lesson for kindergarteners—sorting by concepts and building vocabulary. As you watch, think about the following questions:

Enhanced eText
Video Example 47.2

1. How does this lesson help build English vocabulary?
2. How does partner work give students more opportunity to use their English?

Peer tutoring (Thonis, 1994) is a strategy in which a student who has already achieved certain skills works with a classmate to help him or her acquire the skills. It differs from partner work because partners work together, sharing the responsibilities. Peer tutoring is effective with English language learners for several reasons. A peer who has mastered a higher level of proficiency in academic skills and English usage can often support learning by explaining the assignment in

FIGURE 47.1 Suggested Formats, Learning Tasks, and Pairing Schemes for Partner Work

Format	Learning Tasks/Procedure	Pairing Scheme
Think-pair-share	Group discussions, literature studies, problem solving, reviewing of content materials for tests. Teacher presents question or task. Students think about their responses and then share and discuss their responses with their partner.	One strong English model
Buddy read	Reading of content material, challenging text. One student reads; the other listens or takes notes. They stop periodically to discuss and create a graphic organizer for study.	One strong reader
Research interview	Content material in science, social studies, and any informational writing. Students do individual research on a topic or aspect of a topic. Partners interview each other to gain the knowledge obtained by their partner. When sharing with another pair or whole group, each partner reports the material learned from the partner. The original researcher has the responsibility of monitoring the report by the partner to guarantee its accuracy.	Equal partners or one strong reader
Conversation role-play	Oral language development, adjusting to social situations, situational vocabulary. Partners role-play certain social situations such as a birthday party, a job interview, meeting new people at a nonfamily party. Appropriate language is introduced by the teacher in advance, and the partners pretend to be a part of the social situation. After a while pairs are combined into groups of four, and the partners must introduce each other to the new pair, providing appropriate information they have gained from the initial conversations.	Equal partners
Convince me	Problem-solving tasks in science or math. Teacher presents a problem to be solved. The students work independently to find innovative solutions to the problem. The students are then paired to try to convince each other of the viability of the two solutions or to combine their solutions to make a better solution. They then meet with another pair, and the foursomes must decide on and present their best solution to the whole group.	One strong English model

the student's first language or model what is expected. The peer tutoring situation often lowers anxiety for the learner because questions can be answered more readily on a one-to-one basis and the students are less likely to be inhibited. Questions can even be answered in the home language when the students have the same language background. Peer tutoring also provides the tutor with positive feelings of self-esteem and accomplishment as the tutee gains knowledge and English proficiency.

Step-by-Step

The steps in implementing skills grouping are the following:

• *Observe and document language levels*—Set up a method for observing and documenting students' language levels, learning, and classroom performance. See the anecdotal records and performance sampling sections in the Theoretical Overview section of this text for suggestions.

• *Review needs for instruction*—Frequently review the records you keep of the students' levels of functioning and needs for instruction and look for commonalities on which to base instruction. Form skills groups based on these commonalities.

• *Design and implement lessons*—Design a lesson to teach the skill for which the group has a common need. Explain the skill, model it, and give the group opportunities to practice using the skill under your guidance. As a follow-up to the lesson, give the students an authentic task that requires the use of the skill just taught. Observe the students' use of the skill in the assigned task. Celebrate with students who are using the skill effectively, and plan another lesson focusing on the same skill for those students who need more instruction. See Figure 47.2 for the cycle used in forming and teaching skills groups. Note that the skills groups are flexible because future groups are formed on the basis of need. The students who achieve the objective of the lesson are not included in the next group of students reviewing the skill.

FIGURE 47.2 The Cycle Used in Forming and Teaching Skills Groups

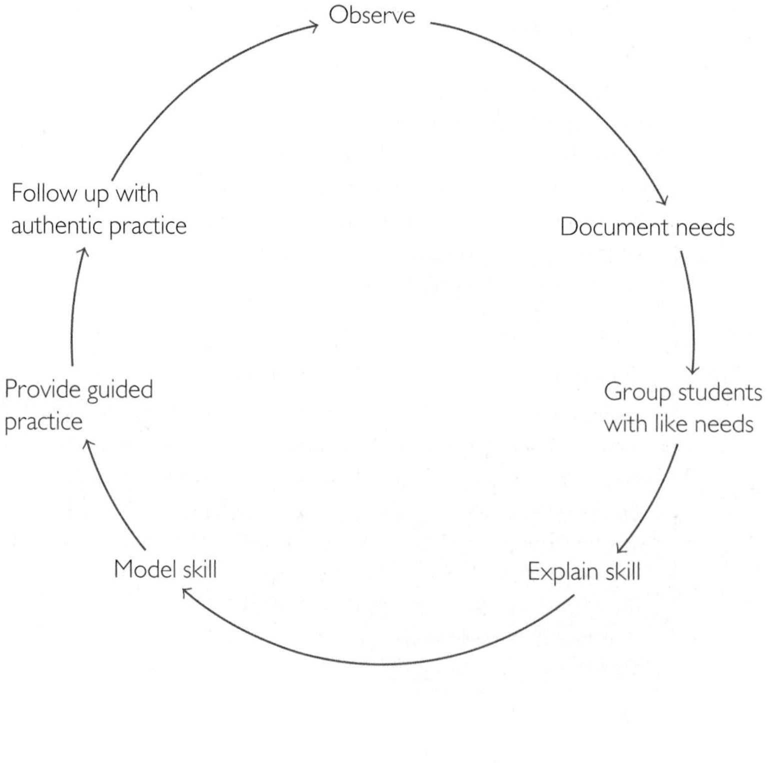

Step-by-Step

The steps in implementing partner work are the following:

- *Pair the students*—Decide the purpose of the partner work to be done before you assign the pairs. If language development is one of the main purposes of the pairing, make sure one of the partners can provide a strong English model.
- *Identify and train potential tutors*—If one student is going to work as a tutor for the other, the student acting as a tutor must receive some training instead of the students working together. Identify students who have proficiency in the academic areas selected and who could tutor other students. Provide training to the peer tutors in:
  - How to pose questions that support thinking
  - How to break the task into manageable pieces
  - When to explain in the first language
  - How to support English vocabulary development

- *Match students*—If the object of the partner work is peer tutoring, match the students who need tutoring with peer tutors, considering factors such as gender, home language, and personality.
- *Model the task*—Choose one student to act as your partner in modeling the task and walking through the steps to be done. List the tasks and the expectations of what will be accomplished on a chart or chalkboard to serve as a reminder during the process.
- *Provide support and practice*—Circulate among the pairs during the activity, giving them feedback on the way they are working together and communicating. Support pairs who are struggling by entering into their interactions and modeling strategies they can use to get the task done.
- *Share progress*—Provide an opportunity for the pairs to share their process or product with another pair or the whole group. Celebrate their accomplishments and review the language they were able to use.

Applications and Examples

Mr. Santiago's second graders are listening intently to his reading of *Wilfred Gordon McDonald Partridge* (Fox, 1985). He is planning a lesson to help his students "describe the overall structure of a story, including describing how the beginning introduces the story and the ending concludes the action" (CCSS.ELA-LITERACY.RL.2.5). When he finishes reading the book, he reviews the story by creating a flip book labeled *Beginning, Middle,* and *End.* He asks the students to tell the things that happen at the beginning of the story. As they mention the elements in the beginning of Mem Fox's wonderful book, he reviews them: "We meet the characters Wilfred Gordon, Miss Nancy, and the other old folks at the home. We learn about the setting—that Wilfred Gordon lives next door to the old people's home. We learn about the problem—that Miss Nancy has lost her memory." As he talks about the elements, Mr. Santiago lists *Characters, Setting,* and *Problem introduced* under *Beginning* on the flip book. Mr. Santiago repeats the process for the *Middle* section of the flip book and writes *Problem gets worse, Characters are developed.* Under *End* on the flip book, Mr. Santiago writes *Problem solved.* His flip book now looks like the one shown in Figure 47.3.

Mr. Santiago asks students to think about a memory they have that they could write about. He gives them time to think and jot some notes about their memories. Next, Mr. Santiago asks Erina to come up front and act as his partner so he can show the students what they will be doing next.

"I have written some notes about my memory. I will use my notes to tell you my story. As I tell you my story, I want you to take notes on this flip book labeled *Beginning, Middle,* and *End.* You are to take notes about my story because you will help me decide if I need to add anything to my story so that it will be more interesting. You will also be watching to see that I have included all the important parts of my story."

FIGURE 47.3 Mr. Santiago's Flip Book

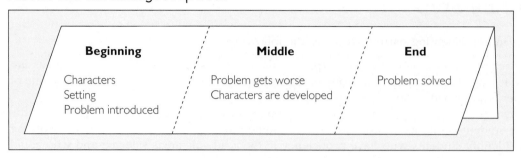

Mr. Santiago then tells his story, and Erina writes the names of the characters by the word *Characters* on the *Beginning* section of the flip book. As he tells about the setting, she writes a few words by *Setting* and then writes a few words by *Problem introduced* as he tells about the problem. Erina continues to take notes as Mr. Santiago completes his story.

"Now that I have told my story to Erina, I want her to look at her notes to see if I have left out any important parts. Erina, what do you think?"

"I don't have any notes in the *Middle* section under *Characters are developed*. I think you need to tell me some more about the characters in the middle of the story to make it more interesting."

"Good, I can do that when I actually write my story inside the flip book. That will be the next part. For now, we need to work in pairs to tell our stories to our partners. Then they can take notes and help us to make sure we have all the parts to make our stories as interesting as Mem Fox's story about Wilfred Gordon."

Mr. Santiago gives the students time to think about their stories and jot some notes. Then he pairs up the students, making sure that there is a strong English speaker in each pair. The partners tell their stories to each other, creating the *Beginning*, *Middle*, and *End* notes on the cover of the flip books. Once everyone has told their stories and received feedback from their partners, they get to work writing the stories in the flip books. They know exactly what to write now that they've told the stories and received advice from their partners.

* * * * *

Mr. Tyler is reading his 11th graders' essays, and he notices that a number of the students are still having difficulty with the proper use of the homophones *there*, *their*, and *they're*. As he reads the essays, he makes a list of the students who are still confusing these words. A little later he notices several students are confused about when to use an apostrophe in *it's*. Several of these same students are also using apostrophes inappropriately with nouns, sometimes creating possessives when they really need plurals. After Mr. Tyler completes the reading of the essays, he has three skills group lists and decides that he will use some of the class time each day for the next week to work on these specific skills. In forming these skills groups, Mr. Tyler wants his students to "develop and strengthen writing as needed by planning, revising, editing, rewriting, or trying a new approach, focusing on addressing what is most significant for a specific purpose and audience" (CCSS.ELA-LITERACY.W.11–12.5).

Mr. Tyler has identified the need for skills grouping in his classes. He has an additional problem because his classes meet for only 50 minutes, and he must find time to teach skills groups while not wasting the time of the students in his classes who do not need this instruction. Although he is surprised that the students he has identified as misusing simple grammar and vocabulary in their essays are not all in his basic writing class, he realizes that he cannot ignore these errors for students nearing high school graduation.

Mr. Tyler designs a group assignment lesson that will enable him to teach the skills he has identified and still maintain the momentum for the rest of his class. He divides each class into cooperative groups. He calls students into a skills group to work with him on the skills he has identified. The rest of the class works in cooperative groups to identify a writing goal and design a presentation for the class using literature to demonstrate the ways in which different authors accomplish this goal. Mr. Tyler begins the class by conducting a brainstorming session where the class identifies some of the writing goals it has. The list includes writing good dialogue, building tension in the plot development, using a rich vocabulary to make the writing interesting, developing interesting characters, understanding the use of metaphor and simile, and determining approaches to creating and developing a problem and solution.

After the list is generated, Mr. Tyler divides the students into cooperative groups, placing one student from his skills group into each of the cooperative groups. The cooperative groups each identify a goal they want to research and begin to look at the literature they have been reading for good examples.

Mr. Tyler calls his skills group together and introduces the problem he has discovered in reading their essays. "I will be working with this small group for a short time each day for a while to help you to overcome a problem that I discovered in reading your essays," he begins. Mr. Tyler gives an explanation of the differences among the homophones *there*, *their*, and *they're* and how important it is that the words be used correctly. He sends the students back to their cooperative groups to begin to look for the examples needed for the group presentations on the way the professional writers approach the goals identified by the class. The members of the skills group has one added task: They are to find sentences in the literature that demonstrate the correct usage of the homophones they are studying and copy at least one sentence that employs each of the homophones. For homework that night, the skills group is assigned a paragraph to be written about an imaginary group of people. The skills group is to find a way to use all three forms of the homophone in the paragraph.

Mr. Tyler follows his instruction with partner work in which one of the students from the special skills group is paired with another student. The partners work together to proof their papers before submitting them. The students proofread each other's papers, giving the student working on special skills two chances to identify the correct usage of the homophones and apostrophes.

Mr. Tyler finds that the system he has set up works well. He identifies needs for skills groups and then provides time for cooperative group work, which can continue while he conducts quick skills instruction. He follows up with short assignments in which he monitors for understanding of the skills.

He uses one additional technique to help the students monitor their own progress. He duplicates copies of the skill or vocabulary rules for the students to attach to the inside cover of their writing folders. Before they turn in any assignments they must work collaboratively with another student on editing by proofreading their writing for the types of errors that give them difficulty. Mr. Tyler finds that making the students aware of the errors they are committing helps them to self-monitor and self-correct. They are refining their use of the English language (Swain, 1993).

Conclusion

Skills grouping is a way to provide focused instruction for small groups of students with shared needs. Because skills groups are created to address a specific need, they are not long-standing groups. Instruction is given, skills are practiced and monitored, and the groups change. If some students require further instruction, that instruction is provided, but only for those who need it. This form of grouping is effective because students receive lessons tailored to their needs and the other students in the class receive assignments that allow them to practice their skills at appropriate levels without being bored by instruction they do not need.

Partner work can be used in many ways across the curriculum. By pairing students to support one another in the successful completion of the task or to review materials and prepare for an assignment, the students have opportunities to interact verbally, practice relating facts and concepts, monitor each other's understanding, or provide home language support. English language learners can be paired in several ways depending on their stages in English acquisition. If a student needs home language explanations, then a perfect partner for that student is another student who shares the same home language but is also more fluent in English.

FIGURE 47.4 Self-Evaluation Form for Group Work

Group Members	Participation	Achievement	Contribution to Group
	E G F P	E G F P	E G F P
	E G F P	E G F P	E G F P
	E G F P	E G F P	E G F P
	E G F P	E G F P	E G F P

Note: E = excellent, G = good, F = fair, and P = poor.

If an English language learner is fairly fluent in English but needs more practice in speaking and writing English, then choose a good English-speaking role model as a partner. To create **bilingual books** and labels, versions of favorite literature in various languages, or illustrated books, match English language learners with partners who are strong in writing and illustration. Partnerships can also be used effectively in math and science by pairing students with strengths such as writing and science or art and science.

Small groups and partners should document their work to provide practice in self-evaluation and demonstrate the active involvement of each of the members. Figure 47.4 provides an example of a self-evaluation form that can be used for this process.

Examples of Approximation Behaviors Related to the TESOL Standards

PreK–3 students will:

- use gestures to ascertain the location of items in the classroom.
- use simple questions to elicit information needed.
- express needs and ideas.
- engage in verbal interaction in English.

4–8 students will:

- ask who, what, where, when, why, and how questions to obtain needed information.

- ask a series of questions to build knowledge.
- follow both implicit and explicit oral directions.
- elaborate on the ideas of others.

9–12 students will:

- ask questions to generate descriptive terms.
- use verbal interaction to resolve conflict.
- participate actively in small-group interactions.

References

Common core state standards. ELA-LITERACY.RL.2.5 © 2010. National Governors Association Center for Best Practices and Council of Chief State School Officers. All rights reserved.

Díaz-Rico, L. (2018). *The crosscultural, language, and academic development handbook: A complete K–12 reference guide* (6th ed.). Boston, MA: Pearson Education.

Fox, M. (1985). *Wilfred Gordon McDonald Partridge*. Brooklyn, NY: Kane/Miller Books.

Gibbons, P. (2015). *Scaffolding language, scaffolding learning: Teaching English language learners in the mainstream classroom* (2nd ed.). Portsmouth, NH: Heinemann.

Haley, M., & Austin, T. (2004). *Content-based second language teaching and learning*. Boston, MA: Pearson Education.

Krashen, S. (1985). *The input hypothesis: Issues and implications*. New York, NY: Longman.

Meyers, M. (1993). *Teaching to diversity: Teaching and learning in the multi-ethnic classroom*. Toronto, Canada: Irwin.

Peregoy, S., & Boyle, O. (2013). *Reading, writing, and learning in ESL: A resource book for teaching K–12 English learners* (6th ed.). Boston, MA: Pearson Education.

Swain, M. (1993). The output hypothesis: Just speaking and writing aren't enough. *The Canadian Modern Language Review, 50*, 158–164.

Thonis, E. (1994). The ESL student: Reflections on the present, concerns for the future. In K. Spangenberg-Urbschat & R. Pritchard (Eds.), *Kids come in all languages: Reading instruction for ESL students*. Newark, DE: International Reading Association.

48

GIST
Exploring Tough Text

Enhanced eText
Video Example 48.1

Generating interaction between schemata and text (GIST) is a strategy for supporting comprehension of informational text (Cunningham, 1982). GIST is especially helpful when students are required to read long texts that contain a significant amount of new information. Students work in cooperative groups, but read sections of the text silently. After each short section is read silently, the members of the group work collaboratively to generate one sentence that summarizes the *gist*, or main point, of the passage. In some very dense text, this summary sentence is generated paragraph by paragraph. Learning to generate a summary sentence has been found to positively affect language learners' reading comprehension (Geo, 2017). Once a sentence is generated, members of the group write it on their own papers so that each group member ends up with a concise summary of the text. The teacher circulates among the groups to facilitate and provide support. This is a particularly effective strategy for English language learners because the group members discuss and clarify meaning as they decide on the best summary sentence for the section or paragraph (Echevarria, Vogt, & Short, 2010; Goldenberg, 2008).

Watch the Strategies video on DVD #12 to see how the GIST process works. Think about the following questions as you watch:

1. How does the group discussion help the students to clarify meaning?
2. How does GIST support students in learning how to summarize?
3. How could the teacher use the paragraph summaries to teach study skills?

Step-by-Step

The steps in implementing GIST are the following:

- *Identify appropriate text for GIST*—Identify text that may cause some difficulty for students. Decide whether the text must be read and summarized paragraph by paragraph or section by section, and determine logical stopping or summarizing points.
- *Group the students*—Divide the class into cooperative groups and identify a leader for each group. Make sure that each group contains a strong English speaker and reader. If possible, group English language learners with other students of the same language background who can provide first-language support if needed. If your main purpose is to facilitate understanding of the text, the discussion of the meaning and the negotiation of the best summary sentence can be done in the students' first languages and later translated to English. If your purpose is facilitating

FIGURE 48.1 Sample of a Summary Point Chart

Stop and summarize at these points:
1. Page 3, at the subheading
2. Page 7, at the bottom of the page
3. Page 9, after the chart
4. Page 13, at the subheading
5. Page 18, at the end of the selection

English communication, then the discussion should take place in English with first-language translations made only for the purpose of clarification.

• *Demonstrate the strategy*—Demonstrate the strategy by discussing background knowledge and informing students that they will be working in groups to create a summary of the material to be read. Post the summary points—the points in the reading at which each group is to stop—then discuss and summarize. See Figure 48.1 for an example of a summary point chart. Instruct the students to read the passage silently to the first summary point and then stop and write a one-sentence summary of what they read.

• *Discuss summary sentences*—After the students have completed their summary sentence, ask one of the students to share his or hers with the class. Discuss the sentence as a group and add details that the class thinks will enhance the sentence. Instruct the students to write the summary sentence on their papers. The teacher serves as facilitator and quality controller, making sure that the summary sentences capture the *gist* of the paragraphs. It is important that the quality control be done in a supportive manner through questioning and supporting the students' understanding of the text.

• *Read and summarize paragraph by paragraph*—Explain to the students that they will be reading the entire selection in this manner. They will all read to each summary point, as indicated by the chart that is posted. As each student waits for the rest of the group to finish reading, he or she should be thinking of the main points in the section—formulating a summary sentence in his or her mind or writing it on a scrap piece of paper. The group should then discuss the section and negotiate the best summary sentence it can write. Once the group has decided on a summary sentence, each member of the group writes the sentence on his or her own paper, and the process begins again. Having worked through this process, you might want to review the earlier video and note how the teacher supports the students' understanding of the text. After reviewing the video, ask yourself these questions:

   ○ How did the teacher make sure that his students understood the process?
   ○ What was the teacher doing as the students were working?
   ○ What did the teacher do when a group included a misconception in its summary?
   ○ How would using this strategy support students in improving their language abilities?

• *Read and compare summary sentences*—Once the selection has been completed, have the groups read and compare their summary sentences. This provides an effective review of the passage read and affords an opportunity to correct any misconceptions. Again, the teacher serves as facilitator and questions the students to lead them to capture the meaning and nuance of the text.

• *Assess to document student involvement and participation*—The group work time in this strategy is a perfect opportunity for the teacher to circulate around the room and listen. This is a good time to take anecdotal records—documenting student interactions and writing language samples for inclusion in the students' portfolios. It is also a good time to create checklists, like the one shown in Figure 48.2, for documenting specific behaviors exhibited by the students.

FIGURE 48.2 Checklist for Documenting Student Interactions and Contributions during a GIST Activity

	Marcos	Juan	Diana	Carol	Carlos
Listens to *others*					
Contributes to summary					
Defends own ideas					
Participates verbally					
Takes leadership role					
Presents to class					

Applications and Examples

The fifth graders in Ms. Menashian's class have been studying the American Revolution. They have read the Jean Fritz biographies of the great men and women who lived at the time of the Revolution and the contributions they made. Ms. Menashian wants to conclude the unit of study with a reading of Henry Wadsworth Longfellow's poem *"The Midnight Ride of Paul Revere."* However, she wants her students to understand the significance of the poem, so she assigns the chapter *"A Centennial Celebration"* in Augusta Stevenson's (1986) biography *Paul Revere: Boston Patriot*.

Ms. Menashian divides the fifth graders into cooperative groups to read and summarize the chapter. Because her class has a number of English language learners, Ms. Menashian makes sure that each group has a strong reader and several students in each group who speak the same home language. She posts a chart of summary points, and the students begin reading and summarizing the selection. As she moves among the groups, she hears some interesting discussion.

"I don't understand this chapter. It says it was 1875," Andre says. "That's a hundred years after Paul Revere's ride."

"I think that's why it's called a centennial celebration. That's a celebration after a hundred years," Juanita says. "I think this chapter is going to talk about how they were still celebrating his ride after a hundred years."

"Oh, I get it," Andre says. "What should we write for our summary sentence?"

"How about this?" Tyra asks. "A hundred years after the famous midnight ride of Paul Revere, the people of Boston were still talking about how brave he was."

"That's good," Margaret says, "but it also said that they were proud of him because of his silverwork too."

"But they were more proud of his patriotism," Juanita says.

"What is patriotism?" Mario asks.

"It's being loyal to your country," Juanita answers. "He risked his life to warn the soldiers that the British soldiers were coming." Juanita says this in English and then repeats the explanation in Spanish.

"OK," Mario says. "So the people of Boston are proud of Paul Revere because he was a great silversmith, but more because he was a great patriot."

"That's a good summary sentence," Andre says. "Let's use that one. Say it again, Mario."

As Mario repeats the sentence, everyone writes it on their papers, including Mario. The group then reads the next section of the chapter.

When the group has completed reading and discussing the chapter, its summary looks like this:

The people of Boston are proud of Paul Revere because he was a great silversmith, but more because he was a great patriot.

On April 18, 1775, eight hundred British soldiers were going to Concord to seize the patriot ammunition and guns.

Patriot troops had to be warned that the British soldiers were coming so they could move the powder and guns.

John Hancock and Samuel Adams also needed to be told to leave Lexington before they were arrested and hanged for speaking against the king.

The patriots chose Paul Revere to make the ride to warn the troops that the British were coming.

It was a very dangerous ride because British soldiers and warships were guarding the whole area.

Lanterns in the Old North Church belfry would tell Paul Revere how the British soldiers had gone.

There would be two lanterns if they had gone by water, one lantern if they had gone by land.

Paul Revere went to the sexton of the Old North Church and told him to put the lanterns in the church belfry when he knew how the soldiers were coming. Then Paul Revere rowed across the river.

Patriots across the river waited with Paul Revere while they watched for the lanterns.

Paul Revere stopped at all the houses between Boston and Lexington and warned everyone that the British were coming.

The patriots all grabbed their guns and kept the British from getting to the guns. They also gave John Hancock and Samuel Adams time to escape.

Ms. Menashian was very pleased with the summaries the students wrote about the ride of Paul Revere and with the discussion of the importance of the ride that took place as the groups shared their summaries. As she concluded the study of the Revolution with the reading of the poem "The Midnight Ride of Paul Revere," she was sure that the students really understood the words and the significance of the event to American history.

* * * * *

Some of the reading in Ms. Hughes's 11th-grade literature class is extremely difficult for her students to understand. Although she is sure that her students will enjoy reading Mark Twain's most famous works, she is concerned that they will not understand the political significance of his work and its place in history. Because of the difficulty of some of the vocabulary in the biographical readings about Mark Twain, Ms. Hughes decides to encourage her students to work in cooperative groups. Being in groups allows them to discuss the vocabulary, to consider the politics involved at that particular time in history, and to comprehend the nuances in meaning that they might otherwise miss.

Ms. Hughes groups her students for the reading of Bernard deVoto's (1984) introductory chapter in *The Portable Mark Twain*. She posts a chart that tells the groups to stop and summarize after each paragraph they read, and she walks the class through the steps in the GIST procedure. She explains the double meanings of the term *gist* and the procedure name, which connects schemata and text.

"Who knows what it means to 'get the *gist* of things'?" Ms. Hughes asks.

"It means that you get the general idea," Leon answers.

"That's exactly right and today you are going to participate in an activity called GIST. You and the rest of your group will work together to figure out what the reading means. Because this introductory chapter is what I call 'tough text'—text that is difficult to read and understand—I want you to stop after each paragraph and discuss the meaning. Your group will write one sentence to summarize each paragraph. When you are finished reading the introductory chapter and writing the summary sentences, you should have a good understanding of Mark Twain and his place in American history. We will talk about the chapter after you have completed the reading."

As the groups work their way through the chapter, Ms. Hughes circulates among them and occasionally gets drawn into the discussions. Because there are a number of difficult words in the reading, she also gathers words from the groups to add to the word wall. First-language translations for the new vocabulary are added to the word wall as necessary.

At the end of the period, Ms. Hughes asks the groups to share their summaries, and they choose the best sentence for each paragraph to create a class summary of the chapter.

After the groups have read and summarized the introduction to the Mark Twain volume, Ms. Hughes asks the students to think about what they have learned and give an overall summary of the history of the time in which Twain wrote.

After the discussion of the introduction, Ms. Hughes assigns the students the first reading in the Mark Twain anthology. First, they discuss some vocabulary and background that they will need in order to understand "The Notorious Jumping Frog of Calaveras County."

Conclusion

Students of all ages and at all stages of language development benefit from the use of collaborative strategies such as GIST. By placing students in heterogeneous groups, with a strong English reader and writer in each group, teachers can encourage discussion of a reading and give students a chance to clarify meaning and vocabulary. The group task of writing a summary sentence for each paragraph that is read provides an authentic assignment that requires the students to discuss the meaning of the paragraph and agree on a sentence that conveys the important information. Once the paragraphs are read and discussed and summary sentences are written and read, each student in the group has a concise summary of the reading assignment.

When several groups read and summarize the same text and then share their summaries, further discussion of the main ideas and supporting details frequently follows. This gives students additional opportunities to hear the information discussed and new vocabulary clarified.

Examples of Approximation Behaviors Related to the TESOL Standards

PreK–3 students will:

- collaboratively write a summary of a paragraph.
- support their opinions in a group setting.

4–8 students will:

- identify main ideas in text.
- write summary sentences of paragraphs.

9–12 students will:

- discuss nuances of word meanings and negotiate with peers to summarize bodies of text accurately.
- explore specific word meanings related to content in the collaborative summarization of text.

References

Cunningham, J. (1982). Generating interactions between schemata and text. In J. A. Niles & L. A. Harris (Eds.), *New inquiries in reading research and instruction* (pp. 42–47). Washington, DC: National Reading Conference.

deVoto, B. (Ed.). (1984). *The portable Mark Twain.* New York, NY: Penguin Books.

Echevarria, J., Vogt, M., & Short, D. (2010). *Making content comprehensible for elementary English learners: The SIOP model.* Boston, MA: Allyn & Bacon.

Geo, Y. (2017) The effect of summary writing on reading comprehension; the role of mediation in EFL classroom. Reading Improvement, *54*(2).

Goldenberg, G. (2008). Teaching English language learners: What the research does—and does not—say. *American Educator, 32*(2), 8–44.

Stevenson, A. (1986). *Paul Revere: Boston patriot.* New York, NY: Aladdin.

49

Tutorials

Closing the Achievement Gap

The **continuous improvement model,** or **CIM,** is currently being used with great success in many states (Davenport & Anderson, 2002). In this model, the daily delivery of instruction follows a set sequence that includes the following elements:

• Warm-up—This is a review of previously taught material to support the students' use of background knowledge. It also supports maintenance of skills, concepts, and strategies.

• Lesson for the day—New material is introduced and guided practice provided. This may involve several cycles of instruction, modeling, and guided practice. Guided practice means the teachers are on their feet monitoring and guiding students as they work.

• Independent practice—Students are given the opportunity to use the material independently. The teachers are still monitoring but instruction and support is more limited.

• Daily quiz—The students are given a quick quiz to determine their understanding. From the results of this quiz the teacher determines which students need additional instruction and which students are ready to move forward. If most students need more instruction, additional lessons are planned. If a small group of students needs additional instruction, a tutorial is provided specifically for those students. If a small group of students is ready for enrichment activities, those are also provided.

This model is based on the premise that all students can learn and that additional instruction must be planned and provided for those who need it. Teachers work in teams to provide the tutorials and enrichment activities their students need. Time is scheduled at the end of each school day (and sometimes after school) to make sure each student experiences success and continuous improvement. Additional time and opportunities for practice have been shown to improve the success of English learners in several recent research studies (Goldenberg 2008). This model is described in depth in *Closing the Achievement Gap: No Excuses* (Davenport & Anderson, 2002) and was first instituted in the Brazosport Independent School District (ISD) in Brazosport, Texas. It has since been used in many school districts across the United States with great success. "Once the Brazosport ISD teachers became convinced that all students could learn, they did something they had never done before: They refused to let them fail" (Davenport & Anderson, 2002, p. 102).

The Brazosport teachers raised their expectations and restructured their programs and the result was an amazing turn-around for all students, including at-risk students in the district. The high school with the highest percentage of low-income students and dropouts eventually outscored the high school that traditionally led the district in achievement. The school also lowered its dropout rate from 6.7% to less than 0.01% and its discipline referrals from about 30% to about 10%.

Tutorials are used to make sure everyone meets the standards. Some students will always need more time and instruction than others. Others will easily meet and exceed standards and need enrichment to achieve their learning potential (Barksdale & Davenport, 2003). Surprisingly, or maybe not, some students need tutorials on some standards and enrichment on others. The solution to the challenge of offering these types of programs, for Brazosport, was what they called Team Times—instructional teams that taught different tutorials and enrichment activities at different times during the day. Additionally, team members (faculty) might sometimes teach tutorials and lead enrichment activities at other times. The faculty teams felt the "tutorial" or "enrichment" labels carried too much baggage for the students and decided it was important that tutorials not connote punishment or "classes for dummies."

Step-by-Step

The steps in implementing tutorials are the following:

- *Plan time for tutorials within the school day*—Identify a 30-minute period during the day when you can work with students who need additional instruction in order to meet standards.
- *Use assessment and observation to identify students who will benefit from tutorials*—Observe as you teach to determine which students need additional instruction and which can be involved in extension or enrichment activities. Make sure that you are maintaining high standards and expecting all students to be able to meet standards, even if they require additional instructional time.
- *Plan activities that approach the standards to be taught in innovative ways*—Don't teach tutorials or extension activities as "more of the same." See Figure 49.1 for Web-based resources on planning tutorials and making them effective.
- *Assess frequently to ensure mastery*—Schedule quick assessments at the end of each tutorial session to determine which students need to continue with more tutorials.
- *Continue to schedule tutorials until students are meeting standards*—As students master standards, move them into extension or enrichment activities. This step may require some innovative use of time.

In addition to time for tutorials during the day, Brazosport uses an "extended day" intervention program. For 3 weeks before the state assessment test, teachers work with at-risk students after school. Each teacher has 10 students, grouped by standard, non-mastery level. They meet from 3:30 to 5:30 p.m., Monday through Thursday. As an incentive, snacks and transportation home on the bus are provided. This is funded with summer school money. This makes more sense if you are trying to prepare students to pass the test since summer school takes place after the state assessment test. The students take their snack break immediately after school and then each teacher takes the 10 students assigned to him or her and they review the standards that were not mastered. Just as with team time, the teachers are rotated so students are assigned to someone other than their own homeroom teacher. Some of the mastery-level students even volunteer to serve as teacher aides.

As a result, 92% of the students considered to be below grade level passed the state assessment test after this 3-week review. After the initial 3 years, Brazosport no longer offered summer school for students who had passed the grade but had not mastered all standards. They found this extended day program more effective for remediating standards.

FIGURE 49.1 Resources for Planning Effective Tutorials

http://www.microsoft.com/education/lessonplans.mspx
http://www.wfu.edu/~ylwong/balanceeq/balanceq.html
http://www.coolmath-games.com/
http://www.mathplayground.com/games.html
http://www.primarygames.com/reading.htm
http://www.starfall.com/
http://www.adrianbruce.com/reading/games.htm
http://www.microsoft.com/education/teachers/guides/freetools.aspx?WT.mc_id=freetools_google
http://www.fcpsteach.org/docs/BrownFinal.pdf

Assessment to Ensure Effective Instruction

The CIM requires frequent assessment. This assessment can be in the form of observation, quick-writes, simple assignments that demonstrate understanding, or short versions of the standardized test questions that students will be expected to pass. The scheduling of daily tutorials requires teachers to be extremely aware of the learning levels of each student. The quick assessments at the end of each tutorial should not take more than a few minutes so that they do not encroach on teaching time. One quick assessment that works well both as an assessment and a review is a "jeopardy" game; another is the "show-me" card game to review the correct use of the homophones *there, their,* and *they're,* as depicted in Figure 49.2.

Applications and Examples

Mrs. Crane is supporting her students in addressing Common Core State Standard ELA-Literacy.W.3.3.b.

FIGURE 49.2 "Show-Me" Card Game for Assessing and Reviewing the Uses of *There, Their,* and *They're*

1. Make sets of large cards with one of the words *there, their,* and *they're* written on each card. Distribute one set to each student.
2. Review the rules with the students before beginning.
3. Using a transparency of the sentences below, revealing one sentence at a time.
4. Each student is to show the card with the correct spelling of the homophone for each sentence that is revealed.
5. The student who displays the correct card and can explain *why* it is the correct card gets 5 points. All students who display the correct card get 1 point each. To support English learners, display the explanation of the meanings of the homophones so that they can identify the correct reason for each choice by simply stating the number of the correct choice. For example:

   1. There = a place
   2. Their = something belonging to them
   3. They're = they are

6. Use a checklist of the students' names to keep track of their ability to respond to the questions and plan further instruction for students who are still confusing the homophones.

Sample Transparency/Chart/Interactive Whiteboard

1. _____ going to the movies.
2. I borrowed _____ lawnmower.
3. I live right over _____.
4. _____ are two stoplights in front of the school.
5. _____ mother has blond hair.
6. Are _____ any more cupcakes?
7. How many are _____ ?
8. _____ going to sing now.
9. What is _____ last name?
10. When is _____ party?

"Use dialogue and descriptions of actions, thoughts, and feelings to develop experiences and events or show the response of characters to situations."

To begin this process, Mrs. Crane employs the CIM lesson sequence in teaching her third-grade class the use of quotation marks in writing direct quotes. She conducts a warm-up activity by having her students say a sentence and then writing their words on a large chart. She explains that when we write another person's exact words we call this a "quote." After writing several quotes from her students, she introduces the quotation mark and adds words to each quote on the chart to show who said the words. To the quote "I have a white cat," she adds the words *said Elena*. She demonstrates the use of quotation marks to separate the exact words a person said from the part that identifies who was speaking. Before she adds the quotation marks to each sentence, she has students come to the chart and place one of their hands at the beginning of the quote and the other at the end. This gives the students a physical representation of the length of the quote and confirms their understanding for the teacher.

To provide guided practice, Mrs. Crane writes a statement about herself on the board and asks the students to copy the statement on a sheet of paper at their desk. She then asks them to add words to the sentence that will show who said the statement. Finally, Mrs. Crane asks her students to place the quotation marks at the beginning and end of the actual statement that she made. During the exercise, she walks around checking to make sure that all students are succeeding at the task.

For independent practice, Mrs. Crane asks each student to write a sentence that is true about themselves and trade sentences with a partner. The partner then adds words to show who said the sentence and quotation marks to show exactly what was said. The students repeat this activity several times while Mrs. Crane circulates, observing, helping, and taking notes. She completes the lesson with a short quiz that consists of a written paragraph of a simple two-person conversation to which the students must add quotation marks.

During Mrs. Crane's extension and practice session at the end of the day, she provides an additional activity for the students who were successful in the morning lesson. These students write paragraphs requiring the use of quotation marks, trade paragraphs, and use highlight tape to identify the direct quotes in the paragraphs.

The group of students that needed more instruction after the morning lesson work with Mrs. Crane for additional guided practice. Using a large chart, Mrs. Crane writes a sentence about a student in the group, such as "Jose has a new baby brother." She then has another student, Maria, read the sentence and add the words *said Maria* at the end of the sentence. She asks what Maria said when she read the sentence, and has the students paste macaroni pieces to simulate quotation marks in front and at the end of the exact words Maria read. Mrs. Crane and the students repeat this exercise with sentences about each student, and then she gives them a short quiz in which the students again use macaroni to indicate the direct quotes in a written paragraph. Mrs. Crane notes that all the students are able to identify the direct quotes, place the macaroni correctly, and even orient the macaroni pieces so that they actually look like opening and closing quotation marks. The students in the extension activity group are equally successful in completing their task.

* * * * *

Students in Mr. Behar's seventh-grade language arts class are learning to write business letters. Mr. Behar plans to address Common Core State Standard ELA-Literacy.W.7.4.

"Produce clear and coherent writing in which the development, organization, and style are appropriate to task, purpose, and audience."

He begins the lesson by reviewing the format for friendly letters and comparing it to the business letter format. He then gives each student a blank business letter format page and walks them through the writing of a simple business letter. He gives them some suggestions of times when they might need to write a business letter such as the following:

Requesting free materials to use in a school report
Asking a professional to review his or her science project before submitting it

Requesting an appointment to observe a professional as a part of a job-shadowing project
Asking someone to make a presentation to your class

Once Mr. Behar walks the class through writing a business letter using the format page, he encourages each student to write a letter independently, choosing their own topic and using the format page as a resource. (See Figure 49.3 for an example of a business letter format.)

During the Team Time at the end of the period, Mr. Behar gives assignments to one group of students to write letters of application for jobs. Mr. Behar has invited a local business owner to work with the students on the type of material to include in an application letter.

Mr. Behar works with the students who need additional instruction. He prepares several business letters, cuts them into sections, places magnetic tape on the back of the pieces, and asks the students to place the parts onto a magnetic board so they form a correctly formatted business letter. After they complete this task several times as a team, each student is given a letter to format individually. Once they format their letter, they are given magnets with the words to identify each part of the letter and they place these on the letter to indicate the names of the parts.

The next day, Mr. Behar asks the business owner to work with the second team on understanding the items to include in an application letter, guiding them through the writing of a letter while the first group writes application letters independently.

Conclusion

One of the most valuable lessons to come from the use of the CIM in highly diverse schools is the understanding that students who have traditionally been low achievers can meet state standards with daily additional instruction. The planning that is involved in providing tutorials benefits all students in the classroom because it requires teachers to expand their teaching strategies and to find new, innovative ways of delivering instruction.

FIGURE 49.3 Business Letter Format Page

_____ (Your return address)

_____ (City, state, zip)

_____ (Date)

_____ (Name of the person receiving the letter)

_____ (His/her address)

_____ (City, state, zip)

_____ (Salutation: Dear Sir/Ms.)

_____ (Body of the letter)

_____

_____

_____

_____

_____ (Closing: "Sincerely/Yours Truly")

_____ (Your signature)

_____ (Your name and title typed)

Examples of Approximation Behaviors Related to the TESOL Standards

Pre-K–3 students will:
- participate in activities to move them into grade-level curriculum.
- demonstrate understanding of basic curriculum concepts.

4–8 students will:
- use writing to express their understanding of grade-level curriculum.

- write paragraphs on specific curricular topics.

9–12 students will:
- use academic language to write reports.
- demonstrate understanding of different genres of writing.

References

Barksdale, M., & Davenport, P. (2003). *8 steps to student success: An educator's guide to implementing continuous improvement K–12.* Austin, TX: Equity in Education.

Common core state standards.ELA-Literacy.W.3.3.b © 2010. National Governors Association Center for Best Practices and Council of Chief State School Officers. All rights reserved.

Davenport, P., & Anderson, G. (2002). *Closing the achievement gap: NO EXCUSES.* Houston, TX: American Productivity & Quality Center.

Goldenberg, G. (2008). Teaching English language learners: What the research does and doesn't say. *American Educator.* Summer 2008. 8–44.

Haycock, K. (2002). Closing the achievement gap. *Educational Leadership, 5*(8), 6.

50

Combining and Scheduling Strategies

Supporting Learning through Differentiation

Today's classrooms look very different from classrooms of the past. Learning centers, technology in many forms, and speakers of many different languages present challenges even for the most innovative teacher (Peregoy & Boyle, 2013). The best teaching strategies can only be implemented through thoughtful planning and organization. In this final chapter, suggestions for classroom organization will include ways to schedule instruction and provide meaningful follow-up and practice. In order to differentiate instruction for your students, small-group instruction will serve as an important part of the school day. This can only take place when all students are engaged in a meaningful activity that supports learning.

Step-by-Step

The steps in setting up and maintaining an effective classroom are the following:

- *Establish classroom routines and expectations early*—As a teacher, you are responsible for establishing classroom routines and expectations. You cannot provide a supportive learning environment if the students don't know exactly what is expected of them. However, a classroom where students are actively engaged is not a silent classroom. If students are expected to learn to speak English, they must have opportunities to practice speaking English. They must also have confidence that their practice will be validated. Daily use of the strategies provided in predictable routines and signals (Chapter 1) combined with total physical response (Chapter 2), modeled talk (Chapter 3), and realia strategies (Chapter 5) will help support students' understanding of how to participate successfully in the classroom. Figure 50.1 lists other combinations of strategies that support student learning.

Enhanced eText
Video Example 50.1

- *Provide a print-rich environment*—Include a wealth of varied print in your classroom. Posters, charts, many books in both English and the students' first languages, and magazines are all forms of print that should be included in your classroom so that students have numerous opportunities to

FIGURE 50.1 Combining Strategies to Support Learning

Objective	Strategies to Use	Special Considerations
Lowering affective filter and providing comprehensible input	Predictable Routines and Signals Total Physical Response Modeled Talk Visual Scaffolding Realia Strategies	Individual student language development Ages of students Number of ELLs in class
Supporting students' movement into English reading	Vocabulary Role-Play Collecting and Processing Words Read-Aloud Plus Moving into Reading Close Reading Bilingual Books and Labels Cloze Microselection Read, Pair, Share Guided Reading	Individual student language development
Developing fluent oral English production and increasing vocabulary	Vocabulary Role-Play Verb Action Syntax Surgery Cognate Strategies Story Reenactment Language Focus Lessons Cooperative Learning Small Groups and Partners GIST	Student confidence level Supportive classroom environment
Developing student understanding of their own involvement in their learning	Collecting and Processing Words Reporting Back Close Reading Cloze Syntax Surgery Checking for Understanding Language Focus Lessons Guided Reading Learning Strategy Instruction	Student confidence level Opportunities for student choice GIST Tutorials

read and discuss print in varying forms. As you view the print-rich classroom in this video, ask yourself the following questions:

- How could this environment be changed to fit students of a different age?
- How can all this print be used to further students' English and content development?

- ***Strive for full implementation to meet the needs of all students***—Teaching and learning strategies must be fully implemented to meet the needs of all students in your classroom. It is not enough to use these approaches occasionally. When you are explaining something, you should be modeling the talk and using gestures, visuals, realia, and whatever else is appropriate to ensure that students comprehend and learn. Students should always be given opportunities to use any new vocabulary introduced, both in speaking and writing. Teachers who support the needs of their students are rewarded with obvious growth in the students. When you, as the teacher, notice a student who is not making progress, you should move into RTI (see Chapter 25) mode and attempt to discover the reason for the lack of progress.

• *Monitor and assess on a regular basis*—To document student progress and make sure all students are advancing, monitoring and assessment must be part of your instructional process. You should observe, provide opportunities to create work samples, and discuss students' work with them. And in order to do this effectively, you have to have a plan. You need to schedule time for observing students, reviewing anecdotal records, and creating student portfolios. When students are actively involved in the process, it greatly improves their commitment to and pride in their accomplishments. Figure 50.2 shows one teacher's assessment and monitoring plan.

• *Use self-evaluation and reflection to improve your instruction*—Reflect on your teaching strategies, assessment, and monitoring plans to determine the level of implementation of effective teaching strategies in your classroom. Also evaluate the ways in which you are documenting student growth and differentiating instruction. Maintain a plan for continued self-improvement and monitor your own progress moving toward full implementation of instructional differentiation. The self-evaluation rubric in Figure 50.3 can help you move into full implementation of exemplary practices.

Applications and Examples

Mrs. Doran and her third graders are working together to document their progress through the use of portfolios. The classroom is arranged so that students can actively practice the skills they are learning. Although Mrs. Doran's class has mostly English-speaking students, she has five students who are English learners at various levels of development. Mrs. Doran finds scheduling to be crucial in providing differentiated instruction in her classroom. When Mrs. Doran teaches a

FIGURE 50.2 Assessment and Monitoring Plan

Daily	Weekly	Each Marking Period
Observe three students during learning center time to document participation and language development.	Conduct running records with students in one reading group.	Have students choose a writing sample for their portfolio and discuss this sample with them.
Observe students during group writing to document what part of the writing they are able to contribute. Note on writing checklist.	Document student engagement and participation during group discussions. Note on group participation checklist.	Review all students' reading journals with them and set goals for the next marking period.
Observe during math everyone responds (ER) activity to determine which students need further instruction.	Give timed math facts tests, have students chart their progress, and put into their portfolios. Confer with students who are not making progress to establish study plans.	Confer with students and parents to establish study plans and intervention strategies, if needed.

FIGURE 50.3 Implementation of Exemplary Practices: Teacher Self-Evaluation Rubric

Beginning	Developing	Accomplished	Exemplary
Aware of exemplary practices and trying some.	Implementing some exemplary practices.	Implementing exemplary practices and adding new ones when students show the need.	Implementing and refining exemplary practices daily. Adding new ones when students show the need.
Starting to assess students and document their progress.	Assessing students to determine their individual needs. Documenting their progress on a semi-regular basis.	Assessing students to determine their individual needs. Documenting their progress on a regular basis. Adapting instruction in response to documented student needs.	Assessing students to determine their individual needs using an assessment and implementation plan. Adapting instruction in response to documented student needs.
Students are not always involved in their own assessment, goal setting, or progress celebrations.	Students are actively involved in reviewing their work and setting goals for themselves.	Students work with the teacher to build their portfolio and set goals. They help to identify areas of need.	Students and parents are actively involved in student assessment, goal setting, and celebrations of progress.

group lesson, she always presents the new material using modeled talk, visuals, and sometimes realia. She adheres to the time-tested Madeline Hunter (1993) model of presentation:

1. Anticipatory set—Build or activate the students' background knowledge.
2. Objective—Establish what you want the students to know or be able to do at the conclusion of the lesson.
3. Instructional input—Explain the concepts you are presenting using modeled talk, visuals, realia, and so on.
4. Teacher modeling—Demonstrate what the students will be doing.
5. Check for understanding—Ask questions or have students show that they understand.
6. Guided practice—Walk around and observe the students practicing actually doing the work.
7. Independent practice—Give students who are ready to practice independently an assignment, and have them work by themselves, in pairs, or in small groups to complete the task.

This model gives Mrs. Doran an opportunity to provide additional guided practice to any students who need it before they move to independent practice. This group may consist of her English learners and almost always some other students who aren't quite ready for independent practice. Only the students who need additional guided practice are included in this group. The other students in the class go on to practice independently what they have been taught.

Mrs. Doran uses literacy learning centers to engage her students in reading and writing for a purpose while she conducts small-group instruction in reading. The students are currently reading and writing folktales, meeting in literature groups to discuss the books they are reading, and giving each other feedback on the tales they are writing. This gives Mrs. Doran time to work with small leveled groups on reading skills and language development.

Later in the morning Mrs. Doran and the other third-grade teachers teach mathematics groups that are arranged by skill level. Mrs. Doran meets with the group that is working on grade-level math skills. Other teachers are working with groups that are addressing basic skills. All of the teachers use manipulatives, realia, modeled talk, and other exemplary practices to ensure that their students are understanding instruction. Because there are English learners included in all the math groups, all the teachers work on math vocabulary as they build math skills.

At the end of the day, Mrs. Doran's school has set aside time for tutorials and enrichment groups to ensure that all students are getting the instruction they need to meet the Common Core State Standards. Some teachers work with larger groups in enrichment activities so other teachers can meet with smaller groups, providing the additional instruction they need to develop English skills or achieve standards in math or language arts.

* * * * *

On Friday afternoons all the teachers support their students in working on school projects designed to apply the skills they are learning to accomplish real-life activities like a community garden or a covered structure for a picnic area on the playground. They use their math, science, and reading skills to accomplish these projects. This also provides an opportunity for parent involvement and community building.

Providing instruction and differentiation at the middle and high school levels presents some different challenges. One high school schedules English language development classes during first period so that the students have a solid block of English instruction at the beginning of each day. The students are then scheduled into regular classrooms where the teachers provide instruction using strategies that support comprehension. They have been trained in exemplary practices for English learners, and they communicate with the English language development teacher about needs they observe in their students so that there is cooperation among the instructors.

Many states are now requiring all teachers to take certification classes in teaching English learners so that they know how to adapt their instruction to the needs of these learners. Some schools have added a period at the beginning or end of the school day to provide additional English instruction. Many secondary teachers are devoting part of their class periods for differentiated small-group instruction. Technology is facilitating English instruction in many classrooms as well. Scheduling and innovation are being used all around the country to provide exemplary instruction for students in all subjects. This video explores some approaches that can be used successfully in small-group instruction at the secondary level.

Enhanced eText
Video Example 50.2

Conclusion

Combining strategies and scheduling time for differentiated instruction are major concerns for all teachers. Some districts have found innovative ways to address these concerns at a school or district level, but many teachers are implementing their own solutions within their individual classrooms. It is obvious that many English-only students need extra instructional time and they should not be ignored. Teachers can identify students who need extra instruction through careful observation and documentation. The goal should always be full implementation of exemplary practices to ensure that all students receive the attention and instruction they need in order to succeed.

References

Hunter, M. (1993). *Enhancing teaching*. New York, NY: Macmillan.

Peregoy, S., & Boyle, O. (2013). *Reading, writing, and learning in ESL: A resource book for teaching K–12 English learners*. Boston, MA: Pearson Education.

Teacher Resources

An Informal Multiple Intelligences Survey

I. Linguistic Intelligence

Reading books makes me feel

Listening to the radio makes me feel

Nonsense rhymes, tongue twisters, or puns make me feel

Playing word games like Scrabble, Anagrams, or Password makes me feel

Using big words in speaking or writing makes me feel

In school, English, social studies, and history make me feel

When people talk about books they've read or things they've heard, I feel

When I have to share something I have written, I feel

II. Logical-Mathematical Intelligence

When I'm asked to compute numbers in my head, I feel

In school, math and/or science makes me feel

Playing number games or solving brainteasers makes me feel

Finding ideas for science fair projects makes me feel

Having to "show all my work" on my math papers makes me feel

Finding errors in someone else's math or logic makes me feel

Measuring, categorizing, analyzing, or calculating makes me feel

Watching science and nature shows on television makes me feel

III. Spatial Intelligence

When I am asked to "close my eyes and visualize," I feel

When I'm asked to draw in pencil and not allowed to use color, I feel

When I read a book without pictures, I feel

When I read a book with actual photographs as illustrations, I feel

When I do jigsaw puzzles, mazes, and other visual puzzles, I feel

When I have to find my way in an unfamiliar building or neighborhood, I feel

When I have to do math without writing it down or drawing pictures, I feel

When asked to draw something from "a bird's-eye view," I feel

IV. Bodily-Kinesthetic Intelligence

When I play sports or other physical activities, I feel

When I have to sit for long periods of time, I feel*

When I work with my hands at concrete activities such as sewing, weaving, carving, carpentry, or model building, I feel

When I spend time outdoors, I feel

When I have to talk without using my hands or body language, I feel*

When I have to look at something without touching it, I feel*

When riding on a roller-coaster ride, I feel

When asked to try a new physical movement, I feel

V. Musical Intelligence

When asked to sing "Happy Birthday," I feel

When someone is singing off-key, I feel*

When listening to music an iPod, the Internet, or compact disks, I feel

If I had to take music lessons, I would feel

If I had to listen to music without tapping my fingers or feet, I would feel*

When someone asks me to sing a tune, I feel

If I had to study without listening to the radio, I would feel*

If there were no more music programs in school, I would feel*

VI. Interpersonal Intelligence

When someone comes to me for advice, I feel

When we have to play team sports at school, I feel

When I have to work out a problem without talking to anyone about it, I feel

When my friends are all busy and I have to spend time alone, I feel

When I have to teach other people something, I feel

When I have to be the leader of my group, I feel

When I go to a party with a lot of people I don't know, I feel

When I have a chance to join a club, I feel

VII. Intrapersonal Intelligence

When I spend time alone reflecting, or thinking about important things, I feel

When I don't get picked for something, I feel

When I spend time with a hobby or interest that I have to do by myself, I feel

When I think about important goals for my life, I feel

When I think about my own strengths and weaknesses, I feel

If I had to spend time alone (safe) in a mountain cabin, I would feel

When my friends want to do something I don't want to do, I feel

If I had my own business, instead of working for someone else, I would feel

Source: Adapted from *7 Kinds of Smart* by Thomas Armstrong (1993). New York: Putnam.

Scoring Instructions for the Informal Multiple Intelligences Survey

All people possess all seven intelligences in some combination, and this exercise gives you an idea of the relative strengths of your personal intelligences. For most of the items, add the total of your points for each question in each section using the scale of 0–1–2–3–4 (from left to right, crying to big grin) for the face you marked. For the items marked with an asterisk, simply reverse the scoring from left to right, 4–3–2–1–0. Add the total points scores in each section. The sections in which you score the most points indicate your strongest areas of intelligence. The lower scores indicate your weaker areas of intelligence. The stronger areas of intelligence are those in which you will learn and demonstrate understanding most easily.

Developmental Profiles for Documenting English Language Development

GRADES K–2

Listening and Speaking			
Early Production	**Speech Emergence**	**Intermediate Fluency**	**Fluency**
Speaks single words or short phrases.	Beginning to be understood when speaking (may still have inconsistent use of plurals, past tense, pronouns).	Asks and answers instructional questions using simple sentences.	Listens attentively to stories and information on new topics and identifies key concepts and details both orally and in writing.
Responds to simple questions with one or two words.	Asks and answers questions using phrases and simple sentences.	Listens attentively to stories and information and identifies important details and concepts with verbal and nonverbal responses.	Demonstrates an understanding of idiomatic expressions by responding appropriately or using the expressions correctly.
Responds to simple directions with actions, pointing, or nodding.	Responds to simple directions appropriately.		Negotiates and initiates social conversations by questioning, restating, and soliciting information and paraphrasing the words of others.
Uses simple repetitive phrases such as "Good morning" or "Thank you."	Orally communicates basic needs and recites familiar rhymes, songs, and simple stories.	Uses consistent standard English with some minor grammatical errors, retells stories using descriptive words.	Consistently uses appropriate ways of speaking and writing that vary according to purpose, audience, and subject matter.

GRADES K–2

Writing			
Early Production	**Speech Emergence**	**Intermediate Fluency**	**Fluency**
Penmanship—Copies letters of the alphabet and words posted in the classroom legibly.	Writes one or two legible sentences.		
Organization and Focus—Writes a few words or phrases about a story read by the teacher or a personal experience.	Writes simple sentences about events or characters from familiar stories read aloud by the teacher.	Writes short narrative stories that include elements of setting and characters (may include inconsistent use of standard grammar).	Proceeds through the writing process to write short paragraphs that maintain a focus.
Capitalization—Writes own name using a capital letter.			Uses capitalization to begin sentences and proper nouns.
		Uses a period or question mark at the end of a sentence.	Edits writing to check for correct spelling, capitalization, and punctuation.

GRADES 3–5

Listening and Speaking			
Early Production	**Speech Emergence**	**Intermediate Fluency**	**Fluency**
Speaks single words or short phrases.	Begins to be understood when speaking but may have inconsistent use of plurals, past tense, and pronouns.	Uses standard English grammatical forms and sounds with some errors.	Listens attentively to complex stories and information on new topics. Identifies main ideas and supporting details.
Answers simple questions with one-or two-word responses.	Asks and answers questions using phrases and simple sentences.	Asks and answers instructional questions with some supporting elements.	Recognizes appropriate ways of speaking that vary according to purpose, audience, and subject matter.
Retells familiar stories and participates in short conversations using gestures, expressions, or objects.	Orally identifies main points of simple conversations and stories that are read aloud using phrases or simple sentences.	Retells stories and talks about school-related activities using expanded vocabulary, descriptive vocabulary, and paraphrasing.	Summarizes major ideas and retells stories in detail, including characters, setting, and plot.
Uses common social greetings and repetitive phrases.	Orally communicates basic needs and recites familiar rhymes, songs, and simple stories.	Participates in social conversations with peers and adults, asking and answering questions and soliciting information.	Participates in and initiates extended conversations with peers and adults on unfamiliar topics by asking and answering questions, restating and soliciting information.

GRADES 3–5

Reading—Fluency and Vocabulary Development			
Early Production	**Speech Emergence**	**Intermediate Fluency**	**Fluency**
Reads aloud simple words (nouns and adjectives) in stories or games.	Applies knowledge of content-related vocabulary to discussions and readings.	Uses knowledge of English morphemes, phonics, and syntax to decode and interpret the meaning of unfamiliar words in text.	Recognizes that some words have multiple meanings (present/gift, present/time) in literature and texts in content areas.
Demonstrates comprehension of simple vocabulary with an appropriate action.	Reads simple vocabulary, phrases, and sentences independently.	Reads grade-appropriate narratives and informational texts aloud with appropriate pacing, intonation, and expression.	Uses common root words and affixes to determine meaning when they are attached to known vocabulary.
Responds appropriately to some social and academic interactions (simple questions/answers).	Demonstrates internalization of English grammar by recognizing and correcting errors made when speaking or reading aloud.	Recognizes simple analogies and metaphors used in literature and texts in content areas.	Uses a standard dictionary to determine the meaning of unknown words.

GRADES 3–5

Reading Comprehension			
Early Production	**Speech Emergence**	**Intermediate Fluency**	**Fluency**
Responds orally to stories read aloud by giving one- or two-word responses to factual questions.	Reads and listens to simple stories and demonstrates understanding by answering explicit questions with simple sentences.	Responds to comprehension questions using detailed, complex sentences.	Identifies significant organizational patterns in text such as sequential or chronological order and cause and effect.
Identifies the basic sequence of stories read aloud using key words or pictures.	Orally identifies the basic sequence of events in stories read using simple sentences.	Reads and uses detailed sentences to compare the relationships between the text and personal experiences.	Uses the text, illustration, and titles to draw inferences and make generalizations.
Identifies the main idea in a story read aloud using key words or phrases.	Reads text and identifies the main idea using simple sentences and drawing inferences about the text.	Reads text and uses detailed sentences to orally identify the main idea, make predictions, and support the predictions with details.	Describes main ideas and supporting details, including evidence.
Points out main text features such as title, table of contents, or chapter headings.	Reads and identifies text features such as title, author, table of contents, index, etc.	Reads and identifies all text features including glossaries, diagrams, and charts.	Uses text features to locate and draw information from text.
	Orally identifies examples of fact and opinion in familiar texts read aloud.	Reads literature and content-area texts and orally identifies examples of fact and opinion.	Distinguishes between fact and opinion and cause and effect in text read independently.

GRADES 3–5

Literary Response and Analysis			
Early Production	**Speech Emergence**	**Intermediate Fluency**	**Fluency**
Listens to a story and responds to factual questions using one- or two-word responses.	Reads literary texts and orally identifies the main events using simple sentences.	Uses expanded vocabulary and descriptive words to paraphrase oral and written responses to text.	Identifies and describes figurative language (similes, metaphors, personification).
Orally identifies characters and settings in simple literary texts by using words or phrases.	Describes characters and setting in literary texts using simple sentences.		Identifies the motives of characters in a work of fiction.
Distinguishes between fiction and nonfiction by giving one- or two-word responses.	Distinguishes among poetry, drama, and short stories using simple sentences.		Identifies techniques to influence readers' perspectives, describes themes, and compares and contrasts characters' motivations.
Creates pictures, lists, charts, and tables to identify the characteristics of fairy tales, folktales, myths, and legends.	Using simple sentences, describes characters in a literary selection based on the characters' actions.	Uses knowledge of language (prefixes, suffixes, base words) to form meaning from literary texts.	Describes the major characteristics of poetry, drama, fiction, and nonfiction.

GRADES 3–5

Writing			
Early Production	**Speech Emergence**	**Intermediate Fluency**	**Fluency**
Labels key parts of common objects.	Writes short narrative stories that include setting and characters.	Begins to use a variety of genres (informational, narrative, poetry).	Writes a persuasive composition using standard grammar.
Creates simple sentences or phrases with some assistance.	Writes simple sentences and uses drawing, pictures, lists, or charts to respond to familiar literature.	Writes a series of events in sentence form.	Writes short narratives that include examples.
Uses models to create brief narratives (a sentence or two).	Follows a model given by the teacher to write a short paragraph of four sentences or more independently.	Creates cohesive paragraphs that contain a central idea with almost standard English usage.	Writes narratives that contain setting, characters, objects, and events.
	Writes simple sentences related to content areas (math, science, social studies).	Uses more complex vocabulary in writing (language arts, math, science, social studies).	Writes multiple-paragraph narratives and informational compositions with standard grammar.
	Writes a friendly letter using a model.	Writes a letter independently that contains detailed sentences.	Uses all the steps in the writing process independently.
	Produces understandable independent writing (may have nonstandard English usage).	Independently writes simple responses to literature.	Uses standard capitalization, punctuation, and spelling.

English Language Development

GRADES 6–8

Speaking and Listening			
Early Production	**Speech Emergence**	**Intermediate Fluency**	**Fluency**
Beginning to speak a few words using English words and simple sentence formats.	Speech is clearer but may still use grammar inconsistently.	Listens to information and identifies important details and concepts orally.	Uses simple figurative language such as "light as a feather."
Asks and answers questions using a word or simple phrase.	Asks and answers questions using phrases and simple sentences.	Oral production may still contain some errors in more advanced grammatical concepts.	Questions, restates, and requests information by paraphrasing the words of others.
May still respond to questions nonverbally.	Restates the main idea of an oral presentation in simple sentences.	Participates in social conversations on familiar subjects with peers and adults.	Varies oral production to fit the situation according to purpose, audience, and subject.
Uses common social greetings and repetitive phrases.	Prepares and delivers short oral presentations.	Identifies main ideas and supporting details from oral presentations or literature read aloud.	Speaks clearly using standard English grammar, expression, and prosody.
		Prepares and delivers short oral presentation based on simple research.	Prepares and delivers presentations including a purpose, point of view, introduction, transitions, and conclusion.

GRADES 6–8

Reading—Word Analysis			
Early Production	**Speech Emergence**	**Intermediate Fluency**	**Fluency**
Recognizes and correctly produces English sounds and reads simple words.	Recognizes obvious cognates in reading (e.g., education, educacion).	Applies knowledge of word relationships to gain meaning from simple text (prefixes, suffixes).	Applies knowledge of word relationships to gain meaning from literature and academic texts.
Recognizes and pronounces the most common phrases and simple sentences.	Pronounces simple words comprehensibly when reading aloud.	Pronounces most English words correctly when reading aloud.	Applies knowledge of cognates and false cognates to gain meaning from content-area text.
Produces readable text by using simple English phonemes in writing (phonetic spelling).			

GRADES 6–8

Reading—Fluency and Vocabulary Development			
Early Production	**Speech Emergence**	**Intermediate Fluency**	**Fluency**
Creates a simple dictionary of frequently used words.	Uses context knowledge to figure out unfamiliar words.	Uses knowledge of English morphemes, phonics, and syntax to unlock unknown words.	Reads fluently and uses decoding and comprehension processes (background knowledge, imaging, paraphrasing, etc.) to achieve complete understanding.
Communicates basic needs using simple vocabulary.	Reads simple paragraphs independently.	Recognizes simple idioms, analogies, and figures of speech.	Recognizes and uses metaphors, analogies, and figures of speech in reading and understanding text.
	Recognizes and corrects errors when speaking or reading aloud.	Uses decoding skills and background knowledge to read independently.	Uses social and academic language to read independently.
	Reads aloud with appropriate pacing and intonation.	Recognizes that words have multiple meanings.	
	Uses a dictionary to find the meanings of unknown words.		

GRADES 6–8

Reading—Reading Comprehension			
Early Production	**Speech Emergence**	**Intermediate Fluency**	**Fluency**
Reads simple text and answers factual questions using key words or phrases.	Reads and responds to simple literary and informational text and answers factual questions using simple sentences.	Reads literature and responds to factual comprehension questions using detailed sentences.	Identifies and explains main ideas and critical details in informational text, literature, and academic texts.
Recognizes categories of common informational materials (brochure, advertisement, etc.).	Identifies and follows multiple-step instructions for simple mechanical devices and filling out basic forms.	Understands and orally explains multiple-step directions for simple devices and filling out application forms.	Analyzes and explains rhetorical styles in consumer and informational materials (warranties, contracts, newspapers, magazines, etc.).
Orally identifies key words, phrases, and main ideas of familiar texts.	Orally identifies factual components of simple informational materials using key words, phrases, or simple sentences.	Identifies and uses detailed sentences to explain the differences among categories of informational materials (dictionaries, encyclopedias, Internet sites, etc.).	Identifies and analyzes the differences in and appropriate uses of various informational materials (textbooks, newspapers, biographies, etc.).
Points out text features such as table of contents, title, and chapter headings.			
Orally identifies example of fact, opinion, and cause and effect in simple texts.	Reads simple texts and identifies main ideas and supporting details using simple sentences.	Orally identifies the features and elements of common consumer and informational materials (warranties, manuals, magazines, books, etc.).	

GRADES 6–8

Reading—Literary Response and Analysis			
Early Production	**Speech Emergence**	**Intermediate Fluency**	**Fluency**
Orally identifies different characters and settings in literary texts using words or simple phrases.	Responds in simple sentences to factual comprehension questions about short literary texts.	Paraphrases sections of literary text using expanded vocabulary and descriptive words.	Analyzes the interactions between characters in literary texts (motivations, reactions, etc.).
Role-plays a character from a familiar piece of literature using words and phrases.	Reads literary texts and identifies the main events using simple sentences.	Reads and responds in detailed sentences to factual questions about forms of brief prose (short stories, novels, essays).	Analyzes the setting (time and place) and its influence on the meanings, connotations, and conflicts in a piece of literature.
Creates pictures, lists, charts, and tables to identify the sequence of events from a familiar piece of literature.	Reads a literary selection and identifies the speaker or narrator.	Identifies literary devices such as figurative language, symbolism, dialect, and irony.	Identifies and describes literary elements such as imagery and symbolism.
Creates pictures, lists, charts, and tables to identify the characteristics of different forms of literature (fiction, nonfiction, poetry).	Identifies different points of view in literary selections (first person, third person) and explains in simple sentences.	Describes the author's point of view in literature using detailed, descriptive sentences.	Analyzes the elements of a plot, how it develops, and the way conflicts are resolved.
Recites simple poems.	Describes the thoughts and actions of a character after reading a simple literary selection.	Compares and contrasts literary themes across genres.	Analyzes recurring themes across literary works (e.g. good and evil).

GRADES 9–12

Reading—Word Analysis			
Early Production	**Speech Emergence**	**Intermediate Fluency**	**Fluency**
Recognizes and correctly produces English sounds and reads simple words.	Recognizes obvious cognates in reading (e.g., education, educacion).	Applies knowledge of word relationships to gain meaning from simple text (prefixes, suffixes).	Applies knowledge of word relationships (roots, affixes) to gain meaning from literature and academic texts.
Recognizes and pronounces the most common phrases and simple sentences.	Pronounces simple words comprehensibly when reading aloud.	Pronounces most English words correctly when reading aloud.	
Produces readable text by using simple English phonemes in writing (phonetic spelling).		Applies knowledge of cognates and false cognates to gain meaning from content-area text.	

GRADES 9–12

Reading—Fluency and Vocabulary Development			
Early Production	**Speech Emergence**	**Intermediate Fluency**	**Fluency**
Uses a simple dictionary to find meanings of frequently used words.	Uses context knowledge to figure out unfamiliar words.	Uses knowledge of English morphemes, phonics, and syntax to unlock unknown words.	Reads fluently and uses decoding and comprehension processes (background knowledge, imaging, paraphrasing, etc.) to achieve complete understanding.
Recognizes simple affixes, synonyms, and antonyms.	Reads simple paragraphs independently.	Recognizes simple idioms, analogies, and figures of speech.	Recognizes and uses metaphors, analogies, and figures of speech in reading and understanding text.
Responds in social settings with short phrases or single words.	Recognizes and corrects errors when speaking or reading aloud.	Uses decoding skills and background knowledge to read independently.	Uses social and academic language to read independently.
Produces simple vocabulary or short phrases to communicate basic needs socially and in the classroom.	Reads aloud with appropriate pacing and intonation.	Recognizes that words have multiple meanings.	Uses and understands the meanings of common idioms and analogies.
	Uses and understands the meanings of connectors (first, next, last, after that, etc.).	Identifies variations of the same word in text and understands how affixes change the meanings of words.	

GRADES 9–12

Reading—Reading Comprehension

Early Production	Speech Emergence	Intermediate Fluency	Fluency
Reads simple text and answers factual questions using key words or phrases.	Reads and responds to simple literary and informational text and answers factual questions using simple sentences.	Reads literature and responds to factual comprehension questions using detailed sentences.	Identifies and explains main ideas and critical details in informational text, literature, and academic texts.
Recognizes categories of common informational materials (brochure, advertisement, etc.).	Identifies and follows multiple-step instructions for simple mechanical devices and filling out basic forms.	Understands and orally explains multiple-step directions for simple devices and filling out application forms.	Analyzes and explains rhetorical styles in consumer and informational materials (warranties, contracts, newspapers, magazines, etc.).
Orally identifies key words, phrases, and main ideas of familiar texts.	Orally identifies factual components of simple informational materials using key words, phrases, or simple sentences.	Orally identifies important points made after reading a persuasive piece of text.	Identifies and analyzes the differences in and appropriate uses of various informational materials (textbooks, newspapers, biographies, etc.).
Points out text features such as table of contents, title, and chapter headings.	Reads and identifies specific facts in informational text using key words and phrases.	Explains examples of how clarity of text is affected by the repetition of important facts.	Identifies and analyzes how clarity is affected by patterns of organization, hierarchical structure, repetition of key ideas, and word choice.
Orally identifies examples of fact, opinion, and cause and effect in simple texts.	Reads simple texts and identifies main ideas and supporting details using simple sentences.	Orally identifies the features and elements of common consumer and informational materials (warranties, manuals, magazines, books, etc.).	Prepares a brief research paper in a content area, using ideas from multiple sources.

GRADES 9–12

Reading—Literary Response and Analysis			
Early Production	**Speech Emergence**	**Intermediate Fluency**	**Fluency**
Orally identifies different characters and settings in literary texts using words or simple phrases.	Responds in simple sentences to factual comprehension questions about short literary texts.	Paraphrases sections of literary text using expanded vocabulary and descriptive words.	Analyzes the interactions between characters in literary texts (motivations, reactions, etc.).
Orally identifies the beginning, middle, and end of a simple literary text.	Reads literary texts and identifies the main events using simple sentences.	Reads and responds in detailed sentences to factual questions about forms of brief prose (short stories, novels, essays).	Analyzes the setting (time and place) and its influence on the meanings, connotations, and conflicts in a piece of literature.
Creates pictures, lists, charts, and tables to identify the sequence of events from a familiar piece of literature.	Reads a literary selection and identifies the speaker or narrator.	Identifies literary devices such as figurative language, symbolism, dialect, and irony.	Identifies and describes literary elements such as imagery and symbolism.
Creates pictures, lists, charts, and tables to identify the characteristics of different forms of literature (fiction, nonfiction, poetry).	Identifies the theme, plot, setting, and characters of a piece of literature using simple sentences.	Describes the author's point of view in literature using detailed, descriptive sentences.	Analyzes the elements of a plot, how it develops, and the way conflicts are resolved.
Recites simple poems.	Describes the thoughts and actions of a character after reading a simple literary selection.	Uses detailed sentences to identify ways in which poets use personification and figures of speech.	Relates literary works to their major themes and historical facts.

GRADES 9–12

Writing			
Early Production	**Speech Emergence**	**Intermediate Fluency**	**Fluency**
Creates simple sentences with some assistance.	Writes simple sentences in response to literature to answer factual questions.	Writes responses to literature that show understanding of the text using detailed sentences and transitions.	Writes in different genres (short stories, informational text, essays, poetry).
Writes a brief narrative that includes setting and some detail.	Uses common verbs, nouns, and modifiers to write simple sentences.	Uses all stages of the writing process including revision to create clear, descriptive writing.	Writes detailed biographies or autobiographies.
Completes basic business forms with such information as name, address, and telephone number.	Creates a draft of a paragraph from an outline.	Develops a clear purpose in a brief essay using facts and quotations.	Writes persuasive expository text using a clear thesis, organized points of support, and addressing of counter-arguments.
Uses common verbs, nouns, and familiar modifiers using classroom resources.	Uses increasingly more words from content areas such as science, social studies, and math.	Uses increasingly more complex vocabulary and sentence structure (complex sentences and devices such as similes and metaphors).	Revises and edits writing to correct grammatical and mechanical errors.
Organizes and records information from selected literature and content area by displaying it on charts, lists, or tables.	Writes a simple informational composition using description, contrast, transitions, and including a main idea and some supporting detail in simple sentences. Collects information from a variety of sources.	Uses basic strategies such as note-taking, multiple outlining, and drafts to create informational text with a clear introduction, transitions, and conclusion.	Writes pieces needed for career development (business letter, job application, letter of inquiry, etc.).

Glossary

academic language—Language used in instruction in the content areas of math, science, social sciences, and English language arts. This, as opposed to "social language," is the language necessary for success in school.

accommodations and modifications—Adjustments made in the classroom to support students beyond the basics provided for everyone. Accommodations are adjustments to the physical environment or delivery of instruction. Modifications are adjustments to the curricula or assignments.

active learning experience—An activity in which students actively participate in teaching and learning strategies that engage and involve them in the learning process, beyond merely listening or taking notes.

adequate yearly progress (AYP)—A report based on standardized test scores that shows the annual progress demonstrated by a student or an entire school population.

advance organizer—An introduction to a lesson that activates students' prior knowledge and prepares them to learn what is about to be presented.

affective filter—Emotions, such as anxiety, that interfere with or interrupt learning.

alphabet strip—A strip of paper or cardboard with the letters of the alphabet (both upper- and lowercase) that is used to support beginning writers.

anecdotal records—Notes taken by a teacher or paraprofessional documenting an observation of a student in the classroom or school activity.

artifacts—Things left over. These could be things found in an architectural dig or examples of work done by students in a classroom. In a classroom, artifacts most often encompass work that exhibits the students' efforts, progress, and achievements in one or more areas of the curriculum.

assessment strategies—Ways of documenting student growth and learning such as observations, test results, anecdotal records, or performance samples.

attribute—A property or characteristic such as color, size, or a personality trait.

authenticity—Related to realness; not false. Education that is *genuinely* connected to real-life situations.

authentic practice—In education, providing actual practice in something that is used in real life.

Autonomous—Acting independently.

author's chair—A special chair where a student author sits to read a piece of writing as part of the celebration of completing the work.

basic theory—Educational theory that is well established and supported by research.

BICS—Basic Interpersonal Communication Skill or social language.

big book—An oversized book created for use in reading aloud so that the students cans see the words and illustrations while seated in a group.

bilingual books—Books written in two languages. Sometimes the text is written in both languages on the same page; other times it is written in one language and then repeated on an adjacent page in the second language.

book walk—An introduction to a book in which an adult and child turn through the book page by page, looking at the pictures and making predictions about the story.

CALP—Cognitive Academic Communication Skills or academic language.

charade—A game in which players try to guess words and phrases that a teammate acts out without speaking.

checking for understanding—Questions asked specifically to determine what an individual student understands in order to clarify misunderstandings before continuing instruction.

checklist—A list designed to identify things to observe in order to document students' understandings.

cinquain poem—A formula poem consisting of five usually unrhymed lines containing two, four, six, eight, and two syllables, respectively.

circular story—A narrative story structure in which one thing leads to another until the story ends where it began.

cloze activities—Written text in which some words are left out and blanks inserted. These activities are used to help students focus on context when reading.

cognates—Words in two languages that share a similar meaning, spelling, and pronunciation.

cognitive demand—The amount of demand on the intellect the language presents, the difficulty of the language.

cognitive strategies—Cognitive strategies are one type of learning strategy that learners use in order to learn more successfully. These include repetition, organizing new language, summarizing meaning, guessing meaning from context.

cohesion links—The important parts of written and spoken paragraphs that connect sentences so that they form a unified, connected whole.

collaboratively—Working together.

collecting words—Teaching strategies that help students to build their vocabularies (see Chapter 7).

Common Core State Standards (CCSS)—The educational initiative in the United States that details what K–12 students should know in English language arts and mathematics at the end of each grade and establishes consistent educational standards across the states to ensure that students graduating from high school are prepared to enter college programs or the workforce.

comparative organizer—An activity used as a lesson opener that serves to integrate new material with similar material already understood by the learner. It focuses on how the new and known material differ.

comprehensible input—Lessons and instruction that are understandable and can be internalized.

communicative classroom activities—Activities in the classroom designed to encourage students to communicate verbally.

concurrent—Happening within the same time frame.

conferring—Having a meeting or conference. Used as a part of the writer's workshop to provide feedback to the writer.

consistent—Always the same.

content-area standards—Grade level standards set by professional organization in the various content areas (language arts, mathematics, science, social studies)

content-area knowledge—Information related to a particular type of content such as math, science, or social sciences.

context—The parts of something written or spoken that immediately precede and follow a word or passage and clarify its meaning.

context embedded—Communication that takes place within a situation that supports the understanding by the participants.

Contextualize—To provide a connection to a certain context; to make clear by connecting information to a given situation or setting.

continuous improvement model (CIM)—An overarching approach to education in which everyone—students, teachers, and administrators—are provided whatever support they need to be successful.

cooperative learning—Working as a group to solve a problem or attain specific goals.

correction tape—Wide (1-inch wide) white tape that can be written on to cover and correct an error a child or teacher makes while writing on a chart.

cueing systems—The cues we use to make meaning of written words, visual cues, phonic cues, and syntactic cues. Using what we know about written language to be able to unlock unknown words and sentences.

data chart—A graphic organizer used to organize data or information collected on a given topic.

decoding—Unlocking a code; using letters and their sounds to pronounce words.

deep processing—Getting below the surface when reading; looking at deeper meaning, the author's intent, and the choice of words to portray emotions or nuances in meaning.

dialect—A regional language variety distinguished by features of vocabulary, grammar, and pronunciation from other regional varieties.

diamonte poem—A formula poem that is shaped like a diamond and uses nouns, adjectives, and gerunds to describe either one central topic or two opposing topics.

differentiated instruction—Adapting instruction to the individual needs of students.

digital—A way of storing data. Computers and cameras can store data digitally.

dimensions of language—The parts of communication that affect its ease of understanding (the difficulty of the words and the situation that may support understanding).

direct instruction—When teachers explain exactly what students are expected to learn, and demonstrate the steps needed to accomplish a particular academic task.

document camera—An electronic device used for lessons, presentations, and training to show live images of documents, flyers, brochures, solid objects, etc. It magnifies and projects the images of actual, three-dimensional objects, as well as transparencies.

drop everything and read (DEAR) time—A program to provide time for self-selected reading during the school day.

early production students—Students who are in the process of acquiring a language and are beginning to verbalize that language.

English language development levels—The levels English learners move through as they make progress in producing verbal and written English; the levels are preproduction, speech emergence, early production, immediate fluency, and fluency.

English language learners (ELLs)—Students whose first language is not English and who are in the process of acquiring English.

everyone responds (ER) activities—A method that allows all students to demonstrate their understanding (or non-understanding) in a non-threatening manner by responding non-verbally without waiting to be called on.

exemplary practices—Teaching strategies that have proven to support learning and are recommended by master teachers.

experience text relationships (ETR)—Making connections between personal experiences and written text.

expository organizer—An activity planned to introduce concepts and principles to learners by creating a bridge between what is already known and the new material to be learned.

expressive, syntactic processing—Formation of words and sentences in order to communicate.

experiential-extension activities—Activities designed to build on new skills and extend them by providing practice in using the new skills.

figurative language—Speech or writing that departs from literal meaning in order to achieve a special effect or understanding, such as "quiet as a mouse."

flow chart—A chart that shows a progression and helps the reader understand the steps in a procedure.

foreshadowing—A hint, sometimes subtle, in a story that gives advance notice of something to follow.

free-voluntary reading—Silent, self-selected reading of enjoyable books written at a student's independent reading level.

generating interaction between schemata and text (GIST)—A strategy used to support students' understanding of text by activation prior knowledge and experiences relating to the text being read.

genre—A category of literature or other form of artistic endeavor.

glossary—A list of words and definitions in a text.

graphic organizer—A visual presentation of information showing relationships between ideas or facts related to a learning task.

guided practice—Providing practice in a skill with guidance from the teacher.

guided reading—A form of small-group reading instruction in which students are given practice and support in using cueing systems to better their reading abilities and comprehension skills.

hand TPR—A form of *total physical response* where hand gestures are added to the ways in which words are represented.

hard copy—A printed copy of text or illustrations.

high-frequency words—The words that appear most frequently in writing.

highlighting—Calling attention to something either by verbal expression or by using a highlighting pen.

indigenous—Native to an area. Indigenous plants are those that grow naturally in a given area.

informal writing sample—A sample of a student's writing usually used to document the student's writing abilities.

instructional reading level—The level at which a student can correctly pronounce 90–94 percent of the words with at least 75 percent comprehension.

integrated curriculum project—Teaching so that several areas of content are presented and their connections demonstrated.

interactions—Reciprocal actions, effects, or influences. When people speak, write, or communicate in order to influence or cause a reciprocal action from another.

interactive journal—A journal in which a student communicates with another student or teacher, taking turns writing and responding.

interactive read-aloud—Reading a story aloud and stopping for discussion, clarification, and responses from the listeners.

interactive whiteboard—A large interactive display that connects to a computer. Users may also control the computer using a pen, finger, stylus, or other device on the whiteboard itself. It may also be equipped with a projector.

interactive writing—A form of directed writing in which the teacher and students plan sentences to write and take turns writing letters, words, or whole sentences depending on the abilities of the students.

intermediate fluency—One of the levels of competency on the continuum of acquiring a language. Students at this level can produce both verbal and written sentences in the target language but are still making errors of pronunciation and such things as verb tense.

interventions—Planned educational procedures that are meant to support students with special needs.

irregular verbs—Verbs in English are irregular if they don't have a conventional *-ed* ending (like *asked* or *ended*) in the past tense and/or past participle forms.

KWL chart—A chart labeled "Know—Want to know—and Learned," used for identifying what students know about a topic; questions they have; and then, after some research, what they learn.

language acquisition—Gradually acquiring a language through receiving and understanding messages, building a listening (receptive) vocabulary, and slowly attempting verbal production of the language.

language development levels—Levels of proficiency in acquiring a new language.

language experience approach (LEA)—An approach to writing whereby students dictate sentences about their experience while the teacher writes their words on a chart. It demonstrates how spoken words can be written and then reread.

language focus lesson—A lesson that contains some content knowledge but also has another objective, that of learning and developing a new language function or structure.

large platform projector—A projector used to show pages of a text on a large screen so that it can be seen by a group of students.

learning centers—Stations in a classroom where individuals or small groups of students engage in follow-up activities designed to expand their experiences and skills.

learning strategy instruction—Lessons designed to teach students strategies to support their own learning.

leveled questions—Questions stated so that students at various stages of language development can respond and participate actively in the lesson.

manipulatives—Physical objects that are handled and moved in the support of learning, frequently used in math and science lessons. They are highly adaptable, however, to a variety of curricular areas.

meaning cues—Cues in reading that help the reader focus on the meaning of the passage. Illustrations serve as meaning cues for young readers.

metacognitive strategies—Using knowledge about the way you learn to help yourself to learn or remember new information.

microselection—Identifying key words in a reading passage.

minilesson—A short lesson designed to support students in acquiring a specific skill.

modeled talk—Demonstrating as you talk.

modeled writing—Demonstrating sound–symbol relationships by sounding out a word while representing the sounds with letters.

modeling—Demonstrating.

motivation—The desire to do things.

multiple examples—Providing more than one example in order to clarify the meaning.

multiple intelligences—The different ways in which human beings are "smart."

No Child Left Behind Act of 2001 (NCLBA)—A United States act of Congress setting standards and expectations for all students across the nation.

nuances—Subtle meaning differences.

pantomime—Using motions to convey a message without spoken words.

parameter—A rule or limit that controls what something is or how something should be done.

without saying it exactly as it was written.

peer tutoring—A procedure whereby one student tutors another.

performance sample—An assignment designed to collect a work sample for assessment.

phonic cues—Using the letters in a word to figure out how to pronounce it. Also called visual cues because you must look at the way the word is spelled to determine the pronunciation.

planning board—A chart in the classroom used to give students assignments. Usually used when they are working in different centers.

pocket charts—Charts with pockets used in the classroom to display words, phrases, and sentences that can be moved around to form new words, phrases, and sentences.

predictable routines and signals—Classroom routines and signals that are followed daily.

preproduction stage or period—The period of time that a student learning a new language is not yet communicating verbally in that language.

preproduction students—Students acquiring a new language but not yet verbalizing the language.

prewriting strategy—Activity planned to help students think of writing topics and plan what they will write.

principles—Fundamental norms, rules, or values that represent what is desirable and positive for a person, group, organization, or community.

problem solving—Presenting activities so that students can learn different approaches to finding solutions to problems.

pyramid poem—A formula poem about a person, place, or thing that is written in a pyramid or triangular shape. (Read more about this at http://www.ehow.com/how_8109202_instructions-pyramid-poem. html#ixzz33RJQVaRo.)

quadrant matrix—A chart that compares the relationships between two things by making a chart divided into four parts (quadrants).

Race to the Top (RTT)—A federal funding program that provides competitive grants to encourage and reward states that create the conditions for education innovation and reform.

read-aloud—An activity in which one person reads a book out loud and others listen.

read-aloud plus—The teacher reads aloud to students while adding visual support, periodic paraphrasing, and/or rewriting as the "plus" or extension of the read-aloud, thus actively involving the students.

reader's theater—Students assume roles and read a script with expression, fostering fluent reading practice.

realia—Real objects used in teaching.

reenactment—Acting out a story previously read.

refrain—A part of a story read repeatedly, for example, "Run, run, as fast as you can. You can't catch me, I'm the gingerbread man."

repertoire—A collection, usually of skills; a "bag of tricks."

replica—A copy of something, usually in miniature.

reporting back—A verbal report of a learning activity.

representative manipulatives—A second level of manipulatives in which concrete manipulatives are replaced, for instance, by pictures drawn to represent them (e.g., tallies, dots, circles, stamps that imprint pictures for counting). They can represent the concrete objects even though they don't resemble them.

response to intervention (RTI)—How a student responds to a special educational strategy designed to support his or her learning.

rubric—An assessment tool that usually consists of four or five points with description of what must be achieved to score the points.

running record—A reading assessment in which a teacher notes the way a student reads, uses cueing systems to enable the unlocking of unfamiliar words, and retells the story.

scaffolding—Providing support so that a student can be successful.

scientific process—A systematic method for experimentation that is used to explore observations and answer questions.

self-evaluation rubric—An assessment chart that is used to judge your own performance.

self-monitoring—Keeping track of your own progress, approaches, and concerns in learning.

self-regulation—The ability to control your own behavior, emotions, and thoughts.

semantic feature analysis—A strategy that uses a grid to help students explore how sets of things are related to one another.

semantic processing—Listening to understand.

semi-concrete—A visual representation of something two-dimensional rather than three-dimensional. See *representative manipulatives*.

seminal research—The process of carrying out original and often influential research in a particular field that may provide a solid basis for future research and thus the development of a field.

Shared reading—Reading a book with a child. The child joins in when they know the words.

shared writing—A form of writing instruction in which the teacher and student work together to create a text.

social/affective skills—Ways of interacting using feelings or personal relationship skills

socioeconomic status—The level of financial income that the person enjoys.

grouping—Grouping students for small-group instruction based on demonstrated needs.

speech emergence level—The level of language acquisition at which the student begins to produce verbalizations in the target language.

standard English—The form of English that follows all the grammar and pronunciation rules.

sticky notes—Small notes that have a sticky edge so they can be attached to another piece of paper; Post-it notes is the brand-name version.

story map—A strategy that uses a graphic organizer to help students learn the elements of a book or story by identifying characters, plot, setting, and important events in the story.

sustained silent reading (SSR)—A time during the school day set aside for self-selected pleasure reading.

syntax—The study of the rules for the formation of grammatical sentences in a language.

syntax cues—Using the structure of a sentence to unlock unknown words.

syntax surgery—Writing a sentence on a sentence strip and then cutting it apart to rearrange it into more understandable pieces.

T-chart—A chart used to list two separate viewpoints on a topic. Topics can include anything that can be easily divided into two opposing views.

think-aloud strategy—An approach in which a teacher reads aloud and stops to verbalize thoughts that help her or him make sense of what is being read. It is used to demonstrate how we make sense of text.

total physical response (TPR)—A strategy that uses physical movement to teach vocabulary.

Venn diagrams—Graphic organizers that use overlapping circles to show where aspects of two texts or concepts are similar. The aspects that the texts or concepts share are noted in the overlapping sections of the graph.

visual—In education, any picture, chart, or illustration used to support student understanding.

visual scaffolding—Using visuals (real objects, pictures, gestures) to support student understanding.

wait time—The amount of time a teacher (or other students) waits for a response from a student. This time must be longer for English learners.

word sorts—An activity where words written on cards are sorted according to set rules (categories, number of syllables, vowel sounds, etc.).

word walls—A list of words displayed on a wall or bulletin board to be used in furthering word knowledge.

writer's workshop—An approach to teaching writing whereby students work through a series of steps: prewriting, drafting, conferring, revising, editing, publishing, and celebrating.

writing journal—A notebook in which students write daily to describe experiences, list possible writing ideas, and experiment with writing formats.

zone of proximal development—The difference between what a child can do with help and what he or she can do without guidance (Vygotsky, 1978). The place where students can be taught new skills with some scaffolding from a teacher.

Index